Praise for REVOLUTIONARY REHEA

"General histories of the neoliberal era are shaped by an overwhelming sense of defeat for radical movements. It is, of course, true that neoliberalism was spectacularly ushered in by shattering working-class resistance in some key workplaces in India, Australia, the UK, and the US. *Revolutionary Rehearsals in the Neoliberal Age*, however, compels us to be attentive to a different view of this era. Tracing revolutionary uprisings from 1989 to 2019, this book is a map of resistance and resilience in the face of tremendous odds. The case studies, as well as the introductory essay, lead us through situations where the victory of capitalism over humanity was anything but assured. And yet the book is not a wistful history about what could have been. Rather, it is a strategic assessment of near-victories to prepare us for the fire next time."
—TITHI BHATTACHARYA, coauthor of *Feminism for the 99%*

"This fine collection of essays deals with some of the most significant revolutionary situations in the neoliberal era. It makes great reading, with powerful arguments, and concludes with a wager on the future: climate change is a terrible danger, but it has revolutionary potential, because it cannot be prevented by partial reforms that do not challenge the capitalist system itself."
—MICHAEL LÖWY, author of *Revolutions* and *Ecosocialism*

"What remains of revolution after decades of neoliberalism? The question is both perplexing and urgent. With realism and radical intransigence, *Revolutionary Rehearsals in the Neoliberal Age* tackles it head-on. Acknowledging the inadequacy of longstanding left-wing models to our era, the authors gathered here also refuse to counsel despair. Instead, they trace emancipatory impulses and upheavals across the scorched landscape of neoliberalism. The result is a provocative, stimulating, and deeply radical set of reflections on the meaning of revolution today. This is a book for everyone who wants to change the world." —DAVID MCNALLY, author of *Blood and Money* and *Monsters of the Market*

"How can popular movements not only topple repressive governments, but also create more thoroughly democratic, egalitarian, and solidaristic societies? This is the question that animates the contributions to *Revolutionary Rehearsals in the Neoliberal Age*, which examines a wide range of revolutionary situations from 1989 to 2019. The case studies, which are well researched and insightful, include Central and Eastern Europe; Africa, including South Africa; Indonesia; Argentina, Bolivia, and the 'pink tide' in Latin America; and Egypt. The theoretical reflections by Colin Barker and Neil Davidson are provocative and challenging. This volume will interest anyone who seeks to understand popular uprisings and revolutions and the ways capitalism motivates, structures, and constrains them." —JEFF GOODWIN, professor of sociology, New York University

REVOLUTIONARY REHEARSALS
IN THE NEOLIBERAL AGE:
1989-2019

Edited by Colin Barker,
Gareth Dale, and Neil Davidson

Haymarket Books
Chicago, Illinois

Published in 2021 by
Haymarket Books
P.O. Box 180165
Chicago, IL 60618
773-583-7884
www.haymarketbooks.org
info@haymarketbooks.org

ISBN: 978-1-64259-468-3

Distributed to the trade in the US through Consortium Book Sales and Distribution (www.cbsd.com) and internationally through Ingram Publisher Services International (www.ingramcontent.com).

This book was published with the generous support of Lannan Foundation and Wallace Action Fund.

Special discounts are available for bulk purchases by organizations and institutions. Please call 773-583-7884 or email info@haymarketbooks.org for more information.

Cover design by Eric Kerl.
Cover photo by Alisdare Hickson.
A boy confronts Egyptian military police south of Tahrir Square, 2011.

Printed in Canada by union labor.

Library of Congress Cataloging-in-Publication data is available.

10 9 8 7 6 5 4 3 2 1

Dedicated to the life, work, and memory of Colin Barker (1939–2019) and Neil Davidson (1957–2020)

CONTENTS

Introduction   1
Colin Barker and Gareth Dale

Part 1: Theoretical Implications

Part 2: Revolutionary Situations, 1989–2019

Part 3: Theoretical Implications

INTRODUCTION

Colin Barker and Gareth Dale[1]

In 1987, Bookmarks Publications issued a volume entitled *Revolutionary Rehearsals*, edited by Colin Barker. It was subsequently reprinted by Haymarket Books.[2] Its topic was the way in which protest movements can develop into insurgent challenges to state power and how regimes seek to contain and repress revolt. It considered five moments when, it seemed, widespread popular insurgency, with vital roles played by workers' occupations and political strikes, posed at least the possibility of socialist revolution. Ian Birchall explored the events of May 1968 in France, with its general strike and factory occupations. Mike Gonzalez considered the year before the 1973 military coup in Chile, placing emphasis on the *cordones* in the industrial belt. Peter Robinson looked at the Portuguese revolution of 1974–75, with its mass strikes, workplace occupations, and land seizures by agricultural laborers. Maryam Poya dissected the 1979 Iranian revolution, in which industrial action in the oil sector played a pivotal part. Colin Barker analyzed the Solidarność movement in Poland in 1980–81, in which strike committees were the effective force, and added a final chapter that drew out some general patterns from these diverse cases.

Early in the last decade, the editors at Haymarket inquired about the possibility of a "second edition." The present volume, which looks at a series of popular upheavals since 1989—in Eastern Europe, South Africa, Indonesia, Argentina, Bolivia, Venezuela, sub-Saharan Africa, and Egypt—is not a direct sequel to the earlier book, but it does follow a similar pattern and asks the question: What did we see accurately in 1987 and what did we miss? As with *Revolutionary Rehearsals*, we selected case studies that raised questions concerning the potential of revolutionary episodes to break out beyond the anticipated script. We asked authors to look at both processes and outcomes

1

but to avoid the retrospective determinism that assumes the latter were fore-ordained. This would be to miss the "what if" questions that arise specifically within revolutionary struggles. All of this poses questions of what we under-stand by a "revolutionary" rising, so before turning to ask "what did we miss in 1987," let us briefly unfurl the conceptual map.

Revolutions: Definitions and variations

The book is about revolutionary risings. By "revolution" we refer to a polit-ical process with two analytically distinct aspects: a revolutionary situation and an outcome. The first is a specific and temporary political moment in which two or more rival blocs struggle for state power. The category includes not just "successful" but also "defeated" revolutionary attempts, and not only those that feature mass movements (the focus of this volume) but also mili-tary coups, civil wars, and counterrevolutions.

The patterns of causation and the inner processes of revolutionary situ-ations vary widely in the extent of popular involvement and the role played by social movements, in the layers of populations involved and the nature of their activities, and in duration: compressed in time or extended over years. And what begins as one type may turn into another—for example, where a coup sets off a popular mobilization, either to oppose it (as in the 1920 Kapp Putsch in Germany) or to extend and transform it (as in Portugal in 1974). Equally variable are the *outcomes* of revolutionary situations. One or another group of "contenders" may gain state power, displacing the previous regime. Or they may come to some form of compromise with the old regime. Revo-lutions may of course be defeated, if the old regime succeeds in remobilizing its forces.

Defined in this way, revolutionary situations are not "extraordinary" affairs, wholly outside the normal run of political analysis. They are relatively common. Charles Tilly suggests, for example, that Europe alone has seen literally hun-dreds of attempted and successful revolutions in the past half-millennium.[3] On the world scale, between 1900 and 2014, Mark Beissinger has identified 345 revolutionary episodes—defined as "a mass siege of an established government that successfully displaces an incumbent regime and articulates demands for substantially altering the political or social order."[4]

Turning to the *nature* of revolutions, we draw two distinctions. The first is between political and social revolutions. These refer to the outcomes of revolutionary episodes. While both forms involve dramatic struggles between regimes and contenders, political revolutions only alter the character of the state (for example, its personnel or its political constitution) with the overthrow or transformation of a particular government or system of government. Social revolutions in addition alter the underlying societal form, or what writers in the Marxist tradition term the "mode of production." We follow here the "consequentialist" approach to the categorization of revolutions, where the social character of a revolution is judged—after the event—by its effects rather than by its players. An early example was the liberal theorist Benjamin Constant's acclaim of France in 1789–93 as the "happy revolution." "Despite its excesses I call it happy," he wrote in 1819, "because I concentrate my attention on its results."[5]

It should be noted that the nature of a revolution's outcome may be disputed during the drama of an actual revolutionary episode. There may be social forces who seek to achieve more than just a change in the state but also the wholesale reconstruction of social power and property and who nonetheless lose out in the eventual outcome. Famous examples include the Diggers and Levelers in the English Revolution, the *enragés* in the French Revolution, and the Partido Obrero de Unificación (POUM) in the Spanish Civil War. These may be treated by historians with what Edward Thompson termed "the enormous condescension of posterity," but they represented at least the *possibility* of alternative outcomes—and their opponents took them sufficiently seriously to go out of their way to crush them. That said, not every revolutionary episode is characterized by challenges "from below" or "from the left." Some "political" revolutions involve large-scale mobilization of popular forces, while others do not, and the same can be said about "social" revolutions.

Better sense can be made of this if we add in a further distinction, specific to Marxist discussions. This is between *bourgeois* and *potentially socialist* revolutions. Bourgeois social revolutions are those that install regimes that remove impediments to capitalist expansion, establishing the conditions for capital accumulation. These are, in Neil Davidson's summary, "the imposition of a dual social order: horizontally over competing capitals so that market relations do not collapse into 'the war of all against all,' and vertically over the conflict between capital and labor so that it continues to be resolved in the interest of the former"; the establishment of "'general conditions of production,' which individual competing capitals would be unwilling or unable to provide"; and the representation of "internal" capitalist interests in relation to other states and classes.[6] These conditions can be provided by a wide variety of forms of state, including governments formed and led by landed proprietors, military officers, religious dignitaries, social democrats and communists, liberal intellectuals, and tribal chiefs.

Bourgeois social revolutions—the transformation of social reproduction patterns away from those predominant in feudal, absolutist, or tributary society and toward the dominance of capitalist social relations—did not logically require any significant level of popular self-activity and self-organization. They could be and often were accomplished "from above."[7] We should not therefore accept Theda Skocpol's definition of a social revolution, namely as "a sudden, basic transformation of a society's political and socioeconomic structure, accompanied and in part effectuated through class upheavals from below."[8] Upheavals from below were either absent from, or carefully contained in, many revolutions—an example is the Meiji Restoration of 1868— that set a whole variety of countries on the path to capitalist development. It was in an effort to understand this phenomenon that Antonio Gramsci developed the term "passive revolution" to distinguish the Italian *Risorgimento* from the French Revolution and its Jacobinism.[9]

In *some* bourgeois revolutions, members of exploited and oppressed classes pressed claims for more socially just and inclusive ways of organizing everyday social reproduction than were eventually achieved, and thus provided *hints and anticipations of* and *hopes for* a socialist future. In that sense, some bourgeois revolutions—those that did involve such popular self-organization and collective activity—can also be counted as *failed or defeated socialist revolutions*. Most historians and theorists of revolution, their eyes fixed on the eventual victors, ignore or play down the significance of these "utopian" movements, through whose multiple struggles and defeats the outlines of a history of socialism can be traced. This is one reason to insist on stressing the inner narratives of revolutionary situations and actual revolutions.

For socialist revolution, in contrast to bourgeois revolution, a massive upsurge in popular self-activity and collective self-organization is not an add-on but indispensable. This requires emphasizing because these basic distinctions became muddied through the twentieth-century experience of nationalist and other bourgeois revolutions whose leaders attached the label "socialist" to their own class rule, even as they were incorporating and adjusting their systems of social reproduction in alignment with the imperatives of world capitalism.

The question of socialist revolution in the twenty-first century occupies the chapters by Colin Barker and Neil Davidson that begin and close this volume.

Popular involvement and worker militancy

Looking back at *Revolutionary Rehearsals*, it's clearer now than it was at the time that it was conceived and written after the end of a particular epoch in the history of global capitalism, in a period when a whole new global formation was emerging, a new phase for which we still lacked either an agreed-upon name or indeed a clear analysis. In 1987 we might have supposed that the patterns we disclosed would repeat themselves, and hopefully on a still grander scale. There would be a further series of revolutionary risings, typically concentrated in urban settings, with key roles played by militant workforces in large workplaces, and with renewed "revolutionary conjunctures" (on which more below).

Some patterns identified in *Revolutionary Rehearsals* have reappeared in the post-1987 decades. Most obviously, many revolutions have occurred. Indeed, more frequently than before. Beissinger's data suggests the annual rate of "revolutionary episodes" edged up from 2.44 during the first half of the twentieth century to 2.80 during the Cold War (1950–84), then soared to 4.10 during the post–Cold War decades (1985–2014).[10]

A second pattern concerns geographical location. Reflecting the global trend to urban living, most revolutions of the past four decades have been overwhelmingly urban in focus, including those in Iran, the Philippines, South Korea, Latin America, Eastern Europe, South Africa, Indonesia, Tunisia, and Egypt. Again, Beissinger's research brings this out clearly. He identifies the predominant mode of revolution in the late twentieth and early twenty-first centuries as "urban civic revolt." In these, many people mobilize in central urban spaces with the aim of "overthrowing abusive governments," their grievances typically including an absence of civil liberties, repression of protesters, the arbitrary power of rulers, lack of popular representation, stolen elections,[11] and corruption.[12]

What, though, of the militant workers and workplace occupations, the land seizures and the interfactory strike committees? On this, continuity is less apparent.

Consider our first two case studies in 1989–94: Central/Eastern Europe (by Gareth Dale) and South Africa (Claire Ceruti). The first can be traced to precisely where *Revolutionary Rehearsals* left off: Poland in December 1981. Solidarność had dealt the Polish regime a blow from which it could never recover. But in the military coup, Solidarność had been defeated too. It began to rebuild, in the underground, but in the process its leaders shifted their understandings and ambitions. Before the coup its program included a call for democratic control of industry. Increasingly, that was edged aside. Instead the talk was of "freedom," which they came increasingly to understand as "freedom of the market." And it was not only the *opposition* that was converting to the idea of market freedom. So too was the "communist" regime, increasingly aware that the state-capitalist growth model was failing. It, however, had lost the necessary authority to carry through "reform." In 1988, under the stimulus of a small wave of strikes, the regime sat down with the opposition at a "Round Table" where they negotiated free elections. In June 1989, Solidarność swept the board, formed a government, and rapidly adopted neoliberal policies. The former revolutionary socialist, Jacek Kuroń, became minister of labor, offering TV fireside chats on how rising unemployment was a good thing. In Hungary, a similar pattern occurred: one commentator called its transformation a "refolution."[13] In both cases, the degree of popular involvement was small.

If Poland in 1989, with Hungary, exemplified the "negotiated transition" path to regime change, East Germany, Czechoslovakia, and Romania exemplified the "revolutionary rupture" model, in which massive demonstrations and in some cases street fighting were required to dislodge the regime.[14] But what of the workplaces? In East Germany there were small but important strikes, and many workplaces were in tumult. The Czechoslovak revolutionary process included a two-day general strike. Yet on the whole, independent working-class organization and demands did not feature strongly in 1989—unlike Hungary in 1956 or Poland in 1970 or 1980–81. Workers constituted the majority of those demonstrating, but for the most part they did so wearing the lion-skin of citizenship rather than asserting specifically working-class demands.[15] In East Germany most protests occurred *nach Feierabend* (after clocking off).

The events in South Africa followed a similar course. A long struggle, rooted in union and township organizations, finally compelled the Apartheid regime to the negotiating table and pushed the transition to democracy forward, but in ways that the ANC leadership was able to contain within the purely "political" goal of achieving state office. In line with the South

African Communist Party's (SACP's) theory that the transition must be a "two-stage" affair—*first* a democratic revolution and *later* an anti-capitalist social transformation—the ANC was little interested in promoting either the township struggles or workers' battles against their employers, except insofar as they helped lever it through the long and bitter negotiations with the white supremacists. The ANC and National Party leaders became convinced they would have to do a deal and to compel other interests to accept. The ANC and the SACP watered down their plans for economic reform and sought business support. After the achievement of free elections, Mandela's ANC government took office on a vaguely leftist program, but only two years later adopted a neoliberal policy program. No significant progress was achieved in lessening the country's massive inequalities. The advent of democracy increased the potential for protest, for it permitted the legalization of unions as well as space for civic organizations like South Africa's Anti-Privatisation Forum, for NGO activity, and for oppositional parties.[16] However, while the level of everyday popular protest in post-Apartheid South Africa has been among the world's highest, successive ANC governments worked to contain and deflect—and sometimes to murderously assault—popular resistance.[17]

How might we make sense of these different patterns of revolt?

Democratic transition

Looking back, the East European and South African upheavals—alongside the "People Power" revolution in the Philippines (1986) and the "People's Movement" revolution in Nepal (1990)—were shaped by, and helped to define, a new global conjuncture. They marked not its onset, as is sometimes thought, but its climax. It had commenced already fifteen years earlier. It was defined by four transitions. Two of them were era-opening, the other two were era-closing.

The first transition has received the most academic attention, with entire journals devoted to its study. It is the worldwide spread of liberal-democratic government. The construction of forms, norms, and procedures of liberal democracy is of course not new. It had been a defining element of the US and French revolutions, and the model spread and generalized across subsequent centuries—sometimes explosively, as in the aftermath of World War I. Then, from the mid-1970s, liberal-democratic government expanded rapidly and, for the first time, at the global scale. From fascist Spain and Portugal to the military regime in Greece, and then in the following decade to most of Latin America, the Philippines, and South Korea, all were replaced by liberal democracies. The scale of change was astonishing. In 1975, two-thirds of governments were considered "authoritarian." By 1995 this had dropped to a quarter, while the proportion reckoned to be "liberal democracies" doubled over the same period, from a quarter to a half.[18] This formed the backdrop to the uprisings featured in this volume, several of which saw the institutionalization of liberal democracy—in some cases successfully, in others only fleetingly. Alongside Eastern Europe and South Africa, they included Congo and Bénin (discussed by Leo Zeilig), Indonesia (Tom O'Lincoln), and Egypt (Sameh Naguib).

In a few cases, the previous authoritarian regimes collapsed after failure in war: the Greek colonels failed in a coup attempt in Cyprus, Portugal's army was losing its wars against liberation movements in its African colonies, the Argentine military was defeated in the Malvinas. From the standpoint of former fascist or military rulers, this kind of fairly sudden collapse was the most dangerous outcome, often leading to senior figures receiving lengthy prison sentences for crimes of murder and torture. Where they could manage it, leading figures in other authoritarian regimes sought to *negotiate* transitions to democracy, under whose terms they would protect themselves from subsequent prosecution and even strengthen capitalist property rules and relations.

Much of the extensive academic literature on these processes plays down the role of strike waves and mass protest movements, and especially workers' unions and parties, and instead places the spotlight on the tactics of regime and opposition elites—ensuring the exclusion of hawks and radicals on either side and discovering ways of drawing a veil over the past and safeguarding the positions of traditional power holders. Yet in many countries, organized labor played a significant part, not least in *motivating* the democratic transitions, demonstrating its opposition to the old regimes through widespread and militant strike movements that blunt repression could no longer contain. Not only that, but its forces pressed for more democratic outcomes than did the elites.[19]

The classic case was Spain. A movement surge in the late 1960s and early 1970s—centered on students, church groups, neighborhood associations, underground political parties, and industrial action—fed into a spike in (illegal, and usually political) strikes in 1974–75. Within weeks of General

Franco's death in 1975, a renewed wave of strikes compelled a shift in the fascist regime's stance, displacing the old hardliners. The new administration under Adolfo Suárez announced elections, dissolved the secret police, and legalized independent trade unions and the Socialists (PSOE) and then the Communists (PCE)—against the wishes of much of the military. The matter of *timing* was significant. As Sebastian Balfour notes, if the regime had not acted when it did, "it is quite feasible that the movements of protest would have become more radical, giving rise to alternative forms of popular power on a local level."[20] At least some members of the old regime were well aware of this, taking note of recent events across the border in Portugal. Franco's nephew, Nicolás, commented in 1975, before his uncle's death, "We have so many things to learn, both good and bad; because it did not carry through evolutionary changes in time, Portugal now finds itself faced with the uncertainties of a revolution."[21]

In return for the PCE's admission to negotiations, the party's leader, Santiago Carrillo, sought to act "responsibly," abandoning previous rhetoric about a democratic "rupture" and accepting the old elite's leadership of the process, their electoral law, Franco's flag, and the monarchy. The PCE sought a *compromise* with Spanish capital, and with their former fascist opponents, and were granted it weeks before the elections. As Balfour comments, "The multitudinous agitation that shook Spanish society in 1976 thus took no concrete political shape." The mass strikes that broke out in some parts "may have posed a momentary challenge to the local representatives of the State, but they did not throw up new centres of political power."[22]

In the June 1977 elections, Suárez's party claimed first place with 34 percent of the votes, followed by the PSOE, which won 29 percent, with the PCE gaining only 9 percent. A former prominent fascist became Spain's first democratically elected prime minister in decades. Two further measures consolidated his victory. To deal with the socioeconomic problems of inflation, strikes, unemployment, and declining profits, he needed the opposition's support. This he secured with the Pact of Moncloa in autumn 1977, where Spain's political parties and major unions agreed to limit wage increases and strikes.

Spain's "peaceful democratic transition" came to be regarded as a model. Indeed, Adolfo Suárez, former Francoist and then former prime minister, went to Chile in the mid-1980s to discuss his experiences in negotiating with the opposition. As in Spain, so in Brazil and Chile the *pace* and *form* of transition was determined by the military, who retained significant influence within the new "democratic" governments that emerged.[23] In Brazil, during the Constitutional Convention (1987–88), the military prevented a far-reaching limitation on its own institutional autonomy. In Chile, General Pinochet was able to set the timetable for democratization and to shape the "democratic constitution" in important ways. In Uruguay, the military insisted on an amnesty law granting the armed forces immunity for human rights violations committed during the years of dictatorship, extracting this concession as its price for allowing the democratic transition. In all these cases, "negotiated transitions" reduced the "risks" of popular insurgency and created openings for at least the more far-seeing of the old regime to achieve satisfactory "safe landings" after regime change. Politically, they required both a "reforming" wing within the ruling class and, within the opposition, a dominant "reformist wing" prepared to contain popular demands and organizations by a mixture of co-optation and demagogy and by excluding dissenting voices. So far as policy was concerned, both sides needed to treat economic "liberalization" as relatively unproblematic.

An era, a conjuncture, a phase, and a paradox

The second and third transitions, although not on the radar of many social scientists, are of particular interest to socialists. One was the closing of the long era of bourgeois revolution. Its arc, traced by Neil Davidson in chapter 10, began in the seventeenth century and stretched to the 1970s. If its early phase had seen revolutions in the United Provinces, England, the US, France, and Haiti, and later the "passive revolutions" that consolidated a bourgeois political order in Scotland, Germany, Italy, and Japan, a final wave occurred between 1945 and the 1970s, concluding arguably with the liberation of Portugal's African colonies and the overthrow of Ethiopia's feudal-absolutist regime in 1974 or with Zimbabwean independence in 1980.

This was the age of decolonization, of national liberation in Asia, Africa, and the Caribbean along with the wholesale revolutionary reconstruction of China. The period includes the long-drawn-out war of independence in Algeria, the Cuban Revolution of 1959, and the epic struggle of the Vietnamese against the French and the Americans. Whatever their particular histories, these revolutions shared a significant negative characteristic. In none of them did independent working-class organization and initiative play any major part. The Chinese Communist Party, which in the

1920s had been mostly a workers' party, became completely cut off during its subsequent development from the urban working classes. Strikes and urban uprisings played no significant role in Mao's victory. Similarly in Cuba, where a group of radical liberal intellectuals led a guerrilla assault on the Batista regime, urban workers were politically absent from the struggle. Only after taking power did Castro announce that what had occurred was a "socialist" revolution. It was the same story, largely, elsewhere. Many Third World countries lacked socialist organizations focused on working-class forces. Trade unions were often in clientelist relations with states, as with Peronism in Argentina, and in many parts of the global South dependent on middle-class organizers. While, objectively, the working class continued to grow both absolutely and as a proportion of the populations of actual and former colonial countries, its capacity for independent political activity in its own name was limited.

If working-class agencies did not lead these revolutions, other social forces assumed the revolutionary mantle. Leadership came from the ranks of radicalized middle-class intellectuals or, as in Egypt under Nasser, from army officers; in either case, the leaderships were inspired by visions of nationalist development and sought to use the local state as a machine for forcing it through. These revolutionary movements—and their projects—were inherently elitist. It was characteristic that they could be pursued not only by leftist nationalists and guerrillas but also by "progressive" military forces. Not uncommonly, they adopted a language of Marxism, but it was a language heavily inflected by Stalinist "socialism from above" and other national programs for state-led capital accumulation.

The Left internationally was marked by the period. Most believed that there was at least something socialist about Stalin's Soviet Union; they shared with the social-democratic tradition the view that state ownership was somehow non-capitalist or anti-capitalist. Some did break to the left of the Moscow-identified communist parties, in a few cases to join the small groups that developed more critical positions, but overwhelmingly they subscribed to one or another variety of what might be termed "left Stalinism"—above all to Maoism once the split between Beijing and Moscow was sealed in the later 1950s, but also to guerrillaist politics (itself another form of elitism). These forms at least had the prestige of "success" of a kind on their side— even if the essential social character of that success was the founding of new centers of capitalist accumulation, the very mark of "bourgeois revolutions."

By the mid-1970s, to all intents and purposes, the era of bourgeois social revolutions in all their diverse shapes had ended. The entire globe now constituted a single world capitalist economy, with a couple hundred capitalist nation-states, ranging from liberal-democratic political systems with developed welfare apparatuses, to highly authoritarian kingdoms and military dictatorships, to state-capitalist regimes claiming versions of "communism" that might have had Karl Marx spinning furiously in his grave.

If "bourgeois social revolutions" were over, that did not mean that revolutions as such ceased to occur, as the case studies in this volume illustrate. Changing conditions of capitalist accumulation generate pressures to periodically "remake" states, state policies, and states' relations with their subjects, not least in circumstances of crisis. These moments may manifest as revolutions, yet their character—in the absence of any that is genuinely socialist—was inevitably now "political."[24] Some may improve the rights and material conditions of sectors of their citizenries, others may be simply reactionary, in developing new forms of political subjection, as where fascist or military regimes are imposed. In some, mass popular movements have played a role, but mostly, in the neoliberal era, they have not, or not much. The possibility that political revolutions might "grow over" into potential socialist revolution has been small. Working people gained a degree of political freedom from the ending of authoritarian regimes, but their gains were limited.

If the just-discussed "closure" was of a historic era, of bourgeois revolution, the third transition of the mid-1970s also saw a closure, but of a *conjuncture*. As Davidson outlines in his chapter, 1968–76 represented the last of the three revolutionary conjunctures of the twentieth century. The other two were 1917–23 (or 1910–23 if one begins with Mexico) and 1943–49. In his definition, these are processes that extend in space—across states and regions—and in time, normally lasting some years. Participants in them are generally aware at some level that their struggles are linked to a broader moment of potentially systemic global change. Uprisings that take place during such conjunctures gain system-challenging heft due to the instability of hegemonic structures and a coalescence of social movements. All three revolutionary conjunctures in the twentieth century included bourgeois-revolutionary breakthroughs (Ireland in 1916–21; Turkey in 1923; China in 1949; Ethiopia, Angola, and Mozambique in 1974), as well as, in established capitalist states, upheavals with a strong socialist presence and potential (Germany in 1920, Italy in 1943–45, Portugal in 1974–75). All three revolutionary conjunctures arose in the wake of major military conflict (World War I, World War II, Vietnam). All three ignited bursts of democratization. Liberal democracy was introduced to Austria and Poland after World War I, for example, and after World War II to Italy, Japan, and Indonesia. (For the latter, decolonization was the precipitant.) In 1968–76, Southern Europe followed suit.

In all three periods, a key actor was the labor movement, broadly defined.[25] The first, 1917–23, requires no comment. In 1943–49 labor movements played powerful parts in upheavals and revolts in Japan, Italy, Yugoslavia, Albania, and beyond. The third, 1968–76, saw explosive labor struggles in Spain (discussed above), Italy, and West Germany, and in France, Chile, and Portugal—the case studies from *Revolutionary Rehearsals*. The period since that time has been more "normal," specked with struggles of course, but which have not gathered force globally in a radically transformative way and with generally low levels of industrial action. After the mid-1970s, levels of labor militancy tended to slide. In most of the rich countries, union membership went south, often as a direct result of rising unemployment and the destruction of the industrial bases of "traditional" sectors of powerful unionism. In many parts, rank-and-file organization was undermined, and confidence in the possibilities of collective action waned.[26] The studies in this volume, therefore, are of revolutionary situations in a non-revolutionary conjuncture.

The fourth transition was to the neoliberal phase of capitalism. As new patterns of transnational production, capital flows, financialization, and the like ("globalization," for short) became increasingly dominant in the 1960s and early 1970s, state-centered regimes of accumulation came under strain. These included "import-substitution industrialization," corporatist social democracy, and the state-capitalist model that had been one characteristic outcome of mid-century bourgeois revolutions. Then, in the mid-1970s, a global economic recession and stagflation arrived, delivering a crippling blow to the previous Keynesian hegemony. The policy responses offered by the Right, known at the time as "monetarism" and "supply side economics," were later to become known as neoliberalism.

Some accounts of the origins of the neoliberal turn go little further than these political-economic trends and crises, with additional reference to the influence of think tanks and their wealthy benefactors. But it should also be related to the other mid-1970s breaks and transitions outlined above. Thus, the fundamental mission at the dawn of the neoliberal era, in what David-son calls its "vanguard" phase,[27] was to shackle unions, intimidate militants, and roll back the welfare and wage gains that the 1968–76 labor struggles had achieved. In much of the global South, and in China since 1978, the neoliberal agenda—pushed from within regimes and often also by external forces such as Washington and the IMF—centered on the dismantling of the statist economic structures that had resulted from the post-1945 bour-geois revolutions (including decolonization). As Quinn Slobodian shows in *Globalists: The End of Empire and the Birth of Neoliberalism*, decolonization was "central to the emergence of the neoliberal model."[28]

As regards liberal democracy, its interaction with neoliberalism has been complex and paradoxical. The relationship began badly. Indeed, the first un-mistakably neoliberal government was the homicidal despotism of General Pinochet. Yet we then saw liberal democracies, one after the next, implement neoliberal programs. These included governments that issued from "demo-cratic revolutions," such as the Czech Republic in the 1990s. Given democ-racy's universal appeal,[29] the neoliberal program received a legitimacy boost thanks to the coincidence of its own globalization with the globalization of liberal-democratic government. This coincidence was most pronounced in the 1990s, a decade of worldwide liberal revolution. The democracy favored by neoliberal thinkers and policy makers, however, was of the "militant" (or "Hayekian") kind. That is to say, it is understood narrowly as a particular set of procedures (multiparty competition, secret ballots) and rights (to expres-sion, faith, and private property), accompanied by strict limitations that are designed to ensure that the corporate sector is protected from interference by the *demos*.

As neoliberalism strengthened its grip on national and international economic policy-making, the upshot was income polarization, the marginal-ization of the poor, and the cowing of the most consistent and potent force for democracy: organized labor.[30] The ensuing brew of ruling-class hubris, a subdued working class, wealth polarization, social atomization, and the ero-sion of the social position of the poor bred authoritarian politics. Along these lines, the neoliberal turn contributed to a double movement with respect to democracy. Neoliberal reforms undermined the substance of democracy even as formal liberal-democratic government extended its sway. It was a paradox that the Nigerian political theorist Claude Ake, writing in the mid-1990s, captured well. Democracy since the end of the Cold War, he noted, appeared "triumphant and unassailable, its universalization only a matter of time," yet its triumph was only permitted "because it has been trivialized to the point that it is no longer threatening to power elites."[31]

Destabilizing the neoliberal order

The neoliberal ascendancy, as the case studies in this volume will show, altered the conditions under which revolutionary situations developed and the kinds of possibilities that they disclosed.

Following the neoliberal recipe, social welfare programs were cut back, former state-run industries were privatized, economies were opened to multinational investment, and economic policy was subordinated to servicing large and growing debt burdens. Major environmental, economic, and social crises offered speculators and those with privileged access to decision-makers new opportunities—to profit at the expense of their shattered neighbors' lives. Over time, neoliberal norms and policies became embedded in the world economy, which was increasingly dominated by a vast mass of unregulated private capital that demanded lower corporate taxes, grabbed land for "development," privatized every kind of resource, and enforced debt repayments, subjugating everything and everyone to its insistent demands.

All this required breaking up existing patterns of working-class life and inflicting exemplary defeats on labor: the miners in Bolivia; the airline pilots in the US; the Fiat workers in Turin; the miners, newspaper printers, and dockers in Britain; the textile workers in Bombay.[32] Too often, commentators read these defeats as signifying the end of the working class as a focus of resistance *tout court*. What they missed was that the defeats were, as in times past, often the occasion for new beginnings and for the remaking of workers' movements—even though the road thereto may be long and stony. Older industries and occupations might crumble, but new sectors were being driven into the proletariat and could bring impulses to revived insurgency. "White collar" workers came to play a far more central role in popular resistance. The gap between workers and students narrowed, as higher education became a mass bureaucratic-capitalist industry.

Vital signs of anti-neoliberal revolt came from the global South, where "Structural Adjustment Programs," imposed by the IMF and which typically involved sharp increases in food and fuel prices, set off a string of what became known as "IMF riots." Beginning in Peru in 1976, these extended over the next decade and a half to countries across the Middle East, Africa, the Caribbean, Latin America, and Eastern Europe. On the whole, these protest movements, a total of 146 from 1976 to 1992,[33] remained isolated within individual countries and lacked an important element of political generalization, but in some regions, particularly Africa, as Leo Zeilig documents in his chapter, they contributed to "a convulsion of pro-democracy revolutions."

By the early 1990s, after the collapse of the Soviet Union, neoliberalism's ideological pull, pivoting on the claim that "free markets" facilitate freedom and democracy, was at its height. The revolutions in Eastern Europe and in South Africa appeared to fit this narrative. But the gloss was beginning to flake. Across continents popular suspicion and hostility grew toward the privatization of public services, the granting of private property rights to wealthy corporations at the expense of the poor, and the increasing dependence of the poor on food and fuel whose prices are governed by commodity speculators. Increasingly, neoliberalism smelled not of "freedom" but of the corruption of public offices by the lure of wealth, and in popular insurgencies, the interconnections between governments and capital gained renewed attention.

In symbolic terms, perhaps, the appearance in January 1994 of the first declaration of the Zapatistas in Chiapas, Mexico, which tied together opposition to NAFTA, neoliberalism, and continuing oppression, represented a turning point.[34] The poetic "First Declaration of the Lacandon Jungle" made direct theoretical linkages between the struggle of some of Mexico's poorest indigenous peoples and the developing shape of globalizing world capitalism. It may be claimed as the initial manifesto of a new and wider movement wave, and one of the inspirations for the "Global Justice Movement" or the "movement of movements."

From the mid-1990s, new international alliances formed, addressing and campaigning against *general economic inequalities*. Activists began constructing a global movement outline, targeting the structures of contemporary capitalism—albeit with little clarity about how much needed to be changed, or how. The initial actors were as likely to be churches and NGOs as groupings from the Left. One major focus, along with ecological threats, was the suffering of the poor in Third World countries: targets included sweatshops producing for major multinationals, the displacement of peasant farmers, the ills of agribusiness, Third World debt, and unfair trade agreements. Demonstrations were held outside IMF and World Bank meetings. New militant formations emerged to pick up the anti-globalization theme. These initiatives lay behind the November 1999 "Battle of Seattle," where protesters from a variety of campaigns and organizations joined to shut down a meeting of the World Trade Organization, giving a decisive boost to the movement.

If the movement expressed no widely accepted "political economy," it did demonstrate the existence of an expanding audience for one. It made no clear distinction between "reform" and "revolution," nor were most adherents anxious to differentiate on this basis. Rather, new forms of collaboration between different kinds of actors and different kinds of repertoire were being tested. Seattle and its aftermath directly challenged two previously powerful ideas about contemporary social movements: that they had no interest in "Grand Narratives" and that they were focused on issues of personal identity and "postmaterialism." After Seattle, two slogans rapidly became popular internationally: "Another World Is Possible" and "Our World Is Not for Sale."

The "global justice" framework brought together numerous campaigns and struggles that raised claims against a perceived common global enemy; its claims were anti-systemic.[35] Although, in any particular country, it involved only a very small minority of the population, the emerging movement was distinctive. After 1968, Michael Hardt suggests, "struggles . . . did not create chains, . . . did not create cycles." Movements had lost a sense of a common enemy and a common language. But now something else was emerging: "It clearly is a cycle, of sorts, and there is developing a common language and common enemies."[36]

The movement expanded across continents, gathering large numbers of demonstrators at official international policy gatherings, from Prague to Melbourne to Quebec to Genoa. Elizabeth Humphrys suggests that in Australia, at least, the movement was beginning to lose its way by the summer of 2001, in the face of some uncertainty about what it should *do* beyond continued "summit-hopping"—a form of contention restricted to a minority of would-be activists.[37] The advent of the World Social Forum, which held its first meeting at Porto Alegre in April 2001, did not alter this problem.

In any case, the movement's existing forms were thrown into disarray by the attack on the Twin Towers on September 11, 2001. Suddenly official politics was dominated by the "war on terror" and the "clash of civilizations." Much of the steam went out of the original Global Justice Movement.[38] Most activists in the advanced countries focused attention on a swelling anti-war movement, but that too began to fade as the wars in Iraq and Afghanistan dragged on. The World Social Forum became mired in problems about its nature and future. Regional Social Forums, in Europe and elsewhere, also went through a small cycle of expansion, contention, and decline. It seemed that "global anti-capitalism" had peaked and then declined. Its initial forms of expression had partly been exhausted. The problems it addressed had not gone away, but its capacity to focus resistance had seemingly weakened.

Instead, the major arenas of struggle against neoliberal capitalism shifted to the diverse *national* terrains, where movements came up against their local states, as key agencies through which the impulses of world capitalism are translated into everyday life. As Tom O'Lincoln shows in his chapter on the Indonesian revolution of 1998, the immediate background to the fall of Suharto was the East Asian financial crisis and the regime's attempts to impose IMF "solutions." In terms of our periodization of revolutions, Indonesia represents a hinge case. It could be read as a revolution against the "crony capitalism" of the past and impelled by the neoliberal tide; equally, it was widely seen as a response to the East Asia crash and therefore a rebuke to neoliberalizing capitalism.

As our chapters by Jorge Sanmartino, Jeffery Webber, and Mike Gonzalez highlight, it was Latin America that, for half a decade after 2000, hosted the most advanced and widespread popular challenges to the neoliberal project, as it moved from its vanguard phase to its global consolidation. If the movements of previous years had been mostly defensive, they had begun to develop novel ways of organizing, struggling to "recompose" their forces and create new "infrastructures of resistance."[39] The regional economic crisis of 1998–2002 saw them turn to offensive strategies, opening up a period of movement creativity across Latin America, involving new kinds of alliance between workers and peasants, new forms of insurgent collective action, and of deliberative assembly and efforts at self-government, often involving grassroots participatory democracy. Among the high points were the "Argentinazo" of December 2001; the momentous victory against water privatization in Cochabamba that initiated a five-year period of revolutionary upheaval, including the "Gas Wars" that brought down two presidents in 2003 and 2005; the popular uprising in Venezuela that defeated an attempted rightist coup against President Hugo Chávez in 2002; and the popular uprising in Mexico that installed the "Oaxaca Commune," which drove the police and army out of that city for several months in 2006. In any reasonable counting, these events included three "political revolutions" in which large numbers of people engaged in "mass sieges" of the regime, compelling presidents to resign. The streets of Argentina echoed to the cry: "Get rid of them all, every last one." (*Que se vayan todos, que no quede ni uno solo.*)

It was the energies developed in these kinds of movements that lay behind the election of left and center-left governments in South America that together comprised the "pink tide." They came into office in a context formed by popular pressure and greater tax revenues available to fund social reform. Buoyed by a tide of rising commodity prices (fueled by rocketing Chinese demand), governments in states like Brazil, Bolivia, and Venezuela were able to bring in social welfare measures and reduce absolute poverty—but not inequality and not a shift in their dependence on "extractivism." Some called them "compensatory" states. They raised tax rates on multinationals and used the increased funds to expand welfare programs. They did not, however, succeed in breaking the chains of dependency that characterized their general economic situation: indeed, the proportion of low-value primary production in output trended upward. In politics, they offered clientelist opportunities for advancement to *some* movement personnel, seeking to incorporate and contain popular insurgency. Where and when movements opposed them, for example over the expansion of raw material exploitation, their relations with those movements grew antagonistic.[40] From around 2012, raw materials prices started to fall and debt-to-GDP ratios deteriorated, undermining the basis for "compensatory" welfare payments and prompting governments to hike food, transport, fuel, and other prices. Their popular support waned, and the Right went on the offensive. Rather than being precursors of a "21st century socialism," their programs turned into what Webber calls "reconstituted neoliberalism." In the process they disarmed the radical impulses of the first half of the first decade, throwing left forces back into re-thinking and re-assembling.

In their own way, the pink tide governments repeated the processes that marked "reformism" in relation to the popular movements from below that were analyzed in *Revolutionary Rehearsals*: they both "represented" aspects of movements' demands and simultaneously constrained, pushed back, and misrepresented the democratic organizing impulses that those movements also contained. What faded from view were the transformative social visions that characterized the movements in Latin America in the half decade after 2000, to the point where, as Sanmartino puts it, those espousing such ideas "began to sound naive."

Resistance and revolt in the time of "monsters"

If the notion of "labor movement" is open to broadening and contestation, so is that of "class struggle," in terms of its *subjects* and its *objects*. One feature of the neoliberal era has been a broadening of the social composition of the labor movement. Its putative previous sameness was always an exaggeration; nonetheless, its heterogeneity has become more pronounced, with greater involvement of women workers in particular. Another feature has been a shift in its forms and arenas and objectives. As discussed by Colin Barker in the next chapter, questions of "democracy," and "rights," but also those of "social reproduction," have tended to come to the fore, through movements that focus not simply on working conditions but on life in general. As Miguel Martínez notes with respect to the 2014 "Umbrella Movement" in Hong Kong:

> Street occupants raised more criticisms of capitalism than in prior pro-democracy protests. It was not a protest exclusively focused on the goal of achieving a liberal democracy. Rather, property speculation, poor welfare policies and the wealth gap were intimately related to the democratic aspirations. Therefore, the Umbrella Movement represented not a mere challenge to the partial democratic regime of Hong Kong but also a contestation of both its limited political autonomy and the neoliberal rule in which the regime is rooted. . . . Although political liberties and a defence of liberal democracy are allegedly the main motivations of the UM activists, a critique of capitalism and productivism, environmental pollution and economic alienation permeated the discourses coming from the occupations.[41]

The Umbrella Movement was but one in a series of "urban civic revolts" or "urban uprisings" that punctuated world politics in the aftermath of the 2008 crisis. It took different forms in different countries, commencing with Iceland's 2009 "pots and pans revolution" that brought down the government of Geir Haarde. There followed the movements of "indignados" in Portugal, Spain, and Greece, along with America's "Occupy" movement in 2011, the mass demonstrations in Istanbul and other Turkish cities set off by the state's attempt to commercialize Gezi Park, and those in Brazil against higher transport fares in 2013. These were interwoven with and themselves sometimes led to other kinds of mass urban protests and strikes, including a series of general strikes in Greece and the "tides" and "marches for dignity" in Spain in 2012 and 2013, along with a host of different local campaigns and struggles around prices, housing, transport, health and welfare services, police behavior, and so forth.[42] In the overwhelming majority of cases, "political" and "economic" issues were closely intertwined, not least those around "social reproduction"—as Colin Barker discusses in the next chapter.[43]

The zenith of this cycle was reached in 2010–11 with the revolutions in Tunisia and Egypt. The latter case, analyzed in our penultimate chapter by Sameh Naguib, may have appeared to some as a classic "democratic revolution," with urban crowds protesting against gerrymandered elections, but it was far more than that. As Naguib documents, workers' strikes and grassroots neighborhood committees played a major role in the fall of Mubarak's regime, and protesters demanded not only democratization but social justice. The neoliberalization of Egyptian society under Mubarak was sharply in the frame. Egypt's old regime was of course able to fight back and, in 2013, crushed its enemies—the protesters, democracy, and the Muslim Brotherhood alike—in a bloody counterrevolution that was accompanied by others in Syria, Yemen, Bahrain, and across the region. The authoritarian nationalism of Abdel Fattah al-Sisi and Bashar al-Assad formed part of the "black tide" of reaction that pulsed around the world in the postcrash decade, led by the well-known pantheon of ghouls: Modi, Trump, Bolsonaro, Duterte, and Salvini.

How far we have come since the early 1990s, when Francis Fukuyama could propose that "History" was easing toward its terminus with the triumphant globalization of liberal democracy.[44] Not only has that tendency stalled or even reversed, but the other components of the 1990s liberal package—globalization and neoliberalism—are in a rickety (or "zombie") condition. Broader systemic contradictions discussed by Davidson in our final chapter—notably in society-nature relations—loom ever larger, while the neoliberal cycle of debt-driven boom followed by crisis, the socialization of losses, and bitter austerity appears set to continue. Increasing levels of sovereign debt, notes Beissinger, have been reshaping local and national political economies, "compounding popular grievances and rendering states vulnerable to fiscal crisis." Whereas in the past, war was frequently the source "of the fiscal crises that helped to precipitate social revolutions, due to the increased tax burdens that often accompanied it," in the post–Cold War era revolts have more commonly been connected to "fiscal austerity due to excessive foreign debt and government cutbacks of subsidies and jobs."[45] We can expect therefore all manner of social groups to move toward revolt. Indeed, even while completing this introduction in 2019, uprisings have mounted inspirational challenges to, and in some cases overthrown, regimes in Sudan, Algeria, Hong Kong, Lebanon, Ecuador, Chile, Iraq, and Iran.[46] In most cases, old-regime forces deploy the tools of counterrevolution—ballots, corruption, divide-and-rule tactics, co-optation, as well as murderous violence. How might the pattern be broken? Could global capitalism itself become subject to challenge, with social revolution once again appearing on the horizon of possibility?

We should not suppose that any half-realistic vision for social transformation "from below" already exists, awaiting only some form of "awakening" or "embodiment" in new movement practices and organizational forms, or that any exponents of such visions have merely to wait for the masses to turn to them for solutions. Nothing is less helpful than an idealization of the revolutionary tendencies of actual movements.[47] What movements should and can do is always a *contested* matter, and one in which most of the collective learning is undertaken in the midst of actual conflicts. Visions are needed, and ones, moreover, that go beyond simply opposition to the dictates of neoliberalism. This, as we understand it, is what Panagiotis Sotiris, writing on anti-capitalist strategy in Greece after the Syriza government's neoliberal turn, proposes with his notion of "productive reconstruction":

> We must think of "productive reconstruction" not as a "return to growth" but as a process of transformation and intense confrontation with capital, based upon public ownership, self-management, and forms of workers control. It has to be a process of experimentation and learning. Contemporary forms of solidarity, of self-management, of alternative non-commercial networks of distribution, of open access to services, the discussions on how to use the public sector or how to run public utilities are not only ways to deal with urgent social problems. They are also experimental test sites for alternative forms of production and social organization, based upon the "traces of communism" and collective inventiveness and ingenuity in contemporary resistances and everyday gestures of solidarity—something exemplified in the myriad acts of solidarity in Greece during the refugee crisis.[48]

Central to that reconstruction is the expansion of new forms of popular democratic power, of workers' control, of solidarity and coordination that lie beyond the scope, and indeed the competence, of mere parliamentarism. If "social revolution" is again to belong on the agenda of the Left, that is where it must find its center: not simply in a change of government, but in the remaking of power and control across the whole face of society, a remaking that must—here Sotiris cites Antonio Gramsci's *Prison Notebooks*—attend to the "molecular" forms of historical change, that is to say, the multifarious, complex, and non-deterministic ways in which social practices are continually being reshaped.

PART 1:
THEORETICAL IMPLICATIONS

CHAPTER 1

Social Movements and the Possibility of Socialist Revolution

Colin Barker[1]

Introduction

Was there a time when many Marxists believed that the tracks of history led more or less inexorably—even with some delays and retreats—to a socialist future? If so, few such Marxists survive today. Rather, as Cinzia Arruzza recently suggested:

> We are not on a train traveling toward universal liberation and equality. Irreversible ecological disaster is actually at the moment a more likely possibility than a global revolution dispensing with capitalism once and for all. In fact, by connecting us into a "world," capitalism has created only the historical *possibility* for a politics of insurgent universality, not its historical *necessity*.[2]

It is now over a century since the last, indeed the *only* successful attempt at a socialist revolution, the Bolshevik revolution of 1917. That attempt, moreover, ended in the "degeneration" and then the complete reversal of the democratic, egalitarian, and internationalist ideals of "October." Every attempt since has failed. Just as the 1871 Paris Commune was defeated through its isolation in one city, so the revolution in Catalonia in 1936–37 was isolated and defeated; similar fates dogged the Central Workers Council of 1956–57 in Hungary and Solidarność in Poland in 1980–81.[3] To be sure, there have

27

been self-styled "socialist revolutions" that overthrew old regimes and indeed empires but that installed new regimes pursuing state-centered capitalist development, giving a new lease of life to varieties of schemes for "socialism from above," but none of these was centered on the self-emancipation of labor or an explosion of democratic participation. Rather, Rousseau's paradox, adopted by Solidarność in Poland in 1980, remains predominant: "The human being is born free but is everywhere in chains." The chains may now be the insistent demands of debt and vulture capitalism, but they are nonetheless heavy. Perhaps the predominant mood today is what the late Mark Fisher termed "capitalist realism": "the widespread sense that not only is capitalism the only viable political and economic system, but also that it is now impossible even to *imagine* a coherent alternative to it."[4]

It might, then, seem somewhat perverse to be still asking: How *might* social movements prepare the way for a renewed effort at the revolutionizing—the overthrow—of capitalist social relations and their associated system of states? Just when climate change—the result of everyday capitalist competition—threatens the very existence of ever larger numbers of human and other life forms, and when capitalist industry and commerce are throttling the deepest oceans with plastic debris, how *might* such movements "save the planet" and humanity's place upon it? After a century of failures on the left, would we not be better engaged in refining our apocalyptic despair and preparing for a million Jonestowns?

And yet . . . every one of the failures that have branded the souls of today's Left was at least *explicable*. Like Bertolt Brecht's *Rise of Arturo Ui*, every political disaster was *resistible*. If "inevitability" never marked the road to socialism, it also never signposted capitalism's Onward March. Victories have been won—even if they were not the "final victory" we and our forebears wanted. If the old Left has been "rolled back" under neoliberalism, that has happened before and New Lefts have emerged from unexpected quarters and with new vigor. Capitalist society is not characterized by inexorability but by *class struggle*, battles for alternatives, surges of popular opposition, always taking new forms, drawing in new forces, developing new repertoires, broadening imaginations, exploring and refining arguments, testing limits and boundaries.

1. Class struggle and social movements

"Class struggle" is a summary term for the conflicts in modern society whose central axis is the capitalist mode of production itself, that is, the current system of social relations that is doubly driven by competition among its producing and consuming units and by the ongoing exploitation and oppression of its dispossessed majorities. As a system, it generates both needs it cannot meet and variable resources for popular resistance. Class struggle is at least a two-sided affair, in which all sides are active strategists in the pursuit of their opposed aims. Within the Marxist tradition, it possesses an additional feature, as the potential source of systematic change. As Marx told his friend Joseph Weydemeyer:

> No credit is due to me for discovering the existence of classes in modern society or the struggle between them. . . . What I did that was new was to prove: (1) that the existence of classes is only bound up with particular historical phases in the development of production, (2) that the class struggle necessarily leads to the dictatorship of the proletariat, (3) that this dictatorship itself only constitutes the transition to the abolition of all classes and to a classless society.[5]

Marx thus credited class struggle as the means not simply for the pursuit of immediate objectives *within* existing society, but for far-reaching social and political transformation, for *social revolution*. As to why revolution is required, Marx provided a summary two-part answer. The first is familiar: no other method can separate the ruling class from their property and power. But second (and more important), "The alteration of men on a mass scale is necessary, an alteration which can only take place in a practical movement, a revolution"; only active participation in a revolutionary movement can enable the oppressed to get rid of "the muck of ages" and transform themselves into subjects capable of remaking the world.[6] Using other language, Marx expressed the same idea in the opening sentence of the Rules of the First International, "The emancipation of the working classes must be conquered by the working classes themselves."[7] In this light, the central problem facing revolutionary politics consists in identifying and overcoming the multiple obstacles and difficulties that the exploited and oppressed face in developing their own collective self-organization and self-empowerment. This was the heart of what Hal Draper, in a brilliant essay, termed "socialism from below" as against all the varieties of "socialism from above."[8] "Subalternity" is how Gramsci dubbed that problem of the muck of ages. His "subaltern" is a term whose usage develops through his *Prison Notebooks*.[9] It first appears in the third Notebook, where he writes:

> The history of the subaltern classes is necessarily fragmented and episodic; in the activity of these classes there is a tendency toward unification, albeit in provisional stages, but this is the least conspicuous aspect, and it manifests itself only when victory is secured. Subaltern classes are subject to the initiatives of the dominant class, even when they rebel; they are in a state of anxious defense.

Hence, he concluded, "every trace of autonomous initiative is therefore of inestimable value."[10]

Subalternity—dependence on the initiatives of the dominant class—manifests itself in practical passivity and in disbelief that our own and our fellows' collective activity has the potential to alter the conditions of everyday life. In its extreme, it is portrayed in Javier Auyero's anthropological explorations of the powerlessness and confusion of the Argentinian poor in the face of both environmental poisoning and welfare dependency.[11] More generally, it is expressed most of the time in what Gramsci terms people's "contradictory consciousness." While it's never the case that popular consciousness is completely dominated by ruling-class ideas, it mostly remains an unstable amalgam, mixing together elements of a conception of the world borrowed from ruling groups along with elements of independent critical judgment that may only manifest themselves "occasionally and in flashes." This second set of elements involves what Gramsci means by "good sense," "the healthy nucleus that exists in 'common sense' . . . and which deserves to be made more unitary and coherent."[12]

> The personality is strangely composite: it contains Stone Age elements and principles of a more advanced science, prejudices from all past phases of history at the local level and intuitions of a future philosophy which will be that of a human race united the world over. . . . The active person-in-the-mass has a practical activity, but has no clear theoretical consciousness of their practical activity, which nonetheless involves understanding the world in so far as it transforms it. Their theoretical consciousness can indeed be historically in opposition to their activity. One might also say that he or she has two theoretical consciousnesses (or one contradictory consciousness): one which is implicit in their activity and which in reality unites them with all their fellow-workers in the practical transformation of the real world; and one, superficially explicit or verbal, which they have inherited from the past and uncritically absorbed. . . . Critical understanding of self therefore takes place through a struggle of political "hegemonies" and of opposing

directions, in order to arrive at the working out of at a higher level of one's own conception of reality. . . . The unity of theory and practice is a part of the historical process, whose elementary and primitive phase is to be found in the sense of being "different" and "apart," in an instinctive feeling of independence, and which progresses to the level of real possession of a single and coherent conception of the world.[13]

Subaltern groups in Gramsci are never simply "objects" of historical development, the products of outside influence, although it can seem that way, especially in periods of time and in sectors of society when organized struggle from below is at a low ebb. Not seeing the potentials of "good sense" within "common sense" involves a one-sided appreciation of popular consciousness, associated with cynicism and elitism: not uncommonly, this can be witnessed among the exploited and oppressed themselves as expressions of defeat. Rather like Gramsci's "fatalism," such cynicism "is nothing but the clothing worn by real and active will when in a weak position." It is always a *partial* stance: "In fact, however, some part of even a subaltern mass is always directive and responsible."[14]

This implies a theory of "ideology," an often misused term, several aspects of whose functioning demand recognition. First, ideologies are inherently practical, action-oriented. They tell us not only what the world is like, and what value-standards we should apply to experience, but also what is and is not practically feasible. As well as telling us who we are, how to understand our relations to the material and social worlds, what counts as good and beautiful, our ideas also suggest what we can hope and what we can do.[15] Second, we think "in groups" and not as isolated monads, forming our ideas in ongoing, never-completed interactive conversations. Language and thought are, as V. N. Voloshinov, the Marxist philosopher of "signs," insisted, intrinsically "dialogical."[16] Third, ideologies are consequently open-ended, self-transforming, and hence operate in a condition of "disorder."[17] Our formulations are constantly being "tested" against material and social reality, hence—even when we believe them to be fixed and certain—are always provisional.[18] Fourth, there is commonly a disjunction between what people think "privately" and what they say and do. One source of this is their practical caution in the face of power, exercised both by those in superordinate positions but also by relative equals. The American anthropologist James C. Scott offers a very fruitful account of the critical but "hidden transcripts" of the powerless, which too easily escape the attention of historians and social scientists.[19] Fifth, there is "unevenness" and a lack of homogeneity within the thinking of all classes and groups, such that collective responses to situations must always be negotiated and argued.[20]

Often, the "provisional" character of ideological containment is too little stressed. At any given moment, a majority of people may feel that key aspects of the social structure are unchangeable. But such feelings are rooted not in some fixed and unchanging permanent "self-mystification" generated by social relations, but in the context of ongoing critical dialogue and action. People give challengeable reasons for their sense of "unchangeability," and these reveal pragmatic judgments about social forces and experiences. "Socialism is impossible—look at my husband"; "We can't strike, the miners were defeated"; "Most workers are just stupid—how else did the Tories get back in?" Pragmatic judgments are experiential, hence fluid.

2. Social movement heterogeneity

Under what conditions might we expect the balance between "common sense" and "good sense" to shift away from "subalternity," or dependence on initiatives by others?[21] When might "rebellious" activity lose its feeling of "anxious defense" and assert itself more confidently? To attempt answers to such questions is to inquire into the potentials contained in collective activity and organization from below, in short into "social movements."

"Social movements" are a shorthand term for the forms through which the exploited and oppressed engage together in struggle against aspects of their conditions of life. They are the phenomenal forms in which class struggle from below appears.[22] Defining social movements has been accounted a "theoretical nightmare";[23] it is certainly impossible outside the conflicts in which they emerge. People associate together in an effort to oppose some pressing feature of the situation in which they find themselves, and in the process establish informal or formal organizational links among themselves through which they can determine how their mutual activity might ameliorate or remove the obstacles to their needs, and how they may act in concert.[24] Movements then develop through their practical interactions with their opponents and with those they seek to draw into their ranks and as they work to make sense of their own existence and the tasks they undertake.

The social phenomena that comprise movements range enormously in scale, from "local" formations contesting particular offending situations to broader "campaigns" all the way to society-wide revolutionary challenges to states and capital.[25] Movements at any scale in their development are varied in their composition, and what makes them a relative "unity" as entities is the emergence among them of some kind of shared "project" for change. They combine together individuals and groups with particular interests and grievances, always to some degree overcoming differences among them yet at the same time remaining heterogeneous.

In this view, movements are not so much fixed entities following predetermined pathways as developing fields of activity and argument. Romanticist commentators sometimes miss this: they see the relative unity that movements sometimes achieve but miss their inner differentiation. Therewith they also miss the "cycles of learning" that movements undergo in their dealings with opponents and their efforts to steer themselves.[26] Movements are bodies engaged in popular learning and experimentation of a practical and theoretical character, processes involving internal debate and the practical testing of strategic and tactical conceptions.

Where the actions and organizational links that mark the presence of social movements have any degree of longevity, the activists whose networks form their core architecture are liable to develop systems of communication among themselves, woven through the everyday networks of work, community, and other forms of associational life. Alan Sears conceives of these as "infrastructures of dissent," referring to

> the means through which activists develop political communities capable of learning, communicating and mobilizing together. This process of collective capacity-building takes a variety of forms, ranging from informal neighborhood and workplace networks to formal organizations and structured learning settings. The infrastructure of dissent is a crucial feature of popular mobilization, providing the basic connections that underlie even apparently spontaneous protest actions.[27]

The development of such systems of communication or infrastructures of dissent is itself shaped by ongoing processes of (re-)composition of classes, through the impact of shifts in the forms of production, patterns of employment and of urban life, inward and outward migration, available means of communication, and the shapes and extents of state intervention. Such communication systems and infrastructures are themselves not "given" but are directly *built* through the activity and imagination of activists. They are also, as we shall discuss further below, liable to decay and weaken in effectiveness, to splinter and to collapse under the impact of external changes, and not least in the wake of movement defeats. New generations thus have to re-imagine and re-make them out of the material possibilities that await discovery in new forms of capitalist society. The "making" and "re-making" of "subordinate classes" and their cultures of resistance mark the history of all capitalist societies; they present themselves as sets of political tasks that are the work of social movements, locally, nationally, and internationally.

One claim made for recent movements needs to be discounted: namely that relationships among participants are "horizontal" and marked by "leaderlessness." This is to "flatten" the idea of the networks that comprise movements, and to overlook how they *move*, shift focus, adopt new tactics and forms, etc. As the Brazilian Marxist Rodrigo Nunes suggests, movement networks are actually "leaderful"; their patterns of development consist in a succession of leadership initiatives or "vanguard functions" being performed by particular hubs and nodes within their networks. These hubs and nodes make "readings" of the movement around them, offer proposals for collective action and organization, and meet with a variety of accepting or rejecting responses from other connecting nodes.[28] "Leadership" may thus pass from one hub to another, or draw different hubs together, forming new chains of influence, new communication systems, and opening up new lines of thinking, action, and organization.[29] The decade beginning in 2010 has been full of instances of this kind of development, with new ideas hopping across national boundaries and being tested and modified as they travel. The fruitfulness of Nunes's ideas appears strongly if they are applied to the quite different movements analyzed by E. P. Thompson in his classic work, *The Making of the English Working Class*.

The character of these communication systems or infrastructures shapes the possibilities open to movements. The comparison Gareth Dale makes in this volume between Poland and East Germany is instructive: in East Germany after 1953, working-class activist networks gradually atrophied, but in Poland they were kept alive and renewed in surges of working-class militancy (1956, 1970–71, 1976, and 1980–81) but also in the years between these surge periods, via informal and semi-organized networks that linked workplaces. These in turn facilitated the formation of the *interfactory strike committees* that organized the anti-regime movements of 1971 and 1980 and provided the underlying organizational shape to Solidarność.[30] Nothing comparable happened in the 1989 revolutions in East Germany (or Czechoslovakia), despite the extensive participation of workers.[31]

Such "infrastructures of dissent" should not be thought of simply as autonomous centers of popular militancy. They are also interwoven into all manner of political, social, cultural, and religious networks, across which participants collaborate with and challenge each other over which ideas and practices should be valued and which should be marginalized. In the neoliberal era, activists in the West might look back fondly at the extensive popular networks that shaped working-class resistance in previous decades, when trade-union membership figures were much higher, and when strikes were far more common than today. They risk forgetting the powerful tendencies to *conservatism* within those networks and the relative power of union bureaucracies and rightward-moving social democratic and communist party formations. The *defeats* that workers' movements experienced, notably in the later 1970s and the 1980s under what Neil Davidson has termed "vanguard neoliberalism," were in principle *resistible*, but the labor movements of the time were ill-equipped for this.[32] If for a time, during the 1960s and early 1970s, rank-and-file oppositional movements within and around trade unions posed the possibility of pulling the movements to the left, by the mid-1970s conservative and bureaucratic tendencies were again in the ascendant—notably in the UK, Italy, and the US—and rank-and-file movements proved incapable of organizing effectively to prevent major defeats in the 1980s.[33]

Nor is "militancy" in itself a sufficient resource for movement success. South Africa in recent years has been denoted "the protest capital of the world," yet its oppositional movements are separated from each other:

> From 2004, South Africa has experienced a level of ongoing urban unrest that is arguably greater than anywhere in the world, and its strike statistics reveal the highest number of days lost per capita per annum. Although there is widespread sympathy between actors in these two movements, evidence of unity is minimal.[34]

Peter Alexander and Peter Pfaffe insist that the two kinds of movement they explore—township revolts and workplace struggles—are both collective expressions of a shared working-class situation. The two groups of participants, unemployed township youth and employed workers, both belong to the same working class, one as an employed section, the other as part of the "reserve army of labour." Yet, while their "core" opponent, South African capitalism under the ANC government, is the same, their forms of action are distinct, sometimes directly contradicting each other. The two "wings" of the movement—whose personnel, of course, move back and forth between them over their lifetimes and who often share common residential patterns—are not synchronized in the means of contention they deploy or the forms of association they develop. Alexander and Pfaffe draw parallels with earlier work done in two different settings, by Ira Katznelson in the US and Manuel Castells in Spain. Katznelson, generalizing about US history, distinguished between "work and community-based conflicts" and concluded that "the links between (them) . . . have been unusually tenuous. . . . Each kind of conflict has had its own separate vocabulary and set of institutions. . . . Class, in short, has been lived and fought as a series of partial relationships, and it has therefore been experienced and talked about as only one of a number of competing bases of social life." This experience, he suggested, helps account for the relative weakness of radical politics in the US. Castells, writing about "the largest . . . urban movement in Europe since 1945," identified two components in the Spanish movement of the later 1970s: the labor movement and neighborhood associations. Rather like Katznelson, he recorded that the two wings "fought separate battles, even if they often clashed with the same police and exchanged messages of solidarity. . . . They were allies not comrades."[35] Those neighborhood associations barely survived the advent of elections: "The vigorous neighbourhood movement that flourished in Madrid and Barcelona during the late Franco period for the purpose of demanding a wide array of social services alongside civil and political freedoms . . . did not live to see the success of the democratic transition. Right before the 1977 elections, most neighbourhood associations went into a period of crisis and eventual decline."[36]

As I write this in early 2019, it seems that some workers' militant movements in the US are moving toward erasing former boundaries between themselves and other movements and other claimants. The teachers' strikes, beginning in Chicago in 2012, were notable for including in their demands calls for improvements in their students' conditions and for organizing solidarity from both students and their parents. Fighting not only for their own pay but also for wider social gains gave their struggle enormous added power but also caught the attention of and brought inspiration to other teachers across the country. They struck at once against the general running down of public education, and, equally, against state racism and for communal solidarity. 2018 saw major teacher strikes across five "red states," followed in January 2019 by a massively successful teachers' strike in Los Angeles, taking up issues of "social reproduction" as well as teachers' pay and conditions.

Considered as a whole, popular movements are normally heterogeneous in their manner of assembling people into activity, uneven in their patterns of development, variably resource-rich, prone to different repertoires of collective action and organization, bound by distinct types of social ties. They are "segmented" in all manner of ways, even if—from the standpoint of the analyst (or of the committed activist)—their different "parts" are all responses to the same general sets of problems with common roots in a definite mode of production and a definite social formation. One of the first Marxists to draw theoretical attention to this was Rosa Luxemburg in *The Mass Strike*—her account is one in which the differences between segments played a positive role, as each *energized* the others:

> Every one of the great mass strikes repeats, so to speak, on a small scale, the entire history of the Russian mass strike, and begins with a pure economic, or at all events, a partial trade union conflict, and runs through all the stages to the political demonstration. . . . [And each] political action, after it has attained its highest peak, breaks up into a mass of economic strikes. . . . With the spreading, clarifying and involution of the political struggle, the economic struggle not only does not recede, but extends, organizes and becomes involved in equal measure. Between the two there is the most complete reciprocal action.[37]

As Luxemburg stresses, this "reciprocal action" is a feature chiefly of *revolutionary* periods. In like manner, Alexander and Pfaffe recall that the "hinge" that has opened in post-Apartheid South Africa's movements was largely closed in the course of the struggle against Apartheid in the 1980s, when township and trade-union struggles were mutually reinforcing. In other periods, and other situations, systems of communication or infrastructures of dissent may express and organize divisions within and among movements as much as they may unite them. Indeed, it was part of the work of classical social democracy to maintain a distinction of "spheres," keeping "political" questions as the preserve of a parliament-oriented party, while "economic" questions were left to trade unions and cooperatives and especially to their leaderships.

3. Are movements inherently reformist?

Part of the difficulty in defining movements is that they refuse strict classification. They are themselves realms of inner contestation as to their purposes, the means they use, the inclusivity of their "memberships," the nature of their targets, and so on. They change over time and in the course of their struggles, and they contain multiple possibilities. This view of social movements requires the rejection of some other characterizations—one very influential one coming from Charles Tilly: "A social movement consists of a sustained challenge to powerholders in the name of a population living under the jurisdiction of those powerholders by means of repeated public displays of that population's *numbers, commitment, unity and worthiness*." Tilly summarizes these qualities as a population's "WUNC." In general, he suggests, social movements center on *indirect* forms of action:

> actions that display will and capacity, but that would not in themselves accomplish the objectives on behalf of which they make claims. *Social movements call instead for powerholders to take the crucial actions.* While obviously applicable to campaigns for civil rights, women's suffrage, or peace, this *indirectness* also characterizes movements for environmental action, Third World solidarity, abortion rights, or sexual preference; they organize around the demand that powerholders recognize, protect, endorse, forward, or even impose a given program.[38]

Thus, while Tilly defines movements in terms of their interactions with the powerful, he limits them to engaging in what we might term "militant lobbying." They remain on the terrain of "petitioners," even if the forms of collective action they deploy are apparently radical, including various forms of "direct action," "civil disobedience," "mass strikes," etc. What Tilly's movements *don't* do is seek to accomplish their aims by *removing* powerholders and placing themselves in the seat(s) of power. In short, social movements are *reformist* and always *dependent on the initiative of others* in their overall orientation. In Gramsci's term, they remain "subaltern."

If Tilly's limitation sets social movements apart from any questions about *social revolution*, it also seems unnecessary. There seems no good reason not to treat movements as the bearers of *multiple possibilities*, all the way from the most timid petitioning to full-blown social revolution. Indeed, it is not uncommon for them to contain among their ranks protagonists of these and many other possibilities, all seeking with greater or less effectiveness to win adherents to their distinct standpoints. These inner debates, along with the outcomes of movements' various encounters with their opponents, shape their actual developmental paths—which remain, in principle, *open*.[39]

4. "Protest waves"

This openness is found at every scale or level of movement development, but it assumes particular significance when movements take on a "mass" scale, as in the "waves of protest" that irregularly—and often surprisingly—mark the history of political development in different capitalist countries, sometimes indeed spilling across national boundaries. Such protest waves provide the moments when new possibilities are most likely to emerge.

The very emergence of a popular movement on any significant scale involves a change in the political and social landscape, and not least for movement participants. They must make sense of the newly emergent situation and occupy themselves with questions that, for most, were previously outside their immediate concerns. Once collectively active, they are compelled to begin to think about fundamental strategic and tactical questions, summarized by Marvin Gaye and V. I. Lenin: *What's going on?* and *What is to be done?* The two sets of questions are interconnected and have multiple aspects. Who are *they* and why are they acting this way? How strong are they, and what are their vulnerabilities? Who are *we*, and what might we *become*? Who might we win to our side? Who, if anyone, does not belong with us? What should we be demanding or making happen, and how—and is it enough? How should we organize ourselves, who can we trust and who should we treat with suspicion? What might be better and worse ways for us to conduct ourselves? How did what happened *yesterday* affect what we might do *today and tomorrow*? And so on . . . None of these questions allows simple answers. They are *problems*, to which stock solutions commonly do not apply, and which require discussion, exploration, drawing on past experiences but also creatively imagining, modeling, and testing new ways of handling them. They are occasions for argument but also for innovative and productive new agreements. Wrestling with them demands *dialogue*, often marked by a new urgency. All manner of individuals and groups may contribute to the ongoing debates—including those who are *opposed* to the movement's very existence or to its further development. To the degree that more people are engaged in collective action, more voices are available to contribute to movement debates, but there is also a greater variety in those voices, with potentials for misunderstandings, confusions, and divisions. On the other hand, the advent of larger numbers also expands the range of conceivable solutions to problems.

The central feature is that, commonly for the first time, large numbers of people are drawn, through their own collective activity, into making a movement, and in so doing also into making that movement's theoretical, strategic, and tactical questions their own. The rise of large-scale popular movements alters the political landscape, and not only for the participants. It centrally involves what Leon Trotsky terms "the direct interference of the masses in historic events." This opens the field of *possibilities* as nothing else can. For Trotsky, of course, this was the central process of *revolution*: "the forcible entrance of the masses into the realm of rulership over their own destiny."[40] Such developments often throw ruling classes into disarray. The normal basis of their rule assumes the relatively "tractable" nature (Edmund Burke) of those they dominate, a condition that depends on their "knowing their place" and—above all—not acting and organizing collectively. "Normality," as historian Lawrence Goodwyn puts it nicely, is a condition where "a relatively small number of citizens possessing high sanction move about in an authoritative manner and a much larger number of people without such sanction move about more softly."[41] The partial or large-scale upsetting of that condition can compel the powerful to stutter and fall back, sometimes to concede something. But only for a while: ultimately, an "organized people" (or "an organizing people") is an intolerable constraint on ongoing exploitation and oppression. By one means or another, by some variable mixture of repression and/or compromise and co-optation, ruling elites will attempt to claw back their position and remove or reduce the threats posed by the very existence of popular movements. They will look for ways to reduce movement impacts, not least by seeking allies from *within* the movement who reject its further potential radicalization. As Alan Shandro remarks, movement ideas, organizational forms and methods of struggle are all within the "strategic sights" of their opponents.[42] The direct and indirect efforts of movement opponents to contain and defeat them, in turn, set up new tensions and dilemmas for those movements themselves. Indeed, many of the events and dramatic encounters that mark movements' developmental paths are generated in the interactions between movement participants and their opponents.

5. New potentials

The question that mass movements pose for Marxism is: *What might they become?* What in the practice and organization of social movements could point toward them becoming core agents in the remaking of society on new, far more democratic foundations? Can they represent a "bridge" between everyday struggles within the framework of capitalism and struggles to over-throw it? If so, how? The very question implies a notion of "immanence": that within the highly contradictory formations that social movements represent there exist, to larger or smaller degree, potentials for large-scale and profound social transformation. "It will be said," wrote Gramsci, "that what each individual can change is very little, considering their strength. This is true up to a point. But when an individual can associate himself or herself with all the other individuals who want the same changes, and if the changes wanted are rational, the individual can be multiplied an impressive number of times and can obtain a change which is far more radical than at first sight ever seemed possible."[43] To that we must add that some of the ways in which individuals "associate" with others, and some of the joint activities they engage in, are more promising in this regard than others.

Participants in movements make "leaps" in their own development. From "passivity" (itself a complex mixture of practices, impulses, and ideas) they move into *collective activity*. These changes in their activity also involve changes in themselves. Every leap is conditioned by its jumping-off point. For workers who have never before dared to challenge their boss, a small strike or even workplace meeting is a major event, especially if those involved know that all around them others are organizing, taking collective action, voicing their discontents at the same time. Solidarność's victory in August 1980 set off many such local struggles in the following months. Andrzej Gwiazda, the union's vice-president, later described his experiences at a meeting of workers in the book trade: "There I could see with my own eyes how a workers' assembly, divided into groups and grouplets, terrified by the presence of the manager and other official figures, and with absolutely no faith in the possibilities of success, transformed itself into a fighting, democratic organization after four hours of discussion."[44] Martin Luther King Jr. argued that the civil rights movement advanced the self-respect of black Americans:

> Our non-violent protest in Montgomery is important because it is demon-strating to the Negro, North and South, that many of the stereotypes he has held about himself and other Negroes are not valid. . . . In Montgomery we walk in a new way. We hold our heads in a new way. Even the Negro reporters who converged on Montgomery have a new attitude. One tired reporter, asked at a luncheon in Birmingham to say a few words about Montgomery, stood up, thought for a moment, and uttered one sentence: "Montgomery has made me proud to be a Negro."[45]

In like manner, joining in collective action in the context of a mass movement enhances everyday citizens' sense of their own powers and their own role in history-making. By the multiplication of apparently small events a mass movement can grow very fast, with its participants all making their own self-transformative leaps in mutual confidence, organization, and understanding.

At the same time that some are finding the courage and the incentive to engage for the first time in already familiar forms of organization and activity, others may be pushing ahead by inventing new forms. Periods of mass insurgency witness an expanded use of already developed "repertoires of contention" (workplace strikes, joining and forming unions, demonstrating in the streets with banners, attending political meetings, and the like), but such periods of mass insurgency, or what Sidney Tarrow termed "protest cycles," are also often marked by *innovations in methods of struggle*: "Cycles of protest are the crucibles within which the repertoire of collective action expands."[46] Such new methods can *spread* rapidly to become additions to a cultural *repertoire* in political circumstances where not only are more layers of people engaged in collective action, but also they are more aware of and more actively connected with each other and thus capable of *learning* from each other.

Because mass movements activate larger numbers of participants than is normal in the political life of capitalist societies, all manner of things that previously seemed unchangeable move within the horizons of possibility. An oppressive police force can be driven from the streets, whether in Petrograd in 1917, in Oaxaca in 2006, or in Cairo in 2011. Hated and corrupt bosses can be driven out: unpopular foremen were "wheelbarrowed" in Russia in 1905 and 1917; former fascists were subjected to *saneamento* (cleansing) from public, private, and union offices in Portugal in 1974–75; Polish workers forced the removal of corrupt officials in 1980–81; and Egyptian workers demanded *tathir* (purification) of autocratic bosses and owners—demands that strengthened and spread during 2011 and 2012, shifting the "frontier of control" in workplaces and the state alike.[47]

Commonly, in mass movements people begin to establish their own collective control over aspects of everyday life that were previously beyond their normal reach. They occupy premises and spaces, establish their own control over entry and exit and their own rules for the use of what they have taken. The Petrograd soviet in 1905 took over control of food supplies, and similar developments marked other movements, as in the French general strike in Nantes in 1968.[48] In Seattle during the 1919 general strike, the citywide strike committee took control of local transport, issuing passes to bus drivers for the movement of essential goods.[49] In Barcelona, in 1936, during "the greatest revolutionary festival in the history of contemporary Europe," workers occupied "elite neighbourhoods, church property, business offices, hotels and the palaces of the rich," converting them to new uses. After the National Confederation of Labor (Confederación Nacional del Trabajo, or CNT) called for a return to work, workers' committees collectivized several thousand enterprises under workers' control. The Barcelona Ritz became Hotel Gastronómico no. 1, "a communal eating house under union control providing meals for members of the militia, the urban dispossessed from poor inner-city *barrios*, cabaret artists and factory workers"; "assistance to the unemployed ensured that begging was largely eradicated after July"; the workers' movement developed new schools and medical facilities.[50] Taking over printing facilities and radio stations to challenge state and capitalist media monopolies was a notable feature of the popular revolution in Portugal in 1974–75 and of the virtual recreation of a Commune in Oaxaca, Mexico, in 2006.[51] In Greece, the main public broadcaster, ERT, was placed under workers' control for several weeks in 2013 before the occupiers were evicted by the riot police. They went on to organize an internet-based media service:

> These workers went on to develop innovative ways of organizing the production of shows, challenging previous distinctions between technical and creative roles. It was hard. They were not being paid. So it was not a model for withdrawing from the society. Rather, it was a lived experiment of how democratic participation and control might be extended deeper into the society—if the central structures of economic and state power were brought undercontrol.[52]

In the occupied workplaces of Gdansk, Poland, in 1980, the strike committee's own security details banned alcohol. Inside the Lenin Shipyard, the interfactory strike committee took over the loudspeaker system, keeping thousands within (and outside the gates) informed about their meetings and broadcasting their negotiations with the regime's representatives. They organized feeding and sleeping arrangements, even building "workers' dachas" out of available materials in the shipyard.[53] At the Gdynia port occupation, workers caught stealing cigarettes from the bonded warehouse were sentenced by a popular tribunal to stand on pallets with "thief" placards round their necks.[54] The interfactory strike committee took control of the city's taxis and trams, and reopened a striking canning factory, so as not to waste the fish when the Baltic fleet came into port. The Polish strikers refused even to open negotiations with the regime until it restored telephone communications across the country.

The everyday material necessities of conducting mass struggles provide the setting in which some advances in popular control are made and new social forces are drawn into involvement. In Tahrir Square, Cairo, in 2011, the organization of physical defense, food and drink, medical, and cleaning services was undertaken from within the huge crowds. When the Egyptian police (defeated in the streets, many of their vehicles and stations burned out in the street fighting) withdrew, popular neighborhood committees emerged to defend public safety. There was a similar development in the Oaxaca Commune of 2006.[55] The Uruguayan writer Raúl Zibechi records the growth across Latin America among poor communities of organized "self-defense measures and counter-powers. Initially, these are defensive, but ultimately develop power structures in parallel to the state. Since they are anchored in community practices, these self-defense groups are key to forming a form of power that differs from the hegemonic powers centered around state institutions."[56] In other struggles, buildings have been taken over to run nurseries and clinics. In the 1960s, the Black Panthers provided programs of "survival pending revolution" to America's urban ghettos, including "free breakfast programs for school children and food aid for families; schools, adult education, and childcare; medical care, medical research, and clothing; free plumbing, home maintenance, and pest control; and protective escort for the elderly and ambulance services; cooperative housing; employment assistance; free shoes."[57] In long strikes, like those of the British miners in 1984–85, the organization of food supplies became a vital requirement in the pit villages, drawing in women who then came to play an increasing part in the strike as a whole. Zibechi suggests that such developments have become increasingly central to contemporary struggles in Latin America, noting

> the double centrality of community and reproduction, placing families—revolving around women—at the center of the movements. The community is the political form that the people assume to resist and, in doing so, they change the world by changing the place that they occupy in it. Communities do not pre-exist as collective practices, they are the product of struggle and resistance.[58]

Increased involvement in collective action entails higher degrees of mutual organization. In Tsarist Russia, Rosa Luxemburg recorded that the apparently "chaotic" strikes after January 1905 become "the starting point of a feverish work of organization . . . from the whirlwind and the storm, out of the fire and glow of the mass strike and the street fighting rise again, like Venus from the foam, fresh, young, powerful, buoyant trade unions . . . (along with) daily political meetings, debates and the formation of clubs."[59] In such periods, movement "organizing" can achieve levels that a century of "normal" trade-union recruitment doesn't even approach: thus in a few months during the autumn of 1980, the new "Solidarność" union recruited and activated a far higher proportion of Polish workers than the British Trades Union Congress had managed in a century and a quarter. The impulse toward mutual organization can spread into neighborhoods, among the "self-employed," among the disabled, among those experiencing all manner of oppressions, creating innovative new forms and revitalizing old ones. Party memberships soar. Organizational *experimentation* is common, not only in "single-purpose" associations but also in alliances, coordinations, and coalitions. Through all of this, experiences are widened, schemes are refined and tested (sometimes to destruction). New layers develop skills and competences or rapidly discover the need for them.

Luxemburg's account of 1905 catches the diversity of a mass movement: "It is a gigantic, many-coloured picture of a general arrangement of labour and capital"; it "reflects all the complexity of social organization and of the political consciousness of every section and of every district"; it includes "regular trade union struggle of a picked and tested troop of the proletariat drawn from large-scale industry" and "the formless protest of a handful of rural proletarians," "the first slight stirrings of an agitated military garrison," "the well-educated and elegant revolt in cuffs and white collars in the counting house of a bank," "the shy-bold murmurings of a clumsy meeting of dissatisfied policemen in a smoke-grimed, dark and dirty guard-room."[60] She might have added Russia's *peasants*, except that their revolt only got underway when the workers' movement was already in defeat and recession; so too, she might have made mention of other oppressed groups—including women, religious minorities, whole nations oppressed by the Tsarist Empire's "prison of peoples," Jews suffering brutal anti-Semitism, and so on. For those subjected to all manner of oppressions, mass movements open up possibilities of openly addressing their particular pains; their struggles are variably interwoven with other "economic" and "political" struggles, increasing movements' real diversity and potential emancipatory richness.

An important part of the developmental process of a mass movement consists in the emerging perception among its varied participants that it exists as an entity, transcending local and particular identities and affiliations, becoming a "movement for itself" with a potential to effect social and political transformation. Such perceptions lie behind the "reciprocal action" that Luxemburg identified between different forms of struggle in the Russian movements of 1905. In Pamela Oliver's words, in mass movements an event in one setting becomes "an occasion for deciding" in another.[61] That is, what connects different "parts" of a social movement into a larger whole emerges as a developing sense among participants that they are engaged in something *shared*, even if their immediate concerns are local and particular and there are as yet few direct organizational links between them. This is what permits and encourages organization across locations, between different sectors, among people with distinct grievances. In his research on Bolivia in the early 2000s, Jeffery Webber detects a "combined oppositional consciousness" uniting trade unionists, the urban poor and indigenous peasants, a combination also found in different particular patterns in Argentina's movements in 2001–2, in the "Oaxaca commune" in 2006, and in Tunisia and Egypt in 2011.[62] This consciousness also permits and encourages theoretical generalization, linking issues and finding solidarity with others who are differently exploited and oppressed. Movements thereby promote awareness of the existence of a larger "system" whose varied manifestations make better sense when understood together.

Theoretical and practical issues are closely bound together, for at each stage in a movement's development all the issues of strategy and tactics come to the fore. How to understand the overall situation, and the various forces at play within it? How does what just happened make sense? Who is trying to do what to whom, and what is needed to advance or hinder this? Whose account seems more and whose less trustworthy? No wonder that, as Trotsky remarked of revolutions, mass movements too are very "wordy" affairs. A stable, routine existence can be lived almost wordlessly, since just about everything is known and expected. But in the tumult of great social and political conflicts, as old certainties slip and slide, finding one's place and seeking a way forward become theoretical and practical problems that must be explored through dialogue, through confrontations of ideas and remaking of standpoints. Hence the "torrents of words" that mark large-scale social confrontations.[63]

Collective activity and organization transforms and develops the social individuals who undertake it. Durkheim talked of "collective effervescence" as a creative process. A sense of shared achievement and empowerment. Individuals rise to achievements they did not dream they could make. Acting—and talking—together, people develop their shared powers to solve new problems, in real innovations. Imaginations broaden, as well as aspirations and the boundaries of possible change. Not only do people themselves change, but they also change the relationships with each other. They see powerful people differently, can laugh at them and are not afraid of them. There is a simultaneous enhancement of popular power and of the characters of the newly empowered.

Movements commonly involve the formation of new kinds of organization as well as the proliferation of older forms. Not only do larger numbers form and join strike committees, trade unions, cooperatives, popular assemblies, political clubs and parties, but new bodies arise to coordinate innovative forms of activity, from the *cortes de ruta* (road blockades) of Argentina's *piqueteros* (picketers) to the neighborhood committees that sprang up in Cairo's residential districts to organize local policing in 2011, or the bodies created to organize food and other supplies during long strikes and other struggles. These are politically significant insofar as they draw new layers into collective activity, providing new settings for the exercise of initiative and democratic control and new forums for political debate, as well as for individual and collective self-development. Moira Birss writes about the Argentinian *piqueteros'* organization, the Movimiento de Trabajadores Desocupados (Movement of Unemployed Workers):

> As members of the MTD expressed in interviews, before participation in the MTD they hardly ventured from their doorstep and certainly did not venture into critical political analysis. Going out onto the streets, however, opened their eyes to the systems that had relegated them to life in a shantytown. Said an interviewee, "I went from my house to school [to pick up my children] and from school to home. I would watch TV and [the protests] would seem ridiculous. Why do they go out to cut off the roadways? But now I realize that no, you have to fight for what belongs to you." By engaging in consensus-based collective action these *piqueteros* have awakened their own political consciousness and demanded recognition from the government and labor unions that have often ignored them or silenced them with patron-client handouts.[64]

Such bodies often provide new sources of wider movement initiative, beyond the control of existing movement bodies like unions or parties. Within existing movement organizations, also, new organizations, hubs, and networks emerge to challenge existing leaderships, including "rank and file" and shop steward organizations in unions, as well as radical groupings, as seen within the US black liberation movement in the 1960s, or indeed the American women's liberation movement as it emerged to challenge male hierarchies within the civil rights and student movements of the 1960s.

These developments accompany the expansion and contraction of popular aspirations. What "we the people" want may begin with small reforms, or the removal of particularly hated public figures like Ben Ali in Tunisia or Mubarak in Egypt, but can expand in scope with the expansion of the movement, and especially with its successes. Conversely, movement setbacks can produce disorientation, disappointment, and a retrenchment or redirection of popular demands. In the seven months that followed the victory of the Polish workers' movement in August 1980, Solidarność expanded in size, drawing in new layers and winning victory after victory—until late March 1981, when the sudden cancellation of a planned general strike produced angry confusion. Attendance at meetings dropped off, and working-class candidates for Solidarność's upcoming national congress were hard to find as workers "did not know what to say" in selection meetings.[65]

On the significance of movements in Greece and Spain over the past few years, Kevin Ovenden writes that "we have seen a glimpse of a new way entirely of doing things, one where ordinary people begin to formulate their own answers and their own ways of organising." Such ideas—of "popular, worker control and decision-making as an alternative to being governed in the old way"—appeared during strikes and workplace occupations and "flickered" through many community struggles and through the movements in Greece's city squares in 2011.[66] To an important degree, such "flickers" or "fleeting" appearances of demands that transcend the limits of parliamentarian politics in favor of worker control and direct self-government need to be enlarged and translated into widespread *mass argument and activity*. It is here that the groundwork of a possible revolutionary vision can be laid, in all manner of different activities and organizational forms. The removal and replacement of hated managers, officials, and supervisors, the taking over and reorganizing of public facilities and private properties, the occupation of buildings and workplaces, the building of popular assemblies, neighborhood committees, workers councils, interworkplace committees, self-management bodies, communes, soviets, *cordones*, *shoras*, and the like all contain the implicit possibility of generalization as the basis of a new societal and state form. What matters is, firstly, whether and to what degree such bodies both involve increasing numbers of participants and begin to exercise authoritative, directive power over aspects of social life (as did the 1905 soviet, which went beyond being a strike committee to becoming a potential alternative state, intervening practically in everyday life and issuing instructions to the post office, the railways, and even to policemen).[67] But, secondly, there must also be a *general argument* posed, voiced in many different ways but involving growing numbers of participants, that it is in just such activities that the potential roots of a new societal form capable of solving the crisis may be found.

In some movement struggles, coordinating bodies emerge to link a whole variety of such popular impulses and organizations and to establish situations amounting to "dual power." That is, their existence and activities pose a real alternative to the existing state power and pose the question of a quite different form of social production. These bodies have gone under a variety of names including the "Commune" of Paris in 1871, the "soviets" and "workers councils" of the 1917–19 period that re-emerged in Berlin in 1953 and Budapest in 1956, the *cordones* in Chile in 1972–73 before the military crushing of the Allende government, and "the Popular Assembly of the Peoples of Oaxaca" in 2006.[68] Some emergent bodies have closely approximated the "soviet" form without much recognition on participants' part that this was the case. The Solidarność movement offered a notable example.[69] More precisely, while some participants did perceive this possibility within the Polish movement, they anxiously rejected it as it conflicted with their more limited ambition to have Solidarność *negotiate* with the government but not threaten its existence.[70] But that ambition was itself utopian: the form that Solidarność took, where all workers were part of a single unitary organization regardless of industry or trade and where its members' activities and aspirations regularly threatened to break the boundaries of "trade unionism," meant that the regime was determined to destroy it, by one means or another. When other methods failed, the regime turned to the military option of *crushing* the workers' organization on December 12–13, 1981. They arrested and interned almost the entire national and regional leadership of Solidarność and proclaimed martial law. Numbers of workers were killed, though not on the scale of other military repressions—as for example in

Paris in 1871, in Finland in 1918, in Chile in 1973, in Oaxaca in 2006, or in Egypt in 2013.

Mass movements do sometimes win some gains: they force governments to carry through reforms that improve people's lives, they overturn (some) repressive regimes, they enlarge the rights of different categories of citizens, they organize industries that were thought to be "unorganizable," they beat back some attacks. In that sense, they are indeed part of the process of making and remaking society. But often they win less than numbers of their active supporters believe possible, the victories they do win are hedged about with limitations, they succumb to repressive responses from opponents, their active memberships lose heart and withdraw, and so forth. "Upsurges" are followed by "downturns," and movements can "go into abeyance" for sometimes quite long periods.

6. Reactionary movements

Although the idea of "social movements" is mostly attached to and discussed in the context of what the Communist Party used to term "progressive" causes, the field includes movements that both mobilize non-elite social forces and pursue essentially "reactionary" causes, even if they are often sponsored and steered from "above."[71] Such was the Ku Klux Klan, responsible for the killing of thousands of former black slaves in the decades after the American Civil War and in part responsible for the imposition of "Jim Crow" legislation across the South. Hitler's Nazi Party recruited large numbers of unemployed and workers into its ranks, mobilizing them—especially through its Sturmabteilung (SA) wing—into fighting bodies directed at socialist and communist organizations and events, and borrowing some of the "repertoire" of the Left (red flags, street parades, even the word "socialist"). After Hitler became chancellor, the SA continued its "movement" activities, demanding a larger place in the Nazi administration and looking to carry through a "second revolution" against landed property and large-scale capital. Hitler's response was to organize the murder of large numbers of its leaders (and other enemies) in the "Night of the Long Knives" beginning on June 30, 1934.

The most recent example, discussed in Sameh Naguib's chapter, is the social movement that enabled the *counterrevolution* in Egypt in the summer of 2013. The Muslim Brotherhood government of Mursi, elected on June 30, 2012, faced a continuing tide of strikes and other protests that threatened to deep the revolution of 2011.[72] While Mursi attempted to draw the military high command closer to his government, the military had other ideas. Mursi lacked the will or the means to halt the popular movement and restore "order," and they worked to undermine and replace him. Behind the scenes, from the spring of 2013, their agents steered and aided a *mass movement* to bring Mursi down, promoting a mass petition demanding his removal, building alliances with former "secular left" parties and preparing for a huge anti-Mursi demonstration on June 30, 2013. Millions joined this, in what from the outside looked like a rerun of the revolutionary demonstrations of January–February 2011. Only with a difference: where the demonstrators in 2011 fought the police, now the police joined and facilitated the mass crowds, and the army sent helicopters in *support*. From June 30, Abdel Fattah al-Sisi, head of the military, claiming to express the "will of the revolution," played a more open hand, actively promoting and endorsing mass rallies against the Muslim Brotherhood's "terrorism" that gave him a "mandate" to take all power into his hands and to use army and security forces to massacre over a thousand supporters of the Brotherhood on August 14. With the honorable exception of the Revolutionary Socialists and the April 6th movement, most of Egypt's "liberals" and "left" declared their support for the new dictatorship and in many cases collaborated directly. They falsely accused the Muslim Brotherhood both of an ill-defined "fascism" and of wishing to establish in Egypt an Islamic dictatorship on Iranian lines. After August, there was no more military support for any kind of protest, and in the autumn the regime brought in draconian anti-protest laws.

The Right's success in building reactionary social movements always reveals weaknesses of the Left. In late-Weimar Germany, as Trotsky argued strongly, what was needed was a *united front* between communists and socialists, which could organize a fight to involve the millions of unemployed who were drawn toward the SA Brownshirts and confront them politically. Instead, the Communist Party was induced by Stalin to treat the Social Democrats as "social-fascists" rather than as potential allies. In Egypt, a clear left alternative to the statist, nationalistic, Nasserist and still Stalinist-influenced left, focused rather on the potential power from below of popular movements, was needed. But different politics need clear articulations and numbers to carry them. A handful of Trotskyists in Berlin or the Revolutionary Socialists and the April 6th movement in Cairo and elsewhere were simply insufficient.

7. Intra-movement struggles

Of course, the limitations of movements and their retreats can, in part, be attributed to ruling-class resistance to movement demands. But only in part. Also significant are the inner politics of movements themselves. At the core of these politics is an old argument—between "reform" and "revolution"— which has taken on a wider relevance in the century since Russia's October Revolution. Indeed, there are senses in which "October" does not offer a very useful model for the problems of revolution in the twenty-first century. Because of its particular pattern of political development, the Tsarist state did not witness the development of a modern, "integral" state in which many of the institutions and assumptions of modern "reformism" could flourish and gain widespread popular roots. Certainly the hectic few months between February and October 1917 were insufficient to provide a grounding for such tendencies. In that sense, the Bolsheviks were able to secure their notable victory in October in leading the way to a "soviet" republic without being much hampered or diverted by anything like an entrenched trade-union bureaucracy allied to a strong social-democratic party or an established parliamentary regime. The face of *counterrevolution* in Russia was represented by General Kornilov and later the White armies and their imperial allies, rather than by elected "socialist" politicians and their allies within workers' parties and unions. However, a single year later in Germany, as mutiny and revolution overthrew the Kaiser's regime and brought the world war to an end, the array of political forces would prove very different. The mutiny and popular movement that brought down the Kaiser was if anything larger than that which ended Tsarism, but the Social Democratic Party (SPD) leaders, Ebert and Noske, despite having supported the war to the end, were able to place themselves at the movement's head and to limit its effective aspirations to a democratic republic that could enable capitalism to continue. They allied themselves with far-right army officers to form the Freikorps, who both murdered Rosa Luxemburg and Karl Liebknecht and were regularly deployed to attack strikes and uprisings. In the strictest sense, the SPD leadership played a *counterrevolutionary* role, available to them because they had rushed to the head of the "democratic revolution" that—against their earlier wishes—had brought down the old regime. During the four years that followed, the German Communist Party faced several opportunities to lead the workers' movement in a different direction, but mistaken policies adopted by its party leadership meant that it missed them all.[73]

The practical and theoretical problem of "reformism"—the prominence within popular movements of parties, ideas, tendencies, and practices that simultaneously expressed some degree of opposition to the status quo and set limits to what that opposition might express—became a core question for the newly born international communist movement in the years immediately after 1918.[74] Within Marxism, some of the most interesting examination of the roots of the question was provided by the Italian communist Antonio Gramsci, particularly in his explorations of what he termed the "integral state." Where Marx had argued that the bourgeoisie had revolutionized economic life, Gramsci extended that idea to argue that it had also revolutionized the world of politics and its institutional forms. The integral state created by the bourgeoisie allowed "an organic passage from the other classes into their own" in a way that previous "castal" states did not. "The bourgeois class poses itself as an organism in continuous movement, capable of absorbing the entire society, assimilating it to its own cultural and economic level. The entire function of the State has been transformed; the State has become an educator."[75] The modern state has become "a network of social relations for the production of consent, for the integration of the subaltern classes into the expansive project of historical development of the leading social group."[76] States become implicated in all manner of aspects of social reproduction, far beyond their "classic" tasks of legislation and war-making.

The developmental path of modern states has involved parallel movements of opening and closure. On one side, states became more open to "pressure" and "persuasion" to respond to societal needs and to the recognition of claims to "rights." On the other side, modern states and capitalist classes have permeated their opponents' own movements and formations, intervening in their inner life to limit and constrain their forms and their demands in ways that permit the ongoing dominance of capitalist exploitation. For all its limits, the modern state presents the *appearance* of a flexible instrument, capable of providing an open space for "improvement." It thus offers a grounding for a movement world where "reformism" in its widest sense becomes part of "common sense." Gains, limited though they may be, are nonetheless possible. If the effectiveness of gains is sometimes exaggerated, that in part can be attributed to the fact that reforms are regularly *opposed* by the most reactionary elements within ruling classes. The modern state also offers a ground on which a host of *mediating* bodies and persons can develop, partly tied to the state and its routines and partly tied to the antagonisms of civil society—the most conscious bearers of ideologies of reformism or what Gramsci dubbed "economic corporativism." Here are constructed "the earthworks of civil society" that any *revolutionary* movement would need to traverse as part of any generalized assault on the structures of modern capitalism.

The "common sense" of everyday or integral reformism is perhaps the largest impediment to socialist revolution. For if, as Trotsky suggested, people turn to revolution when "there is no other way out," integral reformism always seems to allow that there *is* another way. Some set of concessions or compromises can be extracted that might offer some relief to immediate problems, even if they leave intact a partially reformatted capitalism—and thus leave the root causes of people's problems still present and capable of regenerating on a still larger scale. Certainly, integral reformism would lead us to expect, at a minimum, that in just about any social and political crisis there will be voices *inside movements* urging that we should *negotiate* with the powers that be, that we should "moderate" our aspirations and demonstrate our "realism," that we should recognize that many people are put off by aggressive militancy but might be won over if we only slowed the pace and narrowed the scope of our demands. Those voices may be "honest brokers" or may be hoping to make their own political fortunes; they may be disillusioned former revolutionaries. Whatever their motivations, their presence and influence can't be wished away.

At some point in the development of any mass movement, "success" for reformist projects requires the marginalization of more radical impulses, the demobilization and division of the movement's popular forces, and their resubordination to the imperatives of ongoing accumulation. The particular means by which this may be achieved can vary widely, from repressive measures at one end to partial incorporation and political taming at the other. Where it is successful, those activists whose ideas and practices embody the aspiration to "go further" are forced into retreat and into efforts to remake and rethink their understandings and strategies, sometimes only temporarily and sometimes for whole periods until conditions for new "waves of revolt" appear. In the interregnum, their ideas may, as with the Argentinian radicals discussed in Jorge Sanmartino's chapter, "even begin to sound naive."

Yet we must insist: such outcomes are not certain, not set in stone. The conflict between "reform" and "revolution" is conducted at once within movements and between movements and their opponents, in actual struggles. "Alternativity" is always present, difference always indicates potential. It is a seemingly regular feature of movements that they divide. If at their birth they seem to represent a new unity, often accompanied by a wave of poetic enthusiasm, the scale and complexity of the problems they encounter are always liable to engender differentiation and division: over their goals, their methods of struggle, their very meaning. Their progress is marked by crises of development, "turning points," and the clashes of alternative conceptions and alternative leaderships. The results of those often dramatic struggles and encounters are never predetermined. What counts is whether there develops, *within* and *across* the whole terrain of movement debate, an *intransigent wing* that has educated itself and its auditors in the dangers of resubordination and that can offer a vision of *going further* and *aiming higher*. Victory for such an intransigent tendency means, not demobilization and disappointment, but still wider mobilization and contestation, up to and including an expansive democratic challenge to the entire power setup. Its capacity to influence the movement is not a one-off achievement, but is learned, developed, and tested in multiple particular conflicts, in small and large crises.

8. New impulses, new possibilities

Internationally, the "movement scene" over the past two decades and more has been highly variegated, full of dramatic incidents, innovations, advances, and reversals. The remaking of movements has been underpinned by ongoing shifts in "class composition" as a new vampiric capitalism—variously termed "monetarism," "post-Fordism," "globalization," "financialization," and "neoliberalism"—has bitten ever more deeply into the social fabric. The old industrial landscape has been savaged, from the rustbelt sectors in China to the decaying steel, shipyard, and mining towns of Europe and North America, abandoned by capital. Manufacturing has been hugely mechanized and robotized, while shifting its locations both nationally and across the globe.[77] China, Japan, Korea, Taiwan, and Singapore together now produce a larger share of industrial output than North America. Along with immensely expanding the numbers of industrial jobs that North America and Europe have shed, they have become major capital exporters; across Latin America and Africa, Chinese capital in particular has become increasingly dominant in the "extractivism" (of oil and gas, minerals, and mono-crop agriculture) that has provided the background to large political shifts on those continents, and that has displaced millions of migrants from the countryside to old and new cities, both within and across national borders. "Services"—a rather ragbag term that includes everything from logistics to education and health care and to finance, fast food, and "security"—has provided a larger share of both secure and insecure employments.[78] Thus from three directions ("industrialization" in the east, "de-industrialization," productive relocation, and expansion in "services" in the west, "dispossession" in the south) the shape of the world's working classes has shifted considerably. Alongside this, the pools of the "relative surplus population"—those experiencing long-term unemployment and semi-employment—have grown, exerting downward pressure on wages and living standards at the same time that the wealth of those at the top has grown at breathtaking rates.[79] Economic pressures mean couples of working age are now mostly "two income" households, altering family life away from the "housewife" pattern of an earlier capitalist phase. Women play more central roles in the new working classes, as they do in labor migration.[80] While there are arguments about the size (and indeed the existence) of a distinct "precariat,"[81] neoliberalism has generated a wider general "precariousness" of labor, speeded up since the 2008 crisis[82] and most marked among migrant workers whose reduced political and civil rights increase their vulnerability.[83] As well as creating some new "homogeneity" of the working classes—notably in the spread of managerial methods formerly associated with manufacturing into services—capitalism's latest phase has generated new forms of *heterogeneity*.

A key feature of the world economy in recent decades has been "financialization": The world economy is, by now, decisively influenced by the unrestricted mobility of a massive pool of unregulated private capital.[84] This has changed the character of states: to attract capital and to pay off accumulating debts, they have competed to turn parts of their own national sovereignty into commodities, offering less-regulated flags of convenience, Export Processing Zones, banking centers, tax havens, land for development, farming and mining: "National economic policy has been dictated by the imperative to induce capital, be it 'national' or 'foreign,' to invest in the national economy. This development has aptly been termed: the transformation of states into competitive states."[85] The scale of state indebtedness has risen at the same time that tax revenues from capital have shrunk. Thus, for example, the average level of Latin American and Caribbean government debt tripled between 1980 and 2005, and then more than doubled again over the subsequent decade.[86] As Jerome Roos writes: "The profound transformation of the capitalist world economy over the past four decades has endowed private and official creditors with unprecedented structural power over heavily indebted borrowers, enabling creditors to impose painful austerity measures and enforce uninterrupted debt service during times of crisis—with devastating social consequences and far-reaching implications for democracy."[87] Most states have adopted vigorous neoliberal programs involving both cuts in all kinds of "welfare" spending and also extensive privatizing of former state enterprises; international and regional financial institutions have exerted strong pressures in the same direction.

As the conditions of capitalist production, realization, and distribution have changed, so too have the conditions under which labor is socially reproduced. Cutbacks in state spending on "welfare"—capital spending, subsidies and grants on food and fuel prices, health care, education, housing, public transport, and the like—were often combined with direct and indirect measures of "privatization" of necessary services. Urban housing costs soared. If neoliberal policies were at first the property of the Right, social democracy soon fell in behind. Even in "social democratic" Sweden, large parts of the welfare state were privatized.[88] In Britain, Labor governments promoted "private finance initiatives" that burdened the education and health sectors with long-term repayments to finance capital, often with extraordinarily high profit returns, while the much-cherished National Health Service became a "brand" umbrella under which a web of public and private agencies compete.[89] In Greece, the initially "left" Syriza government rapidly capitulated to the demands of the European Central Bank.[90] Neoliberalization of "left" parties was not limited to Europe. In South Africa, within two years of the fall of Apartheid, the ANC government adopted neoliberal economic policies. So later did Brazil's Workers Party and the Movimiento al Socialismo (MAS) government in Bolivia.[91] Neoliberalism did not just undermine state welfare systems: in the US, as the unions' strategy of negotiating "benefits" for their members lost headway as large companies cut them back, so also their memberships shrank.[92]

Recent decades have thus seen the whole environment of movement struggles alter quite dramatically. In different parts of the world, the shape of movements looks different. What can be said about North America and Western Europe barely applies to China, South Africa, or Latin America, let alone the Middle East. "There is a very different rhythm of struggle in core countries (Britain, France, Canada, U.S., etc.) than in the 'semi-peripheries' (or newly industrializing) countries. Sometimes we tend to 'flatten' the world, and assume that dynamics in the core countries were setting the pattern for dynamics elsewhere. But—the world is not flat."[93] However, it is not simply that there are "differences," but they are *combined*. The potential movement interconnections between countries and regions are perhaps stronger than they have ever been. New possibilities and new uncertainties have multiplied.

Within the former "core states" of world capitalism, unions have been immensely weakened. The relative security and affluence that a previous generation of workers enjoyed has been lost with the global restructuring of major industries, and the unions that represented them have lost members while failing to organize emerging new sectors of employment. The decline has been at its most stark in the US: private sector union density (percentage of the labor force in unions) declined from 39 percent in 1954 to 10 percent in 1999 and suffered a further drop to 7.6 percent in 2015.[94] Only the public sector unions have gained density, rising from 23 percent in 1973 to a height of 38.7 percent in 1994 and falling to 35.2 percent in 2015.[95] Since the 1970s, union membership overall has declined 45 percent, while strike activity has fallen an astonishing 95 percent. Across the working class, living standards and working conditions have declined, while work has been intensified and degraded through myriad managerial innovations. Hourly and weekly real wages sit below their 1972 level.[96]

Decades of business unionism and concession bargaining in the US have disabled union bureaucracies' capacity to restore their organizations' fortunes. At the worst, some American unions (especially in construction) have pursued narrow sectional interests in direct opposition to environmental struggles, notably in the battle to stop oil pipelines at Standing Rock and elsewhere.[97] Union victories are still possible in the US, but mostly they have required high levels of conscious and deliberate organizing, the displacing or bypassing of conservative leaderships, and the direct involvement of real majorities of members in the running of disputes.[98] In Argentina, the continuing influence of "Peronism" kept the formal union movement isolated from the radical influences of the Argentinazo, as Jorge Sanmartino details in his chapter. By contrast, as Jeff Webber shows, the fact that the two main union federations in Bolivia adopted "social movement unionism" policies brought support and organizational coherence to the movements of 2003 and 2005. The readiness of unions to look outside workplaces for support and simultaneously to broaden their demands to encompass those to whom their workers provide services was critical to struggles in both health and education. Such practices shaped the communal struggle initiated by the teachers' union in Oaxaca in 2006 and, in 2012, student movements in both Quebec and Chile and the strike of Chicago teachers. Victories have also been won by newer, more radical unions in Italy, the UK, and elsewhere who have focused on "precarious" workers in previously unorganized sectors like delivery and warehouse workers, cleaning and security staffs, etc. The very notion of what a term like "labor movement" means, and what its potentials may be, has continued to be fought over and reshaped by new kinds of practice.

One of the biggest changes in the working class has occurred in China, where several hundred million former peasants migrated, over the course of a single generation, to become workers in the exploding cities. Predominantly young—at least at the time of their migration—these workers proved capable of extensive workplace militancy. In the same period, some eighty million workers—the majority of them women—lost their jobs in the older "rustbelt" centers of Chinese manufacturing.

If the notion of "labor movement" is open to broadening and contestation, so is that of "class struggle," and not least in terms of its *objects*. One feature of neoliberalism has been a shift in both the social composition of "protest" and its forms and arenas. In the 1980s, a good deal of commentary sought to explain this growing diversity in terms of a rather facile distinction between "old" and "new" social movements, with the former apparently focusing on "materialist" questions while the latter focused more on "postmaterialist" questions concerning such matters as cultural autonomy and "identity." These distinctions were always dubious.[99] What does appear to be the case is that two kinds of issues have become more prominent in movement struggles and demands: the first centered on matters to do with "democracy," "political representation," and "rights," and the latter on questions around "social reproduction"—with a good deal of overlap and interplay between these.[100]

The earlier phases of neoliberalism were associated with the expansion of formal democracy in significant numbers of states, notably in Latin America, in Eastern Europe, and in Africa, but notably not in China or the Middle East. Where democratization was successful in Latin America, it was initially accompanied by some falling back in popular protest activity during the first part of the 1990s, but this slight lull was then replaced by a marked new upturn in movement activity associated with opposition to neoliberal social and economic policies—now facilitated by the lessened repression.[101] Many of the radical impulses generated in the new wave were channeled into new elected "left" governments associated with the Latin American "pink tide." These, however, after introducing some measures of social reform (in part paid for by a swelling demand for raw materials exports) and reducing poverty but leaving basic inequalities untouched, adopted measures that critics dubbed "reconstituted neoliberalism," limiting and undermining the previous popular advances and posing yet unsolved questions about relationships between left parliamentary parties and movements. In particular, these governments threw into confusion the movements to whose activity they owed their very existence. Zibechi cites the view of Bolivian scholar Huáscar Salazar:

> The cycle of struggles between 2000 and 2005 tended to surpass the state. However, with the rise of Evo Morales, "the state managed, little by little, to reconstruct its base of power and each time strengthened its political monopoly, appropriating anew tasks that society had previously undertaken." The governmental dynamics managed to absorb the communal energy expended during struggles and to dismantle the movements that could have called into question the MAS's management of the state.[102]

Yet, if Latin America's "progressive governments" failed to promote them, the movements of the twenty-first century have, as Jorge Sanmartino's chapter suggests, revealed a popular thirst for a different, expanded form of democracy closer to visions of "self-emancipation" than to older visions of reform from above. Similar aspirations emerged in southern Europe in the Egypt-inspired "indignados" movements of 2011 and in "Occupy" in the US, where calls for "real democracy now" resounded. If that aspiration for a fuller democracy had a rather abstract expression in the "assemblies," it had deeper roots in the communal practices and organizational forms of Latin American indigenous and urban organizations and in such developments as the "recovered factories" of Argentina (and to a degree Greece), where popular democracy was intermingled with forms of practical economic cooperation.

Social reproduction issues have also been at the heart of struggles against cuts in welfare spending and against privatization in Africa, Latin America, North America, and Europe. The sphere of "material interests" is never limited to wages and working hours alone, but includes a whole welter of matters of vital importance for everyday urban and rural life: the supply (and price) of water, fuel, electricity, transport, housing, education, and health and welfare services have provided "flashpoints" for popular struggle in Bolivia and Ireland, in African and Brazilian cities, in the suburbs and centers of

European cities. In Paris's *banlieues* and across a series of American and European cities, anti-racist and youth movements have battled against murderous police: the cycle of revolt that swept Greece began with protests at the police shooting of a schoolboy in Athens, a police killing in north London was the spark that set off widespread riots, and a whole series of racist police murders gave birth to the #BlackLivesMatter movement. If, in the 1980s in Britain, David Bailey notes, the typical protester was a worker in a trade union, a whole variegated mixture of social actors—students, environmental protesters, residents and tenants, immigrants and anti-racists, anti-war and anti-cuts campaigners, and others—have moved toward center stage in more recent years.[103] In different mixtures, the same story could be repeated across continents. The social shapes, and the forms of collective activity, that characterize movements have altered markedly along with the immediate sources of their discontents. Nor is there any iron wall that keeps workplace and social reproduction issues apart: the crisis in jobs and living standards that neoliberalism has brought to hundreds of millions across all five continents is also a crisis of "home" and "community," of *social life*. It is also a major arena of class struggle.[104]

New forms of movements, new forms of struggle engender new kinds of actual and potential alliances. It is no longer clear, as it seemed to a previous generation of activists, where the "center" of popular struggle lies. The boundaries of movement activity are anything but fixed, with actual and potential "spillovers" between sectors and "hybridization" of movement forms emerging.[105] Often the variegated collective actors who populate the movement landscape are isolated from each other, but where they find ways to connect their collective powers—as the experience of the Oaxaca teachers, the Quebec students, the teachers, parents and students of Chicago, the workers and indigenous peasants of Bolivia and Ecuador and others has shown—they can make large leaps in their power.

We live in an age of social and political experimentation. The risk for activists and theorists alike is that we seize too eagerly on this or that particular movement innovation and imagine that *here* we have found the key to movement organization and development for the future, without simultaneously assessing the limits and barriers that each form of practice reveals.[106] What seems correct, as Alan Sears suggests, is that "the next new left" is still in the process of formation. Its discontinuity with the last new left will be considerable and probably in ways we can barely imagine.[107] It will surely be far more "female" and necessarily multiracial. Its emergence may take some time. Kim Moody warns:

> It usually takes a generation for the workforce to realize the power that it has, and the points of vulnerability. This was the case when mass production developed in the early 20th century. It took pretty close to a generation before the upheaval of the '30s.[108]

The key organizing focus of any new left movement in the future may not be the workplace, though it will—somehow—necessarily have to confront and defeat boss power at work; otherwise, a whole part of life experience (which actually absorbs *more* of the time and energy of working people now than it did in the previous generation) will be untouched by movement impulses. And it will have to find ways to get beyond a series of barriers that, up till now, have mostly contained and constrained the movements of recent decades.

The first of these is the *isolation* of movement activity to particular social sectors or particular geographical locations. This may be institutionalized, as in the examples from South Africa, the US, and Spain noted earlier, and in the practice of classic social democracy, which reserved "political struggle" for the parliamentary party and "economic struggle" for the unions. In Argentina the movement of workers in the "recovered factories" was barely connected to workers in "regular employment" where Peronist unionism acted as a restraint on solidarity. The "Oaxaca commune" of 2006 was—rather like the earlier Paris Commune—restricted to a particular city and region and thus open to eventual defeat by organized state power. The difficulty is to find ways to express cross-movement solidarity *in action*. Here strategic questions arise. In Argentina, the Peronist unions held back workers' struggle in 2001, yet they could not just be "written off." Ordinarily, as they have demonstrated on several important occasions over the past decade and more, Argentinian unions have a capacity to mobilize many more forces than does the (very fragmented) left in all its forms. As elsewhere, the problem lies in *converting* unions into fighting organizations with a wider and more transformative perspective than their incumbent bureaucracies. That, after all, was the underlying secret of the Chicago Teachers' victories: an organized left caucus won their union membership to a more vibrant and democratic vision of the very meaning of their union, one that meant reaching out to their students and their parents in a common struggle for the future, not just with regard to teachers' pay and jobs, but education itself.[109] In short, just as "isolation" is not a natural or inevitable condition, but depends on a definite *politics*, so combating it calls for a *different politics*. Further, the nature of that "different politics" itself requires critical exploration. A radical politics that relies, for example, on preexisting "identities" (for example, a narrowly conceived "class membership" or "racial/gender solidarity") is liable to miss both the actual differentiations in experience among those assumed to share the same identity and the real potentials for "cross identity" solidarity among those who share similar problems: mistaken theory and practice on the left can itself *contribute* to maintaining the isolation of movement sectors.[110]

Secondly, there remains a problem with a century-long history: in countries where parliamentary democracy allows the possibility of the election of "left governments," what is—and what can be—the relationship between such governments and popular movements? Does the pursuit of parliamentary office ever aid the aim of radical emancipation, or does it always hinder it? The question has assumed some prominence in recent years, notably with respect to the "pink tide" governments of Latin America, the Syriza government in Greece, and the prospects for new left parties like Podemos in Spain. Is the very existence of parliamentary government an inherent and impassable barrier to social revolution?[111]

Experience to date has not been encouraging to those who seek to *combine* left parliamentary government with social movements as a route to social transformation. In Latin America, as Webber, Sanmartino, and others have stressed, popular movements in 2000–2005 placed an emphasis on mass direct action, grassroots popular democracy often in assembly form, and the "de-professionalization" of politics. The popular organizations they built combined confrontation with the state with the development of new forms of governance-from-below that seemed to "prefigure" a postneoliberal and even anti-capitalist society that many in their ranks aspired to build. However, the initiative in these movements passed to a series of more or less progressive governments, who drew on the movements' energy to get into office but simultaneously limited those movements to "subaltern participation," defined as the pacifying incorporation of popular sectors into the gears of the capitalist state.[112] Movements' capacity for further development of their autonomous and antagonistic confrontations, and therefore also for the further development of alternative visions, has been contained and reduced as they have been "domesticated."[113] None of the left governments managed to alter the underlying pattern of capital accumulation they inherited. Especially once the global economic crisis began to be felt directly in the region, and leftist governments began cutting public spending and services, a space has emerged for some resurgence of the Right. In Greece, where there was no ballast of raw materials exports to stabilize the crisis, the Syriza government simply gave in dramatically to the demands of the "troika," leaving the movements that had put it in office betrayed and disoriented.

It remains a possibility that a pathway to a revolutionary reconstitution of society might *begin* with the election of a left government to parliament. But any such left government would be placed under immense pressure to contain its supporters' hopes and demands and to evade efforts to control it from outside and below. Were it—against form and precedent for such governments—to promote further radicalization of movements, it would provoke a full-scale crisis with capitalist power. In such conditions, any *beginning* with elections would transform quite rapidly into a very different situation of direct confrontation between movements and capitalist power, involving major ruptures and the splitting of political forces, more akin to a revolutionary situation than to "normal politics." At the heart of any such situation would be a critical question: Do those in government (as is likely) seek to temporize with capital and to demobilize the popular forces, or do they contribute to developing the means and the popular will to carry movements' own power forward, laying new and broader bases for a wider emancipation? In such a scenario, any value a left government might have would be outweighed by a developing popular insurgency. Elections, whether of presidents or governments, *happen*. For movements, the question that really matters at such moments is whether they focus on their own self-developing projects and their own self-organization or allow their own self-diminution and disabling by others' priorities.

There is a third barrier, noted by several of our authors. While we have witnessed widespread and active resistance to the priorities imposed by neoliberal states, that resistance has, to date, also been marked by the weakness of *alternative projects* based on enlarging emancipation and democratic control. It's not that they have been completely absent, but they have seemed underdeveloped and only partially articulated, in part because of the sectoral isolation previously noted, and in part because *old* languages of liberation are no longer trusted and *new* ones still await their crafting. Small coteries may be rehearsing them, but their flowering depends on new popular upsurges that affirm their relevance. If, across Latin America, where many of the impulses of the early twentieth century were felt most strongly, the "cycle of revolt" is now in decline, local questioning and reformulation are as likely as an immediate explosion. As Raúl Zibechi commented: "When major historical processes come to an end, and in turn major political defeats transpire, confusion and despondency set in, desire intermingles with reality, and the most coherent analytical frameworks blur."[114] The struggles of the past two decades posed questions and suggested partial answers that will remain part of activist *milieux* as topics for debate and development. One key idea, taking partial shape in popular movements across several continents and now awaiting its next development, was that movements' own self-generated organizations and practices can and should provide the basis for the constitution of society, economy, and politics. It's not likely we have heard the last of that idea.

Fourthly, that idea requires political embodiments in the shape of organizations, networks, and coalitions that take "emancipation from below" as their underlying principle. It's difficult to foresee the forms that such bodies may take and how they may emerge to claim some kind of hegemony within movements. Those who already recognize the practical need for them require healthy doses of modesty and openness to diversity of expression if they are to make headway.

Finally, if the Bolsheviks in 1917 were already clear that their own revolution could only succeed if it *spread*, the further development of global capitalism in the past century has only reinforced that notion. "Socialism in one country" was always a reactionary as well as a utopian idea. But how might practical internationalism be promoted today? In a decade when the inherently global threat of climate change has become ever more prominent, and when millions of migrants and refugees are forced to flee new apocalypses, a new revolutionary internationalism becomes ever more urgent.

PART 2:
REVOLUTIONARY SITUATIONS, 1989–2019

CHAPTER 2

1989: Revolution and Regime Change in Central and Eastern Europe

Gareth Dale

Introduction

From the mid-1970s, the world's political and economic architecture underwent a twin shift. In economic regimes, the dominant models shifted away from Keynesianism and corporatism. From Chile and the US to Britain and beyond, governmental, business, and media elites embraced economic reforms that were later dubbed neoliberalism. Meanwhile, the domain of democracy expanded. From Athens to Madrid to Lisbon, from Santo Domingo to Quito to Lima, authoritarian regimes crumbled, making way for liberal democracy. Political elites in such countries succeeded in co-opting opposition parties and movements—even quite radical ones—and restabilizing the body politic around a moderate, pro-capitalist center. This was a development from which reformist actors in ossified regimes, including in Hungary and Poland, were able to learn.

The acme of this dual movement arrived in 1989 with the transformation of Central and Eastern Europe (CEE). The upheavals there quickly came to serve liberal opinion as exemplars of democratic revolution. They appeared to validate the liberal promise that free markets and political liberty walk hand in hand. They seemed to have infused history with a newly vital and progressive political spirit, one that was uprooting the atavistic and absolutist past in the backward zones of Europe and realigning them with the moving benchmark of Western modernity, introducing the territories lost between 1917 and 1949 to the liberal agenda of capitalist progress. They appeared to represent, in Jürgen Habermas's phrase, a "revolution of recuperation," a transformation that reconnected CEE to the locomotive of modernity, enabling the region to "catch up," by way of the (re)introduction of liberal institutions—the market economy and constitutionally secured parliamentary democracy.[1]

In countering this narrative, critics have kept a vigilant eye on post-1990 trends and statistics, highlighting those that contradict the liberal-triumphalist view. For example, while one may concede that economic growth across CEE had been low in the 1970s and 1980s, and standards of health and life expectancy had been stagnating or even declining in the same period, few areas of social and economic life experienced upticks following the 1989–90 transition, and some underwent bitter regression.[2] One can point to persistently low productivity, repeated economic crises, and an increased vulnerability to global downturns, self-serving Western involvement, the decimation of the professions, retrenched forms of servitude and "managed democracy," an undergrowth of rent-seeking and corruption that has flourished in the new market environment, and ongoing environmental deterioration. (In an illustration of the latter, former Soviet-bloc territories account for fully one-third of the fifty most ecologically destructive countries as identified by the World Wildlife Fund.)[3] Despite the roughly equal presence of women and men in the 1989 demonstrations in CEE, their aftermath saw little change in the proportion of women in positions of power; instead, many countries saw the removal of maternity entitlements, restrictive abortion laws, and the revival of "family values" conservatism.[4] The social consequences of the region-wide depression of the 1990s were cataclysmic. Double-digit inflation scythed through personal savings in Belarus, Bulgaria, the Baltics, and beyond, and in no country affected by the Great Depression of the early 1930s did real wages decline as steeply as in CEE in the 1990s. Even ten years after the transition, only in the Czech Republic had the average wage crept back above its 1989 level, and in many countries it remained below half that. In the light of immiseration and social regression on this scale it is little wonder that, when asked if life in their country is now harder than it had been before 1990, many answer in the affirmative: 62 percent of surveyed populations in Bulgaria and Hungary, 72 percent in Ukraine.[5]

Homing in on such exploitative and inegalitarian outcomes of 1989 may help to puncture the liberal-triumphalist argument, but it still leaves questions concerning the revolutionary content of that year. From one angle, 1989 was, at most, a "passive" revolution, a transition convened from above. In some versions, the accent is placed on Western intervention, in the form of political confrontation (Washington ratcheting up the New Cold War) or economic seduction (Bonn's mammoth loans to Hungary and the GDR).[6] At the extreme, the argument is that Western agencies directly organized the upheavals: the Romanian revolution, for example, as a coup orchestrated in Langley and executed with assistance from the Hungarian intelligence community. Others emphasize Soviet structural exhaustion and the ensuing reform programs—*perestroika* and *glasnost*. From the mid-1980s the Kremlin's imperial grip loosened rapidly. (And its intentions were becoming harder to divine. As Georgi Derluguian quipped, "Few believed that Gorbachev could really mean what he was saying but everybody assumed that this seasoned apparatchik knew what he was doing. The truth was exactly the opposite.")[7] Elite divisions in Moscow reverberated throughout the bloc, paralyzing hard-line leaderships from Berlin to Bucharest and exacerbating the "loss of faith" that was gnawing at Communist Party members and functionaries. One Czechoslovak survey from early 1989 revealed that as many as 57 percent of party members and 52 percent of functionaries possessed "no trust" in their party and state leaders.[8] Across Eastern Europe, reformists made bids for power, in some cases with encouragement from their backers in Moscow. At the extreme, the argument is that the Russian intelligence services organized the upheavals: that the Romanian revolution, for example, was a coup orchestrated by the KGB, with assistance from high-ranking Romanian functionaries.

The "extreme"—external subversion—claims can for the most part be briskly dismissed. There is no significant support for them—although when we come to the "colored revolutions," below, the picture changes somewhat.[9] Equally obviously, imperial interventions mattered, and these connected to structural factors internal to the countries of CEE. But what of the role of social movements? Some accept that revolutions took place in 1989 but play down the element of collective action. Habermas managed to write a

tome on 1989 without as much as mentioning the role of protest movements, while Claus Offe accorded them a marginal, reactive role. It was not
the movement that brought victory, writes Offe of the East German events,
but vice versa: "The obvious weakness of the state apparatus encouraged and
triggered the growth of a democratic movement." East Germany in 1989,
he concludes, was an "exit revolution" not a "voice revolution." The GDR
was not brought down by "a victorious collective struggle for a new political order; instead, massive and suddenly unstoppable individual emigration
destroyed its economic foundations." Similarly, for the Marxist philosophers
Robert Kurz and Wolfgang Fritz Haug the GDR's collapse was occasioned
by an exodus that expressed not conscious action but, respectively, "blind
and helpless flight" and a mix "of psychosis and plebiscite," and was later
overlayered by a protest movement driven by "nothing but unconscious and
untamed resentment"—rather like, Kurz adds superciliously, crowd behavior
during a New York power outage "or when fire breaks out in a prison."[10]

In a counterblast to these eructations of elitism masquerading as argument, Harvard historian Charles Maier has inveighed against the (largely
West German) scholars and pundits for whom "the East German popular
movement seemed actually embarrassing," such that the vocabulary they
grasped for spoke of the GDR's "implosion," as if "some worn-out machine"
had simply broken down.[11] The implosion thesis presumes structural shifts
in CEE to have occurred that *only then*, in 1989, contributed to an expanded
space for social movements. In reality, its history had from the outset been
shaped by struggles between the regimes and movements. In the late 1940s
the Communist parties and their associated "mass organizations" (such as
the state-run "trade unions") were reshaped through their role in subjugating resistance, a redesign that was then consolidated in the 1950s, most
dramatically through the crushing of revolts in the GDR, Poland, and Hungary. But although mass protests were crushed, and protest in general was
systematically suppressed, with even quite "innocent" forms of collective
self-organization corralled by state institutions, nonetheless, "infrapolitical"
forms of resistance, and small-scale industrial action, still influenced the
regimes across CEE, affecting myriad social and cultural issues—from the
toleration of Western rock music, to the role of the Church, to work quo-
tas. Then, in the 1980s, Solidarność in Poland lit the fuse that was to bring
Soviet domination of the region to an end. In East Germany in the middle
of that decade, emigration and niche social movements became serious irri-

tants to the regime and served as seedbeds from which organized resistance was soon to spring.

In 1989, state crisis and the blossoming of social movements were mutually conditioning processes. Even where, as in Poland and Hungary, Communist structures were negotiated away behind closed doors, the process was accompanied by manifestations of popular will—in Poland, strike waves and the June 1989 elections; in Hungary, the demonstrations of March 15 and the public theater surrounding the re-interment of Imre Nagy.[12] If, in Poland and Hungary of the late 1980s, the masses played a cameo part, in East Germany, Czechoslovakia, and Romania, at each critical juncture, collective action, however hesitant at first and however wracked by doubts later on, played a pivotal role. Mass action precipitated the revolutionary conjuncture to a head and influenced its course of development.[13] This was particularly evident in East Germany. Here, the spirit of protest manifested itself in the summertime border breakthroughs and embassy occupations before shifting to the Saxon town of Plauen, and thence to Dresden, where a large-scale pitched battle took place. The year 1989 was not quite as velveteen as is sometimes supposed. Wherever the police attacked, protesters fought back. In Dresden, the "People's Police" beat, and fired water cannon at, the crowds that had gathered at the main station. The crowds responded robustly, building barricades, hurling stones and Molotov cocktails, torching a police car, and demolishing some of the station (including all its doors, as well as a shop and ticket machines).[14] It was a moment that abruptly illuminated, in stark relief, the relationship between state and society—a relationship that had long been enacted behind masks and through choreographed protocols. The police recoiled, taken aback by the torrent of abuse they faced ("Nazi swine!," "Fascists!," "Red pigs!," etc.), with one officer even reporting that, after he received an injury, the doctor who treated him quipped that as a member of the "cudgel police" he had received his just desserts.[15] Under pressure of this sort, the security forces began to buckle. In one week in Dresden and Plauen alone, forty-five soldiers of the National People's Army, including five officers, refused to obey orders.[16]

That same week, in early October, witnessed similar scenes in Leipzig. Baton-wielding police attempted to prevent protesters from gathering. The latter replied with cobble stones, in a series of confrontations that, according to sociologist Detlef Pollack, "strengthened the demonstrators' will to resist, even though many of them had been injured."[17] On October 9, again in Leipzig, public protest achieved its breakthrough, when the scale of the demonstration overawed the local leadership of the Sozialistische Einheitspartei Deutschlands (SED) and the city's security forces, sapping the will to use arms. It was only now—*after* a series of showdowns with the mass movement in which the state's aura of omnipotence was irreparably punctured—that the old regime truly began to "implode." It was collective action in Leipzig, and again on November 9 in Berlin, that pushed the process of state erosion beyond the point of no return. In terms of numbers, the movement crested in the first week of November. In addition to demonstrations of around two million, that week alone saw some 230 reported political meetings, attended by over three hundred thousand people.[18] The East German mass movement peaked twice more, in early December and in January. And it helped to trigger a chain reaction, with a similar movement in Czechoslovakia (it kicked off in mid-November when police attacked a demonstration in Prague)[19] followed by the distinctly less velvet uprising in Romania in December. Together, these movements toppled dictators, political regimes, and their associated rules and habitus of oppression, as well as sharply accelerating the collapse of Soviet power.

1. Exceptional Poland

The revolutions in East Germany, Czechoslovakia, and Romania were noteworthy for the level of working-class participation, on which more below. But they evinced a contrast with earlier uprisings in the region, such as East Germany in 1953 and Hungary in 1956, or indeed the uprising that in a sense fired the starting pistol for this final unraveling of the Soviet system: Poland in 1980–81. It had centered on collective action in workplaces and was led by an organization, Solidarność, that had arisen from strike committees. The movement began in dockyards and factories, its most powerful weapon was the strike, and its key coordinating centers were strike committees and, in several towns, interfactory strike committees. What accounts for this difference between 1980–81 in Poland and 1989 in East Germany and Czechoslovakia?

If one looks at the institutional structures and forms of rule that characterized Poland on the one hand and East Germany and Czechoslovakia on the other, it is the similarities that stand out. The economic and political systems were cut from the same cloth. In the factories and offices of Poland, workers were subjected to similar types of oppression and compulsion as prevailed west of the Oder-Neisse, in East Germany, and south of the Tatra, in Czechoslovakia. In all three countries, independent workers' organizations were obliterated in the late 1940s and replaced by a state union, and lateral connections among workers were systematically suppressed.[20] There are also parallels in the experience of mass struggles: in Poland and the GDR, workers in the mid-1940s set up independent works councils, which were abolished (although not without robust resistance).[21] In the mid-1950s all three nations were rocked by labor unrest, which culminated in workers' rebellions in the cities of Pilsen (Czechoslovakia) and Poznań (Poland) and a nationwide workers' rising in East Germany.

But from around 1970 the Polish experience began to diverge quite sharply. The years 1970 and 1971 saw strike waves, protest marches, and riots in the cities of the Baltic coast of greater dimensions than those of 1956–57. In Sczezcin a citywide strike committee was established, and a series of short general strikes were called, during which "workers' militias patrolled city streets and strikers published their own newspapers and broadcast their own radio programs."[22] In 1976 there were more workers' risings, centered on the region around Warsaw, in Radom, and in Łódź. In the next four years around a thousand strikes took place, which culminated in the strike waves of summer 1980 that gave birth to Solidarność and broke the Communist Party's monopoly of power.[23]

In Poland, then, the development of workers' organization tended to curve upwards from 1956 to 1980–81, both in scale and geographical scope. The 1956 movement was concentrated in a few major plants in the big industrial centers only; that of 1970–71 centered on the coastal belt around Gdansk and Szczecin and reached workplaces elsewhere; in 1976 perhaps three-quarters of the country's largest plants were affected; in 1980–81 the movement encompassed the whole nation.

To explain the contrast between the Polish and Czechoslovak/GDR experiences, a variety of arguments offer themselves. The latter two regimes were more repressive, whereas the former placed greater emphasis on containment of protest through reforms—for example, with substantial concessions granted to private farmers. In Czechoslovakia and East Germany social conditions were never quite so desperate. They did not experience the roaring boom followed by sharp crash that so destabilized the Polish economy in the 1970s, and their tighter labor markets enabled greater scope for workers' demands to be achieved through factory-level bargaining. In Poland, external resources capable of assisting workers' movements were present to a greater degree: the Catholic Church was a more powerful institution than were the churches in the country's neighbors and afforded some protection to the independent trade unions. Workplace-based movements were able to draw radical intellectuals behind them, too.[24] Supporters of KOR (Committee for the Defense of Workers), to take the best-known example, helped to produce the newspapers and leaflets of Poland's underground workers' movement.

Yet an equally important, and widely neglected, difference was the degree to which networks of militants in Poland succeeded in keeping alive collective memories of resistance. The familiarity of sections of the workforce with the industrial-action repertoire and with trade-union norms and values were important factors that contributed to the success of strike action in the 1970s and 1980–81. Thanks to the research of Lawrence Goodwyn, Roman Laba, and others, we know that the uprisings of 1956, 1970–71, 1976, and 1980–81 were no mere litany of disconnected events. They seemed to erupt as if from nowhere but each in fact followed upon months and years of intricate organizing.[25] Even during periods in which industrial action was subdued, militants in certain factories and regions succeeded in maintaining contact with one another, keeping alive memories of past struggles. An accumulated memory of strategic knowledge, tactical repertoires, and organizational skills came to be embodied in such networks. It was particularly among these groups of militants, who had acquired self-education through self-activity,[26] that class identities were reproduced and regenerated and those tactics developed and tested, notably the sit-down strike, that were to prove so successful in challenging the regime in 1970–81. Why, Goodwyn asks, did Lech Wałesa and other militants at the Lenin shipyards act with such assurance in 1980? Because they had a wealth of experience and had been discussing "the politics of self-organization" at least since the massacre of 1970 if not before.[27]

Summarizing the findings of Goodwyn and Laba, Cyrus Zirakzadeh has described how "the strikes of 1970 and 1976 were etched on the collective memory of the Polish working class." The "ongoing warfare between workers and the party-state," especially the strike waves of 1956–58, 1970, and 1976, "played a key role in the political education of the future leaders of Solidarity."[28] Linda Fuller echoes this argument in her instructive comparison between workplace politics in Poland and the GDR. In the decades before 1980, Polish workers "amassed a tremendous, varied, and interconnected store of political knowledge and skill." They learned how to organize sit-down strikes, how to establish interfactory strike committees, and how to set up communication networks. They absorbed lessons about politics—such as "how, where, when, and with which management and party personages to negotiate"—as well as some "subtle lessons about one another as individuals, upon which the success of their next action sometimes hinged—who did what well and not so well, who could be counted on for what, who had the personality for which tasks."[29]

2. East Germany: Fading traditions

Compared with Poland, the trajectory of workplace-based protest in Czechoslovakia and East Germany could scarcely have been more different. In the GDR it slanted downward from 1953, and there may well be truth in Axel Bust-Bartels's contention that it was from around then "that the tendency toward withdrawal into the private sphere, and accommodation with the existing order began to prevail."[30] From the early 1960s onward, strikes were few and far between. In the 1980s only a smattering occurred, almost all of which were defensive in nature, small in size, only a matter of hours in duration, and restricted to individual workplaces.[31] That said, it would be misleading to suggest that the workforce was thoroughly atomized or individualized. Camaraderie was a natural part of most workers' existence, based on a perception of common conditions and grievances as well as strong shop-floor bargaining positions and endemic "infrapolitical" struggle. Despite the quashing of open resistance, wars of attrition were pervasive. By the late 1950s, decentralized, factory-level bargaining between management and work teams had become an axial industrial relationship,[32] and over subsequent decades industrial relations settled into a pattern that Jeffrey Kopstein has described as "a continuous, yet hidden battle over work norms and wages," in which neither workers nor employers gained clear-cut victories.[33]

As a result of workplace resistance, "a conscious frontal antagonism towards management" prevailed among the bulk of industrial workers, in the words of one sociologist of GDR industrial relations.[34] This was commonly accompanied by a rudimentary class consciousness, a sense that the life chances of "us down here" and "them up there" contrasted sharply and that the interests of the two groups were at least sharply divergent if not diametrically opposed. It could be heard in the ubiquitous grumbling that managers and functionaries were to blame for economic mismanagement such as bottlenecks and other problems hindering the production process, the costs

of which would be unfairly borne by workers, and that the privileges and isolation of the *nomenklatura* blinded them to the real situation of ordinary people—that "them at the top . . . have their luxury suites [but] don't know how
bad it is for us at the bottom."[35] This, however, was not a class consciousness
brimming with self-confidence. There was little sign of what one sociologist
has called "corporate class consciousness," where a worker identifies herself
and her interests "with the corporate body and the interests of the working
class as a whole," let alone hegemonic consciousness, in which "a worker
identifies the revolutionary interests of the working class with the interests of
society as a whole."[36] Ideas of this sort tend to flourish when working-class
organization spreads beyond the walls of individual workplaces, and above
all when workers' movements directly confront the state—such as, in the case
of Germany, in the Wilhelmine and Weimar periods, the immediate postwar
years, and June 1953. Folk memories of the labor-movement achievements,
values, and norms of these periods could only survive unharassed in spaces
sanctioned by the SED. Maintaining collective memories of the 1953 rising
was all but impossible. Even whispered exchanges were tracked down and
punished by the ever-vigilant Stasi.

Connected to the absence of corporate or hegemonic class consciousness, moreover, was the eclipse of memories of pre-1933 labor traditions. The
milieux of social democracy, having survived Nazism—albeit in a drastically
weakened condition—were marginalized in the late 1940s, through incorporation into an increasingly Stalinized SED. The co-opting of social democrats
into positions of power may have contributed more effectively to the demise
of their traditions than the repression directed against those who resisted.
Grassroots Social Democratic Party members witnessed SED policy being
explained and defended by well-known functionaries from "their own" camp.
In the 1950s and 1960s, identifiably social democratic identities and heritage
gradually faded from the scene. Even in their traditional strongholds, established networks of social democrats crumbled and dissolved, as some took
positions as functionaries in the economy, state, SED, or state-run "union"
(FDGB) while others retreated from the political and industrial fray.[37]

The outcome was that although low-level forms of industrial action were
endemic, and although managerialist and quota-busting behavior was widely
frowned upon and egalitarianism and solidarity were positively valued, organized socialist (or syndicalist) currents distinct from and critical of the SED
were marginalized and, by the 1980s, only a tiny minority of the working

class had experience with militant industrial action. Few would even have known a participant in strikes, unless a parent or grandparent had been involved in 1953 or in the struggles of the Weimar years. Even thinner on the ground were individuals with experience of independent trade unions or works councils. After 1948 (in the case of councils) and 1953 (in the case of strikes), memories of these forms of contention faded. Whereas the shipyard workers of Gdansk in 1980 remembered previous struggles (1976, 1970–71, and 1956), either on their own account or in the form of practical knowledge kept alive by networks of militants, their counterparts in Leipzig or Prague rarely did.

There were exceptions. The first works council to be established in East Germany in the autumn of 1989 was initiated by an elderly worker who had been active in the works councils' movement in the 1940s.[38] There are also cases of workplace activism in 1989 that tapped into recent experiences.[39] For the most part, however, strike action and works councils in 1989 drew less upon hands-on experience than abstract knowledge. Although the strike and the works council were familiar concepts, they derived from the West German media and from history lessons and literature. Workers who picked them from out of the industrial-action toolbox were not always sure how they functioned. The collective of workers who instigated the formation of one of the early works councils in 1989 illustrated the uncertainty that resulted. They had some idea of its nature and purpose and, one of them recalls, were adamant "that we needed it." However, "we didn't even know what a works' council looks like, we just didn't know."[40]

3. Where was the working class?

Some have taken the low degree of working-class *organizational* presence in the 1989 upheavals to signify a low level of working-class involvement *tout court*. In the case of East Germany, the most sustained and forceful argument of this sort is advanced in Linda Fuller's *Where Was the Working Class?* She begins from the axiom that the class structure of the GDR was dichotomous, pitting workers against "intellectuals, who, on the basis of specialized knowledge acquired primarily through higher education, carried out the redistribution of the surplus that workers produced."[41] Equipped with this analytical device, she makes the case that the 1989 revolution was a battle between two segments of the ruling intelligentsia. The protests that toppled the regime were "sponsored" by intellectuals and dominated by the educated middle classes, while workers "stayed out of politics altogether, aside from sometimes discussing events among themselves."[42]

On one point, this case is unarguable. There is no doubt that many of those who emerged from the 1980s opposition to found and lead the GDR civic movement were educated to tertiary level and were more likely than the average citizen to hail from the middle classes and to pursue professional careers. Two-thirds of the founding members of the civic movement organization Democratic Awakening and almost half of the forty-three founding members of SDP (in its 1989 refounded iteration) were theologians.[43] When Democratic Awakening established a regular leadership body in October, it included two lawyers (one of whom also worked for the Stasi), a sociologist, a musician, two pastors, a physicist, a lecturer, an engineer, and a mechanic. New Forum was the only group that was not founded by clergy, but only 10 percent of its leading members were classed as workers. In Czechoslovakia a similar picture applied. Although a good many spokespeople of Civic Forum / Public Against Violence (hereafter CF/PAV) self-identified as laborers as well as "farmers, drivers, smiths and pensioners," there were many church ministers, doctors, and managers, too, and overall an over-representation of individuals with university degrees.[44]

This was less true of the rank-and-file membership. Many had either not entered or had dropped out of higher education. In the GDR, quite a few worked in menial jobs, often in the employ of the Church, yet the "intellectual" sections of the middle classes were also present to a disproportionate degree, with a significant over-representation of graduates. One survey of the membership of "Democracy Now" gave the following breakdown: 51 percent academics, 20 percent managers and white-collar workers, 15 percent skilled workers, 9 percent students.[45] A survey of the Berlin New Forum membership found that almost three-quarters were educated to the tertiary level. Thirty-nine percent described themselves as "intelligentsia," 10 percent as "managers," and 10 percent as "students and apprentices." Only an eighth described themselves as "workers," and only 1 percent as unskilled workers.[46]

Fuller castigates the civic movement for ignoring the working class and explains this behavior in terms of the intelligentsia's privileged material circumstances.[47] Intellectuals were rewarded for their state-supporting roles as guardians of scientific progress, gatekeepers of opportunities and information, and managers of legitimation. Social life in a middle-class milieu instilled intellectuals with a confidence in their ability to negotiate with powerful people and to engage actively within the body politic. In the process, they gained familiarity with speaking to public gatherings, chairing meetings, debating alternatives, constructing coalitions, evaluating options, isolating opponents, and so on.[48] Furthermore, the "political confidence" of intellectual dissidents was in some cases (although by no means always) buttressed by a relative immunity from state sanctions. In the case of pastors, the contract between state and Church provided a significant degree of security. For others, it resulted from personal contacts, public prominence, or their unique skills. In short, oppositional intellectuals benefited from an array of resources, including skills and leadership qualities, which had been cultivated in their professional lives and social milieu. Elitist justifications of privilege were commonplace in these circles, as was disdain for the masses—widely regarded as uneducated, greedy, slothful, and pampered.

This, Fuller surmises, explains why workers' sympathy with the opposition was essentially passive. But this is an assumption that much evidence contradicts. Opposition groups such as New Forum gained a hearing in countless workplaces, New Forum activists themselves encouraged workplace militancy, and some groups of workers approached New Forum to seek advice. The street demonstrations and the civic movement, on one hand, and workplace discussion, protest activities, and FDGB meetings, on the other, were not separate worlds. They overlapped. The events, demands, and discourses of one fed into the other. In Francesca Weil's phrase, workplaces were the "relay stations" of the protest movement. In some Leipzig workplaces those who attended the "peace prayers" in the early autumn would return to work the next day and describe the experience to colleagues, sparking political debate.[49] Indeed, many workplace networks of militants were born not on the shop floor but from encounters at peace prayers or civic movement meetings.

Fuller does concede that "some workers" attended the public protests. But, she insists, according to the survey data of "[Karl-Dieter] Opp, Voß, and Gern, opposition group members, whom we have seen were overwhelmingly middle-class, joined demonstrations more often than those who were not."[50] In fact, the data set of Opp and his colleagues shows that "people holding a university degree on the average reported the *lowest* frequency of demonstration participation"—lower indeed than all categories of workers.[51] It may be that intellectuals were *underrepresented* in demonstrations.[52] Moreover, there is reason to suppose that most "intellectuals" present were white-collar workers rather than from the middling layers, let alone members of Fuller's "ruling intelligentsia."[53] The core participants at the Leipzig demonstrations, according to Bernd Lindner, were "overwhelmingly manual and white collar workers."[54] Elsewhere, in Saxony and Thuringia, the smaller industrial towns often witnessed higher rates of participation in protests than did the big cities, which, being administrative centers, contained higher concentrations of functionaries.

Simple arithmetic suggests that these findings may be generalized. Between August 1989 and April 1990, twenty-six hundred public demonstrations and over three hundred rallies took place in the GDR, as well as over two hundred strikes and a dozen factory occupations.[55] The largest three demonstrations each attracted well over one million people. No accurate figures exist for the total number of participants in demonstrations and public protests. That it was in the millions is indisputable. One researcher has estimated the figure at over five million.[56] Yet there were only 1.6 million graduates in the land. Even had they all mustered on the streets, they would have composed only a minority of the crowds. To see in 1989 a "revolution of the intellectuals" is to elide "the people" with the intelligentsia, to mistake the composition of social movement organizations for that of the movement as a whole, and to allow the light directed at its spokespeople to leave the crowds in shadow. (The public prominence of intellectuals, moreover, was not a novelty of 1989. It is hardly uncommon for lawyers, doctors, priests, and teachers to act as spokespeople in revolutionary situations.)

The thesis of working-class non-involvement in 1989, in short, holds no water. Workers, in very large numbers, were actively involved. But one can go further and argue that, at critical moments, their role was decisive. A case in point is the early phase of the revolution in East Germany. In September and October, Stasi units were showered with reports attesting to the increasing urgency with which economic and political reform was being demanded in the workplaces.[57] Their sources warned that if supply shortages were not overcome, "spontaneous strikes could occur."[58] The strikes that did break out were typically in response to political issues rather than, or in addition to, workplace problems. Stasi reports indicate that discussion of the pros and cons of industrial action was roiling in workplaces across Saxony and Thuringia.[59] Several strike threats were issued, not only in reaction to the closure of the border to Czechoslovakia (on October 3) but also in protest at the deployment of paramilitary "factory battalions" against the street demonstrations.[60] News of these activities undoubtedly gave state leaders food for thought. They must have realized, writes Bernd Gehrke, that a crackdown on mass protests in Plauen, Dresden, or Leipzig "would have sparked strike action which, to have been checked at all, would have necessitated a state of emergency."[61] In late October, an assessment for Soviet diplomats in East Germany found the "mood in the workplaces" to be so "unfavorable that there is the danger of the formation of parallel structures."[62] Similar concerns were voiced at a SED Central Committee meeting in early November. One member warned that "the working class is so enraged they're going to the barricades! They're shouting: get the Party out of the workplaces!"[63]

Despite the anxieties of Stasi generals and SED chiefs that the ferment in the factories could boil over, the decisive part that workers played in 1989 was not in workplaces but in the public squares and streets. It was when the public protests in Leipzig and elsewhere were joined by tens of thousands of working people that the regime's hard-line tactics were defeated. The demonstrations, in the words of sociologist Hartmut Zwahr, "gained their decisive, system-destroying power thanks to the mass participation of workers."[64] In East Germany, in short, the movement was not simply a *Feierabend* (after-work) affair. Rather, one of its chief bases was the workplace, and the decisive factor in its success was the entry of workers—and in this, the GDR was not atypical. In late November 1989, Czechoslovakia experienced a two-hour general strike supported by around half the entire labor force, with a further quarter or so expressing symbolic solidarity.[65] In Romania, the late 1980s witnessed major expressions of working-class discontent, as in the 1987 mass strike in Braşov, while the event that unleashed the uprising in December 1989, the liberation of Timişoara, commenced with workers leaving their workplaces en masse and marching to the town center. In a range of other countries of the region, notably Albania, a high proportion of overall protest activity in the late 1980s and early 1990s consisted of industrial action.[66]

4. *Trasformismo*

During the early, "flower" phase of the 1989 transitions, the overwhelming sentiment was that all social layers were finding solidarity and common purpose in defiance of and opposition to the despised old regime. In some countries, social interaction became extraordinarily intense, even intoxicating.

"Suddenly we all want to assemble as much as possible, to listen as much as possible, and to speak as much as possible," reported one Slovak journalist.[67] The language of renaissance was ubiquitous. "We were all born on 17 November," rejoiced one Czech student. Others characterized the atmosphere as a "beautiful fever" akin to "falling in love" (as Tomáš Hradílek, a spokesman for the dissident initiative Charter 77, put it), or being "drunk on new wine" (in the words of Czech folk singer Jaromír Nohavica).[68]

It would be an exaggeration to say that civil society was being invented anew. Under the old regimes, people had been involved in clubs, self-help groups, citizens' initiatives, and the like. Nevertheless, the countries of East Germany, Czechoslovakia, and Romania in 1989 witnessed an extraordinary eruption of civic activity. Opportunities were opening up for all manner of projects that had been illegal or indeed still were. In the GDR, two to three applications to register new associations reached the Interior Ministry every day. Houses were squatted, in some of which art galleries and bars were opened, and students created independent unions. Feminists set up women's centers, cafés, and libraries, and an Independent Women's Association was formed, which helped to make formerly taboo topics, such as spousal abuse or same-sex love, subjects of open discussion.[69] Another feminist group, Lilac Offensive, demanded that March 8th be made a women-only holiday.[70] Waves of protest in some cases led directly to the formation of new institutions. In Erfurt, a member of "Women for Change" noticed containers being loaded and driven away from the local Stasi headquarters and smoke rising from its chimneys. She urged acquaintances to action, and before long several dozen people were blocking the road; all lorries were prevented entry or exit; cars were allowed through only after being searched. This precipitated the formation, nationwide, of committees to launch investigations into brutality by the security forces.

These periods of combativity and delirious unity, these utopian conjunctures in which traditional authority structures were crumbling and campaigning groups could force their way into newfound political and cultural space, were, even in the GDR, Czechoslovakia, and Romania, relatively brief. Outside that group, they were relatively tepid and were vitiated by nationalism and racism. In Bulgaria, for example, the opposition movements of 1989 were weakened by their susceptibility to anti-Turkish racism.[71] In Yugoslavia, a formidable upsurge in industrial action in the 1980s, with wildcat strikes and a widespread public hostility toward the entire ruling elite,[72] precipitated the fall of "communism," but its progressive thrust was ultimately derailed by wily operators such as Franjo Tudjman and Slobodan Milošević, who were able to stabilize the new order by playing the "national card," thereby postponing Yugoslavia's "1989"—in the case of Serbia until the "Bulldozer Revolution" of 2000.

The dominant strategy through which to engage the opposition movements, however, was to gradually concede their democratic demands, in the mode of *trasformismo*: the organization of a loose alliance between regime and moderate oppositional forces, in order to marginalize radical currents. In this respect, as in so many, Poland blazed the trail. In 1988 it underwent roughly what its neighbors experienced in 1989. The situation in both cases was objectively similar: mass collective action was forcing a divided and faltering regime to reform, with the old order cautiously coming to recognize the advantages of containing revolt by means of political concession in the form of parliamentary democracy.

The imposition of austerity and other proto-neoliberal reforms would proceed so much more smoothly, it appeared to Poland's military dictator, General Jaruzelski and his team, if the Solidarność leaders were to propose it. Just as *glasnost* could help advance the case for *perestroika*, democracy could prove an indispensable means of selling the pain of market reform to a recalcitrant population. In Jaruzelski's recollection, the regime had learned from the past:

> The first crisis arose in 1956. We had to send tanks onto the streets; there were deaths. The second serious crisis then followed in 1970, and the third in 1980. In 1981 we had to send tanks onto the streets again. In 1988, a new crisis. In May and August—strikes. But this time we attempted to resolve the crisis without violence, without bloodshed. For if we had endlessly followed that road, the gap between us and the working class would have perpetuallywidened.[73]

On another occasion, in late 1989, he put the point in a most illuminating way.

> As a result of major economic problems we have faced difficult experiences. I'm thinking of December 1970 and August 1980. We undertook a series of attempts to reform, but these ended in failure. In each case, the obstacle was our population. The Party, the government, was not in a position to win the majority to acquiesce to unpopular decisions. However, these decisions, now being carried out by the current coalition government, are being accepted fairly quietly, even though living standards are worsening. Strikes

are rare. This shows that the population places greater trust in this form of government.[74]

In addition, he anticipated, "with this [coalition] government we are more likely to receive Western assistance."

Here, then, is the chain of events, from 1956 to 1989, highlighting resistance on the part of the Polish masses. But it also hints at another chain. It, too, connects 1956, 1980–81, and 1988–89—but this chain modifies the heroic narrative, outlined above, of Poland's protest trajectory. In this narrative, 1956 is the year in which Moscow sent tanks to crush the uprising in Hungary, repeated in Czechoslovakia twelve years later. These acts spread a fearsome pall over opposition movements across the region. In 1970s Poland, the prominent activist Adam Michnik declared that opposition must develop as a gradual process, for if it does not, the tanks will roll again. Michnik's KOR comrades, such as Jacek Kuroń, agreed: Yes, do agitate, organize, talk, and what have you, but keep within the law![75] This was the "self-limitation" precept that came to guide the Solidarność leadership in 1980–81 and which emboldened the regime in its bid to inflict a humbling defeat on the popular movement.

It was in the aftermath of Jaruzelski's crackdown of December 1981 that the ground was prepared for the closed-door "negotiated transition" to democracy, based on "Round Table" talks, that was to become the model across the region at the decade's close. Both sides were weakened. The regime had been exposed as enjoying minimal popular support. Solidarność had been revealed to have insufficient will to overthrow the regime when it came to the crunch—and its efforts to avoid confrontation, as Jack Bloom has documented, "made it increasingly suspect in many people's eyes."[76] Both sides were bruised and humiliated—and external events played a part too. Regime hardliners were weakened by the developments in Moscow. For their part, movement radicals were dispirited by the global social-movement downturn of the late 1970s and 1980s, which encouraged oppositionists in Poland and across CEE to turn away from conceptions of grassroots social transformation and toward liberalism—initially around the slogans "market socialism" and "civil society," and later for "democracy, markets and Europe." In Poland, the notion of "self-limitation" shuffled, step by step, toward a skepticism and even hostility—egregiously, in Michnik's case—toward working-class activism *tout court*.[77] By 1986, the regime was issuing amnesties to Solidarność members, at precisely the moment at which their organization reached a nadir in terms of effectiveness and popularity[78]—and then, when in May 1988 a rash of economic strikes broke out, "official Solidarity knew almost nothing about it."[79] Solidarność, as David Ost has documented, was able to push instead for political strikes, forcing the Round Table talks, in which, however, "workers all but disappeared."[80] This is the secret of the riddle of Poland's 1989. The election result of June was extraordinary, dramatic, momentous, and historic. It took the Communist Party by surprise (it didn't believe that it could possibly lose as badly as it did) and Solidarność swept the board.[81] But Solidarność was a shadow of its previous self. It had come to accept the basic structures of social order, had shelved radical aspirations, and now idealized the liberal institutional framework.

In demonstrating that an authoritarian regime could be brushed aside, and in its willingness to uncritically embrace liberal institutions, the Polish experience typified, and powerfully shaped, the 1989 upheaval as it rippled across the region. In East Germany, the attitude of the opposition leaderships toward public protest was initially tepid, and toward industrial action they were dismissive.[82] This was particularly apparent during a strike wave in early December that began to enthuse local branches of New Forum. "The readiness to strike," one New Forum leader recalls,

> was at that time greater among the workers than in the divided opposition movements in which intellectuals and pastors set the tone. . . . The call for a general strike at this time, which came from places like Plauen and Magdeburg, was ridiculed within our own ranks. When the time was ripe we did not act.[83]

Instead, the opposition groups opted to form pacts with regime forces, at Round Table talks, and in the form of "security partnerships" with the police and the Stasi. (This, incidentally, permitted these institutions to regroup and to destroy a good deal of evidence of their crimes.)[84] The movement followed a similar trajectory in Czechoslovakia. Following the November general strike, which led directly to the toppling of the regime, the CF/PAV attempted to demobilize the citizenry. It called for an end to mass demonstrations and encouraged strike committees to metamorphose into branches of CF/PAV for the purpose of negotiating with municipal leaderships.[85] While the streets pulled CF/PAV toward more radical positions in certain instances, its general trajectory was toward behind-the-scenes machinations and interelite negotiation. Its decision-making assemblies were summoned less and less, with committees close to Václav Havel now making all the key decisions. When discontent among the grassroots membership arose in response, Václav Klaus was able to tap into it, steering it in a populist-rightist direction—notably with his privatization plan, presented as a tool with which to break the power of the *nomenklatura*. Velvet revolution gave way to velvet corruption. The demos was levered out of "its" revolution—and when celebrations were called to mark its first anniversary, students in Prague pointedly refused to join in, arguing that basic demands of the previous year remained unfulfilled. The revolution was not velvet, they spat, but "stolen."[86]

Having achieved the institutional breakthrough, many of the reformers who had headed the struggle for democracy began to push a market-fundamentalist agenda, encouraged by Western advisers, foundations, and governments.[87] The market-fundamentalist juggernaut that was storming toward CEE encountered surprisingly little organized resistance. More than the intellectuals of the old dissident coalitions or even than the bulk of the former party elites, it was workers, especially women, who bore the brunt.[88] The ensuing bitter disappointment and rage, as Ost describes in the case of Poland, was consistently directed, above all by Solidarność, "*away* from class cleavages and toward identity cleavages."[89] Ultimately, the main beneficiary was conservative nationalism, headed by the Kaczyński brothers in Poland, Klaus in the Czech Republic, and Viktor Orbán in Hungary.

Conclusion

Following 1989, the structures of bureaucratic state capitalism and one-party rule in Central and Eastern Europe transmuted into liberal market economies and parliamentary democracy. The direction was broadly the same, even if the modalities and tempi varied widely, whether with respect to market reform, the predation of state assets, the extent of lustration, and the degree to which the political system resembled an orthodox or a "managed" parliamentary democracy. The underlying causes of the transformation included the weakening of Soviet hegemony and of the command-economic system, which prompted a turning of reformist heads toward Western-style systems. But, as with episodes of democratization elsewhere and in earlier eras, mass, working-class collective action played a central role in the transformation. Popular movements brought to a thunderous end the torrid decades in which independent political and industrial activity had been systematically stifled throughout CEE. At least in East Germany, Czechoslovakia, and Romania they did so with élan, displaying tremendous courage, creativity, and wit, as well as tactical nous in their confrontations with the forces of "law and order." In the uprush of grassroots activism, debate, and initiative, protesters discovered hitherto unsuspected capacities and provided a glimpse of the potential that arises when established order crumbles in the face of collective action. In all three countries a sense of "alternativity" arose, a feeling that "anything might happen" and "everything is possible," accompanied by a widespread sense of "collective effervescence."[90] Those who had been impotent discovered new powers and the ability to influence the political process. Radical questions welled up. What is the nature of this or that aspect of society? Should it be so? Can it be changed? If so, how do we get there?

The democratic gains were momentous: civil liberties, the formal accountability of government to the citizenry, and the right to organize politically and industrially. But once the impetus from the mass mobilizations subsided and new institutions of social control and the disciplining of labor were consolidated, those achievements were put under pressure. This coincided in the 1990s with soaring inequality and a regional Great Depression that impoverished millions, further sapping the strength of labor. In this context, and exacerbated by the global crisis of 2008, economic grievances fed into the surge of support for conservative nationalist and authoritarian populist currents, from Putin in the east to Orbán in the west. With hindsight, then, 1989 serves as a reminder that the masses taking temporary ownership of the streets means only so much unless it is the precursor for their taking permanent ownership of society.

Postscript: The "color revolutions"

The 1989 revolutions were at the meridian of an arc of change that commenced in Gdansk in 1980 and concluded in Moscow in 1991 (or, arguably, with the "electoral revolution" in Belgrade nine years later). Some would go further and propose that CEE and the post-Soviet territories, perhaps even extending into the Middle East, experienced an ongoing liberal-democratic revolution in the 2000s too. The evidence for this consists essentially of the "color" (or "flower") uprisings of the mid-2000s: the Rose Revolution in Georgia (2003–4), its Orange successor in Ukraine (2004), and the Tulip Revolution in Kyrgyzstan (2005) as well as the Cedar Revolution in Lebanon (also 2005). In each case, in a context of forthcoming or recently held elections, opposition parties and civil society campaigners, organized or headed by NGOs, accused corrupt, old-regime forces of rigging the system and demanded a free and fair electoral process.[91] In each case, the regime remained obdurate, prompting thousands of people to protest, while opposition groups, legitimated by the crowds on the streets, negotiated political change.

The case that these colorful episodes should be understood as revolutions rests on three main arguments. First, they exhibited high levels of popular mobilization and significant levels of confrontation with the security forces. In Georgia, over one hundred thousand took to the streets, and when the president, Eduard Shevardnadze, opened parliament, hundreds of followers of the opposition leader Mikheil Saakashvili stormed the building.[92] In Ukraine, demonstrations in Kiev numbered in the hundreds of thousands, with smaller protests taking place across the country.[93] In Kyrgyzstan, a succession of demonstrations, in 2002, demanding justice for citizens killed by police at an earlier event, combined with outrage over the parliamentary manipulation by the Askar Akayev regime and ignited an explosion of protest. There were mass meetings, demonstrations (of ten thousand or so in Jalalabad), and occupations of airports and roads. These culminated in insurrection in the capital city, Bishkek. Government buildings were occupied, a TV station was seized, and the presidential palace, known as the White House, was stormed.[94] Second, they exhibited hearty doses of what Lenin once referred to as the "festive energy of the masses."[95] The Orange Revolution, explains Andrew Wilson, should be seen as "profoundly revolutionary," in part because it was a manifestation of "real people power." There were "carnival-like street parades" and a genuine desire "for regime change, not just for a new president." The mood in the Maidan Nezalezhnosti (Independence Square), he goes on, did not just indicate personal support for the leading opposition politicians Viktor Yushchenko and Yulia Tymoshenko; rather, "it was the articulate anger of a people finding their voice. . . . The key sentiment was 'kick the bastards out,' and that is what revolutions are all about."[96] Third, the movement for regime change went beyond mere expressions of desires and grievances but culminated in real political-systemic shifts, particularly with respect to democracy. All of the color revolutions, it has been argued, not only overthrew corrupt incumbents—Shevardnadze, Akayev et al.—but also hoisted into office new governments that were populated by committed democrats.

Critiques of this position take two principal forms. In one, domestic conflict is reduced to geopolitics, with protests explained as the fruit of external intervention and manipulation. There may have been a popular element to the movements, but they possessed little autonomous spirit. In all three countries, the fingerprints of US and Russian embassy officials could be descried in some events, and the EU and United States' funding and training of numerous NGOs, including those that agitated against vote rigging, was well documented. In Ukraine, the Western powers favored Yushchenko while Russia backed his rival, Viktor Yanukovych. The West monitored the elections, through the Organization for Security and Co-operation in Europe, while Russia provided political advisers and some funding, alongside its media organs' presence in southern and eastern Ukraine.

Although it is self-evidently the case that significant external meddling and influence peddling occurred in all three uprisings, its role should not be exaggerated. In Ukraine, for example, Western organizations did provide funding for NGOs but only a fraction of their overall income.[97] The weightier counterargument to the notion that these were in any meaningful sense revolutions is a different one—namely, that regime change was cosmetic, not structural and socially transformative as it had been in the GDR, Czechoslovakia, and Romania. Georgia, following its roseate redecoration, was presented to the world by its Washington backers as a democratic success story, even though its new president had been elected—in echo of the vote shares achieved in the USSR under its notorious Georgian leader—by a staggeringly implausible 96 percent of the popular vote, and he then proceeded to co-opt the NGOs, neutering "civil society" opposition, before launching a harsh crackdown on demonstrators in 2007.[98] In Ukraine, "revolution" and "counterrevolution" rapidly came under the sway of the major political parties, which themselves were acting overtly as vehicles for business elites. The Orange Revolution, in essence, represented the "transfer of power from an unpopular government to an opposition through elections"; it "replaced one part of the Ukrainian elite with another."[99] Even in Kyrgyzstan, the one case in which popular movements pushed toward full-scale insurrection, there was, for all the personnel change at the apex of the political hierarchy, no significant change of regime. Here too, the movement was steered by wealthy elites,[100] and the new regime, of Kurmanbek Bakiyev, was no slouch in deploying authoritarian techniques when its support base began to erode—and all this with the vocal support of Washington, concerned as it was for its military base at Manas.[101]

It is in this sense that the color revolutions could appear to have been overtaken by geopolitics. This is not to say that geopolitics, most obviously

Soviet hegemonic decline, was not a fundamental determinant of the 1989 revolutions. Nor is it to say that agency in the color revolutions can be reduced to external interference. Rather, in the context of a movement sector that had not thrown up significant organizations of its own but attached itself more or less closely to existing elite-dominated parties, the economic and geopolitical connections of those elites, including of course to the great powers of Russia, Western Europe, and the US, came to play an important role. This included, against the mainstream narrative of "permanent liberal-democratic revolution," Western support for the stalling or even reversal of democratic reforms in Georgia, Ukraine, and Kyrgyzstan after their color-revolutionary episodes.

CHAPTER 3

The End of Apartheid in South Africa

Claire Ceruti

1. Reading the story forward

The South African transition has been variously described as a rainbow miracle, an unfinished revolution, a giant sell-out that blessed established capital, and insurrection deflected. Pinning it down is complicated by the perfectly natural compulsion to read the story backward—framed by how on earth we got *here*—even when it's told forward.

"Here" is "South Africa Inc." to borrow a phrase coined when Cyril Ramaphosa, the country's new president at the time of writing, chatted on TV about returning to politics after seventeen years as a key beneficiary of big capital's narrow foray into "black empowerment." Naturally, the broadcast avoided entirely the hand of the former mineworker-unionist and 1990s negotiator in criminalizing strikers in the days leading to the Marikana massacre.[1] Ramaphosa's role in that brutal restoration of profit-making encapsulates the sometimes awkward position of the few selected by the dominant faction of a remade liberation movement to bind afresh the deeply personal ties between the new owners of the state and old established capital. Despite considerable rewards for interceding between those worlds, Ramaphosa only made it to number twelve on the country's 2011 rich list, making him

93

the second-richest black South African. This, too, is emblematic of the ruling party's enthusiastic embrace of the discovery that, instead of acquiring command of a national economy when they acquired the state, they had acquired only the executive machinery of an entrenched (and therefore still very white) ruling class. The face of the state is transformed but not its role, and the greatest change in the distribution of the "commanding heights of the economy" has been its relisting in stock exchanges abroad.

How did South Africa Inc. get so far removed from the vision, widespread in the 1980s movement, of a victorious ANC implementing radical nationalist policies, let alone socialist ones? Must we concede that our younger selves were, "if not naive . . . unrealistic nonetheless, as events were soon to prove"?[2] Looking back, it is easier to see the transition's place in a much longer arc, where the end of Apartheid was the closing act of a failed attempt at reform from above in the 1980s (rooted in the '70s crises of accumulation), which neither contained the resistance it triggered nor, consequently, achieved the restructuring intended. And we can see that the transition was, simultaneously, the opening act of a more successful restructuring that temporarily stabilized South African capitalism, producing quick dividends for some, but at considerable cost to the proletariat, marginalization for much of the black "middle class," and persistent racism.

The danger, however, of telling the transition only as the backstory to the present is that it is easy to walk away impressed mainly by the cunning of the ruling class, because of how things *actually* turned out. Even those of us in the movements who predicted that the proletariat could not be satisfied by nationalism's "broad church" were surprised at how blatantly capitalist restructuring rode in on the back of "liberation." It is easy to read back into the transition only the triumph of neoliberalism over liberation—to see a skillful manipulation of the anti-Apartheid movement by capital, to complete the restructuring it could not achieve under Apartheid. This is superficially accurate, but it obscures an entwined tale of squandered possibilities for mass action.

There were good reasons in the 1980s to believe South Africa might buck the "continental pattern . . . criticized by Fanon" where the new national bourgeoisie would "'be quite content with the role of the Western bourgeoisie's business agent'" and "'merely brandish'" the state "'to supervise the pacification of the people.'" Saul expected the intransigence of white settler minorities "to radicalize any opposition" because it "tended to imply the need to mobilise people to a more committed level of involvement than would be the case in situations where the nationalist leadership was ... merely ushered into power by the departing colonists."[3] In practice, the settler state, with nowhere to depart to, was later compelled to negotiate. The exceptional size of the South African proletariat, implicated in increasingly substantial urban uprisings and strikes, sketched insurrectionary possibilities.

Those who supported negotiated compromise in the 1990s justified themselves partly by the absence of a revolutionary situation. Looking back, the transition was obviously neither a narrowly averted insurrection nor a rehearsal for one. But looking forward from inside a transition imposed by two clichés of a revolutionary situation (the rulers could not rule as before and the people wouldn't be ruled), it is less clear that nothing more could have developed. The transition was much trickier for the ruling classes than the carefully orchestrated process suggested by some characterizations of a "managed transition"— despite the sophisticated intentions of the National Party (NP), which had already, in the 1980s, begun to consider "reform" as a counterrevolutionary strategy.[4]

The South African transition should alert us to the immense structural difficulties that drove ruling classes onto the tricky road of "managed reform," and the immense dangers of managing an emboldened resistance when they did. Racial engineering was no white froth—as implied by the South African Communist Party's (SACP's) two-stage theory encapsulated by "national liberation first, then socialism"—but the very fabric of capital accumulation in South Africa; it was never going to be easy to unravel.

The transition was an intensely contradictory process, brutally contested outside the negotiating chamber. Undeniably, it tested new methods for containing radicalizing movements and consolidated a retreat from radical economic nationalism. It was the crucible in which the ruling class was forged anew around hitherto unlikely friendships, such as Ramaphosa's with Roelf Meyer of the National Party and Bobby Godsell of the mining corporation Anglo American. It consolidated moderate strategy inside popular organizations, gradually subsuming them into the ANC, and the ANC to its Executive. But neither should we forget that the movement won much more than F. W. de Klerk originally intended. Looking back on how smoothly capital seemed to change horses, it is easy to forget that his bold gambit never intended to sacrifice his own party on the altar of corporate continuity and that the mass movement whipped the transition forward on several critical occasions.

From inside the transition, it was possible to glimpse possibilities that rested neither on fantasies about the depth of the ANC's radicalism nor fanciful estimations of the movement's real strength. While "elite pact" adequately describes what replaced Apartheid, this was not built on mass quiescence. How did the new elites successfully surf the forcible entry of a proletarian movement into history?

The period was, after all, punctuated by lessons in the effectiveness of taking matters into collective hands, even if it was "difficult to take out of workers' minds that ANC are the leaders," as one unionist said. A group of young ANC members interviewed around 1994 defended their leadership's compromises, but also insisted that

> we managed to force the government to agree with us on the record of understanding, where the government was to arrest people carrying dangerous weapons, fence the hostels [and so on]; all those things, mass action actually brought. The whole thing that ensured that the process of negotiations becomes fast ... was [mass action] after we lost comrade Chris Hani [a popular commander of the ANC's armed wing, MK].[5]

The grand paradox of Apartheid's end is that mass action, in driving through a settlement, laid the basis for a political restabilization that the old order was too deeply invested to achieve for itself, while the ANC's negotiators might have compromised too much for a stable settlement. It was mass action that, time and again, restored the negotiations and ultimately imposed the relatively peaceful handover that ushered in a surprisingly long window of legitimacy for the state, during which capital could at last advance its hitherto fraught attempt to draw the movement into a corporatist framework to oversee privatization and massive labor redundancies.

It was easier to see from inside the transition that this owed less to the cleverness of an embattled ruling class than to how the politics dominating the movement constrained the movement's understanding of its strategic choices at this specific historical conjuncture. An important mechanism deflecting proletarian power was the substitution of political power for social power in the two-stage frame. Under oppressive accumulation, the democratic demand penetrates economic, social, and political questions, producing contradictory possibilities: of growing over into socialist struggle, but also of deferring social questions to the political kingdom.

Explaining how we got here—and where we did not go—starts before the transition. What had become of the movement that put insurrection back on the ANC's agenda in the mid-1980s?

2. Shuffling toward a stalemate

By 1989 the "mass democratic movement" was battered. Despite "spontaneous instances of resistance . . . [and] explosive issues in the schools," wrote Webster and Friedman, a "mood of political quiescence" prevailed; "for the most part, the ponderous weight of four successive states of emergency has borne down on progressive organizations and in some areas, completely destroyed democratic structures."[6] An estimated thirty thousand people were detained under emergency regulations between 1986 and 1988.[7] Rape, other tortures, and murder became common.

State strategy was shifting to lengthy trials, targeted detentions, and banning specific individuals, meetings, funerals, and organizations such as the United Democratic Front (UDF, an umbrella for anti-Apartheid organizations inside the country). The four-year-old trade union federation COSATU was restricted to activities "related to employment and the workplace," and police raided its offices.[8] Its special congress in 1988 had been crucial to a 2.5-million-strong national stayaway against detentions and banning orders, mobilizing shop-floor networks and circumventing emergency restrictions on "civic" organizations and church groups by inviting them to the congress. Vigilante groups, break-ins, fire-bombings, assassinations, and kidnapping supplemented legal repression.[9]

Mass detentions took activists out of society but brought a movement into the prisons (and drew new layers into a movement they meant to stamp out, through the Detainees' Parents Support Committee and a growing campaign for international sanctions). A hunger strike by about seven hundred detainees across the country, in January 1989, precipitated the release of eight hundred. Liz Abrahams, a union member detained in 1986 while doing civic work, describes an experience of depression and mistreatment punctuated by resistance:

> On 9 August—[South African] Women's Day—we occupied the prison's surgery as the doctor was not there and had a meeting. What a discussion! When we were done, we rose and sang the [liberation] anthem. The matron came and said, "Come, come, you had enough outings—the time is up." But we stood firm and sat and somebody told her, "You must wait until we have finished praying and singing, and then we will come." So we prayed, shouted "Amandla" and *toyi-toyi*ed all the way to the gate. From there we all went back to our cells.[10]

Another time, Abrahams and her twelve cell mates sat down at the end of exercise time, demanding reasons for their detentions, and had to be wrestled back into their cell, where the bruised, annoyed warders teargassed them.

The disruption inside the prison system showed that a militant movement of some breadth and depth, powerfully linking workplace and community, had developed since 1984's township uprising (more on which below). Abrahams met many other members of her union inside:

> You went to the exercise yard in the morning and the branch secretary from Grabouw was detained. The next morning there's another one from Saldanha Bay. . . . When we had discussions we never excluded anyone because we wanted them to understand how a union works, how you must act to build up a union. They were all interested even if they did not belong to a union.[11]

But could that movement survive this beating?

It is odd trying to get one's head around this question looking backward, because we now know that Mandela would walk free less than a year after Webster and Friedman's grim prognosis. In 1987 the ANC drew up preconditions for negotiations but could not agree to the regime's preconditions.[12] ANC exiles were debating the merits of people's war to overthrow Apartheid versus those of armed struggle to force negotiations while, inside the country, the "internal movements" such as UDF debated defeating Apartheid and capitalism in stages or simultaneously.[13] Inside the country, it did not feel like negotiations were around the corner.

What switched the course of events was, as is often the way, banal chance: President P. W. Botha had a stroke in January 1989. "The Old Crocodile" was a former defense minister who built the most powerful army in the region, then presided over an attempt to devolve the cost of Apartheid onto its victims via political "reform," sparking the 1984 uprising. De Klerk assumed leadership of the National Party in February, and his "enlightened" faction squeezed Botha out of cabinet by August.[14] Their enlightenment did not extend to majority rule, but De Klerk's faction understood that four states of emergency reflected a loss of control as much as an exercise of power. De Klerk moved quickly to release five Rivonia trialists (those imprisoned with Mandela in the early 1960s) by mid-October—largely because he had little time to waste.

In the uncertainty following Botha's stroke, the movement revived, buoyed on a swelling "tide of expectations."[15] The involvement of new, often respectable, suspects such as clergy and white organizations may have helped, but the restricted organizations, despite real damage from the Emergencies, remained key. COSATU and the UDF had launched the National Defiance Campaign on July 26:

The response was overwhelming throughout the country. White facilities were invaded, and banned organisations declared themselves "unbanned," initiating a period of open and mass defiance of Apartheid laws.[16]

The softening hand of the state surely helped the campaign, but the movement was already emboldened, months before the velvet glove was donned, by its own analysis of Apartheid's weaknesses. Take the September 2 demonstration, unusually in Cape Town's (white) city center, against upcoming elections (in which the majority—classified "Africans" by Apartheid—had no vote, while whites, so-called Coloreds, and so-called Indians could vote for separate, unequal parliaments, known as Tricamerals, established in 1984). This protest, automatically illegal under emergency laws, became known as the "Purple Shall Govern" protest (a play on "the people shall govern") after police used a dye-filled water cannon on protesters who, upon receiving orders to disperse, sat down in the road a few hundred meters away from parliament. One protester briefly diverted the water cannon to spray surrounding buildings, including the National Party headquarters.[17] The purple chaos immediately came to signify a faintly ridiculous police state losing control. The police were perhaps restrained by disproportionate numbers of white people, since buses from townships had been blocked, but we should not mistake the arcs of dye for the indigo stripe of the coming rainbow nation. This novel form of crowd control was after all intended to mark for arrest those who escaped teargas and batons; a thousand people and fifty-two journalists were arrested for protest around Cape Town that day.[18] Four days later, police massacred about twenty people by shooting into a crowd in a township during a three-million-strong anti-elections stayaway that was probably larger than the turnout for the elections.[19]

It is therefore not surprising that the movement was deeply suspicious of De Klerk's sincerity, and even the exiled ANC suspected "a genuine attempt to create a climate conducive to negotiations—but on debt rescheduling [with imperialist powers, due in July 1990], not on the end of apartheid."[20]

2.1. Apartheid's cul-de-sac

To the movement, De Klerk's subsequent decision to permit marches on September 13 and 15 signaled "a necessary state accommodation of persistent mass struggles"[21] rather than De Klerk's benevolence:

The nature of current resistance and defiance suggests that those with allegiance to the Mass Democratic Movement believe they have the government in a corner. There is no sign that action based on this belief will stop, and the sense of achievement generated by the "Pretoria spring" of the mid-September marches will fuel this.[22]

But, if the movement's easy revival hurried De Klerk's faction toward genuine talks, his trajectory hadn't been hatched in those few months following Botha's stroke. Decades later, De Klerk recalled (in curiously soft focus) its roots in earlier, failed "reform":

> In 1986 the National Party embraced the idea of a united [!] South Africa . . . but with very effective protection of minorities. Then my predecessor lost his enthusiasm. When I took over, my task was to flesh out what was already a fairly clear vision, but we needed broad support. We needed negotiation.[23]

Botha had not "lost his enthusiasm." He'd sown a whirlwind that blew him off course. Later in the interview, De Klerk is clearer that his own trajectory was one of few remaining escape routes from an epic failure to rejig Apartheid:

> The third phase—which coincided with my entering cabinet but was not started by me—was a shift towards reform. It focused on making separate development more acceptable while still believing it was just. But by the early 1980s we had ended up in a dead-end street in which a minority would continue to hold the reins of power and blacks, outside the homelands, really did not have any meaningful political rights. We had become *too economically inter-dependent* [my emphasis]. We had become an omelette that you could not unscramble.[24]

The omelette was Apartheid's Achilles' heel: white-minority rule rested entirely on black labor.

Racial accumulation had long outgrown simple dispossession. By the 1970s it was poking holes in the elbows of grand Apartheid. The state and capital were no less dependent on black oppression than before, but attempts to cut a new suit from the same cloth caught on several knots, chief among them that adapting Apartheid's architecture to the economy's half-blind self-restructuring provoked explosions in which people found and flexed new powers. Consequently, whatever restructuring the state achieved was too shallow to properly recalibrate Apartheid with the economy and came at a very great political and monetary cost.

The 1984 township uprising was a stark reminder that the notion of a permanently temporary, migrant proletariat had a shelf life. Influx control (pass laws) had secured high mining profits that then needed to roost in other sec-tors of the economy—with different labor needs. By 1985, 75 percent of the workforce was in secondary and tertiary sectors, up from 56 percent in 1960; the white labor force was insufficient.[25] Semi-skilled black workers now out-numbered unskilled black workers in manufacturing, and by the mid-'80s the color bar in white-collar occupations was breaking down.[26] Especially after the 1973 strikes and the Black Consciousness Movement, differential incorpora-tion can only have sharpened these workers' sense of dissonance between their place in the work process and their place in the social order. For the Apartheid state and capital, the need for a more stable *section* of the workforce rubbed uncomfortably against established geographies and ideologies of Apartheid. The state wanted manufacturing expansion, but it didn't want to pay more for state housing and it balked at hefty ideological concessions to black urbaniza-tion, which might affect cruder forms of labor control still desired in mines and agriculture. A government-appointed commissioner reconciled contradic-tory priorities by proposing a social border inside which the new kind of black worker was a little less restricted and outside which the old forms of racial labor control were tightened up: the Riekert Commission recommended in 1979 that black workers who were already stable in urban areas should be allowed to bring dependents, to build or buy their own houses in the townships, and to move a little more easily between jobs and towns—and be required to pay for upgrading the townships; everyone else who was black would be chased away.[27] About six million "Africans" made it through the eye of Riekert's needle out of sixteen to twenty million.[28] Many town dwellers were "repatriated" to distant Bantustan villages they had sometimes never seen before.[29] If the commission initially raised any hopes, the state's "reforms" after Riekert emphasized how completely arbitrary any specific black life remained in Apartheid's realloca-tions of black bodies as urban worker, migrant laborer, or "surplus."

And the friction that had built up within the machinery of separate devel-opment was, by now, enormous. Riekert's proposals couldn't stem the numbers defying pass laws, as much to escape the Bantustan crisis as to gain urban rights. The Bantustans were foundational to the separate-development ideol-ogy that framed the low-wage, circular migration at the heart of racial capi-talism's previous phase of accumulation, and the "outside" in Riekert's map of the black labor force. In these scattered fragments of some of the most useless land in the country (figure 2), black South Africans were meant to plant all yearnings, whether for stable family life, accumulation of capital or cattle, social recognition, or citizenship. Above all, those surplus to requirements in the part of the country designated white were supposed to politely rot there. By the '70s, writes Harold Wolpe, "we witnessed the dumping of unwanted labour in the reserves, not to reproduce their labour power [subsidizing wages in his argument] but to perish."[30] "Perish" in the literal sense. As more people were removed to the Bantustans, even subsistence agriculture became unsustainable. Border industries, Apartheid's ultimate solution to keep white a country dependent on black labor, seldom outlasted outrageous subsidies (5,700 rand, or R5,700, per employee in 1967).[31] By 1981, Pretoria had granted "independence" to four Bantustans, transforming millions of South Africans into "foreigners." But the Bantustans were never going to be self-sufficient, deputized as they were to rule unemployed people and those too old, young, or sick for "white" South Africa. Little of Pretoria's "foreign aid" was left for alleviating social crisis after bankrolling their legislatures and the armed forces required to suppress popular opposition. By 1985, the Bantustans' actual population hovered around half of their *de jure* populations.[32]

The social crisis in urban areas was different, not less. Besides the bureaucratic and banal vagaries of race supremacy, material conditions for black people were dire. The conditions that primed schools for 1976 persisted into the '80s, such as classes of fifty to ninety students. The state froze spending on black housing early in the '70s but forbade the private sector from providing housing until the release of the Riekert report. White South Africans sprawled out with swimming pools for the richest and tiny back rooms to accommodate a domestic worker for the average white, while pressure grew on the township "matchboxes" where kitchens regularly doubled as extra bedrooms. Only seven thousand new houses were built across ten townships in the fast-growing, light-industrial region east of Johannesburg in the seven years before 1980, but the population of just one, Katlehong, doubled over that time.[33] After Riekert, white contractors thought townships were risky business, black workers could not afford to have houses built, and no rental market developed since most housing stock remained state-controlled. By the end of the '80s, more than seven million black people were defying the law to live in zinc shacks in urban informal settlements.[34] The thin slice counting as middle class who could afford their own houses still had to live in the same townships as the proletariat with the same inadequate services, dirt roads, and intense social disruption, so the state's attempt to foster a politically pliable black middle class to buffer radicalism failed.

The debacle of the state establishing Black Local Authorities (BLAs) but not devolving any power onto them sparked the township uprising late in 1984. BLAs were indeed black, and indeed local, but completely without authority except to collect rents and levies from residents to make the townships "self-sustaining." Their unpopularity predated the announcement that rents would increase to at least R50 a month against wages of R60 a month in the Vaal Triangle,[35] amid large-scale redundancies in the steel industry, before which fewer than 8 percent of adult residents had voted in council elections.[36] The state's strategy had people cornered: by 1984, thirty-five thousand households in the Vaal (an urban-industrial complex 60 kilometers south of Johannesburg) were in arrears on rents, which had risen 400 percent since 1978.[37]

But people were not an inert fuse: it was the so-called civic organizations' attempts to organize that set things off on September 3. One residue of the 1970s was a blossoming of tiny nodes of organizing. To oppose the Tricameral elections, around six hundred grassroots youth and civic organizations launched the UDF in 1983, while others launched the smaller National Forum. The Vaal Civic Association (VCA), three months old in January 1984, reports these modest activities: a working committee of seven in Sebokeng Zone 12 was "busy mobilising . . . and expect to form and elect an area committee within . . . three months"; twelve members in Zone 7 were "very busy on house meetings and will arrange a [mass] meeting to elect a committee" and had also "organised twenty parents around the issues in schools" (forced resignations of teachers and getting students readmitted who had failed exams); in Bophelong, there was a youth congress and an active committee.[38]

The uprising spread via an ad hoc regional committee, then to other parts of the country, and did not stop at rents. The judge in the Delmas treason trial later complained that "the [rent] increase was revoked on 18 September 1984 and in 1985 and 1986 there were no rent increases at all and yet only 18 percent of the residents pay their rent and the riots continued."[39] The spread and resilience of organizing into the '80s and beyond owes something to the way these organizations framed their work. The judge continued:

[The VCA] was clearly not intended as an organization with purely local civic objectives. At its inaugural meeting resolutions were passed on matters of national concern like the education system, the Black local authorities system, the Koornhof Bills and President's Councils constitutional proposals, the homeland system, the Ciskei government and the banning of the South African Allied Workers Union.

Not only had Botha's securocrats failed to impose the financial costs of oppression on the oppressed, they had conjured a more expensive problem. Townships were terrorized by conservative vigilantes and soldiers, denting the movement but disrupting the stable labor force the state desired. Municipal elections in 1988 confirmed that co-option had failed: less than 10 percent voted in most "African" areas.[40]

By 1989, De Klerk would have been keenly aware that securitization was not the surest way out of the crisis. Conscription brought the crisis to Apartheid's white voting base, while internal repression weighed on an economy already taxed by border wars with liberated neighbors, quadruplicate administration (one for each "race"), and propping up Bantustans. By 1985, Pretoria had racked up and defaulted on $13 billion in debt. The default was a turning point for its friendships in Washington and London. Some $9 billion left the country in the four years following, increasing Pretoria's sensitivity to the international pressure for a settlement.[41]

That wasn't all: the economy was not earning enough from raw mineral exports to cover imports feeding a growing manufacturing sector. The price of its main export, gold, had become unpredictable. Inward-looking development was straightjacketed by the economy's dependence on race-based low wages, which had boosted growth and profits but inflexibly narrowed the domestic consumer base. Liz Abrahams's defiant exchange with her interrogator in prison highlights another dimension:

> He said, "Hey Liz, up to now, what did the people get from you and your struggle?" I replied, "I can tell you what. I started working for the union and people earned 75c, now the people are earning more than R100."[42]

Inflation in 1989 was 15 percent, but some unions were securing increases of 20 percent (while executives were taking 30 percent).[43] The increases did not expand the consumer base much, given rising unemployment, but a workforce flexing new powers since the 1973 strikes was squeezing the quick and dirty profit margins that Apartheid-capital had come to rely on. As the color bar wavered and Apartheid's attempts at reform foundered, the "new" black workers exercised new kinds of leverage. While the township uprising buckled under repression, days lost to work stoppages, illustrated below, rose during the first two states of emergency.

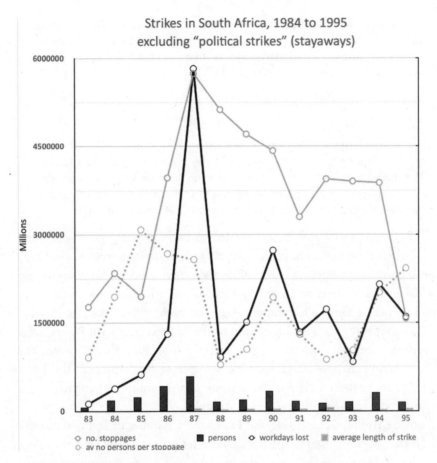

Strikes in South Africa, 1984 to 1995
excluding "political strikes" (stayaways)

Compiled by the author from *South African Statistics 2001*, Statistics South Africa.

Government statistics excluded "political" strikes: the graph's decline in person days lost in 1988 depicted in the graph disguises 9 million person days lost that year to massive stayaways, including the first successful three-day stayaway in twenty-seven years, called by COSATU against the new Labour Relations Act (LRA).[44] It also obscures adaptive organizing in struggles simmering around workplaces. Workers copied preachers, turning train carriages into political meetings on long commutes to dodge meeting bans.[45] Two shop stewards described their 1988 workplace campaigns against the LRA, which aimed to challenge government by putting pressure on employers:

> People feel the bill will take us back and kill our struggle. If we have no union . . . management will do as he likes. We protest at lunchtime every

Tuesday. But we take some extra time, five or ten minutes. We take this time from management . . . to show that we don't like the bill. . . . We have approached management to write a letter [to government against the LRA amendments] . . . but we are still waiting.[46]

Moreover, the workplace had become a site for struggle around issues beyond it:

[The restrictions] must not succeed. The UDF is also workers. . . . We told management we are going to stay away on Monday to commemorate Sharpeville. Management sent out a memo that who wants to work on Monday should approach them to make special arrangements. It shows that we are ruling the company. We are workers. The company cannot do anything without us.[47]

Employers who wrote letters tended to be equivocal; most welcomed the bill's intention to rein in wildcat action and solidarity boycotts. The Wiehahn Commission, Riekert's workplace twin, had tried to domesticate the new black trade unions by ensnaring them in an industrial conciliation machinery separate from white unions, but that backfired. Unions had mobilized combatively to materialize some of the limited new legal rights, such as workplace recognition, building a potently shop floor–based movement while rejecting the overall framework of separate development. The LRA amendments proposed clawing back some of this ground—but provided a new occasion for generalizing union struggles.

Bokkie Botha, representing the Federated Chamber of Industries, fretted: "If the Bill were used to roll back labour reforms it would have the effect of undermining rather than encouraging labour stability."[48] Employers welcomed the states of emergency but feared the repercussions and were looking for political solutions to politicized unions. Botha continued:

There is no doubt from a businessman's point of view you cannot operate in an unrest situation. It's disruptive. So there is a belief that we need to contain unrest [but] at the same time you have to find a solution that allows people to talk. . . . We are extremely concerned that the real voice of the people is being restricted, and the result is to develop a new underground. . . . That is the sort of thing business is talking to government about. . . . Senior business people are making contact with people on the left.[49]

Anglo American had met with the ANC in Lusaka in 1985. By the time De Klerk became president, the writing was clear on the boardroom wall.

De Klerk wanted a public bear hug that would pin the opposition's arms while he whirled out of the corner his regime was backed into. But the global legitimacy waltz required a partner. What made the movement willing?

2.2. The crisis of militant nationalism

The move to talks can be attributed to a kind of stalemate, except the movement's stalemate was not entirely imposed by objective circumstances. Here we must examine the ANC's motives, but also why the internal movement gave the ANC the wheel.

The reform and collapse of the USSR was a key pressure on the ANC. It was no accident that it published preconditions for negotiations toward the end of 1987, nor that a "senior ANC leader" said in 1986, at the height of the uprising, that its objective was "to force Pretoria to the negotiating table," not military victory.[50] The Soviet funding squeeze made the ANC more vulnerable to the pressure also bearing on the regime from the incipient fashion among world powers for controlled settlements in turbulent countries of interest to them. It also drove home the limits of conducting an armed struggle from exile against the regime of a highly industrialized country. Tom Lodge argued that it had become a pressure tactic rather than a way to seize power because of the difficulties of prosecuting guerrilla war with a "persistent imbalance of military power . . . over very long lines of communication," worsened by the ANC losing its Angolan base in the 1989 Namibian settlement.[51] South Africa was relatively urbanized. White farmers dominated the countryside, doubling as reservists for an extensive military network and exercising very great power over the bodies and livelihoods of black farmworkers. Conventional guerrillas could not move undetected.

Yet the ANC failed to center its politics on the powers flexed in 1973 and 1976, preferring to juggle the bomb and negotiating agenda. Its 1983 perspective, *Planning for People's War*, occasionally stretched to hoping for "a long-lasting national work stoppage backed by our oppressed communities supported by armed activities aimed at bringing the regime to its knees,"[52] but in practice, members of its armed wing who were active in the '80s movements could not easily harmonize their clandestine military activities (such as recruiting individuals from the movement or distributing hand grenades) with mass strategy such as organizing self-defense units. The competing negotiation strategy gained momentum through having a practical channel—one that was more at the exiled leadership's fingertips than an arduous internal strategy. The ANC unilaterally suspended armed struggle in August 1990, against the wishes of the

UDF and COSATU, who still distrusted De Klerk.[53] Its core politics framed the state as the key instrument of national development and therefore of liberation; compromise was as good a means to lay hands on a state as conquest.

It is more difficult to judge whether the internal movement had reached a limit. Were the workplace struggles the last kicks of a dying uprising or the seeds of its revival (or, simultaneously, the contradictory beginnings of domesticating unions)?

This was not dual power as one or two romantic commentators imagined, despite accusations that the UDF was "making the townships ungovernable."[54] The state's plans were in tatters, but it substituted localized military rule for collapsed local authorities. Organs of alternate power were, at best, incipient. Street committees developed in some townships during the uprising but were not generalized, and shrank under the states of emergency, sometimes into undemocratic, unpopular bodies.[55] COSATU's failure to build solidarity for the mineworkers' strike in 1987 and its subsequent defeat was a serious blow to the balance of power.[56] On the other hand, when the movement revived after Botha's stroke, the memory was still fresh of the civic movement having briefly constituted the only authority in a handful of townships such as Alexandra, and of the massive stayaways that turned strikes into a political weapon.

Experimenting with these templates was superseded by "genuine negotiations," which were attractive because they proved the movement's power and promised an easing of repression (which turned out illusory). It made tactical sense to exploit spaces opened by De Klerk's overtures to push further.

But why surrender leadership so easily to the ANC?

The regime opened negotiations with the ANC, not the internal movement; many UDF structures and members felt an affinity with the ANC via the Freedom Charter. Despite fierce debate in the late '80s, the "populists" dominating the UDF followed the SACP in framing the struggle as primarily anti-Apartheid for its first stage because, they held, race obscured class, requiring cross-class unity of the oppressed—encapsulated in the unbanned ANC's "broad church." Initially, the UDF continued organizing independently after the ANC's unbanning, but it was proposed that the ANC would handle "politics" and the UDF "socioeconomic" and local issues. Since the separation was artificial in the first place, more and more of the UDF's turf was covered by the ANC, while civic groups claimed local issues. Neglected UDF structures collapsed as many of its leaders were drawn into ANC structures.[57] In 1991, the front dissolved.

Meanwhile COSATU had joined the alliance between the SACP and the ANC the previous year. Before the alliance met in November, there were already complaints about "whether the ANC alone is involved in the talks or [if] the talks [are] the project of the Alliance," but the alliance nevertheless seemed to promise COSATU independence and influence simultaneously: the meeting agreed that allies should consult each other without being expected to agree.[58] While it was patently inaccurate for the SACP to claim that "workerism" had led COSATU to abstain from politics in the late '80s, the "workerists" never exceeded syndicalism organizationally. Winning unions to adopt socialist programs readily turned to lobbying the coming ANC government to adopt union programs, especially under subtle pressures to social corporatism, in a vacuum of specifically socialist organization.

All this is foundational to the compromise ahead, but it is questionable whether even limited bourgeois democracy would have resulted from a transition left entirely up to ANC and NP negotiators.

3. How taming the state tamed the transition

The balance of forces during the transition was neither static nor all on the regime's side. It was an intensely contested process in which, as demonstrated below, mass action broke "logjams" in the negotiations and forced the process forward—sometimes at the behest of the ANC, occasionally independently of it, and, on at least one occasion, despite it. In a process that took half a decade, why did these experiences not ferment increasingly revolutionary practice? Apart from the lack of structures of alternate power, the absence of a deeply rooted revolutionary political frame is a fragment of the puzzle, but it can't explain why such political frames (which did after all exist at the time) did not become more popular during the transition. Another key element was the old regime's compulsion to negotiate, despite its very great need to stamp its own will on the process. In this context, the effect of mass intervention was, paradoxically, to restore the ascendancy of the moderates in the movement, by getting the negotiations back on track in the very moment of proving the efficacy of taking matters into collective hands. The effect was the opposite of exposing the limits of bourgeois democracy.

The length of the transition needs explaining. South Africa's bourgeoisie were "no mere clients or puppets of Western capitalism, but a rich, powerful and well-entrenched ruling class."[59] They ruled a country where the bulk of industry was locally owned but with a marked increase in global linkages in the preceding period, despite sanctions.[60] Since the negotiations did not follow a military defeat of the old order, the ANC entered talks from a position of military weakness with a government that retained the entire state machine. The regime's lack of alternatives made it at the same time very stubborn and very committed to the process. Negotiations became a terrain of intense struggle.

The old regime tried multilateral negotiations to numerically load the dice against the movement, alongside hidden and open violent destabilization. Mass action was the last thing left in the armory after suspending the anyway-failing armed struggle, but the ANC's attitude to mass mobilization was consistently inconsistent: tension between negotiations and "other terrains of struggle" consolidated a decisive strategic shift toward compromise over the course of the negotiations. Time and again, the ANC's reluctance to wield this weapon threatened the possibility of transition altogether.

Enormous rallies greeted the ANC's unbanning, but it did not immediately exploit the legal space to harness mass confidence and regain the initiative from De Klerk, who "employed a strategy of decisive and rapid movement to maintain the initiative . . . until the scandal of government funding of Inkatha more than a year later."[61] When police killed protesters in Sebokeng, the ANC threatened to withdraw from negotiations but soon "clarified" that statement, allowing its commitment to negotiations to dominate. Mandela, on his release, said that "our struggle has reached a decisive moment . . . now is the time to intensify struggle on all fronts" but also that he hoped the crowd would "disperse with discipline. And not . . . do anything which will make other people say that we can't control our own people."[62]

In May 1990, "talks about talks" committed the ANC and the regime to negotiate a political settlement, resolve violence, and develop terms for exiles' return and political prisoners' release. In August, after uncovering an MK network, the NP insisted that armed struggle was the main obstacle to negotiations. In the first of many sacrificial logjam breakers, the ANC agreed to suspend it, without consulting its allies, with no progress on the May commitments, and without any commitment to control state forces. This was a 180-degree turn from the 1989 Harare Declaration, which made suspending armed struggle conditional on removing obstacles to negotiating.

It was widely held that the ANC gave away more than it got in August. Even the SACP's journal grumbled in October: "If [the masses] become mere spectators then our negotiating hand is weakened."[63] In December, the

ANC was sharply criticized at the conference it called to consult with its allies, especially since the regime had, far from keeping promises about prisoners and exiles, maintained a veto on indemnity. The conference resolved to "launch a programme of mass action and all other actions to achieve our objectives as quickly as possible."[64] It wanted the ANC to withdraw from negotiations if obstacles were not removed within four months, but the leadership changed this to "considering" withdrawing.

People on the ground displayed better instincts about the crack opened by Apartheid's impasse. Struggles around housing and residential services went on. There were strikes of health workers, teachers, and Mercedes-Benz assemblers. But there was no attempt to link these to national issues, and the official ANC was removed from them except when Mandela appealed for the health workers and the autoworkers to go back to work.

Violence spread from Natal to Johannesburg in July as the NP's sweetheart Inkatha, a conservative Zulu nationalist party, tried to carve itself out of its regional limitations, with covert government support. COSATU's July stayaway against the violence was the only national action of 1990. More than three million workers responded to the call. What the regime liked to call "black-on-black violence" became their excuse to clamp down. The ANC leadership defended communities' right to form self-defense units against these attacks, but in words only. No attempt was made to replicate COSATU's stayaway, and the unions increasingly believed that further mobilization would worsen things.

Although 1991 was declared "the year of mass action for people's power . . . the first days of January made it abundantly clear that negotiation initiatives would continue to be generated at a leadership level."[65] Mass action was meant to push the negotiators to agree to an interim government and constituent assembly, but now even that was softened to accommodate compromise "in the national interest": the ANC was now proposing an All Party Conference to draw up constitutional principles, which would have given the old order a disproportionate say in the constitution. Walter Sisulu explained: "Our approach is to persuade all the people of South Africa to unite behind democratic ideals." Negative responses from Inkatha and the white Conservative Party should not deter the ANC from "its duty to persuade them as much as possible by exchanging views."[66]

For a time, the movement seemed to get serious about mass action. In February, large marches in Pretoria and Cape Town, coinciding with the opening of the white parliament, demanded a constituent assembly. But a stayaway, called in a commandist fashion and without properly consulting COSATU or ANC branches, flopped.

Struggles simmered around local issues, particularly in northern and eastern Transvaal where the UDF remained well organized until its dissolution. There was also a teachers' march, consumer boycotts in municipalities where authorities were not allowing marches, school protests, and demonstrations on May Day (not yet a public holiday) and against Republic Day (commemorating white South Africa's independence from Britain). Authorities were not completely tolerant of these actions, but the ANC's Albertina Sisulu and Joe Slovo focused on chastising marchers who burned an effigy of De Klerk on Republic Day.

Negotiations slowed to a snail's pace. The NP was quibbling about what constituted armed struggle and was slow to release prisoners. Inkatha violence was beginning to seriously destabilize the process. As the April deadline approached, the ANC finally found the backbone to threaten withdrawing if the state did not act to stop the violence. The state, of course, was actively supporting it. In the midst of peace talks called unilaterally by De Klerk, it emerged that "black-on-black violence" was state-on-opposition violence: the government was directly funding Inkatha. The scandal pushed the NP and Inkatha to sign a peace accord in September. But the ANC saw only an opportunity to restore negotiations, missing the chance to mobilize outrage and alter the balance of forces decisively. Inkatha, by contrast, shamelessly mobilized thousands to march through Johannesburg on the day the peace accord was to be signed, in defense of their right to carry "traditional weapons." Violence resumed around Johannesburg within weeks, but the accord introduced new mechanisms for controlling the police and the army and therefore "signalled that the phase of negotiations over preconditions . . . had largely ended."[67]

Two developments outside the talks guaranteed their continuation beyond preconditions. The first, the Patriotic Front conference in October, gathered ninety organizations (many outside the ANC's tradition, such as the Pan Africanist Congress, or PAC, and some Bantustan leaders and Tricameral parties) to demand an interim government and constituent assembly. The second was formally unrelated to negotiations: 3.5 million stayed off work for two days in November against the imposition of Value Added Tax (VAT). The stayaway clobbered the violence: for two days, only one incident was reported in the whole country. The strike did not defeat VAT, but it advanced the transition by challenging the regime's "right to reshape economic policy unilaterally. . . . The impact on the negotiations process was undoubted . . . the popular force which had been central in propelling the white minority government to the negotiating table had not dissipated."[68]

Despite the strike's power, its value for the leadership—even the union-ists—lay mainly in how it affected the talks. COSATU's general secretary com-mented: "The government has now learned that it is not going to introduce anything in a unilateral way. . . . Sections [of big business and the government] are beginning to see that only genuine negotiations could solve problems."[69] The single-minded focus on negotiations reflected that the majority of the ANC's national leadership was already transforming the organization, in their own minds, from a liberation movement to "a force geared to electoral compe-tition—rather than the broad multifunctional movement which the UDF had embodied so powerfully," in which "the main function of the branches was to give substance to the ANC's authority and leverage at the negotiating table."[70] The ANC journal *Mayibuye* complained in July that the leadership viewed ne-gotiations as the main terrain of struggle, and readers' letters complained more frequently about "mobilis[ing] by decree" as a secondary tool, without coordi-nated work on the ground. Alfred Nzo suggested to the ANC conference at the end of 1991 that lack of "creativity" about the forms of action were limiting its success. Yet the common forms of action were yielding results on a local scale, as Lodge points out. The problem was the lack of coherent organizing.

That same year, white far right-wingers fought (white) police to disrupt a De Klerk meeting in Ventersdorp, cementing a sense of white-right griev-ance. The new phobia that a right-wing backlash would derail the whole process became the reason not to move too fast or too firmly.

Negotiations proper began in December 1991. The first Codesa (Con-ference for a Democratic South Africa) was numerically loaded against the movement, which had three delegations out of nineteen, while the National Party gave itself two. The PAC and Azapo, on the left, and the Conservative Party and AWB (in Afrikaans, "Afrikaner Resistance Movement"), on the white right, stayed outside. Codesa agreed to take binding decisions by "suf-ficient consensus" and to negotiate Bantustans' reincorporation. But when the talks jammed again, the ANC immediately considered major conces-sions, such as federalism, to satisfy Bantustan regimes.

De Klerk, under right-wing pressure, unilaterally called a whites-only ref-erendum that the ANC rejected as racist, but left branches to decide whether to mobilize, resulting in little action. Budget day protests one day after the referendum did not link issues. The NP claimed the "yes" result as a mandate to protect white-minority rights in Codesa, where, as COSATU's Moeletsi Mbeki put it, "the mass of people are not involved. So in a meeting of political parties, the NP has the trump cards, because it has power on its side."[71]

Grassroots frustration and militancy was growing amid mounting evidence of state complicity in the violence, public confidence about "real" negotiations starting, and the VAT stayaway's success. Although only thirty thousand people demonstrated in Cape Town on budget day, the crowd blocked parliament for twenty minutes, then took an unauthorized route back. This defiance of the authorities also defied ANC leaders' constant calls for discipline. That mood continued into 1992 in the host of localized boycotts and marches around rents and service charges, occupations of schools, protests at five universities, a week-long train boycott, and self-defense units resisting Inkatha in Alexandra.

Codesa's skewed composition came home to roost when the NP insisted on requiring a 75 percent majority to change the future constitution. The ANC compromised all the way from 50 percent to 70 percent before with-drawing from Codesa and launching a program of "rolling mass action" with its allies, giving the regime until the end of June to set an election date and an interim government. The deadline coincided with COSATU's deadline, set earlier that year, for a general strike demanding its direct participation in the negotiations. COSATU added demands for an interim government and a constituent assembly. But forcing a transfer of power was not the ANC's aim. "The aim," said Thabo Mbeki, "is to ensure that the alliance's resolve to make negotiations a terrain of struggle will be enhanced."[72]

For a time, those arguing for sustained mass action gained the ascendancy in the ANC. Barbara Hogan (an ANC member charged with treason during Apartheid) argued that the train boycott "showed that there is militancy on the ground, that the conditions exist for mass action, [that] protest is a much more effective form of extracting concessions"; the ANC program now cautioned: "Mobilisation . . . can't be a process which is switched on and off; where people are only called on where there is a deadlock or problem."[73] This time, the action was better organized, with extensive consultation, greater coordination, and a proper buildup to the strike through marches and occupations of white-desig-nated areas of cities. This owed something to COSATU's greater commitment to, and experience in, building from the ground up. The regime and business were alarmed, threatening to lay off workers who participated. The buildup sparked other struggles. A strike wave included a hospital strike that lasted nine months; two hundred thousand marched against the Boipatong massacre, where there was strong evidence of police complicity in the murder of forty-five residents, ostensibly by Inkatha.[74] Still, the ANC's commitment to action remained tempered by its attempts to restrain spontaneous militancy. An exception was a march in Bisho, in the Bantustan of Ciskei, where the crowd, with the cooperation of some adventurous ANC leaders, refused to remain in the stadium, but were then massacred by Ciskei soldiers.

The effort building the stayaway paid off. Four million stayed away in August. De Klerk had to back down and conceded a sovereign constituent assembly. Several army generals and senior civil servants were dismissed. The regime agreed to elections by the end of 1993 and an interim government to oversee them (but wrangled over its precise form for months). Most significantly, the regime agreed to bilateral negotiations.

The stayaway tipped the balance in favor of the ANC—but also, internally, in favor of a *moderate* ANC. Sporadic protests continued for some time after, but the stayaway was hardly over when Mandela called a "cooling-off period" to await De Klerk's response. The action, impressive though it was, remained focused on getting negotiations back on track. And in the face of resounding proof of the potential to mobilize, counterarguments were already stampeding the Alliance. This current, building off the Bisho massacre, argued that compromise and conciliation were essential to South Africa's future stability.

A decisive strategic shift from mass action to conciliation was now consolidated in the ANC, around the fears of the government-in-waiting that the ANC's top leadership had become. Back in February, Mandela had said:

> We realise the importance of a government of national unity, both during the interim period *and when a democratic government has been installed* [my emphasis—CC]. We think we have a very good chance of [forestalling a counterrevolutionary onslaught] if we are able to form a government of national unity as a result of a decision of any majority party which will emerge after the general election.[75]

Note that he proposes a coalition government not to reflect the relative weaknesses of contending parties, but as a concession from the *victorious* party. The formulation was previously that compromise was necessary because mass action did not have the capacity to decisively defeat the regime. The formulation now gathering steam was that mass action could harm the prospects of a successful compromise. Although the May 1992 issue of *Mayibuye* argued that "people's actions should determine what happens at the negotiating table," Mbeki, then on the ANC's National Executive Committee, asserted: "Clearly you can't have a stable political order and a stable society if half the population rejects the constitution" (highly unlikely) and "mass activity must assume different forms. . . . We need to begin a mass campaign of education, for instance, around elections. That's mass activity."[76]

According to an article in the August *Mayibuye*, rolling mass action was "not a programme for insurrection. . . . There is a growing realisation that this task [of reconstruction] belongs to all South Africans. After all, a climate of fear, uncertainty and a lack of investor confidence affects ordinary people's lives as much as it undermines productivity and disrupts the whole economy."[77]

The shift reflected the bit-by-bit resolution of some contradictory aspects of the ANC's character as a nationalist liberation movement forced to sometimes rely on a large, powerful, and frequently self-organized working class, as well as the tension between its main aim—gaining decisive control of a state—and its need to ensure political stability for that state's future.

In late 1992, prominent communists consolidated the shift ideologically. The state as the key instrument of two-stage liberation overshadowed the power of the recent stayaway. Joe Slovo began by asserting that "there was certainly never a prospect of forcing the regime's surrender across the table" and negotiating "is neither the sole terrain for struggle nor the place it will reach its culmination."[78] Slovo's "place of culmination," however, was an increasingly gradualist accession to a state. The negotiations were a stage within a stage to

> bring about a radically transformed political framework in which the struggle for the achievement of the main objectives of the national democratic revolution will be contested in conditions far more favorable to the liberation forces than they are now. . . . We can realistically project the possibility of an outcome for the negotiating process which will result in the liberation movement occupying significantly more favorable heights from which to advance . . . if, amongst other things, the tricameral parliament is replaced by a democratically elected sovereign body and executive power is led by the elected representatives of the majority. [Then] the balance of forces will obviously have shifted in our favour.[79]

Deflecting counterrevolution required power sharing, he concluded. The SACP's Jeremy Cronin, musing over the "unresolved coexistence" of three tactical approaches to negotiations, rejected elite deals and using mass action as merely a lever, but equally discredited "the capacity of mass action to play a role in sweeping regimes out of power" when the international and local balance of forces was "unfavourable." Pallo Jordan rejected reading the balance of forces as "a preordained reality impervious to human will," and the ANC Youth League, espousing a practical perspective, pointed out:

> A study of the short record of negotiations does not give evidence that we have made any gains by making compromises. . . . There is more evidence that the breakthroughs we have made so far have been the result of unrelenting struggles.

But Cronin derided these critiques for "wish[ing] away apartheid structures," and the notion of a government of national unity became central to the ANC national executive's statement at the end of that year.[80]

Fortunately the rank and file, unlike the leaders, had not put mass action on the back burner. When the popular MK commander, Chris Hani, was assassinated in April 1993, people at rallies hissed and booed leaders' calls for restraint. ANC leaders realized that they would not be able to control this movement if they did not leap to its head. Two stayaways within a week were each accompanied by giant marches; 90 percent stayed away in the intensely industrialized region around Johannesburg, Pretoria, and the Vaal, and 88 percent in Natal. A mammoth march occupied central Johannesburg on the day of the funeral. The scale "made Hani's funeral a state event . . . [and] revealed the ANC, backed by the tripartite alliance, as the real future government."[81] Cronin, admitting not a shred of irony, later commented: "These events were all pulled together in a matter of days, and clearly relied enormously on the spontaneous self-organisation of thousands of people," which he linked to "pent-up mass frustration and a general sense of disempowerment produced by the drawn-out transition and our overemphasis on a (probably elite) negotiations process."[82]

The specter of the 1984–86 township risings on repeat kicked the regime to set an election date and at last initiate a transitional government to oversee elections. But again, the lurch forward secured negotiations rather than encouraging a rethink about insurrectionary potential. The negotiators returned to considering regionalism to lure the black right and the white right into elections. Meanwhile another kind of compromise was sneaking in the back. ANC negotiators had to backtrack rapidly to avert a general strike after agreeing to guarantee the right to lock out in the constitution alongside the right to strike. But COSATU itself was, by now, debating a social accord among labor, government, and business.

The elections became a focus for further compromise, but also of further struggle. The Bophuthatswana uprising stands out. It was sparked by a strike of civil servants—previously considered conservative—who were worried about their pensions after reincorporation. It escalated into a full-scale uprising, supported by students and sections of the Bantustan army and police, which developed beyond those initial concerns into a tiny insurrection, except that alternate organizations of power did not form. An NGO worker recounted reluctantly "looting" a bottle of orange juice because cashiers had abandoned shops. A police station was surrounded and the police inside were told they could leave, but not as policemen. Footage shows one stripping off her uniform and walking out in her petticoat, to be welcomed unmolested by the crowd. The white-right AWB were rousted "like goats" after rushing into the main city, Mafikeng, to "restore order" by driving around taking pot shots at black people. The threat of the white right evaporated like the puff of smoke it was, after national TV broadcast a Bophuthatswana soldier executing three AWB members who had crashed their Mercedes while trying to flee the scene. More importantly, the uprising dented an important base for Pretoria in the black right wing. Overthrowing the regime of Lucas Mangope had neatly removed the key obstacle to Bophuthatswana's reincorporation. Ciskei, Venda, and Lebowa quickly abandoned regionalist demands when similar strikes started in their realms.

Regionalism conflicted with the ANC's vision of strong central government, but it was involved in these struggles only via grassroots initiatives of its members. The NP were no longer the only ones fearful of a specter more threatening than the '84 uprising. The top echelons of the ANC, now in an interim government with the old regime, concentrated on bringing the Bophuthatswana crises to a negotiated resolution, then speedily restored order in the region.

The uprising briefly strengthened the appeal of mass action. An ANC-led march through Durban drew thousands, but a follow-up march to Buthelezi's capital, Ulundi, was canceled under the imperative of luring Inkatha back into elections. Buthelezi was undoubtedly more dangerous than Mangope. In contrast to the heads of most Bantustan governments, Buthelezi had built a popular base with a small, hard-core group, creating an uncomfortable tension for the ANC as a government-in-waiting: it made Inkatha much more threatening to future political stability, thus making its neutralization infinitely more pressing as the organization continued rampaging through Johannesburg against its marginalization, but it also meant that toppling Buthelezi would require far more sustained mobilization than the Bophuthatswana uprising. At the eleventh hour, Inkatha re-entered elections at the hefty price of leaving the Bantustan state and police force essentially intact for the five years of the "sunset clauses," which had also provided the

NP a place in the new government. The Independent Electoral Commission admitted, in a convoluted way, that it never finished counting the votes for Kwazulu-Natal, and Inkatha was given a majority in that province's cabinet.

4. Storing up contradictions

The landslide vote for the ANC sealed the defeat of the old regime who, despite clumsy management of a settlement, were delivered comfortable retirements and allowed to be a drag on the first five years of bourgeois democracy, but denied the permanent power sharing they had envisaged. The ANC won overwhelmingly in the areas that had seen recent upsurges in struggle, but narrowly missed the two-thirds majority required to change the constitution. Days later, Mandela publicly expressed his relief.

Behind these intensely contested political scenes, a matching set of compromises had taken shape in the ANC's economic policy, replacing the command economy with a "mixed economy" during the transition and—within two years of coming to power—replacing that with a self-professed "home-grown Thatcherist" program subordinating redistribution to growth. Not only had its leadership narrowed the options for the black working class in South Africa: it had narrowed its *own* options to decisively control a national economy. Capital was able to remain all but invisible in the compromise because the ANC's nationalism, sensitive to the "realities" of the global economy through its aspiration for a state, did all the work for capital, while the collapse of the USSR did the work of herding those who'd seen it as socialist into the neoliberal stampede.

The national question was formally solved, but this was black power only to the extent that the new government got in formation with dominant global trends, which were pulling "marginal" economies unequally back into the world economy. That greatly reduced the already limited wiggle room available to liberation governments to set independent economic policy without confronting gargantuan forces. The dominance of entrenched corporations, now poised on the edge of their national nest, ensured the wiggle room had never been very large in South Africa in the first place. But the attendant existence of a large working class, racially oppressed as well as exploited, repeatedly suggested a power to confront those forces.

The decisive role in the transition, to echo Trotsky, fell to "the masses" while the ANC's core, easing into place as late-arriving, aspirant bourgeoisie, proved to be, if not conservative, less than consistent in defeating the prob-

lem of white-minority rule. The ANC's ability to deflect mass power into liberal democracy as the era of state-capitalist liberation governments drew to
a close depended on subverting the potent connection between political and
economic oppression. The political kingdom was, at first, presented as the
road to the economic kingdom, only to then substitute economic restructuring for economic transformation in a way the NP could never have achieved.

The ANC's core politics militated against it taking the masses beyond the
negotiations, even in its own interests, but I have also tried to explain why people didn't take themselves beyond the ANC, after repeatedly demonstrating a
capacity to organize to force through the organization's best interests despite
its own intentions. Clearly, many of the networks that made the '80s uprisings
possible persisted past the dissolution of the UDF, informally or through civic
groups, youth organizations, newly formed ANC branches, and the unions. The
fact that radical alternatives suggested by the '80s' struggles had neither won
ideologically in the movement nor taken shape in organizations of alternate
power is crucial, but needs explaining as much as providing explanation. The
prospect of peace was a powerful incentive to compromise, but the reality of the
transition was that there was already a people's war in terms of civilian casual-
ties, while the big mass actions stamped down much violence.

One element of explanation is that the ANC was an almost mythical organization returning from distant exile to a country that had until recently
practiced extreme censorship. The reality of the ANC's compromises was not
enough to shock people out of their loyalty because, while the leaders exercised
undue control over the final direction of the organization, they could not mo-
nopolize its identity. People on the ground were able to believe that *their* actions
constituted the "real" ANC as much as the leadership's until very, very many
shocks to the contrary. Because the leaders *were* eventually deposed by the mass
upsurges, at a height that they could claim as everyone's victory, all these cases
of grassroots mobilization appeared as tactical zigzags integral to the organization's success, thus appearing less contradictory than they actually were.

Framing the struggle in stages helped these contradictions to coexist.
People in movements do not merely learn from "successive approximations,"
as Trotsky put it; we approximate from inside political models, which shape
what we learn from experiences and also *what we are trying to approximate.*
Without a more radical frame brought practically to bear on the situation
through actual organization, people learned that the old regime was negotiating in bad faith, but bourgeois parliamentary democracy, of which we

had no *direct* previous experience, could appear as good an approximation of democracy as any other version we had flirted with, and was presented as a better one than the model associated with 1960s national liberation movements and discredited with the collapse of the USSR. The existing two-stage model facilitated the new idea that taking over the existing state, with mild modifications, could make limited bourgeois democracy a possible route to other forms of power and democracy, thus allowing a half-baked solution to the national question to temporarily defuse the social questions.

The South African transition, then, allowed the economic wing of South Africa's ruling class to use the liberation movements to save themselves. But it was and remains a risky business with a shelf life, because, while reaching many parts that the old state could not, it stored up new problems for the future as the former opposition took on the role of managing discontent, throwing a new generation into conflict with the limits of bourgeois democracy within living memory of the previous experiments. The disillusionment with the ANC in contemporary South Africa can go in many directions, some of them very conservative, but it is also another opportunity to approximate a radically different political frame for transformation.

Figure 1: University students march to several residences in Cape Town in October 2015, mobilizing for fees to fall. Photo: Masixole Feni, "The Day the Students Stormed Parliament," GroundUp, October 21, 2015, www.groundup.org.za/article/day-students-stormed-parliament_3420/.

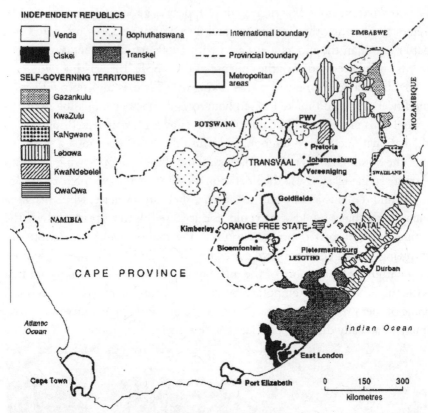

Figure 2: Map of Apartheid Bantustans by the late 1980s. Bophuthatswana had seven fragments, KwaZulu more than twenty. The industrial heart was the PWV region (Pretoria, the
Witwatersrand east and west of Johannesburg, and Vereeniging, the northernmost point of
the "Vaal Triangle"). Source: Washington State University Libraries, https://history.libraries.
wsu.edu/fall2014/wp-content/uploads/sites/3/2014/08/samagif.

CHAPTER 4

Uprisings and Revolutions in Sub-Saharan Africa, 1985–2014

Leo Zeilig, with Peter Dwyer

Introduction: Zaire 1991

Tired of miserable pay, high inflation, and the slow progress of political reforms, the Thirty-First brigade of the Zairian Air Force mutinied. On September 23, 1991, they led a riot across Kinshasa. Baptized the "People's Army," they marched into the city center, encouraging the city to join in. Soon thousands of men, women, and children from the city's poorest neighborhoods were marching. Shops and warehouses were gutted. Locks were blown off cold-storage units and banks with machine-gun fire. The houses of wealthy businessmen and members of President Mobutu's inner circle were targeted. The houses of expatriates were attacked. The headquarters of the Mouvement populaire de la révolution was ransacked, with the rioters scribbling on the ruins of the building, "All's bad that ends bad." Witnesses described a "carnival-like ambience." Looted goods were passed from soldier to civilian. The riot went on for days, turning rapidly into a citywide rebellion against the dictatorship.

For more than four years, the protest movement blossomed. Students were joined by the masses of the urban poor, workers, informal traders, the unemployed, and the army. When President Mobutu agreed to accept political changes in April 1990, he had no idea of the extent of the rebellion that he was about to unleash. The dictator looked as though he might be consumed by the popular revolt. Riots, general strikes, religious marches, and political meetings punctuated the Congo's rebellion, the most serious popular challenge to state power since the struggles against Belgian colonialism in the 1950s.

The Congolese rebellion emerged from a number of important social bases. The Catholic Church helped to generate the early resistance. In the late 1980s, church groups across the country set up coordination committees charged with organizing meetings, often drawing their specific motivation from "the wind of perestroika which shook Eastern Europe."[1] By 1992 the Church struggled to keep pace with the radicalization in society. Gustave Lobunda, a young priest from Kisangani, went on hunger strike in 1992 in protest of the closure of the National Conference, a body charged with planning the transition to multiparty democracy. He described how his actions were animated by a combination of ideas, including the inspiration of the life of Jesus and other sources:

> My hunger strike was also inspired by Gandhi and Martin Luther King, for whom I have always had a profound admiration. I have seen the film of Gandhi at least nine times. . . . I had time to get to know him in the book *This Night, Freedom*. And learnt about Martin Luther King through articles and by his biography written by Stephen B. Oates. Gandhi and King have helped me to understand the value of human freedom, which is a gift from God . . . this consciousness of freedom is so strong that I cannot continue to live under a dictatorship.[2]

On February 16, 1992, a demonstration was organized by Comité Laic de Coordination, made up of many members of the National Conference, but also local parish militants who had been active for a couple of years and were able to mobilize their neighborhoods. José Mpundu from Le Groupe Amos was one of those activists invited to attend a meeting of the Comité in February when the idea of a demonstration was first discussed. Parish activists spread the word in their neighborhoods:

> People of God, this call comes to you from men and women from all levels of society: researchers, teachers, employees, trade unionists, members of NGOs, businessmen, students. . . . Everyone who are called by their Christian faith and animated by a profound sense of justice . . . who see every day the suffering endured by the people of God.
>
> People of Zaire, this country is a gift from God. It belongs to us all.

The political, economic and moral crisis that has shaken Zaire for three decades demands a response.

Our country, potentially, one of the richest on the planet, finds itself paradoxically, among the poorest of the world . . .

In this situation the regime has thrust us into intolerance, ethnic hatred and state terror.

Today, like yesterday, Zairians are constantly victims of a society expressly organized for one aim, to assure the profits and the power of a minority, through denying the rights of the overwhelming majority . . .

Respond to the last man to the call that our churches have made: the *Conférence Nationale Souveraine* is irreversible.

The *Marche d'espoir* will take place on 16 February 1992. This day of the Lord, the people of the capital will descend into all of the streets of Kinshasa to demand the return of the *Conférence Nationale Souveraine*.

Rise up Christians, free the people of God.[3]

The Comité was essentially a group of lay delegates in the National Conference. The only way they could call an effective demonstration was through an appeal to the parishes where local militants were organized. They called for people to support the Marche d'espoir (March of Hope) on the authority of the churches of Zaire. The National Conference needed the "people of God" to force the regime to back down, but they could not organize these people independently of the structures that had been set up over the last two years. José Mpundu describes the day of the demonstration, "On the day itself we only had one mass at 6 am. . . . I must confess that I was a little scared. Scared that there wouldn't be a large enough turnout. But when I saw the number of people at the assembly point my fear disappeared." He estimated that some two hundred members of his parish and neighboring parishes had gathered. Shortly after they had set off they encountered an obstacle, "the army blocking the route. . . . We sat down together according to our plans . . . the soldiers then tried to disperse us, by kicking us. . . . We left the avenue and reassembled in a parallel street where there were no soldiers."[4]

Demonstrators marched holding crosses, Bibles, images of the Virgin Mary and other icons. The crowds sang hymns and prayed. One eyewitness explains what happened when the police started to fire: "We were scared by the firing and were advanced slowly towards the soldiers. Priest, nuns . . . Christians were on their knees praying and brandishing branches, bibles . . . as the soldiers fired into the air. The crowd were singing. Thirty minutes later the soldiers had exhausted their ammunition and we continued singing religious songs, and we had crossed the first military barrier."[5] Another eyewitness writes, "Despite the fact I couldn't walk easily as a result of being hit by the police, a young man saw I was having problems walking and supported me though the march. There were lots of similar gestures. Even our behaviour towards the soldiers— we tried to make them understand the reasons for the march." Expecting the police to use tear gas,

> We had prepared ourselves: we had handkerchiefs and water, and we put these wet cloths against our eyes. The soldiers had nothing. I saw how mothers and fathers were helping the soldiers, wetting their faces. I saw how soldiers who had nothing to drink were given water. The soldiers were asking themselves, "What has happened to us?" They could not understand. . . . It was in this way that the march took place. Nothing was stolen from small shops among the route, nothing! Everyone had the door of their house open to help the demonstrators: people were leaving and entering and nothing was stolen. Really this was a march of non-violence.[6]

Nor was the movement limited to Kinshasa, the capital. Other marches took place in Kikwit, Kananga, Mbuji-Mayi, Kisangani, Goma, and Bukavu. The repression varied. In Kisangani and Mbuji-Mayi, however, the demonstrations were brutally suppressed. Lobunda, who was on hunger strike at the time, describes the Catholics of Kisangani responding to the call from Kinshasa at merely a day's notice. Young Christian militants from Mangobo, a poor neighborhood in the city, wrote and signed a leaflet and distributed it to all the parishes in Kisangani on Saturday morning. "The result: despite the short amount of preparation all the parishes of the city marched even if the numbers from parish to parish varied."[7]

Many were killed, more than thirty in Kinshasa. Activists convened meetings to discuss the march, exchange stories, establish who had been killed, and plan for the next mobilization. A female activist describes how "two days later we had a meeting with the Comité to evaluate the march from across the city. We attempted to get those who had been imprisoned out, and organised visits to the hospital. . . . And as the government had not ceded to our demand to reopen the National Conference, we wanted to organise a further march the following Sunday."[8] Anyone who has been involved in a demonstration will be familiar with such "evaluation" and the planning for the next action.

Some commentators question the motives of the demonstrators. De Villers and Tshonda write of the "imaginary world" of the Christian Marchers. They observe that "people chanted psalms and demonstrated with bible in hand. They were motivated by the hope of a new Christian reign. . . . This Catholic crowd had the deliberation, calm and peacefulness of . . . a procession. Its strength was belief rather than politics."[9] Yet in this context, it is wrong to set belief and politics against one another. The aim of the demonstrators was not a "new Christian reign" but, much more practically, the reopening of the National Conference. The demonstration was motivated by the ideas of nonviolence inspired by a range of political movements. In 1992, Catholic churches were synonymous with protest, encouraging communities to become involved in the changes sweeping the country. There was a widespread belief in the involvement of the church in liberation. Inevitably the movements were contradictory and the tactics sometimes questionable, but people were drawing on their own experiences in which religion played a part.

Though the role of mismanagement and corruption was important in the deterioration in the Congo, it was policies recommended by the international financial institutions and implemented by the government that were ultimately to blame. Despite its great mineral riches, by 1988 the Congo was ranked the eighth poorest country in the world. The World Bank reported that it had a per capita income of $160 a year, while real incomes had fallen to just 10 percent of their pre-independence level. Between 1973 and 1985, the average income fell by 3.9 percent a year. The agricultural picture was no better. By the late 1980s Zaire had gone from being a net food exporter to paying out more than 20 percent of its foreign exchange on food imports. Twenty-eight years after independence the country was saddled with a $7 billion foreign debt.[10] The road and transport infrastructure had almost completely crumbled, cutting off agricultural producers from their buyers in the cities. As Zaire approached the 1990s, people in the countryside retreated to subsistence existence and in the cities to an informal economy. The rapid decline in nutrition levels and health care was killing a third of children before the age of five. Yet this was not the picture for everyone. Journalist Blaine Harden observed privilege in high places: "Mobutu, his family, his European business partners, his CIA friends, and the eighty or so nimble-footed lick-spittles who continue to play musical chairs."[11]

The background to the expansion of the informal economy was a profound crisis in the Zairian economy that stretched back to the 1970s. As we have seen, mining in Zaire was crippled by the collapse of world prices and by state-led plunder and corruption. Mining production took a downward turn from 1988 onward. The future of copper production was evident for all to see. The sharpest fall in production cut right through the period of transition. Between 1987 and 1995 annual production of copper fell from nearly 500,000 tons to a mere 25,000.[12] In February 1989, the prime minister, Léon Kengo Wa Dondo, claimed that only Générale des Carrières et des Mines (Gécamines), a major state parastatal, was still sending any money to the state treasury. The international copper market was becoming increasingly competitive. Other world producers, such as Chile, established new open-cast, lower-cost mines. In the period 1990–93, production was further hampered by strikes, theft of equipment, technical problems, and a worsening political situation. Nor was Gécamines immune to corruption and misappropriation. During negotiations for an IMF loan between May and June of 1989, it was revealed that $400 million had gone missing in copper revenues. This amounted to some 30 percent of annual earnings.[13]

During this period, diamond production grew. By 1995, this new mining sector accounted for approximately 47 percent of export earnings, compared with just 19 percent from copper. Much came from small-scale operations. After the legalization of artisanal extraction in 1981, small-scale "production" expanded rapidly, and within seventeen years had become responsible for 70 percent of all diamond exports.[14] Still, the impact of this new mining sector on the overall economy was limited. Even in 1990, copper production by Gécamines was still responsible for more than 50 percent of national export earnings. Yet, as MacGaffey and Bazenguissa-Ganga have shown, "by 1994, Gécamines, the copper mining company that had been Zaire's principal exporter, was barely producing."[15] The fall in copper production was devastating. Diamond production continued its seemingly relentless upward spiral, expanding further in the 1990s, with the opening up of new diamond beds in the country's northeast region. In 1994 it became the main source of foreign exchange, a process that was inextricably linked to the expansion of the informal economy.[16] Although the artisanal diamond industry had officially replaced the mining of copper by the 1990s as the principal source of foreign exchange, three-quarters of diamonds mined were being smuggled out of the country.[17]

The collapse of Gécamines had a profound effect on the economy of the Congo. Thousands of professionals, doctors, academics, engineers, and skilled workers suddenly found themselves without work. Many who had spent years working directly or indirectly for the company in Katanga now migrated to South Africa. By 1992, Zairians made up approximately half of the migrant workers in South Africa, largely because of the relative ease of securing South African visas. Many more traveled to South Africa illegally on the trucks that drove from Lubumbashi loaded with copper and cobalt. Once in South Africa, many Zairians became involved in the now ubiquitous circuits of informal trade.

At the center of all these developments was Gécamines. By the mid-1990s it was a shell of its former self and faced corruption, collapsing infrastructure, and a hemorrhaging of capital. In 1995–96, the country launched a privatization initiative in certain parts of the mining sector. The decline of copper from the 1970s was symbolic also of the end of a specific economic regime, the collapse of state intervention in the economy with the onset of systematic privatization: the phenomenon now known as neoliberalism. The measures introduced by the government in the early 1980s to legalize artisanal production of diamonds were the valedictory gestures of a state that was increasingly powerless to control the circuits of the informal economy. The rise of the diamond industry was not going to bring about an influx of "foreign direct investment," as promised by the IMF; on the contrary, diamonds were hand-dug in privately owned plots and frequently sold through criminal networks that made use of the preexisting informal economy.

Ever resilient, Mobutu managed to manipulate and disorientate the leaders of the opposition, who were only too willing to bargain with the great dictator. One observer, Loka Ne Kongo, a minister of higher education in a transitional government between 1992 and '93, characterized the opposition leadership in the following terms in 1994: "[They] suffered failure after failure, in large part because of their own impotence; all of the paths that could have led to the removal of the dictator, by non-violence, had more or less been exhausted."[18] These failures eventually destroyed the rebellion and the social movements that had risen up against the Mobutu regime.

1. Across the continent

The changes that were taking place were not exclusive to Zaire. On the contrary, reform was now sweeping across many parts of the continent. There were a series of revolutions following the earlier ones that accompanied decolonization. An extraordinary array of uprisings and rebellions have taken place in sub-Saharan Africa since the mid-1980s. Many of these revolutions were, in large part, a consequence of the quickening pace of structural reforms to African economies—what has been described as the "second wave" of revolts against IMF- and World Bank–imposed reforms. The first wave was caused by the initial implantation of structural adjustment in the late 1970s. The revolutions in question were organized around a set of democratic demands, sparking the pro-democracy transitions that spread across Africa from 1990 onward. The extent of these uprisings, triggering major transitions in political power, is under-researched and extraordinary. Africa exploded in a convulsion of pro-democracy revolutions that saw eighty-six major protest movements across thirty countries in 1991 alone.[19] However, as with nationalist movements before them, the unity displayed by these "pro-democracy" revolutions in ousting dictatorial regimes commonly masked profound divisions regarding the outcomes they wished to see from this process of political and economic transformation. Coinciding as it did with the collapse of Soviet Communism and the emergence of a unipolar, US-dominated world, political liberalization, the immediate legacy of these revolutions, coincided with the dominance of market-based economic liberalization as the singular solution to the economic problems of the world in general, and of Africa in particular.[20]

Throughout this chapter we refer to "revolution" to describe the unfolding and radicalizing events that included, in each case, strikes, demonstrations, riots; frequently, the revolutions included alternative sites of popular power. Though there is a great deal of variety between the revolutions in the Congo, Zimbabwe, Burkina Faso, and beyond, each was curtailed in two senses. In Cameroon, Togo, Zimbabwe, and Zaire, for example, the ruling parties managed to ride the wave of the mass protests and reassert themselves—the revolutions were *curtailed* by the regime. In the academic language of this period, these transitions were "frustrated." However, for those countries that saw ruling parties fall, in Zambia, Mali, and Malawi, as examples, new political formations established themselves. Multiparty elections were frequently held for the first time since independence. Yet, these too were "curtailed revolutions," and the new parties resumed the politics of structural adjustment once in power, pacifying the popular movements and co-opting activists. Renewed projects of structural adjustment were introduced in country after country, now working under multiparty conditions—austerity, deindustrialization, and market fundamentalism resumed.

Therefore, the revolutions we describe in this chapter are "political." Broadly, in these political revolutions, as Neil Davidson has written, "the class that was in control of the means of production at the beginning will remain so at the end ... and the class that was exploited within the production process at the beginning will also remain so at the end."[21] Yet, however fleeting, or frustrated, serious meaningful political change took place. In each of our case studies there were forces, parties, groups, organizations who sought more for their revolution and wanted to continue beyond a democratic transition to a full social revolution. These groups envisaged breaking the pattern of the recycled elites and, in some cases, envisaged linking national revolutions to a single process of regional and continental revolutionary transformation. Along with a host of other factors crippling the development of these politics, the parties and groups who could have argued, organized, and built for such a "social revolution" were either puny, unable to decisively influence events, or not even in existence. However, repeatedly, movements and groups attempted to push beyond the compromises and deals of the democratic transitions as the actual revolutions were taking place.

The economic downturn of the mid-1970s was a key turning point in postcolonial African history. The oil crisis, the collapse of commodity prices on which many African economies depended, and the end of the postwar consensus destroyed the developmental assumptions on which new African states had been constructed. The limited achievements and authoritarian nature of many postcolonial states were increasingly exposed. The acquisition of vast and, in retrospect, unpayable national debts undermined the sovereignty and authority of many African states and led to the imposition of increasingly neoliberal economic policies by the international financial institutions. The desire of nationalist elites to retain power despite the collapse of their popular legitimacy led to increasing numbers of one-party states and military-led regimes. This crisis of postcolonial nationalism created, if anything, an even more oppressive environment for the operation of resistance.[22]

Although the economic crisis of the late 1970s was international in its reach, the pain of the consequent adjustment was carried by the global South, and particularly by those that relied heavily on importing oil and borrowing for heavy machinery from the West. For many African states, the results were catastrophic. For example, by the mid-1970s two-thirds of exports from Ghana and Chad were coffee and cotton respectively, while the fall in copper prices meant that in 1977, Zambia, a country that depended on copper for half of its GDP, received no income at all from its most important resource.[23] As the global crisis spread, loans turned into debts, and national adjustment and restructuring became a requirement for further loans issued by the IMF and World Bank. More and more African states saw their macroeconomic policies shaped by the conditions imposed by IMF and World Bank experts. New voices were now calling for "belt tightening" and austerity.

The result was a period of increased social unrest, which began in Egypt in 1977. The government's decision to raise food and petrol prices, as part of a program of financial stringency under the auspices of the IMF, provoked fierce rioting in major cities across the country. Labeled the first wave of popular protest, this involved Morocco, Mauritania, Algeria, and Tunisia. Throughout the same period a wave of popular protest against similar austerity measures was noted across the sub-continent.[24]

The removal of consumer subsidies led to substantial increases in the cost of living among the urban population in the early and mid-1980s. This came in a context of rising popular discontent with the failures of the postcolonial state to address the expectations that had been raised in the transition to independence. However, there were limited possible avenues for the expression of legitimate public discontent. Most independent civil society organizations and social movements had either been suppressed or incorporated into the state structures, a position from which they were no longer free to criticize state policies. In these circumstances, some incorporated civil society leaders began to express limited criticisms of specific government policies while expressing their overall loyalty to the one-party state. Meanwhile, although many nationalist parties had initially been vibrant organizations throughout many parts of their countries, local structures of the parties had rapidly atrophied, removing another possible avenue for the expression of discontent.

In this context, the lack of formal official leadership led to discontent with the removal of food subsidies, which in a number of countries took the form of riots and social disturbances, at a level that had not occurred in most countries since independence. In Tunisia, for example, the abolition of food subsidies in December 1983 by the ruling "Destour" party led to a doubling of bread prices and substantial riots. Destour, like ruling parties elsewhere, had incorporated trade unions, youth and student bodies, and women's groups into its structures. Tunisian trade unions had specific representation in parliament, and eight trade-union MPs voted against the removal of food subsidies; however, the official trade-union body did not endorse any public demonstration of discontent. Zghal illustrates how riots were organized on a local level by the unemployed and by young women and how the ruling party lacked any significant structures on the ground. What was noteworthy was that President Habib Bourguiba reversed the decision on food subsidies, angering donors but assuaging public opinion. African ruling parties, apparently all-powerful and in control of society and the economy, had their weaknesses revealed both by their inability to control unrest and by their reversal of policy.[25]

Similar events unfolded elsewhere. In Zambia, the early 1980s saw a series of conflicts between the ruling party United National Independence Party (UNIP), its international donors, and the Zambian public. As the economic situation worsened, the IMF and World Bank took increasing control over day-to-day economic policy. Urban Zambians were discontented with many aspects of ruling party policy, and this proved the straw that broke the camel's back. UNIP had sought to position itself as a popular party that spoke for the poor; its supremacy over all aspects of public life was crucial to maintaining its power. It could therefore not be seen to be forced to implement policies simply because donors told it to. President Kenneth Kaunda therefore endorsed the removal of food subsidies in December 1986. When food prices rose, riots followed; crucially, these were not directed primarily against the IMF, but against the ruling party—on the Copperbelt, workers and the unemployed fought with riot police, attacking UNIP offices. As in Tunisia, the government was forced to reintroduce the subsidies. Donors responded by reducing financial support. Major strikes now took place, as workers demanded pay increases to compensate for inflation. Kaunda claimed that "the initiators of the strikes were politically motivated." There were major clashes with the trade union movement, which heavily criticized the removal of food subsidies.[26]

The prime minister claimed that the government still had the capacity to direct economic policy. Such a statement had potentially dangerous consequences: if UNIP was the powerful and effective force it claimed to be, it had to take responsibility for unpopular policies; if responsibility lay with external agencies, the weakness of the one-party state was exposed. Ultimately, popular discontent proved more influential than the IMF. On May Day 1987, Kaunda froze the price of essential goods and introduced new controls over the economy. The World Bank concluded:

> The early demise ... of the adjustment package imposed by the IMF resulted from an unrealistic ... assumption that the majority of middle and lower income urban Zambians would tolerate pauperisation.[27]

Although UNIP sought to retain state controls over the economy for a while longer, their dependency on international donors meant that this could not be sustained. More crucially, structural adjustment, while unpopular with many ordinary people, had an unintentionally positive impact for social movements. By exposing the ruling party's weakness in preventing popular unrest and, in particular, demonstrating the potential for such unrest to achieve the removal of unpopular policies, it encouraged dissidents of various kinds to more openly criticize the one-party states.

The strength and effectiveness of this first wave of struggle was based on wide coalitions of the popular classes, with the working class in a narrow sense usually centrally involved through the trade-union movement. The impact of unrest also depended on the participation of the wider "African crowd," including the lumpen-proletariat of the shanty towns, unemployed youth, elements of the new petty bourgeoisie, and university students.[28] Generally "spontaneous" and directed predominantly toward current economic reforms and austerity measures, the struggles also contained elements of a critique of regime legitimacy and deployed notions of social justice.[29] Given their limited degree of political organization, these movements generally had a restricted political effect, but in some cases, they took on the character of a political opposition, challenging policies and changing the prevailing political configuration. In most cases they served to redefine the terrain of struggle and to provide the basis for the emergence at a later stage of political movements aimed at changing governments rather than just policies.

The "focus" of these protests and uprisings were often the international financial agencies (particularly the IMF), but also the governments that adopted the austerity policies and the representatives of the big corporations (foreign and national) that benefited from "liberalization." In Nigeria, for example, it was students who spearheaded the fight against the government's homegrown structural adjustment program (SAP) in the 1980s. Under the auspices of SAPs, universities suffered major funding shortfalls, and students frequently organized the first protests. One commentator maintained that in the escalation of student protest since the introduction of SAPs in Africa in the early 1980s, there has emerged a new "pan-African student movement, continuous in its political aspirations with the student activism that developed in the context of the anti-colonial struggle, and yet more radical in its challenges to the established political power."[30] The effects of SAPs proletarianized the African student body, breaking them from their postcolonial past as members of the elite and in the 1980s forcing them to instigate some of the first anti-government protests.

As elsewhere on the continent, Nigerian students were no longer an iso-lated (and relatively privileged) vanguard. The collapse of conditions in the country's universities saw declining student status converge with a general societal meltdown. Fuel price increases in 1988, demanded by the World Bank, led members of the National Association of Nigerian Students to ini-tiate nationwide anti-SAP protests. Dibua explains: "Students viewed the increase in prices . . . would visit untold economic hardship on the majority of Nigerians while making it difficult for impoverished parents to finance students' education."[31] While the "demand for economic liberalization" may have weakened formal democratic structures, in some cases it created an ex-plosive and unpredictable cocktail of social forces. However, we argue that the first wave of protests did not result in an immediate political transforma-tion. In most cases ruling parties weathered the storms. It was during what the scholarly literature describes as the "democratic transitions" that this wave of protests gave way to a prolonged period of revolutionary struggle as regime after regime on the continent was overturned.

2. Political rebellion: 1990–98

The wave of political revolutions that swept across Africa in the early 1990s is often portrayed as a singular and unexpected event, with little connection to what had gone before. While the influence of events in Eastern Europe's anti-communist revolutions was considerable, particularly on the *timing* of Africa's revolutions, this was the spark that lit an already smoldering bonfire of popular social and economic discontent, resulting in particular from the impact of structural adjustment policies that, by the late 1980s, were being implemented by governments of all political persuasions.[32] The fact that the eventual outcome of these revolutions was the wholesale implementation of economic liberalization programs by most of the new democratic govern-ments, while a bitter irony that reflected the collapse of alternative ideologi-cal approaches in the wake of the collapse of communism, should not deflect attention from the material basis of many revolutionary movements.

Indeed, the protests that marked the start of the 1990s were eloquent testimony to the devastation that structural adjustment and the free market had already brought to the continent. The effects of the IMF and neoliberalism in the region at the end of this period had only one benefit: it brought together, on an unprecedented scale, workers, peasants, and the poor, who fought with extraordinary militancy and courage against food and fuel rises and political oppression, and often for wholesale political transformation. For more than ten years, many African states had been forced to implement "reforms" by the IMF and the World Bank. They insisted on cuts in the public sector, including the reduction of subsidies and reductions in health and education budgets as a condition of new loans.

By the early 1990s a second wave of popular protest had entered a revolutionary period, now more explicitly political and with more far-reaching aims and objectives, spreading across the continent like a political hurricane. From 1989, political protests rose massively across sub-Saharan Africa. There had been approximately twenty annually recorded incidents of political unrest in the 1980s. By 1992, many African governments had been forced to introduce reforms, and in 1993, fourteen countries held democratic elections. In a four-year period from the start of the protests in 1990, a total of thirty-five regimes were swept away by protest movements and strikes and in elections that were often held for the first time in a generation. The speed with which these changes took place left commentators breathless: "Compared with the recent experiences of Poland and Brazil . . . African regime transitions seemed frantically hurried."[33]

In 1989, the full scale of the second wave of uprisings movement started in Bénin. Students demonstrated against the government in January, demanding overdue grants and a guarantee of public sector employment after graduation. The government, crippled by financial scandals, capital flight, and falling tax revenue, thought it could respond as it had always done, by suppressing the protest. But the movement grew during the year to incorporate trade unions and the urban poor. In an attempt to preempt the movement, the president, Mathieu Kérékou, declared that his party, the People's Revolutionary Party of Bénin, had jettisoned "Marxism-Leninism" and agreed that multiparty elections could be held in the future. In a pattern followed by other countries, he set up a commission that would eventually create a national reconciliation conference that included the opposition movement, trade unions, students, and religious associations.

Emboldened by events, trade unionists, led by postal workers and teachers, left the government-controlled National Federation of Workers' Unions of Bénin. By the end of the year the seat of government, Cotonou, was convulsed by mass demonstrations. When Kérékou attempted to befriend demonstrators during one of these protests he was jeered and threatened, forcing him to flee. In February 1990 the National Conference of Active Forces declared itself sovereign and dissolved Kérékou's national assembly. Obstinately he still insisted, "I will not resign, I will have to be removed." After being defeated in the presidential elections held the following year, he asked humbly for forgiveness and asserted his "deep, sincere and irreversible desire to change."[34]

Meanwhile, mass demonstrations and general strikes forced the pace of the revolutionary changes on the continent. Unions, together with a variety of popular forces, fought regimes hanging on to power in Burkina Faso, Burundi, Cameroon, the Central African Republic, Chad, Comoros, Congo, Côte d'Ivoire, Gabon, Ghana, Guinea, Kenya, Lesotho, Madagascar, Mali, Mauritania, Nigeria, Swaziland, and Zaire. Even if elections were not held and heads of state clung to power, the pattern was the same: trade unions "sought not simply to protect the work-place interests of their members but ... endeavoured to bring about a restructuring of the political system."[35] The African trade-union movement demonstrated greater independence and militancy then at any time in its history.

This revolutionary wave was in many respects similar to the nationalist movements that came together to achieve independence from the colonial powers thirty to forty years previously. Often movements came together quickly from a range of social forces, sought unity around a single common goal, and, in many cases, rapidly evolved from single-issue movements into political revolutions. New parties were formed, and, having agreed only on what they were *against*, they were in some cases thrust into power with little time to consider what they were *for*. In new multi-party movements, trade unionists who had fought against structural adjustment found common cause with businesspeople who hoped multi-partyism would lead to a further opening of the economy. All the country's problems were blamed on the existing ruling party, and the slogans offered simple solutions—that with political change all problems would be overcome. As with nationalist movements, this temporary unity undoubtedly smoothed the path to new democracies—but as with nationalism, it also created unforeseen difficulties regarding the direction of these states after their achievement and the extraordinary revolutionary movements that had directed political change.

But much of this ideological vacuum meant that movements that arose from the resistance to SAPs could not craft coherent and offensive programs of radical reforms. By the early 1990s the collapse of state-socialist regimes in Eastern Europe and the Soviet Union was being heralded as the "end of history" and the final victory for liberal capitalist democracy. This left many trade unionists, students, and activists without their ideological moorings. The political revolutions of the second wave, fueled by a popular revolt against SAPs, became a general appeal for multiparty elections, and new governments, where they were elected, maintained the same economic trajectories. Movements rallied around the slogans of "change" (literally *chinja* in Zimbabwe and *sopi* in Senegal), with little ideological content.

This wave of political revolutions in Africa during the 1990s accordingly took diverse forms and attracted diverse social elements, often giving rise to serious misgivings about the extent of their progressiveness among leftist commentators, particularly in areas where the populists used the religious ideology of Islam or Christianity to mobilize support. While some of these political movements remained closely linked to working-class struggles, others, particularly those rooted in the rural areas, took on the dimensions of ethnic, tribal, and religious struggles.[36]

For example, the "great turn" toward militant Islam in the 1990s constituted a major development in northern Africa, as the popular classes discovered an "authentic" voice in which to express their profound disillusionment with capitalist development and with the corrupt and authoritarian regimes that presided over such "development." The possibility that these Islamist movements were also themselves corrupted by populist authoritarianism and might aim to establish even more oppressive and sectarian regimes greatly preoccupied the Left. Mesmerized all too often by the terrorist violence of the most extreme militant Islamists, the very considerable variation between the different Islamist and Islamic groups and movements, and the extent of popular support for the broader-based, more "moderate" groups, has all too often been missed, and the possibility of accommodation, complementarity, and even fusion of popular working-class movements and Islamic revolutionary traditions has been underestimated.[37]

One of the major results of these curtailed revolutions in the early 1990s was the further acceleration of economic liberalization by the new governments that the revolutionary movements had helped put in place.[38] The opening up of hitherto relatively closed economies to market forces led in most countries to the closure of local uncompetitive companies and a consequent fall in formal employment. The removal of subsidies on basic goods led to a rise in the cost of living that particularly affected the poor. The introduction of charges for social services—health, education, water, and sanitation—led to a decline in the standard of living, for example a decline in literacy, a reduction in life expectancy, and increases in infant mortality. The partial demolition of state-provided health services coincided with the devastating impact of HIV/AIDS in Africa. Agricultural producers were supposedly the main beneficiaries of liberalization. While some countries saw a modest rise in cash crop production, this widened the gap between the most prosperous farmers and the vast majority of poorer peasants. It also left them dependent on world market prices and placed further power in the hands of Western buyers. Although the removal of state controls on agricultural prices was widely welcomed, the dismantling of government agricultural support was generally damaging to farm production—the market did not step in to replace the withdrawal of state support of, for example, fertilizer, seeds, and tools. In some countries, farm and wider business lobbies argued for the re-establishment of state agricultural support.

Arguably, a third wave of protests and revolutions emerged on the continent, initially linked chronologically, if not organizationally and politically, to the anti-capitalist movement that spread unevenly across the globe after the Battle of Seattle in 1999.[39] Some of the protest movements in this third wave sought to complete the unfinished business of the democratic transitions (Senegal and Zimbabwe, for example), others protested against food prices rises and continued liberalization (notably South Africa, Burkina Faso, and Nigeria). Adam Branch and Zachariah Mampilly also make a convincing case for the appearance of a third wave of rebellion, documenting ninety popular uprisings in more than forty African states since 2005. They write, "By our measure the heralded North African protests of 2011 represented not the first ripple of a wave, but rather its crest, with 26 African countries (including Burkina Faso) experiencing popular protests that year."[40] However, in the cases we illustrate below, elements of the different waves of protest are evident.

For us, two examples stand out. During the 1990s Zimbabwe, in southern Africa, experienced the compression of both the first and second wave of protest. The remarkable radicalization in the second half of the decade culminated in the formation of a mass-based opposition party in 1999. Ultimately, however, Zimbabwe's political revolution failed to either unseat the ruling party, let alone reach beyond the narrow parameters of the democratic transition. Burkina Faso is illustrative of a third wave of protest that has developed on the continent since 2000, and particularly after 2006. The revolutionary movement in Burkina Faso has developed at a quickening pace since the countrywide uprising in 2011, until the unseating of the president by the mass movement at the end of October 2014.

3. The Zimbabwean crucible

Zimbabwe underwent a relatively late period of structural adjustment that savaged public services and industry in a country that had been relatively diversified industrially and more prosperous than many of its continental cousins. As a reaction to this economic adjustment in the first five years of the 1990s, there was growth in an opposition, which developed impressively in the second part of the decade into a mass movement. This movement unified an array of forces: war veterans from the struggle against white-minority rule in the 1960s and 1970s, students, street vendors, many of them women, and wide layers of workers organized in the trade-union federation ZINASU.

One of the factors that interests us in Zimbabwe during these years is the role of a small socialist organization, often not consisting of more than a hundred members: the International Socialist Organisation (ISO) of Zimbabwe. The revolutionary Marxist ISO played an important, indeed entirely disproportionate role in the street battles, political education of cadre, and formation of strike committees and even the Movement for Democratic Change (MDC). For the authors of this chapter, studying the Zimbabwe moment in the 1990s and early 2000s, and its subsequent defeat and unravelling, is essential for revolutionaries and activists across the continent.

After Robert Mugabe's removal by military junta in November 2017, Zimbabwe remains in the grip of a crippling economic crisis. GDP per capita is estimated to be the same as it was in 1953. Before dollarization in 2009 the country had the highest inflation rate in the world, soaring to 165,000 percent in February 2008. At the beginning of 2014 an estimated 75 percent of the population lived below the poverty line; today that share is estimated to be more than 85 percent.

The victory secured by the Zimbabwe African National Union–Patriotic Front (ZANU-PF) in the 2008 elections, despite the violence and rigged polls, significantly shaped the next six years. ZANU-PF's dictatorship launched protracted interparty negotiations that started soon after Mugabe's presidential inauguration. February 11, 2009, saw the birth of an inclusive Government of National Unity, with leading members of the MDC assuming significant positions in the new parliament. Morgan Tsvangirai became prime minster. Tendai Beti, a long-standing member of the MDC (and before this a founder of the ISO), became the country's finance minister. But vital ministries and real power remained firmly in ZANU-PF hands.

ZANU-PF's fairly decisive victory in the 2013 elections marked the end of political party collaboration. Mugabe's relationship to his "anti-imperialism," enacted by his promise to speak to the poor and outcast, has always been highly opportunistic, swinging with wild inconsistency between price controls and liberalization. One area that has become contentious is the Indigenisation and Economic Empowerment Act, passed in 2007. Promoted by ZANU-PF as a black empowerment initiative, the act insists on a 51 percent stake to indigenous Zimbabwean shareholders for foreign companies operating in Zimbabwe. Such posturing by ZANU has created a limited social base for itself within Zimbabwe and a large continental and regional influence. The Economic Freedom Fighters in South Africa, for example, point to Mugabe's apparent radicalism as their model.

The MDC has long been characterized by confusing vacillations—calling mass action then retreating from it, seeking to align itself with right-wing policies and accepting shoddy compromises with the regime. Today thousands may still identify with the MDC's radicalism and the confidence of the working class in the late 1990s. Joseph Tanyanyiwa, general secretary of the National Union of the Clothing Industry, recalled in 2011, "The MDC was a rising giant. People are still missing those days. People are always saying: 'Why can't we go back to those good old days where we would really control by means of workers' power?' It is still a deep conviction that we can deliver workers from the bondage of oppression."[41]

Zimbabwe's *biennio rosso* of 1996–98 saw a revolt of students and workers. Strikes by nurses, teachers, civil servants, and builders rippled across the country. In January 1998 housewives orchestrated a "bread riot" that became an uprising of the poor living in Harare's township. The protests, strikes, and campaigns were often explicitly against the government's program of structural adjustment. This resulted in closed factories, sacked workers, and slashing of state funding to the national university and students. Inspired by the largely urban movement, the rural poor, often poor ex-veterans of the war for independence, started to invade white-owned farms. Initially the regime evicted the "squatters" and arrested their leaders. In June 1998 the University of Zimbabwe in Harare was closed for five months and students started to demand that the opposition forces be organized in a national political party—a workers' party.

These years of popular mobilization and political debate were described by one activist as a "sort of revolution." Eventually the revolt gave way to the formation of the Movement of the Democratic Change in September 1999, formed by the Zimbabwe Congress of Trade Union. At this point the new party was resolutely pro-poor, formed by and for the working class. As Job Sikhala, a founding member of the MDC and soon-to-be MP, explained, "it was basically a party of the poor with a few middle class."[42]

As the new party came into formation, attempts were made to stifle the independent voices within the movement. The work of the ISO, which had built solidarity, organized labor forums, set up tenants' associations, and participated in strikes and demonstrations, was obstructed. Despite this, the ISO won an important seat in a working-class area of Harare in the 2000 parliamentary elections as part of the MDC and, despite continued opposition from the party leadership, remained in the party until 2003.

It is hard to exaggerate the role of the ISO, much underplayed by academic accounts of the struggles in the 1990s. Brighton Makunike, who was chair of the MDC at the University of Zimbabwe in 2003, explained, "What I like from ISO is their issue of *jambanja* [resistance]; they don't beat about the bush trying to come up with some alternative, they always have the way forward at their disposal."[43] The ISO in Zimbabwe emphasized self-activity and collective decision-making. This did not turn the organization into a talking shop of endless debates but, by its own admission, decisions were reached through the democratic process of the majority and then acted on. The party's stature rested not only on its pamphlets and debates, but also on action, which included collecting for striking funds for workers, organizing demonstrations, and so on. Ultimately, the ISO was unable to stop the neoliberal turn of the MDC because, according to Zimbabwean socialist Munyaradzi Gwisai, "it lacked the necessary size and penetration . . . to offer a sufficient counter weight to the might of local and international neo-liberal forces."[44]

Other political forces began to flock to the MDC. In the eyes of respectable NGOs, some white farmers, and the middle classes, it was a force that could appease foreign interests and replace ZANU-PF with a government respectful of existing property rights and business interests. So, under the influence of these groups, the MDC did not attack the hypocrisy of the regime, but instead allied itself to those whose farms had been seized and who saw a continuation of the country's SAP as the solution to Zimbabwe's woes.

As the MDC distanced itself from its radical base, ZANU-PF started to develop political defenses in rural areas. Both the war veterans and the youth militias were pillars of the same policy: to create support bases across the country who could physically undermine the opposition and shore up the ruling party. By 2003 the MDC seemed demoralized and without a strategy to challenge the regime.

Zimbabwe's prolonged crisis resulted in serious divisions in all political formations in the country. Mugabe's fall in November 2017 was a graphic expression of these divisions. ZANU-PF faced deep splits in its own ranks. The biggest of these was a faction called G40, led by Grace Mugabe, Mugabe's wife—known, and lampooned, on the streets of Zimbabwe as "Gucci Grace." This was a group of ZANU-PF members who did not fight in the 1970s guerrilla war against Ian Smith's racist white-minority government.

The other main group was supported by Emmerson Dambudzo Mnangagwa—an old general, and the former vice-president, who played a role in the killing of "oppositionists" to the ZANU regime in the 1980s. More than twenty thousand such oppositionists, known in Shona as the Gukurahundi, were killed in Matabeleland in southern Zimbabwe between 1983 and 1987. The Harare-based ZANU government fought the war with the help of the North Korean army, who trained the notorious Fifth Brigade. As a supporter of the IMF, Mnangagwa represented the old guard, as well as the brutal authority of the military—he was regarded as the figure likely to take over from Mugabe in elections scheduled for the following year. However, in early November he was sacked by Mugabe, who decided to swing behind his wife's bid for the presidency. Yet, Mnangagwa emerged as the strongman and figurehead of the junta, which promoted street protests to support its takeover of power. On November 24 Mnangagwa was sworn in as president in front of seventy thousand onlookers.

After Mugabe was finally unseated, much was made of elections, democratic accountability, and the rule of law; the fight was about who had a right to the diminishing "spoils" of state patronage, kickbacks from diamond mining, contracts from the large companies, and shady deals with foreign mining companies and Chinese firms. The opposition formations and the fragmentation in Zimbabwe's ruling party were signs of political decay. The

MDC split several times. New formations emerged, set up by disaffected ZANU-PF politicians. Political opposition to the regime was hopelessly weak, and the government could once more resume "reforms" acceptable to the international community, devastating as they were for the poor. In 2015, to much fanfare, the minister of finance stated that the IMF would loan Zimbabwe $984 million in the third quarter of 2016 after paying off foreign lenders, the first such loan in almost twenty years—in return for which, further "reforms" to the country were promised.

The junta emerged not just on the back of the recent economic crisis, but after the long defeat of the popular, working-class movements that once controlled the streets. As we have seen, these movements briefly lit up the skies across southern Africa, even though they were bludgeoned by the regime, starved by economic crisis, and choked politically. Crucially, the Zimbabwean revolution was also deflected by the leadership of the opposition *itself*, too scared to lead the struggle against ZANU-PF. Today, after Mugabe's bloody and long tenure, there may be the possibility of a resumption of mass action that could become the arbiter for a future Zimbabwe.

4. The Burkinabé revolution

In the 1980s Burkina Faso's president, Thomas Sankara, set a path almost unique on the continent in becoming a beacon of hope against the increased inequality and insecurity as structural adjustment programs were introduced across Africa. Not only did he instigate a state-led project of social reform, but he also became a spokesman against imperialism, the curse of debt bondage on the global South, and the relatively new project of structural adjustment. His murder in 1987 seemed to put an end to a project of reform in West Africa's poorest state. However, in the first half of 2011 Burkina Faso was again in the news with the outbreak of strikes—including a general strike on April 8—mass action, and even mutinies by the presidential guard. Sankara's murderer, the recent president of Burkina Faso, Blaise Compaoré, was not successfully toppled, yet the groundwork for the 2014 revolution that finally forced him from power was established.

By the beginning of the 1990s, international geopolitics pushed the country to start the transition to multiparty democracy and a free market economy. Burkina Faso is now presented as one of the World Bank and IMF's best pupils: a paradigmatic example of Africa's rising. Despite respectable growth rates, largely on the back of high gold prices in seven foreign-owned mines (an extractive industry dominated by the Canadian, Russian, and British), the country is still one of the poorest countries in the world—182 out of 189 countries, according to the 2020 UN Human Development Index, and it has hovered around that spot since 2013—with 46 percent of the population struggling to exist beneath the poverty line. Like many countries in sub-Saharan Africa, the process of neoliberal structural adjustment led to great inequality. One in ten Burkinabé now own half the country's riches.[45] There has also been a pillage of national resources by the presidential clique (senior political officials and senior military figures). Partly as a result, there is high unemployment, especially for the two-thirds of the population that is under twenty-five years old.

Blaise Compaoré was last reelected in November 2010 by over 80 percent of the vote after a quarter century in power (but only receiving 1.7 million votes from an electorate of 7 million). Less than three months later, in the first half of 2011, a powerful popular movement erupted with demonstrations and strikes (but also military mutinies). Strikes took place in many workplaces—for example, at schools, at the Comoé Sugar Company, and in the gold mines, where strikers demonstrated fantastic bravery against the police who were supporting the mine owners. The people turned to those police, saying:

> There is no authority anymore, so we will solve our problems with violence. . . . What we ask you to do is to call Ouagadougou [the capital] and tell them to bring all the riot police. Because we have realized that the policy of the mining bosses is to use the riot police to suppress the local people. While the ministers in charge of the mines are happy to dine with the mining bosses, they never have as much as 30 minutes to talk to the local people. So, let the riot police come. Some of us will fall. We want to see the police shoot at us. But we also have confidence in ourselves. We are sure we will eventually overcome Essakane mine.[46]

Such strikes also demonstrated solidarity from beyond the working class. During a strike by workers at the Comoé Sugar Company, the largest private employer in the country, women, children, young people, other private sector workers, and pensioners demonstrated their solidarity. The exceptionally small working class, composed of an urban contingent and a mining-based one, was not an obstacle to organizing; in fact, the large family and community networks dependent on the salary of each worker amplified the militancy and solidarity of this class.

The authority of Compaoré was further shaken because his authority rested on the army and especially the presidential guard—which mutinied on April 14, 2011. At this stage the government gave in to many popular demands (for example, the teachers), but once order was restored the regime returned to repression against the first group of workers to strike—workers in the Ministry of Finance. As April came to an end, farmers had also joined the revolt, protesting against the sharp fall in prices for their goods.

Since 2008, gold has replaced cotton as the primary source of wealth. By 2012 Burkina Faso was the fourth largest producer of gold in the world. This is based on seven major gold mines, most of which are owned by foreign multinationals with the government owning around 10 percent of shares, giving it the financial incentive to intervene on the side of the owners. The challenges the workers face include casualization and discrimination in favor of expatriate workers. The mines have also had a detrimental impact on local communities, with expropriation or low levels of compensation for peasant land, increasing scarcity of water, banning of informal gold mining, pollution, and the disruption of local life.

The wave of protests continued into 2012. In August of that year, new conflict broke out at Taparko mines, where twenty-nine workers were dismissed for "inciting their colleagues to disobedience" after a union general assembly agreed to take a thirty-minute break during their ten-hour shifts—as stipulated in their collective bargaining agreement. The workers were forcibly expelled with the help of the riot police, and their leaders were dismissed despite the local labor board refusing to accept the dismissals. In the first half of 2014, the small working class led a number of important struggles, scoring certain victories. This period of the year saw increases in allowances for public sector workers following a public sector and teachers' strike in early February; a three-day sit-in at the Ouagadougou municipality headquarters in early May; and a one-day strike by public sector journalists in radio, TV, and print in mid-July over pay and against government interference.

Much of the new wave of protests were coordinated by the Mouvement des Sans Voix, bringing together youth who had been involved in the uprisings in 2011, a group partly influenced by the "indignados" movement in Spain. Another organization was formed in 2013; named Le Balai Citoyen (The Citizen's Broom), it was a grassroots movement led by two well-known musicians that, again, sought to coordinate and mobilize youth in a mission to "sweep" Burkina Faso free of the Compaoré regime. Le Balai Citoyen played an important role in the October rebellion that toppled the president. Serge Martin Bambara, one of the leaders of Le Balai Citoyen, explained how the group had learned from regional movements, including the Y'en a marre (Had Enough) struggle in Senegal that was pivotal in organizing mass action against sitting president Abdoulaye Wade's attempt to secure a third term: "We were inspired by movements that . . . contributed to reinforce the class struggle, as well as the 1970s movements like Black Power."[47]

As in several other African countries (for example, Egypt and Senegal), one aspect of the protests was uncertainty over the future of the president. Constitutionally, his term in office was due to end in 2015, and the immediate cause of the October uprising was Compoaré's attempt to secure a change in the constitution. The shockwaves of the uprising were immediately identified by the *Financial Times*: "Landlocked Burkina Faso is one of Africa's poorest countries, but is an important ally of France, the former colonial power, and the US. . . . Paris and Washington use Burkinabé military bases in their battle against al-Qaeda's affiliates in the semi-desert region of the Sahel, south of the Sahara."[48]

A participant in the October uprisings was the journalist Jean-Claude Kongo, who wrote several weeks afterward about the experience:

> In short, the Burkinabé decided to assume power for themselves and take destiny into their own hands. There is only one way to describe that famous day on Thursday 30 October: quite simply it was a popular insurrection. If the law had passed, permitting Blaise Compaoré fifteen more years, to continue the economic pillage of the country by a circle of his family and friends . . . life would have simply become unimaginable for a population who has already suffered twenty-seven long years. For my part, I was at the National Assembly for the discussions on the proposed change from 28–30 October, and saw it burn under my own eyes. To my wife who didn't want me to participate in the insurrection, I replied that it was impossible to imagine for a second that Compaoré should have the possibility to have control of the country for another fifteen years.[49]

In 1998, Kongo was radicalized by the murder of the investigative journalist Norbert Zongo and the massive protests across the country that followed. Reflecting on this period, he explained, "The crowds of October surpassed those following Zongo's murder. At the moment, we can feel a people recovering their humanity, the tension that had led to a sort of barbarism without limit, has changed, even if we only have a transitional government. The Burkinabé have started again to live, and can imagine a future."

In the uprising in 2014, though power was clearly and decisively on the streets, at the end of October it was to the military that the civil society groups, who had helped lead the uprising, turned. In a dramatic surrender of the popular revolution, which, by October 31, held the major cities and had paralyzed the country and chased out the old elite, representatives of Le Balai Citoyen handed the power of the streets (and strikes) directly to the military command in dramatic footage captured on film.[50]

For a time, during the first days of November 2014, street protests continued with thousands of protesters warning against the betrayal of the revolution, or in seeing the military as a savior to those who had, with their own hands, removed the old regime. Slogans, placards, and chants in a mass protest on November 2 expressed this unease: "Non à la confiscation de notre victoire, vive le peuple!" (No to the hijacking of our victory, long live the people!), or "Zida degage" (Zida, clear off), or even clearer still, "Zida c'est Judas" (referring to Lieutenant Colonel Isaac Zida, who was designated head of the transitional regime).

On November 2, tens of thousands marched in Ouagadougou to the headquarters of the national television and radio, recently occupied by the military. A twenty-eight-year-old trader, Karim Zongo, expressed the general unease: "We do not want the people's victory stolen by the military just after Blaise Compaoré was dismissed on Friday, and a new strong man designated by the military to step into his place. Our struggle now is the outright departure of Lieutenant Colonel Zida." The capacity of the protesters to adapt their slogans, to develop an immediate critique of the seizure of the popular revolution by the army and then launch a renewed offensive was extremely impressive, though ultimately incapable of resisting the bleeding out of the revolution.

Still, why did a movement of such popular power that had managed to overturn one of the continent's most deeply entrenched regimes—a dictatorship despite the veneer of democracy—allow prominent members of the old regime, a recycled elite, to step back into power? What is it about the political economy of Burkina Faso that shapes political action and enables such a political outcome?

We can list some of the relevant issues here. There are fundamental weaknesses of Burkina Faso's extractive, export-based economy that have remained largely unchanged since independence. The country's poverty, the extreme suffering of its people, remains staggering. There is enormous income differentiation: while 46 percent live below the poverty line, one in ten of the population own half the country's riches. Almost 92 percent of the labor force in 2014 was employed in agricultural labor, in subsistence farming and cotton cultivation—statistics largely unchanged since Sankara's radical experiments at pro-poor development in the early 1980s. Agricultural work contributed 30 percent to GDP in 2012. In other words, there is very weak industrialization—thus low levels of proletarianization—combined with a large agricultural workforce. The recent boom in mining has not altered this setup. However, arguably these figures disguise significant changes in Burkinabé society: urbanization has grown as rural poverty drives more people into towns and cities, and the political impact of the country's small working class—employed in mining, the civil service, and teaching—is entirely disproportionate to its size.

The successive waves of protest and uprisings in Burkina Faso have been against both the brutality of the former regime and the immediate manifestations of the continually exploitative relationships, both between the country and the capitalist system, and between the country's highly unequal economic and political classes. Reductions of basic living standards and encroachments on the lives and liberties of the Burkinabé people have been continually resisted, and in 2014—and for particular reasons—acts of great resistance coalesced into more coherent movements for change that linked the struggle for economic and social transformation to the need for effective political accountability and representation. However, there have not been alternate voices and forces—of sufficient strength—to challenge the continued presence of a compromised political class.

Conclusion: From democratic revolutions to what?

The revolutions and uprisings in this chapter, frustrated *and* "successful," were part of a series of waves of change. During the 1990s and 2000s, popular revolutions erupting as a consequence of neoliberal reforms and structural adjustment have so often manifested themselves as liberal movements for democracy and human rights.[51] This arises from the fact that governments implementing neoliberal reforms rely on increasingly draconian measures to suppress popular discontent. Chris Harman described these processes well: "The path that began with neoliberalism ends up in quasi-dictatorship. . . . The effect is to turn social and economic issues into political struggles around demands for democracy and human rights. In the process people can lose sight of the social and economic roots of these political issues."[52] Unless this link is made, protest movements seeking to alleviate the effects of economic liberalization can easily be convinced that the primary answer to their grievances is more formal political or constitutional reform, rather than a deepening of democratic culture and practice and ultimately control of the socioeconomic situation.

In very different ways, the early 1990s saw movements for social, political, and economic transformation across Africa mutate into movements led by an opposition elite for democratization and citizenship. As a recent study has argued, "African protests have too often been co-opted by elites, who, through subterfuge and deceit, subvert its political content into more narrow agendas."[53] In most cases, such elites resumed the imposition of neoliberalism in a new context, eventually setting off a new wave of protests against the effects of those policies. Some new governments successfully co-opted and corrupted leading activists. Political activism was often softened up by the carrot of "participatory democracy" and the stick of economic decline, deforming and distorting activism and agendas. In such circumstances, new waves and generations of activists, frustrated at the failures and compromises of their seniors and elders, came to the fore to seek new and old types of changes, often with little opportunity to grasp why their forerunners had failed to achieve their aims.

We should also draw attention to the striking difference in the scale of political mobilization across the continent. From 1995, Zimbabwe saw what one activist described as a "sort of revolution," with urban (and rural) protests increasing year after year. With each new wave of protest new layers of society would be galvanized, deepening the political movement that was tightening around the government. As Brian Kagoro explained, by 1997 "you had an outright . . . rebellion on your hands."[54]

The crucial element during this period of "rebellion" was that it was generalized. In many respects, the experiences of other countries during the transition—in Senegal, Nigeria, Zambia, Kenya, and Malawi, for example—could not have been more different. The period of the transitions in the 1990s was not always marked by massive urban protest and ferment. In some countries political decisions were made by a political elite that, although drawn from the ranks of the opposition, was not directly accountable to a wider movement. Although there was a popular groundswell of support for the transition, it did not operate in conditions of widespread political protest, let alone "rebellion." Activists did not, as a result, reach the level of political development experienced by activists in Zimbabwe, for example, let alone Burkina Faso.

Some activists, certainly those from a moment in Zimbabwe's uprising, or Burkina Faso's recent revolutionary struggles, talked about the euphoria of having been involved in massive social mobilization. Often, they conceptualized this activism in general terms of liberation and revolution, terms that do not seem transplanted onto their activism but are a product of the scale of the protests—and the period when the transition took place—in which they have been involved. Elsewhere—in Senegal in the late 1990s, for example—activists might remember the excitement of the campaign and the exquisite joy and hope that was generated by election victories, their horizons sometimes fixed on more limited possibilities.

Undoubtedly, one of the reasons why some movements on the continent are weaker than others, and why activists are animated less by broader ideologies, is what Cherif Ba, an activist from Senegal, described in 2004 as the failure of *la formation des militants*—training and education of activists: "Political parties must take responsibility for raising the political level of their activists. But what party does this? . . . Therefore activists don't get the basic training they must. . . . Political involvement is simply engaged in . . . to support the president or further the aims of a political party."[55] However, most of the political left, disoriented after the collapse of Stalinism, has immersed itself in a political circus of recycled elites. In this circus, activists are relegated to the status of cheerleaders, with no real responsibilities except as uncritical supporters of their political leaders. We have argued that after the second wave of political revolutions, new governments across the continent followed, more or less obediently, the advice of the international financial institutions.

The subsequent process of neoliberalism unleashed a succession of protest waves in Africa that widened popular engagement, but elite leaders eventually shepherded and corralled these movements into the narrower and more limited objectives of "good governance" and "liberalization." Economic liberalization—with its devastating whirlwind of job losses and factory closures—has to a certain extent weakened the organizations and coherence of the African working class while strengthening the role of what Frantz Fanon described as an "avaricious bourgeois caste."[56]

The political transitions and the revolutions that ushered in this period in sub-Saharan Africa in the 1990s occurred in a world fundamental-

ly altered by global geopolitics. Struggles in peripheral capitalist societies
have been profoundly affected by the collapse of ideas of national liberation
linked to state-led development. In the period following the collapse of the
Berlin Wall—which signaled the apparent death of state-dominated strategies for development—ideological confusion consumed many of the social
forces that had looked to progressive and left-wing political change. However, uprisings continue to effect political change even in the absence of a
coherent program for socioeconomic change. Indeed, as one study observes
about the political turmoil and unrest on the continent, "Political transformations across Africa have rarely come piecemeal. Instead, they tend to
come in waves, sweeping across the region and leaving massive social transformations in their wake."[57]

Yet the repeated collapse of vibrant revolutions into limited liberal reformism reflects the limited impact of these revolutions. These limitations
typically derive from the same sources: first, the failure of organizations and
social groups within such protests and uprisings to distinguish themselves
clearly from the political weaknesses of wider political forces, and second,
the absence of effective, independent movements that organize in a broad
political and social milieu (in townships, factories, and universities). In the
presence of such organizations, more radical actions could lead to deeper and
more sustained political transitions. Without them, often the uprisings and
revolutions we have witnessed remain isolated and easily manipulated, and
make only a limited impression on the underlying political and economic
fabric of the continent.

The burden of global economic turbulence and speculation continues
to fall unevenly—in particular on Africa. We argue that the rise in financial
speculation, an attempt to make profitable bets in the context of a relative
squeeze on industrial and manufacturing profits, has seen a massive expansion of bets on "softs"—rice, grain, and other staple foods. The result has
been a spectacular increase in the price of staple foodstuffs, to the particular
detriment of the global poor and many countries in Africa. So food price
increases, largely a result of such speculation between 2007 and 2009, led
to food riots, general strikes, and protests in thirty-five countries across the
world, twenty-four of which were in Africa. This has deepened the emergence of a third wave of political uprisings, which continues to spread across
the continent. Eleven uprisings occurred on the continent in that two-year
period, directly linked to increases in the price of cooking oil, bread, and

rice. It is within this new wave of protest and uprisings that the Burkinabé revolution in October 2014 occurred. Burkina Faso expresses, for a number of reasons, the most intense and radical crest of the recent wave, showing how the convergence of political and economic protests can, in the right circumstances, rapidly develop into a mass revolutionary challenge on power. Post-Compaoré Burkina Faso, unsurprisingly, is still threatened by the neoliberal hold that has gripped countries across the continent for more than twenty years. The official opposition remains committed to supporting the mining houses and multinationals who operate in the country. Yet the possibilities of learning from previous failures animate many discussions. Tolé Sgnon, secretary-general of the trade confederation CGT-B, explained just before the president was forced to flee the capital, "We can replace Blaise Compaoré with someone else who will choose the same neoliberal policies. In this sense, we need to develop critical thought towards the various political forces that are attempting to present themselves as alternatives to the current government but which, for the most part, share the basic fundamentals of the neoliberal policies of the existing government."[58]

Despite these failures, democratization, while limited or curtailed in some countries, *has* widened the space available for activists and movements. Globalization has reduced the extent of autonomous, national sovereign decision-making, but also opened up the potential for cross-border cooperation between radicalizing movements to present alternatives to neoliberal globalization. The next decades will express these now informalized realities and possibilities. But the development of further revolutionary waves in Africa and the capacity of these revolutions to shape political and economic change on the continent will depend in large part on their ability to define a political agenda free of structural adjustment, austerity, and the circulation of elites. Such a project requires a process that Antonio Gramsci described as the subaltern classes educating themselves in the "art of government."[59]

CHAPTER 5

"Reformasi": Indonesians Bring Down Suharto[1]

Tom O'Lincoln

Introduction

Indonesian history can't be understood without grasping its uneven development. Throughout the days of colonial rule, and on arriving at independence from the Dutch around 1950, the country lacked a strong national bourgeoisie. Its development had been held back by competition from Dutch traders who gained support from colonial authorities, including the Dutch East India Company. The space was filled by alliances between the Chinese traders and elements of the state. Thus, a certain pattern of development was set; and attempts by the new government to artificially promote "indigenous" capital achieved little.[2] The aptly named "Benteng" (fortress) program failed to achieve breakthroughs in this regard in the early era of Indonesia's first president, Sukarno. Even extensive nationalizations of Dutch firms simply led to their transfer to the military, as the latter was in bourgeois eyes the only social force capable of managing industry.[3]

The main challenger to the military, the Communist Party of Indonesia (PKI), was eliminated as a factor by a bloody CIA-backed military coup in 1965.[4] This brought to power the group around General Suharto, which ruled until 1998. The most common word used to describe the consequences of 1965 is "tragedy." This heritage manifested in the form of extreme caution in activists and the general population for an extended period, but that is less pronounced today. The Suharto dictatorship opened more space for foreign capital than had been allowed by the popular nationalist Sukarno and used the leverage of state power to take some steps in national development, for example, in infrastructure and investment.[5] It also made some use of racist discrimination to shore up its political position in 1965 and after, for instance, by banning Chinese language and celebrations as part of the regime's attempt to associate the PKI with China. Yet alliances between generals and Chinese entrepreneurs continued, Suharto himself collaborating with Liem Sioe Liong, said to be the country's richest man. These alliances served as a lightning rod, causing the dissatisfaction that people harbored toward the social order to be drawn away to the Chinese traders instead.

Still the land wasn't without hope for democrats or merchants. In the mid-'90s, conventional wisdom said economic development would bring democracy to Indonesia. Being the newest Asian tiger, there was room for growth and its economy would continue to boom. The growing middle class would no longer put up with dictatorship. Genteel lobbying would push the old guard into retirement.

The politician who symbolized this prospect was Megawati, daughter of the country's independence leader Sukarno. Suharto became alarmed about Megawati's progress around 1994, as she consolidated her position as head of the previously tame Indonesian Democratic Party. The dictator organized a rigged party congress to get her dumped, but her supporters resisted, occupying the party headquarters in the capital city, Jakarta. Suharto organized thugs to drive them out, which provoked the July 27, 1996, Jakarta riots. At the same time, though it lacked strong links with these protesters, an emerging working class was organizing and becoming more militant, with networks of activists forming and sometimes coordinating industrial action. The number of strikes was still small compared to the size of the working class, and independent union organization was weak. Most strikes included very limited demands. Still, the trend was there. Peasants staged significant local resistance to capitalist development, which offered some opportunities for young leftists to gain experience and build networks in the heat of struggle.

Additional factors putting pressure on the regime were the three regional independence struggles. Of these, East Timor was in the strongest position as the Timorese issue aroused strong feelings in the West. East Timor would

win independence in 1999 after Suharto's fall. The other two independence
struggles were in Aceh and West Papua. Acehnese hopes were dashed after
the massive 2004 Indian Ocean tsunami devastated the province. Conflict
continues in West Papua, with the international Left supporting the Papuans.
In the cultural realm, dissidents like Iwan Fals and Wiji Thukul set a critical
tone. Fals, a Dylanesque performer, was well known among the youth for his
protests against crime and corruption. His best-known song was "Bongkar,"
meaning "expose" or "smash." Wiji Thukul, who was a member of the People's
Democratic Party (PRD), stood further left, as shown by his poem that acknowledged "only one word—resist."[6] He disappeared and is presumed dead.

1. Time of crisis

Before July 27, 1976, there was already a pattern of unrest, with street demonstrations in Ujung Pandang on the island of Sulawesi that forced the government to lower transport fares, and a large workers' demonstration in Surabaya
in East Java led by the far-left PRD. But the July 27th riots were a huge turning point. They were more political than most riots: groups marched along
major streets chanting "Long live Megawati" and "The military are killers."[7]
A public servant acquaintance later told me of confronting the marchers at
the entrance to the Social Welfare Department ("Depsos") and persuading
them to spare the department, given its role in helping people. They acqui-
esced, crossed the road, and set fire to a Toyota showroom instead.[8]

The repression that followed was effective for a while. The PRD was
driven underground and into jail, from whence it issued defiant statements.
("Fast or slow the people will form ranks to make its own history.")[9] But it
was the 1997 election campaign that allowed hostility to the regime to show
itself again under the guise of electoral campaigning. With Megawati side-
lined, few wanted to support her former party, so mass opposition focused
on rallies by the remaining token opposition force, the United Development
Party (PPP). Huge crowds took to the streets a number of times, gridlocking
the capital and other cities, and toward the end there was street fighting.
These actions combined support for Megawati and for the star that symbolized the PPP; this Mega-Bintang ("Mega-Star") alliance showed that mass
hostility was mounting against the regime. The PRD called for a third leg
to the slogan, making it *Mega-Bintang-Rakyat* ("Mega-Star—the People"),
with some success.[10]

The 1997 Asian economic crisis[11] was rich in ironies. For years the experts had hyped the economic boom, portraying local political and industrial leaders as miracle workers, while hot money poured into the Southeast Asian region. Only the Japanese fund managers were cautious; in fact they began pulling out as early as 1995. The rest abruptly followed in 1997, after the "tiger economies" showed signs of declining competitiveness and over-capacity. As Harvard economist Jeffrey Sachs remarked: "Euphoria turned to panic without missing a beat. Suddenly, Asia's leaders could do no right. The money fled."[12]

Initially, capitalist pundits and the International Monetary Fund (IMF) thought that Indonesia would escape the crash, because its economy was supposedly so good in terms of fundamentals. Yet by December 1997, the country was in financial turmoil, its currency plunging from an exchange rate of Rps 2,300 to the US dollar, to Rps 10,000, and it continued to plunge further.[13] Indonesia's external debt soared to $142 billion. It seemed the country's "fundamentals" consisted mostly of keeping an eye on empty office buildings.

The one thing Suharto still had going for him was the grudging recognition that he had presided over economic growth. He was the "Father of Development." But at the end of 1997, the Asian crisis brought development to a shuddering halt. At first the economic crisis dampened the struggle, because so many people were focused entirely on survival. Then a new rhythm of revolt began, based on new social contradictions. For a time, most of the upheavals around the country took the ambiguous form of riots, mostly with a big anti-Chinese component. Even so, considerable dissatisfaction centered on Suharto, his cronies, and the regime. The mood of hope had changed to desperation. Political demonstrations were mostly token affairs. It was not until March 1998 that the students began to mount a national, genuinely political protest campaign movement. This quickly became a mass movement, with regular demonstrations at even the most conservative campuses, such as Trisakti University in West Jakarta.[14]

The student movement began with rallies inside the campus walls, where it was relatively safe. Then they started trying to get into the streets but were usually stopped by the security forces. The resulting clashes provoked new street fighting, so that the authorities could argue against street marches on the grounds that they caused riots. Many students accepted this. The student movement had other weaknesses. It was moralistic, and often the students organized in isolation from other forces. There were those who hoped to somehow inspire the rest of the population, but there was little concept of building concrete links. Most were affected by the image—propagated by the regime over many years—that the students were a "pure" (*murni*) moral force not to be corrupted by mixing with others. Still, they had some impact in society. In late April, the workers, who had been largely quiescent in the face of mass unemployment, began to strike. It wasn't a mass strike movement, and it wasn't always political, but it added to the rhythm.

Suharto invited the IMF to prop up the economy and then spent months trying to avoid implementing its demands. The regime announced that some major projects would be shelved, but they reappeared in a new guise. The clove monopoly of Tommy Suharto, the dictator's son, was supposed to be scrapped; but then it seemed to return in a new form. These games allowed Suharto's family and cronies to cling to their assets, but world money markets were hostile. Unemployment soared; inflation raced out of control, yet Suharto's ruthless political machine handed him another presidential term. Despite the unrest the regime held firm, mouthing platitudes about reform while arranging the kidnapping and torture of activists. Armed thugs seized Pius Lustrilanang, an ally of Megawati and of another liberal reformer, Muslim leader Amien Rais; they also snatched Andi Arief, a prominent member of the PRD. Pius later surfaced telling of brutal mistreatment. Andi Arief eventually turned up in police custody, though none of the cops would own up to actually arresting him.

At the start of May 1998, Suharto arrogantly announced that democratic reform wouldn't proceed until 2003. The students were furious and their demonstrations grew. The public mood hardened perceptibly, as most people concluded reform was only possible if the dictator fell. The student movement blossomed almost everywhere. In the city of Yogyakarta, the students took a member of the local parliament hostage, while in Surabaya they stormed into a radio station and ordered their demands be broadcast. To build this national movement was a great achievement. The regime had made campus political activity extremely difficult by imposing an official organization, the Campus Coordinating Agency, and restricting alternative groups. Students were told to pursue academic goals and shun "practical politics." But in 1998 they shrugged this restriction aside, saying their actions had nothing to do with the rubber-stamp electoral system and thus were technically not practical politics.

On May 4, the regime announced it would implement the IMF's plan to stop subsidizing fuel and electricity prices. The price of gas would rise 71 percent immediately, while electricity would go up 60 percent over the course of the year, on top of all the earlier hardships. Desperately, motorists queued for the last of the cheap fuel, gridlocking Jakarta's traffic. While ordinary workers walked miles to get home, the cars of the rich were conspicuous in the petrol queues. Their chauffeurs filled up, went home to siphon off the gas, and returned for more. This profiteering gave a sharply defined class content to the gas crisis. The press seriously questioned why the subsidies had to be removed. Yes, they cost a lot of money—no less than Rp 27 billion—but the government had previously found Rp 103 billion to bail out the banks owned by its cronies. The oil industry was earning foreign cash at what were now fabulous exchange rates, so why couldn't it give local consumers a break?

Meanwhile a wave of strikes broke out in the industrial estates to the west of the capital. Around two thousand employees in ceramic and chemical plants in Tangerang and Serang stopped work, demanding wage increases to keep up with inflation. Twelve hundred workers at Surabaya's P.T. Famous plant[15] gathered outside the personnel office with placards saying that the bosses were liars and that the workers were not toy robots.

On the surface this seemed unrelated to the political unrest. However, it had become very hard for workers to strike due to mass unemployment. The fact that such actions were now occurring suggested the political struggles were having a flow-on effect. Within days, there were further signs. Around two thousand medical staff from the Surabaya General Hospital demonstrated for democratic reform. They had sent messages to the local parliament but had been ignored, so they felt there was no alternative except to finally take to the streets. The ferment was so great, even craven time-servers in parliament began debating issues and criticizing the government, looking for all the world like genuine representatives of the people. Jakarta was consumed with bitter anger, waiting for a spark. That spark was struck by snipers who killed four students at Trisakti University on May 12.

When I heard the news the next morning, I went to Trisakti.[16] Thousands of students had gathered for what was both an act of mourning and a political rally. Delegations arrived from other campuses, as did every prominent figure of the democracy movement. Megawati spoke (the first time she had said a word about the months of protests) along with the liberal Muslim intellectual Amien Rais. Both pleaded for nonviolence, but mounting tensions and social conflicts had gone too far for that.

Students began to drift into the streets. Here they were joined by workers, the unemployed, and the poor. The police marched up and street fighting began; even those well within the university grounds didn't escape the raw taste of tear gas. Around Atma Jaya University in the heart of the city, office workers left their desks and came into the streets to express their support for the students. By nightfall, riots were spreading and the following days saw Jakarta in flames. Few corners of greater Jakarta were untouched. Some neighborhoods looked like war zones.

Finally the dictatorship cracked. Students invaded the parliament and the authorities made no effort to kick them out. No government accepts such a thing unless it's on the ropes. The media defied the censors, and coverage of the riots was extremely frank. Newspapers held back from issuing editorials that called directly for the president's resignation, but the press did begin to discuss the Suharto regime in highly critical and sometimes insulting terms. Foreign businesses took to their heels. Experts lamented a catastrophic economic position.

What had been a widespread but still diffuse yearning for change became a national consensus. Personal friends of mine share the same sentiments as hardened political activists. So did people in the street. A burly sergeant, followed by a diffident private, dropped in for fried rice at the Hotel Tator and told me emphatically: Suharto had to go. Parliamentary speaker Harmoko, his home burnt to ashes, called on the dictator to quit. Members of parliament backed an extraordinary parliamentary session to seek Suharto's resignation. Thirteen ministers themselves resigned. At Trisakti the poet Rendra had read bitter verses aimed at the dictator. Recalling all the injustices, he concluded:

> Because we are like a flowing river
> and you are a stone without a heart
> the water will wear away the stone.[17]

On May 21, 1998, with students occupying the parliament building and riots in the streets, the population learning instant lessons in politics after a million-strong "people power" rally was barely averted by military bullying, the dictator resigned. Rendra's ardent prophecy was fulfilled. What had brought down Suharto was not the politics of prosperity and middle-class lobbying, but the politics of crisis and mass upheaval.

Who led the May events? To the extent that anyone provided progressive political leadership in May, it was certainly the students. Most everyone sympathized with them, they offered the only political arguments with wide impact, and the first of the 1998 Jakarta riots was touched off by the shooting of Trisakti students. But the May unrest was only partly an uprising. Yes, there were sensational actions directed against the government. But it also involved race riots, rapes, and apolitical mass looting; and a significant number of these incidents were orchestrated. Political observer Vedi Hadiz wrote to me, "From where I was, I could see truckloads of looters going back and forth on the toll roads, and it would have been terribly easy for one military vehicle to have stopped them at either end. One looter even asked me the way back to Jakarta (from Bekasi)—obviously somebody brought in from elsewhere."[18]

On talk radio they complained that the security forces conspicuously held back from trying to stop looting and burning.[19] Unlike 1996, there were no contingents marching in the streets chanting political slogans. Most people I spoke with in the aftermath told apolitical stories (like one about a man who tried to board a crowded commuter train with a looted fridge) or made anti-Chinese remarks. This was possible because the students didn't provide leadership to the wider community. Left activists generally agreed on this point. In addition to their fear of stirring up race riots or facing violence from the security forces, most students showed a certain naiveté. A writer who was at the parliament when the dictator fell, to be replaced by Vice-President Bacharuddin Jusuf Habibie (an eccentric technocrat), wrote:

> The fact is they [the students] are poorly coordinated and are not by and large disciplined activists. They have no true militants and many of them are particularly young and not savvy. The radio broadcast some of their comments about Habibie's cabinet appointments. They were favourable about some of them, showing they weren't clear in their opposition to the entire systematic charade.[20]

Although this judgment may be overstated, there is probably a core of truth. But the students were learning fast.

2. Reform or revolution?

The term revolution was little used during May, except as a bogey. The dominant view was that "Reformasi" (a reform program) was needed to forestall a revolution (which would be violent, ugly, and destructive). In late 1998 this view changed for a time among sections of the populace.

The student movement had suffered from years of government effort to contain student militancy. Suharto had played on nostalgia toward student demonstrations, which had helped him take power once upon a time. He had moved the main campus of Indonesia University outside Jakarta, embedded spies among the students, implemented a permit system for political activities, and forced activists to work through official student councils (Dewan Maha-siswa).[21] In 1998 these constraints were shattered. I myself spoke on Lenin and the Bolshevik Party to the council at UGM University, Yogyakarta.

But in the aftermath of Suharto's fall, the student movement was in disarray. Students had campaigned single-mindedly against the dictator, in some cases without much thought to the aftermath. Moreover, many of the students had seen themselves as a morally pure (*murni*) elite that should stay away from practical politics—a mentality cynically encouraged by the regime, which flattered them while trying to undermine them. Now they suddenly confronted a new government claiming to implement reform. After a fairly short lull, they returned to the streets, now calling for "total reform," but their numbers were comparatively small and the student groups were split.

In Jakarta the whole movement had been coordinated by the cross-campus network City Forum (Forum Kota, soon shortened to Forkot). Now, after a split, a sizable section of Forkot operated as a second network called FAMRED, complaining that some elements within Forkot did not believe in nonviolence, and even making corruption charges. Muslim students sympathetic to Amien Rais had formed another group called KAMMI, which represented a relatively right-wing current. The PRD, meanwhile, was increasingly able to operate aboveground and had established a student organization called KOMRAD.

Students were divided over several issues: whether to act politically or focus on the "moral force"; whether loose structures were adequate as against organized leadership; over nonviolence; and over attitudes to the forthcoming special parliamentary session that was to lay down ground rules for the 1999 elections. Some initially had high hopes for the session (in May, after all, they'd demanded it be held immediately). Others were conditionally supportive, while the left wing was arguing to reject the whole affair, because the parliament was just a Suharto hangover. Arguments over these issues became heated, and at one demonstration on November 9 the more radical students pulled down one of KAMMI's banners.

Finally, as the special session approached, the students moved toward a consensus around three demands. Two were well established by late October: put Suharto on trial and end the military's role in politics. The third, which still required much debate, was for accelerating democratization—here everyone agreed in principle, but not on specifics. By October 28, when ten thousand or so rallied on the Day of the Oath of the Youth (a historic date in the national independence struggle), the center and left of the movement were able to unite under the banner of an umbrella group, AKRAB (People's United Action—*akrab* also means "friendly, intimate"). The name not only implied unity but also an orientation to "the people," a significant development in itself. The students were ready to mobilize the wider population.

In the week beginning Monday, November 9, demonstrations against the special session began. The movement was nationwide, but I will stick to events in Jakarta. At first the numbers were still fairly small, a few thousand perhaps. The demonstrators wanted to hold a mock parliament at Proclamation Square but were pushed out of the square by a crowd of so-called civilian militia ("Pam Swakarsa"), thugs hired by the regime from among the urban poor and quasi-fascist organizations. Only late that evening did the students manage to reclaim the square, helped by local residents. From then on, the square became a major rallying point, and each day the demonstrations grew larger.

By mid-week, tens of thousands of students were marching through the city streets. Much larger numbers of local people gathered at street corners to cheer them on, many joining the march or running ahead of it to confront police. So united and well organized were the students that they could split up and hold more than one march, yet eventually converge again at the parliament. There were many stirring tales; here is one I received by email:

> 2 pm: The mass action arrives at Jatinegara, its numbers reaching around 100,000. The military blocks the road with four trucks and a line of soldiers. The military commander asks for negotiations. . . . The leader of the demonstration won't negotiate and gives an ultimatum. . . . Within five minutes the march will break through the barricade. . . . Thousands of students chant "Oppose! Oppose! Forward! Forward! Forward!" . . . The security forces remove the trucks and troops. The march, by now 150,000 strong, marches on chanting "The people united will never be defeated."

Later, in front of the parliament, the military is too strong, and the demonstrators can't break through. Confrontations ensue: tear gas, rubber bullets, street fighting. "Along the slow lane of the toll road a thousand students calling themselves the Jakarta Front arrive chanting 'revolution or death' and singing 'if you want a revolution, join us.'"

An issue that illustrates a number of problems and possibilities is the third demand of the movement: to replace the existing parliament with some kind of transitional democratic regime. In the early stages, students prodded the four best-known liberal democrats (Megawati, Amien Rais, the Sultan of Yogyakarta, and the popular but erratic Muslim figure Abdurrahman Wahid, widely known as Gus Dur) into meeting and making a common statement. The right wing of the movement hoped these four would take the initiative and demand an immediate transfer of power. This they refused to do, making only vague demands such as a gradual elimination of the military's political role. The students then generally forgot about the "Ciganjur group," as they were known, and relied on direct action. Yet ambiguities remained about their demands.

Forkot and FAMRED called for an Indonesian People's Committee to take power, whereas the PRD and KOMRAD called for a People's Council elected from the grassroots. Many students and most of the wider population still expected figures like the Ciganjur group to lead such a transitional vehicle. On the other hand, some were also open to the PRD's argument that the People's Council should be the peak of a much bigger movement consisting of councils of workers, communities, students, artists, and peasants, which would in turn be based on local committees. While this wasn't the same as workers' councils based in industry, the PRD clearly wanted the establishment of some kind of "dual power." All these ideas were far ahead of the consciousness the movement had displayed back in May. Debate continued about them for some time after 1998, but unfortunately, as the movement subsided their basis in reality diminished.

Compromised though he was by his links to the old regime, Habibie still presided over significant changes to the political system. He offered East Timor an independence referendum, though he could not deliver it without terrible conflict. He cut back the military's parliamentary representation, divided the military and police into separate structures, and held the first free elections since the 1950s. The results resolved surprisingly little. Megawati's vote topped 30 percent; Suharto's organization Golkar, with its roots deep in the state machinery, got over 20 percent. Finishing third with about 13 percent was the National Awakening Party, based on the huge Muslim organization Nahdlatul Ulama and led by Abdurrahman Wahid. Then there were a number of smaller parties. These results shaped the new People's Representative Assembly (the lower house).

Electing the president fell to the wider People's Consultative Assembly (functioning as an electoral college and vehicle for constitutional change), where unelected "functional" delegates including the military had more weight. While on the face of it Megawati should have won, old-guard elements feared her as the champion of democracy and reform, and some religious groups opposed electing a female president. Fierce horse-trading brought Wahid to power.

Gus Dur was likable but erratic. He was viewed as a reformer but had appeared on TV with Suharto when the dictator announced his last cabinet, a collection of cronies and hacks audaciously dubbed the "Kabinet Reformasi." His presidency was unstable, and hopes that he would introduce further reforms were largely disappointed. He promised the people of Aceh, long oppressed by Jakarta, a referendum—but didn't hold it. He spoke of lifting the ban on the Communist Party, but did nothing about it. Within a year, the same reactionary forces that had lined up to block Megawati were using her in an effort to dump Wahid.

At this point most of the Indonesian Left, ranging from NGOs to the PRD, rallied behind him and against Megawati.[22] They argued that pressure for a transition from Wahid to Megawati was linked to rightward trends in society as a whole. They pointed to right-wing military, religious, and bureaucratic groups behind the push to dump Wahid and to Megawati's links with sections of the military. Some rallied outside Bogor Presidential Palace, calling on Wahid to issue a decree dissolving parliament before it could remove him. This was a serious mistake.

Yes, there was a link between the attacks on Wahid and those on democracy; but what was its nature? If we ask which president brought in the most democratic change, surely it was Habibie. Not because he represented more progressive forces, but because in November 1998 the mass struggle of the students and urban poor was at its height. As that struggle subsided, society drifted rightward and reactionary elements raised their heads. They did use Megawati; but hadn't the same people backed Wahid in 1999?

Megawati did have closer ties to the military; her father's party cadres had commonly come from provincial Javanese backgrounds similar to those of many officers. But Wahid was closer to the Suharto family, which was as still a force, and Wahid actually appeared with the dictator on TV in the dying days of his rule.

Wahid, Megawati, and Habibie were all essentially similar capitalist politicians, members of the same social elite. The leftists who supported Wahid had confused cause and effect. And their calls for a decree dissolving parliament were extremely dangerous, given that Wahid could only have done that with the help of the military. Relatively few left activists seemed to thoroughly understand the need for a political stand independent of all capitalist politicians.

After 2001 Megawati and her backers consolidated their position to a degree, but her presidency was ineffectual. Like Peter Sellers, she seemed to have reached the top by simply "being there." For its part, the Left fragmented. In the wake of the September 11 attacks and in the face of Megawati's increasing cooperation with US imperialism, Islamic groups began to make a running as a seemingly radical political opposition. The PRD adopted an electoralist strategy that achieved little.

Given the depth of the Asian economic crisis and the hunger for new ideas, it is no surprise that wide layers were interested in socialism. Activists held numerous discussion sessions and generated much educational material. Opportunities for discussion with visiting supporters were also in demand by all the radical groups.[23]

The dominant strategy developed by the Indonesian socialists envisaged two stages. First there would be a democratic revolution, to remove all the existing dictatorial features, such as the military's "dual function" allowing it to intervene in politics. Then, using the expanded democratic space, the way would be open to launch a struggle for socialism. The more theoretically inclined based this approach on Vladimir Lenin's 1905 pamphlet *Two Tactics of Social Democracy*. There was little awareness that in 1917 Lenin had effectively abandoned the two-stage approach of *Two Tactics* and with the publication of the "April Theses" moved to a conception close to Trotsky's theory of permanent revolution. There were a very small number of Trotskyists in Indonesia, arguing a kind of "permanent revolution" strategy, supported by some foreign activists.[24] The most important of these was Danial Indrakusuma.[25]

If such strategies as permanent revolution were ever to be tested, Indonesia would need an insurgent labor movement. In the post-Suharto era some elements of such a movement began to take shape.

3. Aftermath

In the 1960s, the Communist Party was the main organization representing the working class, although there were perhaps no more than five hundred thousand industrial workers, whereas today there are many millions. Under Suharto (president from 1967 to 1998), the old unions were savaged by repression and then incorporated into government-managed structures. The All-Indonesia Workers Union (Serikat Pekerja Seluruh Indonesia, or SPSI) dominated the scene and was commonly described as a "yellow" union. The term is apt, though some allowance should be made for strikes the union staged to achieve legislated minimum wages and conditions. SPSI sometimes authorized such actions. One of the great accomplishments of 1998 was to clear the way for a rebirth of mass labor organizations from sometimes dubious backgrounds.

In the course of the 1990s, attempts were made to create independent unions. The first attempt was called "Solidarity," but after one big strike it was repressed. At the time Suharto fell, there could not have been more than ten thousand members of independent unions in Indonesia. They have grown rapidly since, while at the same time some of the SPSI unions have become more independent. But the movement lacks tradition and experience.

The Manpower Department, which oversees labor policy, reported that in January 2002 there were sixty-one nationally registered union federations, and beyond that many local union groups. According to an analysis by Poengky Indarti of the human rights group Kontras, nineteen of the national federations were "old unions" derived from the Suharto-era official union federation. Another nine have a more complex history related to the Suharto era. Five were organizations of civil servants, twenty-eight were new unions. The labor force was estimated around eighty million, with important concentrations of factory workers on the fringes of the cities of Java, as well as Medan in Sumatra. That workforce has grown significantly since then.

The biggest industrial issue in 2002 was a series of ministerial decrees about workers' rights. The employers were up in arms about some very modest pension benefits, and had pressured the new labor minister to cut back entitlements. All the unions protested, even the yellow unions from the Suharto era. They now had to compete with new workers' organizations, and were starting to become more active in the promotion of their members' interests. Demonstrations began in Jakarta, then spread to Surabaya, where thousands of unionists from the Maspion factory blocked streets and stormed government offices, and to Bandung, where giant rallies paralyzed the city for three days.

President Wahid refused to retreat but left a loophole: provincial governments could stick to the old arrangements if they chose. Several provincial governments rushed to use this escape hatch including the one in Bandung. But the Bandung workers weren't satisfied; they demanded the new decree be suspended nationally. After two days Wahid caved in. He also postponed fuel price hikes demanded by the IMF.

It was the former yellow unions that initially called the big Bandung rallies, and for that reason, some left activists were suspicious about them. But once workers were in the streets, they gained a sense of their own power and took the struggle further than the union leaders intended. In terms of working-class mobilization, these events were a high point in the aftermath of the upheavals of 1998.

Power still rested with the generals after 1998, and this was not just a "behind the scenes" matter. Megawati followed her father in maintaining close relations with senior officers. Her successor, Susilo Bambang Yudhoyono, was a retired military man. According to one analysis, for General Wiranto, who was commander of the Indonesian National Armed Forces from February to October 1998, "it was not unrealistic to seek the post of Vice President. Despite general public sentiment that the military should abstain from civilian politics, every presidential candidate, in light of prevailing political realities, had considered the possibility of having Wiranto as running mate."[26]

Attempts to rebuild a coherent left-wing movement since the '90s have failed. Remnants remain from the Sukarno era, including a group claiming an association with the legendary revolutionary Tan Malaka, and the social democratic Socialist Party of Indonesia. There is said to be a Maoist current operating underground. Even elements associated with the Communist Party are believed to be active. Several other groups are also active. Perhaps more important is the People's Democratic Party, but it suffered splits and compromised itself by undertaking electoral activity within the framework of bourgeois parties, including Gerindra.[27]

There is a tentative acknowledgment in society that things have become marginally better in economic terms and with regard to democratic change. After Suharto fell, I attended the first legal May Day celebration in Jakarta; it was held on a campus of the University of Indonesia with a few hundred present, half of them students. Today the celebration draws workers in the tens of thousands.[28] The term *reformasi* has been devalued but is still heard, at political rallies and strike meetings, in the streets and the crowded buses. And the millions who think none of this is good enough are at least more able to speak their mind. Such is the legacy of 1998.

CHAPTER 6

Bolivia's Cycle of Revolt: Left-Indigenous Struggle, 2000–2005

Jeffery R. Webber

Introduction

Evo Morales, leader of the Movimiento al Socialismo (Movement Toward Socialism, MAS), was elected president of Bolivia on December 18, 2005, with a historic 54 percent of the popular vote.[1] Not even the "most optimistic [MAS] militants had imagined such a result."[2] The percentage of votes obtained by the MAS exceeded by almost 15 points the top showing of any party since the return of electoral democracy in 1982.[3] Moreover, the electoral turnout was an impressive 85 percent of eligible voters, up 13 percent from the 2002 elections. Morales is the first indigenous president in the republic's history, a particularly salient fact in a country where 62 percent of the population self-identified as indigenous in the 2001 census.[4] As part of a wider shift to the left in Latin American electoral politics since the late 1990s, the government of Evo Morales has drawn both vilification and idolization in the existing literature. To focus exclusively, or even primarily, on the electoral politics of Bolivia's new Left, however, is to miss some of the fundamental social and political dynamics of the current

epoch that are rooted in extraparliamentary social movements with complex histories.

After fifteen years of neoliberal economic restructuring (1985–2000), elitist "pacted democracy" between ideologically indistinguishable political parties,
and the concomitant decomposition of popular movements, left-indigenous
struggle in Bolivia was reborn with a vengeance in the 2000 Cochabamba Water War against the World Bank–driven privatization of water in that city. This
monumental uprising initiated a five-year cycle of rural and urban re-awaken-
ing of the exploited classes and oppressed indigenous majority that gradually
spread throughout most of the country. The rebellions reached their apogee in
the removal of two neoliberal presidents: Gonzalo Sánchez de Lozada, in October 2003, and Carlos Mesa Gisbert, in June 2005. These two moments were
dubbed the "Gas Wars" because of the centrality of the demand to renationalize
the oil and gas industry in Bolivia—the country has South America's second
largest natural gas deposits after Venezuela.

This chapter focuses on the October 2003 Gas War as a prism through
which to analyze the key social forces, ideological currents, and repertories
of revolt at play in the wider left-indigenous insurrectionary cycle of 2000–
2005. The central argument is that during the October Gas War, the largely
informal indigenous working classes of El Alto utilized a dense infrastructure of class struggle to facilitate their leading role in the events. A dialectical
relationship emerged between the rank and file of neighborhood councils
and the formal infrastructure and leadership of the Federación de Juntas
Vecinales de El Alto (Federation of Neighborhood Councils of El Alto,
FEJUVE-El Alto) and the Central Obrera Regional de El Alto (Regional
Workers' Central of El Alto, COR-El Alto). Without the formal structures,
the rank-and-file base would have been unable to coordinate their actions
at a higher scale than their local neighborhoods, while without the self-activity, self-organization, and radical push from the grassroots, the executive
leadership of both El Alto organizations would have been more likely to
engage in the normal processes of negotiation with the state, moderation
of demands, and eventual fracturing and demobilization of the rebellious
movements. Meanwhile, the supportive role played by sectors of the working
class with relatively stable jobs outside the informal economy was facilitated
by the ideological and political orientation of social movement unionism
adopted by the two central organizations of the formal working class: the
Central Obrera Boliviana (Bolivian Workers' Central, COB) and the Feder-

ación Sindical de Trabajadores Mineros de Bolivia (Trade Union Federation of Bolivian Mine Workers, FSTMB).

In addition to working through a complex network of working-class infrastructure—the grassroots neighborhood councils, FEJUVE-El Alto, COR-El Alto, the FSTMB, and the COB—the protests in El Alto drew on the rich popular cultures of resistance and opposition in Bolivian history: indigenous radicalism—associated with migrants from the Aymara *altiplano*—and revolutionary Marxism—associated with the migrants from the tin-mining zones. Both of these traditions had, over decades, left an indelible mark on the popular politics of resistance in the city. These traditions were markedly dense in El Alto but also came to define the protests of September and October 2003 throughout the country more generally.

The *alteño* working classes (i.e. those from El Alto) constituted the most important social force in the insurrection, but depended on alliances with the indigenous peasantry—organized through its own infrastructure of rural class struggle, the Confederación Sindical Única de Trabajadores Campesinos de Bolivia (Bolivian Peasant Trade Union Confederation, CSUTCB), and the Federación Única Departamental de Trabajadores Campesinos de La Paz–Tupaj Katari (Departmental Federation of Peasant Workers of La Paz, FUDTCLP-TK)—the formal working class, and, to a lesser but important extent, sections of the middle class. Social movement leaders effectively employed the call to nationalize gas as a collective-action frame that appealed broadly to peasants, workers, and parts of the middle class. The frame focused on the injustice of poverty in a resource-rich land, the foreign control of the gas industry by multinational corporations, and the long history in Bolivia of colonial and neocolonial abuse related to the extraction of natural resource wealth from the country.

Finally, state repression at various intervals in September and October had the effect of radicalizing the working-class and peasant protests, provoking ruptures within the political elite, and drawing sections of the middle class into the popular movement for change. The Sánchez de Lozada government demonstrated early and sustained reticence for serious negotiation with the mobilized peasantry and urban working classes. Although fierce, the state's repression proved insufficiently strong to destroy the opposition, and thus only fueled an intensified process of political, racial, and class-based polarization in the country. Repression effectively forged new solidarities within those sectors at the receiving end of the state's coercion.

All of these conditions together—a dense infrastructure of class struggle and social movement unionism, oppositional traditions of indigenous and working-class radicalism sustained by El Alto's migrant population, alliances between the informal and formal sectors of the working class, the peasantry, and parts of the middle class, a collective-action framing of gas that appealed broadly to sentiments of the Bolivian populace, and fierce but insufficient levels of state repression—ultimately explain the strength of the massive insurrectionary explosions that forced the resignation of President Sánchez de Lozada on October 17, 2003.

1. A portrait of El Alto

On an average day in the indigenous proletarian city of El Alto, *La Ceja*—the city's commercial heartland—bustles with thousands of women street vendors dressed in traditional Aymara attire—bowler hats, boldly colored *polleras* (gathered skirts), and shawls to protect against the cold winds. Hundreds of minivans, with mainly young boys hanging out of sliding doors yelling destinations and fares to passersby, clog the paved arteries that lead down to the neighboring capital city, La Paz. In September and October 2003, El Alto had features of a revolutionary popular insurrection against a racist and repressive state and the depravities of neoliberal capitalism. Tires burned in the streets, the abundant stalls and fast-food chicken outlets were shut down, and dug-up roadways were made impassable, except by bicycle or foot. El Alto earned its position as the vanguard of left-indigenous struggle in Bolivia and as one of the most rebellious urban locales in contemporary Latin America. Bearing the overwhelming brunt of state repression during the September and October events, *alteño* workers were essential to the overthrow of President Gonzalo Sánchez de Lozada.

The obstacles in the way of working-class collective action in the city were formidable: long workdays; low rates of unionization; heterogeneous work activity and small production units that brought only small numbers of workers together; lack of social protection because of the proliferation of informal jobs; increasing numbers of women and youth in the labor market who had little union experience and knowledge of their rights and were therefore more intensely exploitable; and racist and sexist divisions both within the working class and between the working class and capital and the state. Scholars have pointed out that neoliberal restructuring in Latin

America has caused segmentation and structural heterogeneity within the workforce of the region and the dispersion of workers away from concentrated production sites and stable jobs and into the informal economy. The expansion of the informal economy carries with it structural incentives for informal workers to attempt to solve their problems through individual initiatives rather than through collective action. All of these elements combined act as impediments to class-based collective action.[5] How, then, did El Alto's working classes overcome these structural barriers and take up the leadership of such an impressive series of insurrectionary protests?

1.1 A city of migrant laborers

In a celebrated passage of *The Communist Manifesto*, Marx describes how the advance of industrial capitalism "replaces the isolation of the laborers, due to competition, by their revolutionary combination, due to association." The bourgeoisie, through modern industry, produces its own grave-diggers, the proletarian class, which will eventually overthrow the bourgeois order.[6] In a parallel fashion, Bolivian neoliberalism in many ways is responsible for the creation of El Alto's urban indigenous working-class movement, which subsequently mounted one of the most serious campaigns to bury the neoliberal model in Latin America in the opening years of the millennium. Neoliberalism in Bolivia, by helping to drive dispossessed miners and indigenous peasants into the cauldron of hyperexploitation and insecurity that characterizes the city, nurtured the breeding grounds of what became its most formidable enemy. In this new environment, the revolutionary Marxist traditions of the ex-miners and the insurrectionary heritage of indigenous rural rebellions coalesced in a potent and novel combination of left-indigenous struggle rooted in the complexities of urbanized racial oppression and class exploitation.

Tenuously perched on the edge of the *altiplano*, at over four thousand meters above sea level, El Alto's eastern edge breaks sharply down into the steep hillsides of the expansive basin containing La Paz. The northern neighborhoods are characterized by a greater concentration of Aymara residents, the result of rural-to-urban migration from the *altiplano* departments of La Paz, and to a lesser but still significant degree, Oruro and Potosí. The southern zone is more heterogeneous in sociocultural terms, including, as it does, important neighborhoods with high concentrations of "relocated" ex-miners who are predominantly Quechua. In 2001, 74 percent of *alteños* over the age of fifteen self-identified as Aymara, 6 percent as Quechua, 1 percent as of other indigenous or Afro-Bolivian heritage, and 19 percent as non-indigenous.[7] The city functions as a critical thoroughfare connecting La Paz with the Chilean Pacific coast through the Pan-American Highway that runs through the northern zone. In the southern zone, the Viacha and Oruro-Cochabamba highways carry people and commodities to the towns and rural zones of the *altiplano*, as well as destinations in other departments of the country, such as Oruro and Cochabamba.[8] Blocking roads is one popular repertoire of revolt that can effectively strangle the commerce of the western half of the country when carried out to its full potential, as it has been on several occasions in recent years.[9]

El Alto suffers from an acute lack of adequate housing and basic infrastructure. Simple adobe houses, often constructed with family labor, constitute 77 percent of residential housing in the city. A mere 22 percent of *alteños* can afford to live in brick houses, and 37 percent of households continue to go without access to toilets or latrines.[10] According to official data from the 2001 census, only 7 percent of *alteño* households have all the basic necessities satisfied. El Alto's water utility was privatized in 1999 and handed over to Aguas del Illimani, a private consortium controlled by the French multinational Suez. Almost two hundred thousand residents do not have access to Illimani's water and sewage services because they live outside the "served area" as defined by the contract between Illimani and the Bolivian state. Moreover, an additional seventy thousand *alteños* who live within the perimeters of the served area lack access because they cannot afford the $445 connection fees.[11] Unsurprisingly, in this context social movement struggles have often turned on themes of basic necessities such as access to water and sewage; occasionally, these localized battles are linked to broader political objectives and demands for structural transformation of the state and economy, as was the case in the Gas War of 2003.[12]

In 1950, when El Alto was still a part of La Paz, its population was eleven thousand.[13] Over the next half-century El Alto grew at the relatively rapid rate of 8.2 percent per annum, with an intense growth spurt between 1976 and 1986.[14] In the 1980s, two critical shocks set off a spike in the number of migrants flooding the ranks of El Alto's neighborhoods. The first was a series of El Niño–related droughts between 1982 and 1983 that struck the rural hinterland of the *altiplano* with a vengeance, driving thousands of peasants off their land.[15] The second moment, of course, was the mass firing and "relocation" of tin miners after the privatization of the mines in 1985. By 1992, 405,492 people inhabited the city, increasing to 647,350 by 2001, and a projected 870,000 by 2007 and 943,500 in 2020.[16]

1.2 El Alto's working classes as historical formations

El Alto is a poor city. Official data indicates that, in 2001, 70 percent of the population lived below the poverty line.[17] The structure of the working class in neoliberal El Alto mirrors the broader trends of working-class Bolivian life since the mid-1980s. Thus, 98 percent of the approximately 5,045 production units in industrial manufacturing in the city are small or micro enterprises. The workers employed in such production units constitute 59 percent of workers employed in industrial manufacturing in the city.[18] These jobs are precarious, low-paying, and involve long workdays. Moreover, they do not provide social protection benefits to employees.[19] As table 1 shows, industrial manufacturing constitutes the second most important area of employment for *alteños* and, in particular, *alteño* men. Commerce, restaurants, and hotels employ the most *alteños*, with women predominating in this sector. After these two, in declining order of importance, are social services, construction, and transportation and communications.[20] One consequence of neoliberal restructuring in the city has been "the expansion of a vast reserve army of unemployed or marginally employed people, also conceptualized as an 'informal economy,' from which a few emerge as incipient entrepreneurs but in which the vast majority experience new and old forms of oppression."[21] If the shape and character of the world of work has changed in El Alto as a result of neoliberalism, the working class has not disappeared. In fact, the working classes—defined expansively as those who do not live off the labor of others—have only grown in number.

Table 1: El Alto—Employment by Sector

Sector	Total	Men	Women
Total	276,777	159,389	117,388
Manufacturing Industry	69,799	43,360	26,439
Construction	27,345	26,892	453
Transport and Communications	27,169	26,716	453
Commerce, Restaurants, and Hotels	90,522	26,036	64,486
Social and Community Services	48,220	26,465	21,755
Other Sectors	13,722	9,920	3,802

Source: Rossell Arce and Rojas Callejas, *Ser Productor*, 65.

As has been the case elsewhere in Bolivia and Latin America, the informal sector has been expanding over the last few decades in El Alto at the expense of the formal sector. In 1992, the city's informal sector—excluding the domestic segment—made up an already preponderant 64 percent of the labor market. This percentage increased to 69 percent by 2000.[22] The few large industries that do exist in El Alto have scarcely been subjected to scholarly investigation.[23] What stands out, in any case, is the thinness of the web of large industries in the city. Of the thousands of small production units that exist, activity is focused in textiles, acrylic and natural wool weaving, leather-making, carpentry, metal mechanics, machine making and repairs, shoemaking, and plaster work.[24] Unregulated clandestine tanneries, silver and goldsmithing jewel artisans, machine shops, low-end shoe producers, natural and acrylic wool weavers, and leather-jacket and sports clothing units also proliferate in the *alteño* landscape, alongside street vendors and transport and construction workers.[25] According to the most recent data, of the economically active population (EAP) in El Alto, 41 percent are self-employed workers, 22 percent are manual laborers, and 21 percent are non-manual laborers. Add to these categories domestic servants and non-remunerated family laborers, and one has the contemporary cartography of El Alto's working classes. Together, the working classes constitute 93 percent of the city's EAP. Owners and bosses, together with independent professionals, constitute the remaining 7 percent.[26]

1.3 Political cultures of resistance and opposition

The rich traditions of indigenous radicalism in the rural Aymara *altiplano* and the revolutionary Marxism of the tin miners have left an indelible mark on the popular politics of resistance in contemporary El Alto. Relocated miners and Aymara peasants were inserted into the insecure and exploitative social reality of the urban class structure of the city described above. Migration from the mines or from the countryside is a recurring theme in most *alteños'* recollections of the last twenty years. For example, Roberto de la Cruz, a leading figure in COR-El Alto in October 2003, recalls: "Miners migrated to El Alto, indigenous peasants migrated to El Alto, all in search of work." But the new arrivals to the shantytown often found their hopes for employment and a marginally better life dashed: "Unfortunately, when they arrived they did not find work. As a consequence, since 1985 problems accumulated, necessities accumulated that have never been attended to by the government. At some point this situation had to blow up. That is what occurred when we saw an opportune moment for rebellion in October."[27] Oppositional cultures of resistance competed with other political currents—including populism and neoliberalism—whose agents employed the often effective tools of clientelism to win local elections throughout the 1980s and 1990s.[28] And yet, when economic and state crisis shook Bolivia in the closing years of the 1990s, and left-indigenous struggles began to emerge in waves throughout various rural and urban parts of the country, El Alto's array of neighborhood and community organizations moved away from populism. The period of the Gas War witnessed a remarkable reversal of the depoliticization and fragmentation of working-class and popular indigenous life under neoliberalism, in part through the recovery of historical memories of indigenous and revolutionary Marxist political cultures of resistance and opposition, redefined in light of the new complexities of a radically altered sociopolitical and economic context.

Relocated miners were able to *recreate* and *refashion* their historical memory of the protests, organization, and battles in the mining zones in a way that made them relevant to the challenges and stark realities of an impoverished, cosmopolitan shantytown. In other words, their political organizing in El Alto did not rely on a romantic nostalgia or simplistic longing for the rehabilitation of a past already exhausted.[29] Historical divisions that had often separated mining activists from the rural indigenous peasantry had to be confronted as dispossessed peasants and relocated miners found themselves thrust into the informal working-class froth of El Alto.[30] Many ex-miners began, over time, to recognize and identify politically with their indigenous heritage in a way that was not emphasized in the mines. They began gradually to forge new ties of solidarity with radical indigenous-peasant groups in the neighboring *altiplano* and with ex-peasant Aymara indigenous migrants who had settled in the city.[31] Remarkably, in spite of the despair that migration to El Alto often engendered in the families of ex-miners, their traditions of working-class resistance facilitated the slow rearticulation of their political efficacy through a reconstituted infrastructure of class struggle.

The political impact of rural indigenous migration—and especially Aymara migration—to El Alto has been similar to that of the relocated miners in a number of respects. The most striking facet of the city is that 82 percent of residents describe themselves as indigenous.[32] Politically, this collective indigenous self-identification has expressed itself through the use of the *wiphala* in every major march, demonstration, and strike, and the visible use of *ponchos* by a significant minority of men in protests, as well as the much more prevalent—and daily—use of *polleras* by indigenous women. Remarkably, during the height of the October Gas War, the use of the Aymara language took over the public space in many of the streets of El Alto during different periods of the confrontation: "The people began to speak Aymara in El Alto. . . . They always speak Spanish, but during those days of uprising they began to speak in Aymara, to organize the resistance, the barricades, links between districts, all of this, in Aymara . . . it expressed a sentiment to speak Aymara: 'We are this, we're emancipated, we're rebelling, and we're speaking Aymara. Power speaks Spanish.'"[33]

Like the ex-miners whose lives in El Alto were initially characterized by a deep sense of loss, rural-to-urban indigenous migrants also encountered a city that delivered far below their expectations: "These indigenous sought better opportunities in the cities than they had in the countryside. The reality is that their dreams were not realized, their utopias and illusions about a better life in the city."[34] Like the ex-miners, however, the new indigenous arrivals began to join in collective fights to gain basic services for the city, and eventually to challenge neoliberalism more widely. The indigenous migrants informed these struggles with their histories of rebellion in the rural *altiplano*. "Rural communal syndicalism," Patricia Costas Monje points out, has been important in forging the social movement structures and repertoires of contention in the urban context of El Alto, "above all the [legacy of] the

Aymara emergence in the 1970s. The *katarista* movement (an indigenous movement that linked race and class) has left its mark on the forms of the new scenario of social movements today."[35]

Organizationally, the neighborhood councils of each block, *barrio* (neighborhood), and zone of the city, ascending all the way up to the peak organization of FEJUVE-El Alto, mirror important features of the traditional rural indigenous community structure, the *ayllu*.[36] Little by little, suggests Aymara *alteño* sociologist Pablo Mamani Ramírez, the city of El Alto has become a pivotal urban reference point for the indigenous population of the *altiplano* and Bolivia as a whole. It embodies the reality of urban indigenous working-class social relations in a context of sharp racism and the indigenous traditions of struggle that have been adapted from the countryside within that context.[37] For Mamani Ramírez, it is evident that the popular neighborhoods of El Alto are places where the communitarian organization and collective logics of reciprocity and resistance of the rural *ayllus* and mining zones have been revitalized within a distinct urban context.[38]

2. El Alto's infrastructure of class struggle

El Alto's dense web of informal and formal associational networks help to explain how the oppositional political cultures of the ex-miners and rural indigenous migrants were sustained beneath the surface throughout much of the 1980s and 1990s and how collective capacities for indigenous proletarian class struggle were unleashed as left-indigenous protest began its ascent across the country beginning in 2000.[39] The historical memory of the miners and rural indigenous were maintained as "living legacies of discussion and debate" and were rebuilt, refashioned, and strengthened through "engagement in new struggles."[40] Despite the decline in the rate of unionization and the informalization of the world of work, alternative associational fabric in the communities of El Alto provided space for the slow rearticulation and transformation of these historical memories. The dense infrastructure of class struggle in El Alto was the most important factor behind the incredible strength and militancy of the October 2003 and May–June 2005 Gas Wars. From the often invisible networks at the neighborhood level to the peak functional and territorial associations of the working classes in the city—COR-El Alto and FEJUVE-El Alto—the urban infrastructure was able to mobilize, articulate, and sustain the militant rebellion against class exploitation, racial oppression, and imperialism. COR-El Alto and FEJUVE-El Alto managed to unite community class struggle for basic services with the wide-reaching political demands of the indigenous working classes of the city. The protests were able to go as far as they did because COR-El Alto and FEJUVE-El Alto also built alliances with radicalized peasants of the *altiplano* and the peak national organization of the formal working class, the COB, and of the miners, the FSTMB.

At the base level, the most important formal community infrastructures organized on a territorial basis are the hundreds of *juntas vecinales*, or neighborhood councils, which are then articulated vertically into the citywide FEJUVE-El Alto.[41] On a functional basis, small-scale street vendors and market vendors are organized into associations of their own to protect their economic and political interests. Those workers that have been able to unionize their workplaces or maintain preexisting unions are affiliated to COR-El Alto at the federation level in the city and to the COB at the national level. These various associations and federations represent the formal infrastructure of class struggle in El Alto. Within and around them exists a complex myriad of dynamic and often invisible informal community and workplace social networks that reinforce the capacities of the formal infrastructure.

2.1. FEJUVE-El Alto

The structure of FEJUVE-El Alto today brings together representatives of all the districts of El Alto. An executive committee (EC) made up of twenty-nine secretaries is elected every two years during an ordinary congress of the federation. The results of the election must then be recognized by the Bolivian confederation of neighborhood councils CONALJUVE.[42] The EC provides leadership to FEJUVE-El Alto; ultimately, however, its mandate derives from the ordinary congresses held every two years. These congresses define the strategic objectives of the federation. Four delegates from every neighborhood council in El Alto, elected through neighborhood assemblies, participate in the ordinary congresses.[43] Extraordinary congresses are more regular gatherings that are called by the EC to address specific agendas. *Ampliados*, or general meetings, in which the presidents of each neighborhood council must participate, are convened by the EC on a monthly basis in periods of relative political dormancy. In emergency periods of intense political engagement, they can be held at any juncture to address issues that require urgent attention.

Lastly, the EC itself meets at least every two weeks to coordinate the activities of the various secretaries.[44]

At the base level, neighborhood assemblies are convened on a weekly or monthly basis, depending on the neighborhood and the political period. At these gatherings, organized by the leadership of each neighborhood council, rank-and-file *alteños* express their immediate needs and desires, strategize on how best to address them, and voice their criticisms and/or support for the more general direction being taken by the EC of FEJUVE-El Alto.[45] Presidents of each neighborhood council are then expected to articulate the views of the rank and file to the EC of FEJUVE-El Alto and other neighborhood council presidents at the extraordinary congresses and *ampliados* in which they participate on a regular basis.

Each neighborhood council, in order to be recognized by FEJUVE-El Alto, must represent various zones in the city that together contain more than two hundred residents. These local-level councils have in some ways acted as an alternative organizing infrastructure for workers in El Alto who are unlikely to work in a unionized workplace through which they can effectively organize as workers, given the obstacles that have been highlighted above. Membership in neighborhood councils is based on ownership or rental of a housing unit in an *alteño* neighborhood. Each family or household sends one delegate to attend neighborhood assemblies as their representative; each household representative shares the same duties and obligations at these assemblies.[46] The patriarchal gender dynamics in the majority of homes in the city are such that men are over-represented at all levels in the process, from the neighborhood assemblies all the way to the EC of FEJUVE-El Alto. In the EC established in 2004, for example, only ten of the twenty-nine elected members were women. Each neighborhood council has its own EC with a number of secretaries. These committees coordinate the day-to-day activities of their councils but receive their mandates from the neighborhood assemblies and are expected to reflect the wishes of the rank and file when they represent them at the extraordinary congresses and *ampliados*.[47]

2.2. COR-El Alto

While the depth and breadth of industrialization in Bolivia was always limited, the bulk of industrial manufacturing that did exist in the department of La Paz became increasingly concentrated in the shantytown of El Alto be-

ginning in the late 1960s and early 1970s. This industrial activity, in addition
to expanding working-class formation in various other sectors of the growing shantytown's economy, allowed for the gradual emergence of a series of
labor federations created by workers to defend their immediate material interests as well as the interests of the Bolivian working classes more generally.

The Federación de Trabajadores, Gremiales, Artesanos y Comerciantes
Minoristas (Federation of Organized Workers, Artisans, Small Traders and
Food Sellers of the city of El Alto, FTGACM) was established in 1970, for
example. The Federación de Trabajadores de Carne (Federation of Butchers)
and the Federación de Panificadores (Bakers' Federation) created the Confederación Única de Trabajadores de El Alto (Workers' Confederation of El
Alto, CUTAL) in 1987.[48] In 1988, CUTAL became COR-El Alto, and the
latter was recognized in the same year by the COB at its Seventh Ordinary
Congress. Today, COR-El Alto is a sectorally based organization that seeks
to represent various components of El Alto's working classes. It includes
under its umbrella the FTGACM, the Federation of Market Traders, and a
number of trade unions.[49]

COR-El Alto's executive committee is structured similarly to FEJUVE-El
Alto. There are twenty-seven secretaries in the committee who are elected in
a Congreso Orgánico (Organic Congress), in which representatives from all
the affiliated federations, associations, and trade unions participate. Among
COR-El Alto's founding principles is the continuous struggle for the interests
of El Alto's working class.[50] Because the workers' organization conceives of
those interests in an expansive manner, it was able to form alliances with the
territorially based FEJUVE-El Alto and to participate in high-profile social
movements for basic public welfare in the city. As a consequence, COR-El
Alto was pivotal in cementing ties between community-based social movements and union-based struggle in El Alto during the left-indigenous struggle between 2000 and 2005.

2.3. Dialectics of popular power

Over the course of September and October 2003, and especially between
October 8 and 17, left-indigenous popular sectors of El Alto reinvented
and extended the assemblist and participatory forms of democratic power
from below that we earlier witnessed in the Cochabamba War of 2000 and,
in rural form, during the 2000 and 2001 Aymara peasant insurrections.

FEJUVE-El Alto and COR-El Alto became the peak institutional expressions and ultimate coordinators of the popular rebellion and incipient manifestations of collective self-government of the oppressed and exploited in one city. The state was temporarily replaced in El Alto by the popular sovereignty of the indigenous informal proletarian residents, organized at the highest level in FEJUVE-El Alto and COR-El Alto, but also at the base through spontaneous committees of various sorts, neighborhood assemblies, and the long-established network of roughly five hundred neighborhood councils. A complex dialectic between spontaneous mass actions from below, led and organized by the rank and file, and the higher-scale, citywide leadership and infrastructure of FEJUVE-El Alto and COR-El Alto, made possible the heroic challenge to neoliberal capitalism and racist oppression during the Gas War.

Most activists and scholars agree that FEJUVE-El Alto and COR-El Alto were the most important formal social movement organizations in the city during this period.[51] Yet it would be profoundly misleading to give the impression that the executive leaderships of these two social movement organizations simply issued decrees to which the rank and file subsequently responded. Mamani Ramírez, having lived through the events of October 2003, has made some of the most penetrating observations about how rank-and-file activists in the neighborhood councils and other informal networks often overtook and outpaced the leadership of FEJUVE-El Alto and COR-El Alto.[52]

Every urban space that was occupied by the radicalized residents of the shantytown was eventually governed through neighborhood councils and self-organized "committees in defense of gas," "strike committees," and "self-defense committees."[53] Plazas, although they were often sites of state repression and violence, also became open spaces of organizing neighborhood resistance, deliberating, and deciding collectively on strategies, tactics, and visions of change. Emergency neighborhood assemblies were convened by the leaderships of neighborhood councils and committees in defense of gas to decide on immediate actions, such as blocking an avenue or preparing for an imminent incursion by the military into the neighborhood. Regular nightly assemblies in the plazas were more reflective spaces in which the indigenous informal working-class residents could review the events of the day, evaluate their strategies of resistance, and plan for future actions. As state repression intensified, the leaders of neighborhood councils were often forced to operate in a clandestine fashion, thereby providing even greater space for the constant renewal of informal leaderships at the neighborhood level and more important roles for the self-organized strike committees and committees of other types.[54] These spontaneous grassroots formations can be understood as the informal infrastructure of the rank and file. The very self-organization and self-activity of the mass base of rank-and-file indigenous proletarians of the city through preexisting informal networks is what *strengthened* and *enabled* the dynamism of the formal structures of FEJUVE-El Alto and COR-El Alto and made the rebellion possible.[55]

3. Infrastructure of the formal working class and social movement unionism

What made the older organizational structures of the FSTMB and the COB critical allies in the struggle, despite the dramatic trends in the informalization of the Bolivian world of work over the previous two decades, was their strategic orientation toward social movement unionism. Most important, in this regard, was their perspective of reaching out to all of the oppressed, struggling for the working classes and the peasantry as a whole, rather than for the particular interests of the minority of the working classes who remained formally employed in the opening years of the twenty-first century.[56]

The FSTMB similarly embraced social movement unionism. The miners had always stressed that their struggle was part of the struggle for all of the working classes and the oppressed rather than simply being about improving the material well-being of their own sector's membership. Such a politics is evident in a representative FSTMB communiqué released immediately after the overthrow of Gonzalo Sánchez de Lozada on October 17, 2003. In it, the miners clarify what the objectives of the FSTMB had been during the Gas War: the nationalization of hydrocarbons; the renationalization of all the state-owned enterprises privatized throughout the 1990s; the abrogation of the 1996 Agrarian Reform Law because it subjected indigenous and peasant land and territory to the laws of the market; the egalitarian redistribution of land and defense of the collective rights of indigenous communities to land and territory; the restitution of the social rights of Bolivian workers eroded over the years of neoliberal restructuring; rejection of Bolivian participation in the proposed Free Trade Area of the Americas (FTAA); and the refusal to grant immunity to those in government—the "butchers of October"—who were behind the high levels of state repression in September and October.[57]

The COB and the FSTMB helped to organize and coordinate the struggle at a larger scale than would have been possible if El Alto's infrastructure of class struggle had remained in isolation. The COB was a vital public face for left-indigenous struggle in these months, gaining wide exposure in the media and articulating a series of revolutionary positions. The COB and FSTMB were able to mobilize large numbers of formal sector workers during the Gas War and contributed to the militant energy of the mass demonstrations in which they participated. Finally, the miners carried with them into the cycle of protests their long-standing cultural association with the Bolivian revolutionary Left. Thus, even when they did not contribute the largest number of protesters, the symbolic impact of their participation was frequently enormous.

4. Narrative of the Gas War: Dialectics of state repression and mass radicalization

This section provides an analytical narrative of the Gas War, focusing on the dialectics of state repression and mass radicalization. It highlights the key social forces involved at various stages in the Gas War, key turning points in the months of September and October, and the escalation of protest demands over time, particularly following central moments of state repression.

At the outset of September 2003, the popularity of Gonzalo Sánchez de Lozada's administration was in steep decline. In an urban poll of residents of Cochabamba, El Alto, La Paz, and Santa Cruz, 70 percent of respondents disapproved of the government's record during its first year in office. A remarkable 84 percent of residents of El Alto held this view.[58] The future of natural gas development in Bolivia had already deeply penetrated popular political discussions in the streets and countryside and continued to be a contentious subject in the halls of Congress as well.[59] The state-owned natural gas and oil company, YPFB, was privatized in 1996. Under the administration of ex-dictator Hugo Bánzer (1997–2001), a deal was then initiated between the Bolivian state and the Spanish-British-US energy consortium Pacific LNG and San Diego–based Sempra Energy. Under the proposed arrangement, natural gas would be exported through a Chilean port to markets in Mexico and the Californian coast of the United States. A year after the start of his second mandate as president in 2002, Sánchez de Lozada sought to close the gas export deal, contributing a focal point and unifying issue to the left-indigenous social forces in insurrection during September and October 2003.[60]

The idea of using a Chilean port to export gas was provocative to Bolivian nationalist sentiments across the political spectrum, which have long sustained an antipathy toward Chile, rooted in the latter's annexation of Bolivia's coastline during the Pacific War of the late 1870s and early 1880s. However, much more important than basic resentment of Chile's nineteenth-century foreign relations was a profound sense that since natural gas had been privatized in 1996, the resource had been pillaged by transnational corporations with little to no benefit accruing to the Bolivian population. Re-establishing Bolivian social control over natural gas—and other natural resources—soon was understood by left-indigenous movements as the only way to avoid the cruel repetition of hundreds of years of exploitation of domestic natural resources—silver and tin historically—and of the laborers used by capital to extract them.

4.1. Indigenous–peasant revolt and urban tremors in September

The Aymara peasants of the western *altiplano* were the first to act.[61] The initial "insurrectionary energy" of the 2003 rebellions emerged from the overwhelmingly Aymara indigenous province of Omasuyos, next to Lake Titicaca, and close to the country's capital city.[62] They mobilized initially around a list of demands including broad anti-neoliberal themes as well as more specific conjunctural issues relating both to their sector's economic interests and to defending their collective right to indigenous self-government. Under the leadership of Felipe Quispe, the CSUTCB was central to articulating this peasant mobilization, as was the FUDTCLP-TK, led by Rufo Calle.[63]

A peasant march on September 8, 2003, from the community of Batallas to El Alto, was the first mobilization of the Gas War and had as its principal aim the release of community leader Edwin Huampu. Coinciding with the Aymara peasant convergence on El Alto was a civic strike in the city organized by FEJUVE-El Alto and COR-El Alto against new municipal legislation, *maya y paya*, that would have increased taxes on building and home construction.[64] Two days later, on September 10, with no government response to their demands forthcoming, CSUTCB and FUDTCLP-TK militants, with the help of *jilaqatas* and *mama t'allas* (male and female traditional authorities) from the Aymara peasant communities of the rural provinces of La Paz, initiated a hunger strike in the auditorium of the Aymara-language radio station in El Alto, Radio San Gabriel. The most pressing objective continued to be Huampu's release, but the strikers also opposed a number of neoliberal agricultural policies, the FTAA, and the export of natural gas through Chile.[65] The hunger strike quickly garnered the support and solidarity of several other urban and rural popular organizations, including the COB, and plans to erect roadblocks in the *altiplano* were finalized. *Cocaleros* (coca farmers) of the Yungas and the Chapare regions expressed their solidarity with peasant actions developing in the *altiplano*.[66] In a grim foreshadowing of the repression that was to follow shortly, President Sánchez de Lozada and Minister of Defense Jose Carlos Sánchez Berzaín proclaimed that order would be restored and maintained in the country and that the armed forces were prepared to act.[67] Two days later, the national police and armed forces were deployed at various points in the *altiplano*.[68] By mid-September peasants, teachers, the working-class organizations of El Alto, university students, the COB, and others were radicalizing and announcing protest actions to come. In the face of these conflicts, the government once again emphasized that it would maintain order and the rule of law through the use of the armed forces.[69]

4.2. The collective frame of gas

By this stage it had become clear that the future of natural gas development was the overarching frame tying each movement to the others.[70] The so-called Estado Mayor del Pueblo (Peoples' High Command, EMP) played a role in articulating a more lucid position on this matter, from which the various social movements could draw.[71] The Coordinadora and the MAS were instrumental in calling for a national day of protest in defense of gas, to be held on Friday, September 19. COR-El Alto and FEJUVE-El Alto immediately responded to the call and announced that they would lead mass marches on La Paz from El Alto on the national day of action.[72] The Aymara peasantry of the *altiplano* and the *cocaleros* of the Yungas also pledged that there would be coordinated marches in solidarity with the call for mobilizations in defense of gas.[73] The COB likewise promised to lead a march later on the same day in La Paz.[74] Again, the government responded by reciting its mandate to maintain order and the rule of law. Operatives of the Grupo Especial de Seguridad (Special Security Group, GES) and reinforcements of police troops were deployed to Cochabamba.[75]

Roberto de la Cruz directed sharp words at the president: "Gas will be the mother of all battles, if the gringo government insists on selling off our hydrocarbons at the price of a dead chicken."[76] Morales likewise told the press that "If Goni decides to give gas away to Chile this government will not last 24 hours. We are going to strike and blockade until we recover the gas."[77] Here we can begin to appreciate the call to nationalize gas as the fundamental collective-action frame during the insurrectional episodes of September and October. As Álvaro García Linera puts it, "There is a sort of collective intuition that the debates over hydrocarbons [natural gas and oil] are gambling with the destiny of this country, a country accustomed to having a lot of natural resources but always being poor, always seeing natural resources serve to enrich others."[78] The "injustice" of the frame is clearly delineated: being poor in a resource-rich land. The "us" included the indigenous popular classes struggling for a socially just development model. The structural significance of natural gas to the political economy of Bolivia made the strategic frame materially plausible and accounted for its wide resonance throughout the country.[79] The "them" identified included the transnational gas corporations that formed part of the energy consortium Pacific LNG (Repsol-YPF, British Gas, and Pan American Energy), the neoliberal model personified in the presidency of Sánchez de Lozada, and US imperialism writ large. Finally, the pathways of change advocated by the frame to overcome the injustice it evoked eventually involved the ousting of the neoliberal president and the nationalization of gas. "All of a sudden," one of Bolivia's finest journalists observed, "gas is on the lips of everyone. The unions, popular meetings, congresses, communities, blockades and spontaneous reunions like those in [Plaza] San Francisco" have developed their opposition to the sale of gas under the neoliberal framework as a unifying cause.[80] In the event, the day of national protest in defense of gas was a major success.

4.3. State massacre in Warisata
and the radicalization of left-indigenous struggle

The protests of September 19 demonstrated that while the Aymara peasantry had started the cycle of insurrection known as the Gas War of 2003, by late September El Alto had become the new fulcrum of popular mobilization in the country.[81] FEJUVE-El Alto and COR-El Alto coordinated roadblocks of the principal routes connecting La Paz to El Alto. Schools were shut down, the streets of the city were completely barricaded, and stores and street vendors ceased operations. Thousands of *alteño* marchers snaked their way down the La Paz hillsides to join the large concentrations of people in the Plaza San Francisco. The columns of protesters from El Alto were met in La Paz by teachers, factory workers, peasants, truckers, street vendors, health care workers, and pensioners.[82] The COB let it be known that it would be holding an emergency National Assembly on October 1 in Huanuni, in the department of Oruro, where strategic discussion over a possible general strike and coordinated nationwide campaign of roadblocks would occur.[83] The basis of an insurrectionary alliance led by the largely informal working classes of El Alto, and supported by the peasantry, the formal working class, and sections of the middle class, was beginning to emerge. New levels of state coercion soon acted as the spark that consolidated these forces.

The first shock of state repression since the *impuestazo* of February 2003—the police insurrection and popular rebellion against an IMF-imposed income tax increase on salaried workers—radicalized social movements. On September 20, military troops invaded Warisata and began killing indigenous community members.[84] Rather than suppress the movements of September, this moment of state repression extended, deepened, and radicalized left-indigenous struggle both within the rural Aymara zone where the killing took place, and, crucially, in El Alto over the next couple of weeks. By mid-October, protests, road blockades, hunger strikes, and militant clashes with the military and police forces rocked huge swathes of the country and precipitated the resignation of Gonzalo Sánchez de Lozada. In the context of September and October 2003, the deaths caused by state repression "evoked a feeling of unity, of solidarity, of identification with those abused by power."[85]

The Comisión de Derechos Humanos de la Cámara de Diputados (Human Rights Commission of the Chamber of Deputies, CDHCD), the Asamblea Permanente de Derechos Humanos de Bolivia (Permanent Assembly of Human Rights of Bolivia, APDHB), and the opposition parties within Congress criticized the government for causing the violence against the activists on the road blockades and for not privileging dialogue with the peasant leadership. Evo Morales directly accused the minister of defense, Sánchez Berzaín, of being one of those principally responsible for the indiscriminate use of force.[86] In response, the government simply ratcheted up its rhetoric in defense of law and order. Sánchez de Lozada told the nation that his government would not accede to social pressures and would proceed to take down immediately any blockade of highways, in any part of the country, erected under any pretext.[87]

Felipe Quispe of CSUTCB, still on hunger strike in El Alto, offered an immediate and scathing condemnation of the military incursion in Warisata. He said that negotiations between CSUTCB and the minister of agriculture, Guido Áñez, and the vice-minister of government, José Luis Harb, had been proceeding but now had to be abandoned because of the peasant massacre.[88] "The government extends one hand to us and with the other kills our brothers," said Quispe.[89] Almost immediately, the CSUTCB alerted Bolivians that the peasant organization was in a state of emergency, and blockades were erected in several provinces in the department of La Paz: Río Abajo, Ingavi, Muñecas, Inquisivi, and Pacajes.[90] Rural Aymara-language radio stations served the same purpose as the radical miners' stations had in an earlier era of Bolivian history. Four times daily, the Aymara community radio stations transmitted the resolutions of the different meetings occurring in different communities and the strategic and tactical positions being promoted by the CSUTCB based on these rank-and-file community assemblies. This was the principal means through which ordinary peasants learned of the twists and turns of the struggle as it developed in September.[91]

Recalling this period almost two years later, the October 2003 leaders of FEJUVE-El Alto and COR-El Alto remembered the Warisata massacre as a turning point in the radicalization of the first Gas War. Mauricio Cori, executive secretary of FEJUVE-El Alto at the time, told me that repression in the *altiplano* and the deaths in Warisata in particular enraged the residents of El Alto. In his view, the alliances forged between Felipe Quispe and CSUTCB and the social organizations of El Alto, such as FEJUVE-El Alto, were crucial in articulating an immediate popular response that demonstrated the popular sentiment of the time.[92] The leadership of COR-El Alto felt the same way. Roberto de la Cruz described how the popular movement demands in this period evolved from the nationalization of gas to the resignation of Sánchez de Lozada because of the intensification of repressive tactics on the part of the state: "If Goni hadn't left there would have been civil war, because the people were calling for civil war."[93] Finally, the archival research I conducted in the offices of the COB and FSTMB shows that both of these union federations quickly expressed their solidarity with the peasantry in the wake of the Warisata deaths and took measures to condemn publicly and to mobilize against the state's repressive tactics.[94] Only four days after the events in Warisata, for example, the COB convened an emergency National Assembly in Huanuni. At the assembly, the COB condemned the repression of indigenous peasants in the *altiplano* by the armed forces and police. The workers who had assembled in Huanuni agreed to support "the struggle that peasant comrades are sustaining, and other sectors of the workforce in the country, against a political system that has lost popular support."[95] In short, state repression had only fueled the fire.

4.4. The formal working class steps in

Immediately after the Warisata killings, President Sánchez de Lozada's approval rating fell to 9 percent.[96] From this point forward, the largely informal working classes of El Alto became the indubitable vanguard of left-indigenous struggle in the country, articulated most forcefully through FEJUVE-El Alto and COR-El Alto. While secondary to the informal proletarians of El Alto, the formal working class played an essential supporting role in the insurrectionary alliance. It is important not to minimize, as many scholarly and journalistic accounts have, the strategic importance of the actions of the miners, organized in the FSTMB, and the only nationwide confederation of workers, the COB.

Early in the conflict, on September 12, the COB had already released a "Program of Struggle," from which the wider movement of the indigenous peasantry and informal working classes was able to draw.[97] The program called for the abrogation of the existing Hydrocarbons Law and the nationalization and industrialization of natural gas for the benefit of the Bolivian popular classes. It stressed how recovering natural gas from the transnationals had become a historical imperative in the current Bolivian conjuncture, and a central facet of restoring sovereignty and dignity for Bolivians. The document also demanded that Bolivia not participate in the proposed Free Trade of the Americas. On the domestic front, it called for the restoration of job stability and employment creation and the end of labor flexibilization policies. It demanded increases in public spending on health and education, the strengthening of public universities, and the cessation of the privatization of higher education. The workers' organization defended the Public University of El Alto's right to autonomy, a key demand of the university's student federation. The program also demanded that the state reinsert itself in the productive processes of the economy and in the mining sector in particular. The COB pledged to defend the existing social security system and demanded further improvements in this area, along with better pensions.[98]

The COB's program also defended the collective rights to land and territory of landless peasants and indigenous communities throughout Bolivia. It rejected the politics of coca eradication and defended the right to grow and sell the coca leaf and derivative products, a vital issue for indigenous peasantries in the Chapare and Yungas regions. The COB rejected the commodification and private management of water. Instead, the workers' central, following the lead of the social movements behind the Cochabamba Water War, called for the nationalization of and social control over water resources throughout the country. It also demanded the nationalization of the mines, and all the strategic state-owned enterprises that had been privatized in the 1990s: YPFB, ENFE, ENTEL, COMIBOL, LAB, and others. Furthermore, the COB demanded jobs for the unemployed, and rejected any tax increases that targeted the working classes. Finally, the Program of Struggle denounced the criminalization of protest and defended direct action and popular mobilization as a basic democratic right.[99]

In terms of concrete action, the COB called for an indefinite general strike and a nationwide campaign of road blockades to begin on September 29.[100] On October 2, 2003, the workers' confederation made its most important intervention in the September-October Gas War. It convened an open assembly in the Plaza San Francisco with the largest turnout yet of any gathering, during almost a month of growing rural and urban discontent.[101] The crowds at the assembly unified around the call for the nationalization of gas, but also for the first time consolidated the demand for the resignation of Sánchez de Lozada.[102] Gas and the president's resignation were now the centripetal axes of revolt.

5. ¡El Alto de pie! El Alto on its feet!
Democratic insurgency, state repression, and elite fractures

The beginning of the second week of October 2003 witnessed the efflorescence of grassroots insurgency in El Alto, vicious state repression, and the first major fissures inside the ruling bloc. This period of wide-scale revolt began with the civic strike in El Alto on October 8, the third such strike since the beginning of September. Streets were closed down. Public institutions and private businesses were shut down. There was virtually no circulation of traffic. Fierce clashes between the national police and armed forces on one side and activists on the other shook the shantytown with tear gas, gun fire (from state forces), dynamite, rocks, and clubs. At the end of the day, two civilian protesters had suffered bullet wounds, and many others had been injured by rubber bullets. The *autopista* highway connecting La Paz to El Alto was blockaded and full of people preventing traffic flow in either direction.[103] When eight hundred miners arrived from Huanuni, they announced that they would convulse the cities of El Alto and La Paz the following day.[104] Elsewhere in the country old mobilizations were sustained and new ones sprung to life. A miner and another protester were killed the next day, October 9. The government's response to the conflicts of that day trod familiar ground. A visibly angry Sánchez de Lozada addressed a press conference in La Paz. He stressed that the social mobilizations in the country were entirely lacking in legitimacy, and that, moreover, they were being led by "a minority who wants to divide Bolivia" and to destroy democracy in the country.[105]

El Alto's protests continued.[106] The city's avenues were so tightly locked down with the blockades and barricades by the third day of the strike that scarcely a bicycle could traverse through them. Basic foodstuffs and natural gas were becoming scarce in La Paz after more than three weeks of social protests across the country.[107] That Sánchez de Lozada had to go was clear to all the insurgent groups. FEJUVE-El Alto, COR-El Alto, the COB, the FSTMB, and the CSUTCB pledged publicly to refuse sector-by-sector negotiations with the government.[108] Felipe Quispe pointed out that Sánchez de Lozada "is not only an American gringo, but a butcher," while Jaime Solares of the COB argued: "It no longer makes sense to talk with someone who is rejected by the people. The workers want him to leave government."[109]

On October 11, following an attempt by a caravan of military troops to break the human barricade around the Senkata petroleum plant in El Alto, the armed forces shot indiscriminately into the crowds and surrounding neighborhoods, gunning down men, women, children, and the elderly in the process. Chants of "Goni, Assassin!" erupted in response.[110] But the violence merely intensified over the next two days. By some accounts there were twenty-six deaths on October 12, including one soldier.[111]

Salvaging the existing government had become an impossible task for the ruling class. The role of state repression in undermining the legitimacy of the government was once again underlined. A series of cracks in the governing coalition were pried open, the levels of self-organization, self-activity, and mass mobilization of the *alteño* working classes developed further, and, within a short period, sections of the middle class were drawn to the side of the popular struggle. From the perspective of the left-indigenous popular movements, the government was beyond redemption. As one journalist reported, "The number of deaths grows. All the fears of previous days are transformed into rage."[112] The state violence exacted in El Alto "had opened an abyss between government and society annulling any possibility of negotiation," according to García Linera. "It was no longer important what Sánchez de Lozada offered, he was no longer a morally valid interlocutor."[113]

Explosive state violence and popular resistance persisted throughout the next day, October 13. Bread and meat were scarce in La Paz, and downtown in the capital, vehicular traffic was almost nonexistent. As one hundred thousand marchers from El Alto descended through the working-class hillside neighborhoods of La Paz, large numbers of residents applauded, while others joined the march.[114] Protesters came within three blocks of the Plaza Murillo once they had reached the core of La Paz. They sang the national anthem in an effort to persuade the rank and file of the armed forces to join the struggle against the state.[115] Ultimately, the protesters were convinced by soldiers not to attempt to enter the Plaza Murillo because the armed forces were under orders to use lethal force if such an attempt were made.[116] Wide-scale civil resistance endured in El Alto in the face of another wave of state crackdown. Juan Melendres, of COR-El Alto, and Mauricio Cori, of FEJUVE-El Alto, promised that *alteños* would continue their struggle until the regime of Sánchez de Lozada was ousted from power.[117]

The first visible signs of elite rupture surfaced. Vice-President Carlos Mesa appeared on television saying that his conscience would not allow him to support the government as it implemented a policy of repression and death. Mesa did not resign from his position as vice-president, however. Jorge Torres, minister of economic development, did resign, and the widely respected ex-ombudsperson, Ana María Romero, strongly criticized the government for the violence it was perpetrating against civilians and demanded that the president leave office. José Luis Paredes—the mayor of El Alto and a prominent member of the Movimiento Izquierda Revolucionaria (Revolutionary Left Movement, MIR), which was an integral part of Sánchez de Lozada's governing coalition—added his voice to those calling for the president's resignation.[118] In a derisive response to these splits in his government and the widening disgust with his policies within elite and middle-class circles of public opinion, Sánchez de Lozada appeared on television on the evening of October 13 and denounced the protesters as seditious enemies of democracy. He vowed, in turn, to continue to protect democracy.[119] The US embassy was the last pillar in Sánchez de Lozada's shrinking pool of allies. Richard Boucher, spokesperson for the State Department, stated, "The international community and the United States will not tolerate any kind of interruption in the constitutional order and will not recognize any regime that emerges as a result of anti-democratic procedures."[120]

Meanwhile, the state had lost all control over El Alto. Beneath the waves of repression between October 10 and 17, a collective sentiment of resistance radiated throughout the neighborhoods of the city. Bonds of solidarity and coordination between adjacent neighborhood councils, districts, and zones of El Alto were created. Virtually every space in the city was occupied and controlled by neighborhood councils, in near-constant confrontation with the state.[121] A number of radio stations and TV channels assisted in mass-based coordination from below. These included the reporting and call-in program on Radio Televisión Popular (Popular Radio Television, RTP) and the radio stations Red Erbol and Radio San Gabriel.[122] As the strength of left-indigenous social forces grew and consolidated, the *alteño* working classes began to mirror a process Marx identified as "revolutionary practice."[123] In their struggle to satisfy their needs, the rank and file of the left-indigenous movements came increasingly to recognize their common interests and become conscious of their own social power; through their self-activity they came to see themselves as subjects capable of altering the structures of Bolivian society as well as changing themselves in the process through self-organization and self-activity from below.

The events of the first two weeks of October set the stage for the final mass mobilizations that would topple Sánchez de Lozada's government on October 17. The new strength of middle-class protest at this stage helped set the agenda of what would come after.

6. Middle-class moment: Goni's resignation

In stark contradistinction to the indigenous working-class and peasant protagonists of the uprising in El Alto and the *altiplano*, the sections of the middle class that joined the opposition on October 15 were morally opposed to the repressive tactics of Sánchez de Lozada but desired nothing more than his resignation and a smooth constitutional succession of power to then vice-president Carlos Mesa. This political line overlapped precisely with the position taken in preceding days and weeks by Evo Morales and the MAS. By October 15, the time for negotiations had long since passed for those in opposition to the government. With sixty-seven civilians dead and over four hundred injured in September and October under his watch, Sánchez de Lozada had lost all moral legitimacy.[124] Influential middle-class figures, evoking the memory of mining women in the struggle for democracy against the dictatorship of Hugo Bánzer (1971–78), initiated a hunger strike in La Paz in repudiation of state violence.[125] The hunger strike, organized in the Iglesia Las Carmelitas church, was led by Ana María Romero and brought together a range of well-known intellectuals, artists, religious figures, businesspeople, and human rights activists.[126] The hunger strikers organized their action under the framework of "no more death" and called for peaceful actions by protesters, constitutional succession, and the restoration of the rule of law.[127]

Large demonstrations defined the next two days. A massive march on October 16, led by FEJUVE-El Alto and COR-El Alto, descended once again from El Alto into La Paz, converging with the congregated masses in the Plaza San Francisco. Over three hundred thousand protesters gathered.[128] Evo Morales reiterated the position of the MAS in support of a constitutional exit. "This is the moment to rescue Bolivia from the economic, political and social crises," he told the media. "We are not going to negotiate as long as Gonzalo Sánchez de Lozada continues as President and we support the constitutional succession of Carlos Mesa."[129] Mesa himself reappeared on television ratifying his decision to distance himself from the government without rescinding his position as vice-president of the country; thus his succession to the presidency in the event of Sánchez de Lozada's resignation was becoming a clearer possibility.[130] Mesa's rhetoric appealed to the middle class. "I am not with the philosophy that reasons of state justify death," he told the nation. "But neither am I with the radical banners that the moment has arrived to destroy everything in order to construct a utopia that nobody wants or knows where it is going."[131]

The position of the oppositional sectors of the middle class, the MAS, and Carlos Mesa gathered momentum and, with no clear political alternative to the left of this new coalition, Mesa, the MAS, and the oppositional middle class were able to establish sway over the popular movement. Sánchez Berzaín appeared on television and without irony declared that there was no sense in being against the government because the protesters had lost the battle—"they have no possibility of winning."[132] Gonzalo Sánchez de Lozada appeared on CNN that evening and stated that he enjoyed the support of two-thirds of Bolivians.[133] But in the real world, the tide had turned decisively against the government.[134] The US embassy and a fraction of the political elite were all that remained behind the president. García Linera argues that from October 16 forward there was no longer a government, in effect, and that therefore it was only a question of hours before Sánchez de Lozada resigned or the country erupted into civil war. The intervention of the middle classes had shifted the balance of social forces in favor of resignation and constitutional succession. The masses were united in their absolute resistance to the neoliberal state. They were able to paralyze that state, but had no alternative project with which to replace it. Thus the stage was cast for Mesa to take up the minimum program of the insurgent indigenous proletarians and peasants—the resignation of Sánchez de Lozada, the convocation of a Constituent Assembly, and a new Hydrocarbons Law—without challenging the fundamental precepts of the neoliberal order.[135]

Roughly four hundred thousand protesters filled the streets of downtown La Paz on October 17. The president left his residence in the afternoon and arrived at Military College in La Paz. From there he took a helicopter flight to Santa Cruz and composed a letter of resignation that was faxed to Congress later that evening. From Viru Viru airport in Santa Cruz, Sánchez de Lozada fled to Miami, accompanied by his wife, Ximena Iturralde, six family members—including his daughter, congressional deputy member Alejandra Sánchez de Lozada, Minister of Defense Sánchez Berzaín, and Health Minister Javier Torres Goitia.[136] Carlos Mesa became president at 10:30 p.m., in accordance with constitutional procedures in the event of a president's resignation. All the political parties with representation in Congress supported the constitutional succession.[137]

Conclusion

This chapter has sought to provide a detailed portrait of the working classes of El Alto and how they were able to overcome structural barriers standing in the way of collective action through the use of the city's dense infrastructure of class struggle and combined cultural traditions of revolutionary Marxism and indigenous liberation. Sectors of the formal working class were able to play a supporting role in the insurrections because of the orientation toward social movement unionism adopted by the COB and the FSTMB. Similarly, the CSUTCB and the FUDTCLP-TK provided the radicalized Aymara peasantry with a rural infrastructure of class struggle through which to kick off the September-October Gas War with marches and hunger strikes, and to support the insurrectionary process throughout the duration of the period with road blockades and mass peasant assemblies in the western *altiplano*. Congealing the alliance between the peasantry, the informal working classes, the formal working class, and, eventually, fractions of the middle class was a collective-action frame around the call to nationalize natural gas, and the extensive but insufficient use of state repression against civilians on the part of the government of Sánchez de Lozada. Ultimately, the dense infrastructure of class struggle and social movement unionism, oppositional traditions of indigenous and working-class radicalism, alliances between the peasants, workers, and the middle class, the collective gas frame, and state repression came together to force the resignation of Sánchez de Lozada on October 17, 2003.

Carlos Mesa then assumed office. Son of two of Bolivia's most highly regarded mainstream historians, Mesa was a film critic in the late 1970s and early 1980s, publishing *La Aventura del Cine Boliviano* in 1985. Later he became a radio journalist, before turning to TV journalism where he became well known and well respected in middle-class circles. Mesa also established credentials as a historian by co-writing with his parents a thick general history of Bolivia. Throughout the 1990s, his fame grew as a TV journalist and political analyst on the program *De Cerca*, or *Up Close*.[138] Mesa had never been a member of the Revolutionary Nationalist Movement (MNR), even after agreeing to run as Sánchez de Lozada's vice-presidential running mate in the 2000 elections. He utilized this stature as an independent intellectual without party affiliation to distance himself from a regime in which he had in fact played a key role as vice-president.

Upon assuming the presidency, he pledged to piece together independent forces into the government and to restore the credibility of the political class in the eyes of the Bolivian population. In response to the popular October Agenda for which left-indigenous forces had struggled, he promised a referendum on natural gas, a Constituent Assembly, and modification of the Hydrocarbons Law. While the Constitution established that his mandate ought to last until August 6, 2007, Mesa argued that Congress could convene elections as soon as it deemed it reasonable to do so. Mesa requested a grace period in which social movements would withdraw from mass actions and let him study their demands and proceed with governing the country peacefully.[139] In the midst of the jubilation surrounding the fall of Sánchez de Lozada, Mesa was initially well received by the key sectors that had mobilized in September and October. That would soon change. Between late May and early June 2005, mass mobilizations re-enacted October 2003, bringing down the presidency of Carlos Mesa on June 6, 2005, and then preventing his replacement by two representatives of the far right—Hormando Vaca Díez (MIR) and Mario Cossío (MNR).[140] All of this laid the basis for early elections in December 2005, which witnessed the election of Evo Morales to the presidency as leader of the MAS.

The second Gas War erupted out of a context of deep political polarization in the country, with distinct racial, regional, and class dimensions. These various politicized and interrelated antagonisms expressed themselves politically in the formation and consolidation of *left-indigenous* and *eastern-bourgeois* blocs that contended for power. The balancing act Mesa attempted between the two blocs ultimately proved untenable.

As in the past, when left-indigenous social forces mobilized, right-wing elites reacted out of class fear and racial hatred. However, unlike in the past, Mesa as head of state refused to employ lethal state coercion. The dynamics of state repression were thus distinct in May-June 2005 when compared to the rebellious episodes of the first Gas War. In the case of Gonzalo Sánchez de Lozada, fierce state repression in September and October 2003 was nonetheless insufficient to crush the mass left-indigenous mobilizations and thus helped rather to intensify and strengthen them as new social solidarities were created among the repressed population. Carlos Mesa, adapting to the post-Sánchez de Lozada setting, made opposition to state repression a central facet of the legitimacy of his government from the outset and was therefore highly constricted in his ability to employ the coercive apparatuses of the state when left-indigenous insurrection erupted. Because Mesa refrained from employing sufficient state repression to quell rebellion, while at the same time refusing to concede to the demands of the social movements, the rising tide of revolt in late May and early June could not be restrained.

The indigenous informal working classes of El Alto, organized through FEJUVE-El Alto and COR-El Alto, were again the principal actors in the May-June Gas War of 2005. Sectors of the formal working class played a dynamic supporting role, as they had in the first Gas War. Again, the largely Aymara peasantry of the *altiplano* were important allies of the formal and informal sectors of the working class. All of these sectors together constituted the most essential and radical actors of the 2005 Gas War. They fought for the full nationalization of hydrocarbons and a revolutionary Constituent Assembly.[141] The role of the middle class in 2005 was different than it had been in the 2003 Gas War, however. Whereas in October 2003 sections of the middle class had led a hunger strike to protest the brutal state repression of Sánchez de Lozada, in 2005 they defended Mesa's regime against radical left-indigenous movements. Another key distinguishing feature of the second Gas War was the intensified regionalization of political struggle. Sensing the impossibility of reconquering the state at the national level, the most powerful fractions of the Bolivian capitalist class began to entrench themselves politically in the eastern lowland departments, a defensive measure to protect their interests as best they could against the ascending left-indigenous movements. This defensive move expressed itself in the eastern-bourgeois bloc, which would become the thorn in the side of the Morales government during its first years in office.

CHAPTER 7

Argentina 2001:
Our Year of Rebellion

Jorge Orovitz Sanmartino

Introduction

"Lazy bums," thought Gustavo, when he arrived home to change his clothes before rushing off to the Plaza de Mayo. His friends, one after another, had all said they were busy. "I'll go on my own then," he thought, partly in sadness and partly in anger, on that suffocatingly hot summer morning. From early on there were rumors at the DIA supermarket in Villa Madero, a densely populated district in La Matanza, that there would be looting and rioting. Gustavo worked there filling shelves for twelve hours a day; his wages—400 pesos a month. The boss had sent everyone home, but Gustavo, who was concerned about his job, went back at midday to have a look at the wreckage—broken blinds and windows, empty bins, smashed shelves. Now back home, in La Tablada, he looked around his room, at his bed and his clothes, his CDs and his sound system, the River Plate pennant on the wall beside the poster of Enzo Francescoli, the center forward. "Those guys are just lazy," he said to himself, as he went back into the street determined to "do what had to be done." He had decided to join the protest. He jumped on the 126 bus for the hour and a half's journey to the center of town. When he got off, he was a few minutes and a few yards away from the moment of tragedy.

Tall, pale, and thin, he was an easy target for the shower of bullets that hit him there, on the corner of Chacabuco and Avenida de Mayo, live and direct, in front of millions of television viewers. The terrified boy, his hands on his head, tried to run. He stumbled forward a few meters, before his legs gave way under him and he fell back onto the pavement, while others were falling around him, some of them shouting, "They're firing from inside the bank." It was a miracle that many more were not hit.

Gustavo's mother and sister recognized him on the screen. He was eleven days short of his twenty-fourth birthday. People were standing around him: "Bastards! Murderers!" Shortly afterward, the police reconstruction of the event described how from inside the HSBC bank at number 67 Avenida de Mayo, three policemen and a bank security guard had started firing from the area around the cash machines, even though no demonstrators had attempted to enter the bank. There were fifty-nine bullet holes, all fired out from the bank. Gustavo was already dead when he arrived at the Ramos Mejía hospital at 5:30 that afternoon. He was the fifth victim on a day that was still far from over and that would end with 32 dead and 120 wounded across the country.

The history of the nation, past and present, was crystallized in the body of Gustavo Ariel Benedetto. According to a witness, retired lieutenant colonel Jorge Varando, he had shouted "Shoot, then, you fucking cowards!" at the police who were inside the bank that day, December 20. Varando was a graduate of the School of the Americas, the training school for "counter-insurgency" located in the southern US, and a member of the 103rd Military Intelligence Unit; he figured on the lists of torturers under the last military government and was suspected of having "disappeared" two members of the Todos por la Patria Movement, captured after the attack on the La Tablada barracks in January 1989.

Despite all their efforts, the repressive forces could not clear the area around the Plaza de Mayo. For four hours police and protesters had moved backward and forward in an interminable dance that wore away, minute by minute, the exhausted government of Fernando de la Rua. On Avenida de Mayo and Diagonal Norte, the vanguard were the *motoqueros*—the young motorcycle couriers who had been organizing in a new trade union, SIMECA. These three hundred young people were the seventh cavalry of the popular rebellion. When they advanced in formation against the police lined up in the Plaza de Mayo, hundreds of the three thousand demonstrators filling the avenue hurled stones, driving the repressive forces back and encouraging the protesters. De la Rua had ordered the square to be cleared—it might then be possible, he felt, to reach agreement with the Justicialista Party, the Peronist opposition, and for him to stay in power at the head of a "national unity" government.

But the commanding officer could neither disperse the protests nor hold his own positions. Early that morning they had managed to clear the legendary square using truncheons and clubs; the whole country had seen how the police, mounted on enormous horses, had beaten up the Mothers of the Plaza de Mayo as well as the young people who had tried to protect and defend them. But the cost was very high. They had committed the worst possible sin, in this country obsessed with memory. Thousands of indignant people rushed to the square, where the battle would continue for hours and where the police commander, General Rubén Jorge Santos, could only submit to wave after wave of pushing back and forth, a humiliating game that drove him wild until, once the rubber bullets and gas had run out, he ordered the use of live ammunition by civilian commandos in the area.

The focus of struggle multiplied around the city. The McDonald's on the corner of 9 de Julio and Corrientes had been burning since the early morning. Men and women, youngsters, bank employees and office workers, traders, taxi drivers, all learned how to fight in a few hours. Men in suits loosened their ties and sucked lemons to counter the effects of tear gas; women who knew, who saw, who heard about the dead and the bullets were not afraid and stayed to fight back. Musicians from the Colón Theatre, doormen and concierges gave out water and looked after the fighters from the battlefront when they fell back, wounded. It was this gallery of spontaneous warriors with ten minutes' training, the proliferation of barricades and bonfires on every street corner around the city center, the waves of courageous volunteers moving with the tide that justify the many names—the Argentinazo, mass insurrection, popular rebellion—given to this unprecedented action that split Argentine history in two and that ensured that the country would never be the same again.

The people's cavalry, the motorbikes of rebellion, proved to be an unexpected new weapon that the police could not handle. The hail of bullets began to break up the protests and reclaim the avenue. The first motorcyclist was mown down. When the bike turned, a policeman knelt in the street and fired. Gaston died in the first attack by the motorbike union on the corner of

Tacuarí and Avenida de Mayo. Others would be wounded that day. The bikes regrouped, dividing into smaller battalions for different battlefronts, while others carried information, brought ambulances, escorted the wounded, or distributed lemons and rocks. Things work better with two on a motorcycle. While the driver accelerated against police lines, the passenger would hurl rocks and stones at the police, driving them back over and over again as they retreated before the noise of the bikes. Then a greater danger threatened from behind. The protesters on foot were growing in numbers and they were advancing too, throwing missiles and then retreating. They learned very quickly how to avoid the horses, the water cannons, the infantry, the police patrols, and the motorcycle cops.

Others tirelessly struggled four blocks away on 9 de Julio Avenue. In the pedestrian precincts some withdrew to breathe: "It's refreshing and it doesn't burn." There were women resting now who vowed they'd stay "until he resigns," because "we hate him." Elsewhere, three civilian cars drove the wrong way down the street, firing. The demonstrators stopped cars and passing taxis to take the wounded to the Argerich hospital. El Toba held up the head of a young Rasta who had fainted and then noticed the bullet hole in his head. He was bleeding. El Toba put his finger in the wound to stem the blood, then took it out so that it could clot. In the end the Rasta made it to the hospital and survived, though the bullet would always be there, at the front of his head near his brain, and he would always carry with him the memory of the epic struggles of that day. He would remember to tell his grandkids. And he and El Toba stayed friends for years.

On Rivadavia Avenue a group of protesters were trapped while an armored car advanced on them; but a group of reporters blocked its path by holding up their cameras. They were brutally punished, but the youngsters escaped around the corner. Behind the vanguard, on Diagonal, the left organizations gathered with their banners and placards, though that made it more difficult to run and move with the stampedes. At every street corner there were songs and what became the shouted slogan of the day: "Get rid of them all, every last one." (*Que se vayan todos, que no quede ni uno solo.*) It echoed from building to building down the avenue and swelled with the rage of the demonstrators. They ran up the street, then back again; the more experienced marchers shouted, "Walk, don't run," but their advice was ignored. When they were able to move forward, one group stood on the steps of the Cathedral shouting, "All mad, all crazy, stick your state of siege up your arse."

Others kept their spirits up by singing "El pueblo unido jamás será vencido." (The people united will never be defeated).

The banks in the shopping center had their blinds torn down and their windows broken, their facades destroyed by the enraged demonstrators. Columns of smoke rose all over the city, and opportunists seized the opportunity to loot shops and businesses. The offices of the National Committee of the UCR (Radical Civic Union), the party of government, were sacked and destroyed by demonstrators. Another group smashed windows with baseball bats. There was a strange mixture of emotions in these tense moments: there was deep sadness about the dead and wounded, whose numbers were growing by the minute, and there was fear and desperation; but at the same time the atmosphere was festive, joyful, with the wild hope that this time they'd win, yes this time they'd win and kick out the useless, corrupt politicians. The joy was contagious; people embraced one another, and strangers become comrades. This irresponsible, adolescent optimism gave people the strength to go on. As the sun was setting, the news began circulating from mouth to mouth, and it was confirmed when the helicopter appeared over the Presidential Palace. The president had resigned, taking with him the frustration of a defeat whose cost was many dead and wounded, sacrificed on the altar of governability.

1. Pickets and empty pots

Thursday, December 20, 2001, when President Fernando de la Rua resigned with half his term still to run, marked the end of an era. But the crisis and the mass mobilization that for the first time in the nation's history drove out a freely elected government had been bubbling under the surface for months before accelerating on the previous night, the 19th, when the president appeared on national radio and television to announce the imposition of a state of siege in response to the wave of looting that had spread throughout Greater Buenos Aires and many cities in the interior. His purpose was to intimidate the population and put a stop to demonstrations, flooding cities and strategic points with repressive forces.

But, as so often happens, the attempt by a government to fulfill certain ends had very different results from those it anticipated. That was what happened to Don Fernando. In the minutes immediately after he had finished his speech there was a rumble of pot-banging (*cacerolazos*), but within half an hour it rose to a symphony of protest. From north to south, east to west, across the capital and other cities, the noise of pot-banging spread; shortly afterward, spontaneous marches made their way toward the centers of political power, accompanied by the continuing noise. Hundreds, thousands, tens of thousands and later hundreds of thousands of people left their homes. The answer to the declaration of a state of siege was that the people took their streets, turning that day and the whole night into a carnival of color and hope. The old and the young, whole families occupied the city and filled it with their laughter, their songs, and their chatter. An authentic democratic spring defied the state of siege, and the repressive forces disappeared from the city. Shortly before midnight a massive crowd approached the Plaza de Mayo. In Rosario and Córdoba the response was the same. The purpose of the state of siege decree was to break up the spontaneous coming together of the different movements of the unemployed—many of them part of the *piqueteros* movement—who used barricades across major highways and mass mobilizations to support their demands for jobs and benefits, and the middle classes who were demanding the return of their savings, confiscated by Economics Minister Domingo Cavallo.

But the discontent of the middle classes was not only the result of the confiscation (the *corralito* as they called it); that was simply the last straw. Its cause was generalized crisis, the unemployment that was hitting every layer of the population, the loss of expectations, and the disillusionment with a government that had been elected as a center-left coalition but which now ruled with an iron hand, imposing the structural adjustments demanded by the IMF. The attacks on supermarkets had begun a week earlier in a number of cities, starting in Concordia, in Entre Ríos province, on the 15th; it had the country's highest level of unemployment. Rosario, Concepción del Uruguay, Gualeguay, and other provincial cities like Mendoza, Salta, and Río Negro followed. It finally reached the gates of the capital, Greater Buenos Aires, placing the government on maximum alert. It condemned the actions of Peronist mayors and local officials who, it said, were provoking chaos to bring down the government to make way for a Peronist regime. But, in fact, the situation was the product of the hunger and despair of millions of Argentines. There was no conspiracy; this was a social rising against structural adjustment, and the debt and unemployment generated by the neoliberal policies implemented, whatever the cost, by De la Rua—even if in some areas Peronist officials were also involved in protests. Between December 13 and 20, in just eight days, 864 shops were ransacked, more than the 676 in fifty-two days during the period of hyperinflation under the Radical Civic Union government of Raúl Alfonsín that followed the downfall of the military regime. The images of food trucks being stopped and emptied on the road to Rosario were seen across the world—and this in a country that produces grains, milk, and meat for three hundred million inhabitants. The Peronists were also concerned, and the governor of Buenos Aires province, Carlos Ruckauf, and his mentor and Peronist leader, Eduardo Duhalde, called on the population to return to their homes and did everything they could to calm the situation. For none of them could say with certainty that the revolutionary wave would only sweep away the government party and not the whole political system. "Get rid of them all" was a warning they could not afford to ignore.

2. Social crisis and the collapse of the institutions

How did Argentina, known as "the world's granary," descend into this social catastrophe with 22 percent unemployment, 50 percent of its population in poverty and 20 percent homeless? How did the crisis culminate in the collapse of that pillar of capitalism, the national currency, followed by the breaking of agreed contracts, the freezing of payments, the issue of an alternative currency, and the confiscation of savings? The origin of the worst crisis in the nation's history lies in the implementation of certain economic policies since 1991, which continued and intensified the policies that were first implemented by the civilian-military dictatorship imposed by the military coup of 1976. Argentina became the testing ground for neoliberal policies; for years it was the darling of the ideologists and publicists of privatization, deregulation, and unrestricted trade.

The 1991 program of structural reforms and economic liberalization, called the Convertibility Plan, was implemented against the background of crisis and hyperinflation that assailed the country for almost a decade. The hyperinflation of the late '80s and early '90s swept away savings and economic stability and reduced the value of wages month by month, terrifying society in general and acting as a disciplinary mechanism. Faced with crisis, the only possible objective was stability—at any cost. It was the Peronist president Carlos Saul Menem who brought in Domingo Cavallo as economics minister. Overwhelmed by the evidence, the president with the long sideburns and the air of a regional caudillo turned 180 degrees and called into the most important government ministry a financier and businessman who promised to transform Argentina into a paradise of stability.

This ideological and political turn that many countries in the region underwent, faced with the failure and exhaustion of an economic nationalism based on a hypothetical notion of a progressive national bourgeoisie, was particularly radical and definitive in Argentina. It was presented as the price that had to be paid to achieve stability and to restrain that apparently instinctive impulse to increase wages and prices in an unstoppable spiral. The stabilization plan began with a convertibility fund establishing an exchange rate of one peso to one dollar, and with a prohibition on the indexation of prices. Wages, however, could only rise in proportion to increases in productivity. Thus the peso was tied by law to the dollar, and the Central Bank was obliged to provide 100 percent of the monetary base with its international reserves. This was accompanied by other measures—the privatization of all state enterprises and the opening up of the economy to an even greater degree than in Chile under Pinochet. The plan implied an immediate and rapid shock, bringing inflation under control and stabilizing the economy. This allowed Menem to claim a great success and to win a massive consensus behind the economic plan. Neoliberal hegemony thus rested on an enthusiastic public opinion that accepted massive redundancies and the privatization and auctioning off of emblematic enterprises like the national oil company YPF and the telephone company Entel, as well as the national airline, gas, light, and water companies, ports and airports, the postal service, and many other public utilities under highly favorable conditions for their national and international purchasers.

This model of capitalism in its pure state, which condemned state intervention as a residue of the past and an impediment to modernization and growth, assumed that an economy liberated entirely from all regulation and "fiscal pressures" would guarantee investment and increased productivity in the medium and long term. It also assumed that the elimination of customs tariffs would force local firms to compete with foreign products. This produced a significant inflow of capital, a fall in interest rates, and the reactivation of the economy; the result was economic growth through the first four years and the strengthening of neoliberal hegemony. The free market, consumerism, and the modernization of public services extended neoliberal ideology into daily life, reinforcing possessive individualism, overspending, and the pursuit of individual advancement at the expense of any collective solution, undermining popular organizations, particularly trade unions, which were seen as corporate actors bent on resisting modernization. At the same time, the government had reinforced what its foreign minister called "intimate relations" with the United States and Europe. The slogan of the day was, as Margaret Thatcher had put it, "There is no alternative."

But the pernicious effect of the model would soon make itself felt. The overvaluation of the currency, which helped to bring inflation down at first, together with the elimination of tariffs, began rapidly to undermine domestic industry, inundating the market with imported goods. The local bourgeoisie quickly got rid of its own industries to throw in their lot with the privatized enterprises in association with foreign capital, or to invest in the banking or agricultural sectors. National industry became less competitive and firms began to implement large-scale redundancies. The balance of trade fell into chronic deficit, only compensated at the outset by the influx of private capital for privatization and speculation and by the rise in the interest rate on dollars. But the terms of the equation began to tip against them. The duplication of returns on foreign investment, capital flight, and the growing trade deficit increased the shortage of dollars, compensated initially only by spiraling government borrowing. The debt increased to unprecedented levels and, as a result of the Mexican crisis that hit Argentina very badly, became a key element in the subsequent crisis. Interest on the debt quadrupled in a very short time and the debt never fell below 3 percent of GNP. The convertibility regime was only sustainable with a constant and abundant inflow of foreign currency—yet that was becoming increasingly scarce.

The situation grew even worse when countries like Russia entered their own crisis, and when Argentina's commercial partners, like Brazil, devalued their currencies. It is true that in the beginning some entrepreneurs were able to import capital goods to offset wage increases measured in dollars at parity, especially in the agrarian sector in the humid pampas, the most fertile and productive region of the country; by contrast, the production and intermediate goods industries grew weaker and increasingly disarticulated. At first workers in the more dynamic sectors of the economy benefited, since the cost in dollars of the basket of basic goods fell, but at a cost that the workers had never experienced before, because, paradoxically, unemployment rose exponentially even though the economy was growing. And when the recession was announced in 1998, it shot up with rates above 15 percent, while flexibilization, restructuring, and labor precarity became the norm. A country that had never known unemployment rates above 6–7 percent, even in its worst recessions, now had to live with a rate of 18 percent between 1999 and 2000, reaching a peak of 21 percent at the height of the crisis in 2002. In the long term, demand fell and the working class was divided and fragmented, weakening the historic conquests achieved during the first and second Peronist periods and leaving it at the mercy of a government that was encouraging casualization and flexibility as the condition for attracting private capital. The economy never recovered, and the decline in every area grew more rapid and became impossible to stop.

Unemployment, with its catastrophic impact on the distribution of wealth and its consequence in increasing poverty and homelessness, and the weakening of the internal market, became the country's principal economic and social problem, undermining in turn the political and institutional structures of the state. In the financial sector, the drive toward the foreignization of banks and the dollarization of the economy resulted in the general dollarization of all bank deposits and loans, making it even more difficult to escape the convertibility trap, which would imply security of exchange of change for the banks and massive losses for the exchequer. The alternative was to rush ahead and reaffirm convertibility, to calm the markets and hold back the flight of capital. The fall of international prices in the wake of the Russian default of 1997 and the South Asian crisis, followed by the Brazilian, added one more aggravating factor to the equation. The problem was that as a result of convertibility, the economy had lost its control of monetary and financial policy, so that any external negative element simply multiplied its deleterious effects. In this unrestrained logic, the only variable was an injection of confidence that only the IMF and the World Bank could give—as they had in Mexico in 1995. But the conditions were brutal. When Menem left the presidency, the recession had already begun, but it was under De la Rua, who assumed the presidency in December 1999, that it began to deepen.

It is true that society, remembering the horrors of hyperinflation, still supported convertibility. Every establishment political party had campaigned in its defense. The Alianza, an alliance between the historic Radical Civic Union (UCR) and the progressive FREPASO (National Solidarity Front Coalition), criticized Menem's methods, the shameless corruption and barefaced overspending of his regime, and the social consequences of the model, but it never discussed how to resolve the problem without touching convertibility. Its only proposal was to retain it with greater transparency and commitment. In practice, this ambiguity at the heart of the electoral campaign became a more methodical application of the adjustments demanded by the international credit organizations. In 2000 the government had to address repaying a debt of $11 billion, 20 percent of the national budget. In 2000–2001 De la Rua and his economics minister, José Luis Machinea, lowered wages and pensions by 13 percent and cut public spending as well as introducing laws reforming both the tax regime and the state in an attempt to reestablish market confidence and fulfill the requirements of the IMF in order to obtain a *blindaje financiero* (financial shield), which consisted of loans from the IMF, Inter-American Development Bank, the World Bank, pensions funds, private banks, and the Spanish government for $32.7 billion, plus another $7 billion in bonds. These were not new funds but a new financial guarantee to be released drop by drop if and when the country needed it. This multimillion-dollar aid program was designed to restore the confidence of creditors in exchange for a severe readjustment. Far from resolving anything, this served to reduce consumption and growth even further.

By the beginning of 2001, the effects of capital flight had reached $12 billion in the international reserves. There was a flight of bank deposits that generated a banking and financial crisis. The second response came from Domingo Cavallo, Menem's ex–economics minister and the champion of convertibility, who was once again called upon by the Alianza as one more gesture of confidence toward the markets. Given the crisis within the Central Bank, the lender of last resort, whose reserves were evaporating by the day, the "mega-exchange" was agreed to. Its objective was to delay the repayment of interest and capital on the external debt, exchanging old bonds for new. But the cost of this exchange would be exorbitant, increasing the external debt by more than $50 billion, which is why it was challenged in the courts and questioned for years afterward. In fact there was no formula that would restore the "confidence of the market." The debt was impossible to repay, convertibility in such circumstances was unsustainable, and the flight of capital was unstoppable. Cavallo traveled to New York in an attempt to renegotiate, but the fate of convertibility was sealed. The IMF refused to enter into a new agreement. Like the captain of a sinking ship, Cavallo imposed a block on withdrawals, restricting the right of wage earners and small savers to access their accounts and take out money. This infuriated the whole population. The paladin of capitalist legality and security was confiscating the funds and ultimately expropriating the life savings of millions of people. This marked the collapse not only of the banking system but of the economy as a whole, of the state, and of the prevailing political system.

For ten years the power of capital, in its most aggressive and militant form, had hegemonized social relations and imposed a class perspective that penetrated into the deepest reaches of society. Argentina was subjected to a regime of accumulation based on the absolute power of capital, sweeping aside the social barriers and safeguards that the state had built over decades, dissolving sovereignty and any possibility of an active monetary policy. The result was to eliminate arbitration procedures, discredit the trade unions and put them on the defensive, and reconfigure Argentina's social structure, fragmenting the working class and casualizing labor. In this the dominant block, made up of major national and international enterprises acting together (along with, in a subordinate position, industrialists and exporters), many with the blessing of the international credit providers, won for itself an unprecedented legitimacy. It seemed that a new era was beginning, characterized by the unrestricted domination of capital and the subordination of the oppressed classes, who seemed to be gathering in a suicidal alliance under the banner of their executioners. But this pure capitalism, this fusion of free market and debt, of social discipline and intimate relations produced, out of its own contradictions, the most brutal banking and fiscal collapse in living memory. Without methods of arbitration and with no counterbalance, capital damaged itself and opened cracks through which popular movements could march, after an extraordinary period of resistance, and begin to impose limits and raise demands that seemed to re-emerge from the memories of times past.

It is true that what followed immediately was a devaluation that reduced working-class wages in one fell swoop by 30 percent, and that many people read that as a defeat for the workers. But that would be a one-sided and economistic reading, for the relations between social forces, embracing a popular, democratic agenda that had emerged in a variety of forms and contexts, would modify the panorama for the following decade. The bulwarks of neoliberalism collapsed, the free market ship lost its mast, the legitimacy of private enterprise was undermined, and the IMF strategies were almost unanimously rejected. The ideological conquests of neoliberal capitalism collapsed in disorder, and the agenda was now dominated by the demand for a new, postneoliberal hegemony.

Only a new government capable of recognizing this new reality could put the Argentine state on a new and straight course. After five presidents had been dispatched in a matter of months, it was Nestor Kirchner, a second-level governor from the south, who took note of the extraordinary transformation that Argentine society had undergone, whose high point was the popular rebellion of December 19–20, and acted accordingly.

3. Crisis of the political system

The debacle of neoliberalism implied a simultaneous crisis in the system of representation. The political system as a whole, with its parties, the right of the state to conduct social arbitration, impose the law, and insist that contracts were respected, was in jeopardy. The crisis of the parties was demonstrated clearly in the mid-term legislative elections of October 2001, which heralded the definitive collapse of government. In those elections the Alianza lost five million votes, despite the fact that the Radical leaders, like Alfonsín, ran an almost oppositional campaign, distancing themselves from the anti-popular leaders in the Executive. Its coalition partner, FREPASO, had been rocked by the resignation of its leader, Chacho Alvarez, from the vice presidency as a result of a scandal in the Senate; there were allegations of bribery when the Executive was pressuring for a vote in favor of the labor flexibility it had promised the IMF it would introduce. But Peronism also lost part of its electoral base, its vote declining by 650,000 votes. Blank votes reached 9.4 percent of the total, spoiled ballots 12.5 percent, and abstention climbed to 24 percent. To that we could add the million votes that went to the Left and to a new formation—Elisa Carrió's ARI (Support for an Egalitarian Republic)—that broke with the Radicals on the basis of an ethical discourse critical of the "political class"; it garnered 1.6 million votes.

The reputation of the "professional politicians" had never been lower. This was a response, of course, to many and often contradictory ideological pressures. The withdrawal of the state, the disarticulation of much of its regulatory machinery, and its weakening as a representative of the collective and as the space where social conflicts could be resolved—the vacuum that had been generated in terms of its role as principal mediator of social conflicts—created the conditions. While the liberal right presented a program that completely repudiated the interventionist state, leftist civil society was increasingly skeptical and distant from a state it saw as devoid of real power, a power that had been transferred both to the market and to the international financial organizations; it understood that new forms of political socialization and representation could emerge out of that vacuum. The rise of autonomist and libertarian ideologies, which fueled the expectations of the popular assemblies, the *piqueteros*, and many social movements, had its origins in this weakening of the political institutions. The expectations of the moment were expressed as "thinking politics without the state." New forms of representation were imagined and new ways of understanding democracy proposed. The three branches of state power were also included among the accused and, not coincidentally, became the target of popular rage in those intense days. The Supreme Court, many of whose judges were courtesans appointed by Menem when he decided to increase their number, had supported the juridical structures on which neoliberalism had based its policies since 1991. It was now the object of a general rejection and suffered the daily assaults of popular rage.

Above all, people were imagining new forms of social organization, egalitarian and self-governing, for the state and the market, and beyond. However utopian those dreams might have seemed, in part they challenged the revolutionary strategy of a seizure of state power advocated by the parties of the Left, and they imprinted a new dynamics onto the situation, reinforcing the social movements to the point of nourishing a new form of understanding politics from below that took root in the consciousness of thousands of militants and activists, contributing in part to the gestation of a democratic culture that could persist through time. The fall of De la Rua was not the result of a Peronist conspiracy, as more than one analyst would like to think, but the combined product of a terminal economic and political crisis and a popular rebellion that genuinely emerged from below. Those roots would mark out the road for the decade that followed.

For the first time a government was brought down not by a military coup but by a popular rebellion. For the first time a government was overthrown not to end democracy but to recover it. This central feature of this and other risings across the continent meant that the democratic legitimacy of anti-popular governments could be called into question, as could the restricted nature of formal democracies where real power did not lie in the sovereignty of the people but in the concentration of capital, finance, and the international credit organizations. Unlike other contemporary experiences in Latin America, however, the party system as a whole was not brought down in Argentina, as it was in Bolivia, Ecuador, and Venezuela; indeed, the main party, Peronism, would survive. Peronism's capacity to preserve and transform itself, where elsewhere the historic parties were pulverized by the crisis and the popular mobilizations it provoked, marks the distances and limits of the Argentine process in comparison with those other experiences, where the liquidation of the old parties opened the way for new formations and new popular leaders like Evo Morales and Hugo Chávez. It marks the distance between the programs and actions of constituent assemblies[1] in those countries and the constitutional limits imposed upon the changes that took place in Argentina.

Although it too was the object of protests, Peronism was able to capitalize on the crisis of Radicalism and assume a central role as the party of order and governability. Faced with the presidential succession and having won a minority in parliament, the legislature voted to back Ramón Puerta, governor of the northern province of Misiones, as provisional president. Within days he passed the baton on to Adolfo Rodriguez Saa, another provincial Peronist leader, who accepted the job with the consensus of Peronist governors on condition that he would not stay in the presidency until the end of his mandate in 2003 and that he would call elections within three months. When the noise of pots being struck greeted Saa's unacceptable proposed cabinet, and when his colleagues began to suspect he was intending to hold on to the presidential sash, the ex-governor of San Luis found the ground had disappeared beneath his feet and resigned, passing on the presidency to Eduardo Camaño, president of the Chamber of Deputies, though not before declaring, before parliament and the world, the default on the external debt. It was a formality, since it had really already happened, but his announcement was intended to show him as the champion of the nation against the IMF. This did not so much increase the suspicions about Saa himself as reveal the profound ideological transformation in the consciousness of millions. The assumption of the presidency, two days later, by Eduardo Duhalde, the Peronist leader in Buenos Aires, testified to his political influence and his control of a political apparatus that would be fundamental to maintaining governability. He was sworn in on January 1, 2002, the fifth president in ten days.

Paradoxically, Peronism, which had been the basic instrument for imposing neoliberal economic policies, now entered power as the only option for getting out of the convertibility scheme that De la Rua insisted on maintaining. Duhalde, Menem's vice-president and his rival in the battle for the leadership of the party and the presidential candidacy, now had the task of ending convertibility, devaluing the currency, imposing the asymmetrical return to the peso that liquidated the dollar debts of banks and enterprises, and launching a massive social assistance plan called Plan Jefes y Jefas de Hogar (Head of Households Plan) that would end the looting of shops and permit the situation to be brought under control again. Only when he made a grotesque miscalculation, when he thought he had won control of the situation, and that the time had come to attack the *piqueteros* and affirm his own power, did his presidency collapse, forcing him to call early elections. His plan for leading the recovery and reaping the benefits of doing so in 2003 had failed. The repression of a huge demonstration organized by the *piquetero* movement on the Pueyrredon Bridge, which splits the capital city in two, and the cold-blooded murder of two members of the Anibal Veron Coordinating Committee—Maximiliano Kosteki and Dario Santillán—by the crazed Buenos Aires police, which was photographed by the militant press, provoked new protests and a generalized rejection that made it impossible for Duhalde to continue in the presidency. With no candidate of his own, and threatened by his adversaries Carlos Reutemann and De La Sota, the Peronist governors of Santa Fe and Córdoba, respectively, he thought he had found his candidate in Nestor Kirchner, a picturesque, minor character. The circle of turbulence and of governments with no popular mandate thus closed. A new stage was now beginning, which would bring change, timid at first, later more emphatic, in international economic conditions that would favor the new president.

4. New social movements

During the 1990s, under the presidency of Menem, the workers were defeated in their attempts to stop the privatizations; as a result, four hundred thousand workers were made redundant. Civil servants and teachers were, in turn, the worst affected by the so-called decentralization and budget cuts. But despite the blows that rained down on them, the working class maintained a permanent resistance. In the interior of the country, in 1993, there began a series of spontaneous risings by municipal workers and teachers with mass popular support. This resistance would grow in volume and intensity as the effects of these adjustments began to be felt across the whole of society. So, for example, the teachers sustained a two-year-long struggle, between

1997 and 1999, which won a partial victory but which also became the focus of the political struggle against the government. State workers also launched a series of actions with different demands.

The CTA (Argentine Workers Confederation), the federation that represented these different unions, took on a key social and political role that led later to the formation of FRENAPO, the National Anti-Poverty Front, that gathered over three million signatures in support of the creation of a Work and Education Insurance scheme for unemployed heads of household and argued for the formation of a Workers' Party in the mold of the Brazilian Workers' Party, which its leader, Victor de Gennaro, ultimately rejected. The MTA (Movement of Argentine Workers), led by the truck driver Hugo Moyano, organized mass mobilizations against the economic policies of the Menem and De la Rua government, and launched, in coordination with the CTA, two general strikes that paralyzed the country. He also organized opposition to the so-called bosses' unions that, riding the wave of privatization, were transformed into enterprises that ended up running private trains and private insurance schemes for workers, administering pension funds and enjoying a position among the official trade unions.

But what was new in this period and represented the dynamic forces at the heart of the protests were the new social movements that emerged with unprecedented strength in the context of a new configuration of class forces. The *piquetero* movement arose and grew in the course of ten years of struggle and organization. Its barricades on major highways were its trademark form of protest over unemployment and the loss of hope, but it also occupied public buildings and blockaded oil refineries and other workplaces demanding jobs. Poverty, unemployment, and the casualization of labor shaped a new social map, which Argentina, with its strong working-class movement, its vigorous middle class, and the European levels of income distribution it had enjoyed for much of the twentieth century, had never experienced until then. But the subaltern classes have always inherited the lessons of the past. Although the pickets and the barricades became a majority method of social protest, they did not emerge from nowhere but rather were linked to the best traditions of working-class struggle. Employed in different circumstances and in the face of unprecedented and unfamiliar challenges, the old proletarian knowledges were given new meaning in the face of the new circumstances imposed by capital.

The first expressions of this new method emerged in Cutral Có, in Neuquén, through 1996–97, in Libertador General San Martin, Cruz del

Eje, and Tartagal in 1997, where struggles were transformed into popular risings backed by the people as a whole, whose protagonists were workers dismissed by the oil corporation YPF, which had been privatized and handed over to Spanish capital; railway workers made redundant as the railways were shut down; and young unemployed workers with no future. These pickets, spontaneous at first, became more and more frequent and increasingly well organized, deploying a new repertoire of collective action across the entire country, successfully adapting their struggles and demands to the new circumstances and the available resources. In 1997 there were 140 barricades erected across major highways, in 1998 there were 51, and in 1999 the number grew to 252. As the crisis deepened the number of barricades leapt significantly through the subsequent years—514 in 2000, 1,282 in 2001, and 2,234 in 2002, setting off alarm bells for the economic and political establishment.

Cutting off the circulation of goods and vehicles made visible what until then had been hidden from public opinion in the large cities, and began to forge a new political subject consisting of thousands of new social activists rooted in the social networks of the poorest sectors, particularly in Greater Buenos Aires, where for decades Peronism had monopolized popular representation. While the trade unions, led by a Peronist bureaucracy that had for the most part been complicit in Carlos Menem's neoliberal policies, and even opposition unions like the truck drivers were indifferent to the unemployed, dynamic new social movements were emerging on the margins and became the protagonists of the most important struggles of the decade. A corporate narrow-mindedness seemed to limit the vision of the unions and the range of their demands—and that would later weaken their negotiating power. The CTA, the union confederation that had split away from the CGT (General Confederation of Labor) in the early '90s, was the honorable exception; it recognized the emergence of new forms of organization and immediately acknowledged them as part of the working class, allowing both individuals and unemployed movements to join.

The *piqueteros* movement, which was taking major steps in the development of self-organization, the creation of cooperatives, and self-organized production, gave impetus to autonomist ideological currents, based on a strategy of not taking power and in some cases on going beyond wage labor to the self-reproduction of social life outside capital. The left organizations also joined with the *piqueteros*, in one way or another, at least from 2000 onwards, once they had overcome (though it was not the case with every left group) the workerist prejudices that made anyone not occupying a direct role in production somehow suspect.

One of the most creative and fruitful forms of actions were the factories in receivership (*las fábricas recuperadas*). With the recession and the open crisis beginning in 1998 and intensifying by 2000, a number of factories and service industries collapsed, closing their doors and leaving behind debts, including several months' wages for the workers. Under the slogan "Occupy, resist, produce," the movement represented a defensive response to the most immediate consequences within enterprises of the capitalist crisis. In the context of a rising popular movement, these workers—few of them with any trade-union experience or traditions of struggle—instead of leaving the workplace and looking for new work, and faced with an uncertain job horizon, chose to occupy their places of work, first demanding their back pay and later restarting production. A broad political and legal debate began around the issue of private property and the right to work, not just in academic and political circles, but also in the mass media. The political and ideological battle was consolidated with the formation of cooperatives and the demands for a new bankruptcy law that gave the workers priority among the creditors and the possibility of taking over the plant with state support. These factories demonstrated that a workplace without bosses, based on cooperation and the democratic organization of work where capital had previously dominated, was viable, productive, and efficient. Of more than 500 recovered enterprises, 310 have survived and continue to produce today, employing some 13,400 workers. During the crisis there was talk of a massive collapse of enterprises that did not in fact happen; this reduced the number of workers involved in the movement but did not affect its importance, culturally and ideologically insofar as it offered a popular, class-based response to the conventional notion that it was always the wage earners who should pay for the crisis.

The other outstanding expression of these emerging new subjects in the popular struggle was the popular assemblies. These were formed, basically, out of the popular rebellion, as became obvious in the week after December 20, when in the poor barrios of Buenos Aires as well as of other cities like Rosario and Córdoba, meetings of local residents began to gather in squares and parks and proliferated like mushrooms after rain. There were about 120 of these assemblies in the Greater Buenos Aires area, and around 200 in the country as a whole. And they continued to grow and spread until mid-2002, when attendance began to fall. The movement revolved around the Interbarrial (Coordinating Committee) of Parque Centenario, which organized a National Meeting in the Plaza de Mayo in the center of Buenos Aires with the active participation of some ten thousand assembly members. These assemblies were much more than meetings of people affected by the freezing of bank accounts; they were able to voice a range of demands and aspirations. They were a melting pot consisting of savers and the young, the unemployed and the small traders affected by the crisis, the residents concerned with the deterioration of their area, and public sector workers and teachers whose wages had been cut to the bone by De la Rua.

The assemblies discussed the future of the country, drew up lists of demands like the nonpayment of the debt, the political trial of the Supreme Court, elections for a Constituent Assembly, the nationalization of private firms, the raising of the health and education budgets, and payments for the neediest groups, among many others. And there was complete freedom of expression too. The assemblies were spaces where people could meet for political debate as well as to organize, forge solidarity, and hold debates, and were becoming new institutions of representation and self-government. They emerged as a different kind of democracy that rejected the idea that "the people only deliberate and govern through their representatives." The assemblies deliberated and governed in a new way, power was exercised horizontally, and new forms of citizenship were put to the test. This was an assembly-based state (*estado asambleario*) that expressed the state of mind of the whole country, where everything was questioned, discussed, and challenged and the established power could no longer govern behind the curtain of routine and disinterest. Everything was scrutinized—the assemblies are the most conscious section of the vanguard and the most rigorous of judges. The assemblies discussed issues like human rights—for example, the fight for justice for those killed on December 19 and 20.

Many of them set up communal kitchens to provide for the hungry, and seventeen of them developed a popular economy that included microfactories (textile and crafts), food banks, consumer cooperatives, exchange networks, local market gardens, and markets. They also organized demonstrations against the high cost of public services and discussed a tax boy-cott; held forums on health, the environment, and housing; demanded the decentralization of municipal power and called for a law of communes; and occupied the CGPs (Centers for Management and Participation) to involve the city government in the organization of food, jobs, and benefits. They took up the demands of the unemployed and gave them space to organize, as well as supporting the so-called *cartoneros* who gather food and materials for recycling to sell. Out of these activities emerged the urban recycling cooperatives that years later were regulated and legalized by the city government, transforming them into the main organizations responsible for the recycling of solid waste for the whole city. They organized protests of the Palace of Justice, demanding the resignation of all the members of the Supreme Court for their complicity in the privatizations that sold off the country.

The assemblies became a laboratory for popular organization and a point of unity for all the popular classes directing their attacks at the dominant powers and at those responsible, politically and economically, for the situation, neutralizing the campaigns that set out to split the middle classes from the hungry and unemployed of Buenos Aires. The slogan that articulated this new class coalition—"pickets and empty pots, all one struggle" (*piquetes y cacerolas, la lucha es una sola*)—underlined the potential for a social and political bloc that could offer an alternative to the regime that had ruled for ten years and which was now the object of debate. The acid test of this unity was the march organized by the *piqueteros* on January 28, 2002. It began in La Matanza, one of the poorest areas in the city, with closed factories and shortages of every sort, where drug traffickers and corrupt police abounded, where the trash was piled high on dirt roads, with protesters marching to the Plaza de Mayo. It would last seventeen hours and cover thirty kilometers. The *piqueteros*, marching along highway 3 toward the city, were carrying improvised banners made of cloth or flour bags. The response of the assemblies, traders' groups, and student associations was to offer solidarity, providing breakfast as they passed, and the middle classes, ruined by ten years of neoliberal policies, cheered them from their balconies as heroes, friends, and allies. They were given bread, soft drinks, sandwiches, cakes, and fruit, while the organizations of pensioners in the lovely Caballito district welcomed them and joined the march. In the framework of crisis and a questioning of all the elements of state power, the assemblies made it possible to imagine other ways of doing politics, other ways of making decisions and of running society.

The *piqueteros* and their highway barricades, the recovered factories now managed without bosses, the popular assemblies and their participatory democracy—these are the richest legacy of the social resistance and the popular uprising. They are figures, histories, practices, and experiences relived time and again in the popular memory, brought up to date and revived when the situation requires it. Their methods have even been appropriated by the propertied class, as happened during the bosses' lockout of 2008 when they used barricades across the country in their demand for a reduction in export taxes and freedom of trade for their product. They are methods and organizational forms that have come to form part of the tradition of struggle and the shared knowledge of the lower classes, but which have also contributed to the democratic and revolutionary inheritance of the society as a whole as well as its popular classes.

5. The growth of the forces opposed to the system

The Left and the autonomous movements experienced important growth both in their membership and in their political influence. In national parliamentary elections they received over a million votes, and in the elections to the city council of Buenos Aires the Self-Determination and Liberty Party, led by Luis Zamora, won 10.5 percent of the vote—Zamora had split from the Trotskyist Left and declared his open commitment to horizontal organization in tune with the political climate that prevailed in the popular assemblies. Izquierda Unida (United Left)—a coalition formed by the MST (Socialist Workers Movement), a Trotskyist group, and the Communist Party—came next. Other currents also won parliamentary representation, and the forces of the Left as a whole occupied an important space in the chamber. Furthermore, the "enraged" vote (*voto bronca*) that expressed itself in spoiled or blank papers or abstention in the national elections of 2000 represented a huge degree of rejection of the prevailing political system.

And the radical Left was the center of the opposition victory over the Franja Morada (Purple Fringe), the UCR's student organization, in the student unions of the University of Buenos Aires and other national universities. The autonomist currents, for their part, maintained their anti-institutional posture and rejected electoral participation, as did the Maoist Corriente Clasista y Combativa (Fighting Class Current), which had a high profile as a result of its weight within the *piqueteros* and its leadership of the municipal Perro Santillan union, which had been at the head of the local resistances in the province of Jujuy during the '90s. The autonomous movement in particular called into question, politically and theoretically, participation in elections, insisting on the need to stay out of that arena and concentrate their forces on the social movement. Some of its components did not question electoral politics in principle, but felt that the only genuine candidature was one that emerged as an expression of social forces—like Evo Morales in Bolivia. But that had not yet happened in Argentina.

Nevertheless, as the institutional processes began to return to normal, as the presidential elections of 2003 legitimated the election of Nestor Kirchner and he began to take note of popular demands as he rose on a tide of social activism, the anti-institutional positions became more marginalized and the strategies of "thinking without the state" and the actions that flowed from it came to seem progressively less realistic. And the premise that "politics" (that is, the struggle for state power) could bring no good and could not be used by the popular movement was also contradicted by experiences like Bolivia and Venezuela, while at the same time the star of Zapatismo was in decline. If neo-anarchism during the period of resistance and popular rebellion represented a fresh new utopia, a genuine light cast on the darkest and most conservative aspects of society, the fact was that it could not become a realistic strategic option for the subaltern classes. With the relative stabilization that Kirchner was able to achieve, those ideas even began to sound naive.

Taken as a whole, the radical social and political movements introduced an important element of creativity and combativity that nourished popular culture and were effective instruments in the class struggle, even if their political strategy and their tactical errors (for example, the participation of the Left in the apparatus of the popular assemblies) must be called into question. The Left as a whole did not achieve a radicalization of the process nor did it surpass Peronism as the representation of the people, but it did permeate and nourish with its experience, its militancy, and its sacrifices all the popular movements that emerged with the crisis, a legacy that is carefully nurtured and treasured.

6. A new period

In the presidential elections, Nestor Kirchner won just 22 percent of the votes and should have faced Carlos Menem in a second round—but Menem withdrew, leaving Kirchner to assume the post with a low level of support. The first thing Kirchner did was to travel to Entre Ríos province to resolve a conflict with the teachers, whose demands he promised to resolve. That gave the first signal as to what kind of administration he was planning. He received the Mothers of the Plaza de Mayo and other human rights organizations, as well as the *piqueteros* and other social movements, in the Presidential Palace, but he was careful to keep his distance from the employers' organizations. In one memorable act, he took down the portrait of the genocidal president Rafael Videla from the presidents' gallery and threatened to send the majority of the members of the Supreme Court to political trial. In the end they did resign, to be replaced by members with broad social support like Raul Zaffaroni, a criminologist closer to Foucault than any other theorist of penal law.

To counter the economic depression left by the crisis and the wage cuts that resulted from devaluation, Kirchner announced wage increases by decree at a time when the forces of labor were still too weak to strike for wage increases. Suspicious of the new reality, he hid the Peronist symbols and its liturgy and began to speak of "transversality," which was enthusiastically received by important layers of the middle class who had participated in the rebellion. He withdrew the laws of Obedience to Duty and Final Judgment that prevented the prosecution of military personnel who had committed crimes during the military dictatorship and reopened the trials that had been suspended. He dismissed the leaders of the military hierarchy and invited the *piqueteros* to become part of the legion of civil servants that were required by the Ministry of Social Development. After a series of governments that had imposed permanent adjustments and used repression of the popular movements as a necessary complement to anti-popular measures, Argentina now had a government that acknowledged the new relations of social forces and which implemented measures long since demanded, without which the country would have been ungovernable and with which Kirchner's credibility began to rise rapidly.

With a new role assigned to state intervention and the regulatory role of state institutions, and the new configuration of the dominant economic power as a result of devaluation, there was a change not only in government, but in the institutional and economic system as a whole, based on a new scheme for capitalist accumulation and a new role for politics and the state. The new exchange rate encouraged import substitution and favored exports and local consumer goods industries at the expense of privatized services whose dollar resources now began to depreciate. At the same time, arbitration between classes was promoted and internal demand stimulated. All of this, together with the new situation in the international economy resulting from the rising prices of raw materials and food, pushed the economy, after four years of recession, into spectacular rates of growth—above 8 percent of GNP. The default of 2001 freed up resources for public works and social assistance, and the renegotiation of the debt from 2005 onward, with a 70 percent reduction in the bonds that had been defaulted on, reduced its impact on GNP and the national budget significantly. The withdrawal of the Law of Convertibility returned to the country its sovereignty over fiscal and monetary policy and subordinated the Central Bank to the Executive rather than the IMF.

From the ranks of Peronism—that party with its instinct for power; that most successfully sniffed out changes in the international political climate and pragmatically knew which way the wind was blowing; that had been nationalist between 1950 and 1970, democratized in the '80s, and became neoliberal in the '90s—there now emerged the figure who would restore to the political system and the state the stability demanded by the powerful economic groups, the media, and ultimately society as a whole. In a new strategic turn, Peronism became neodevelopmentalist, riding the wave of rising prices for raw materials, profiting to the maximum from the high productivity of export agriculture, and placing both the national state and the figure of the new president at the heart of power, displacing the axis of its alliances from international capital and the banking sector to a multipolar class consensus that left Peronism in place as the mediator between economic forces and the central pillar of the new governability.

The new scheme did not imply a return to the old economic nationalism. The alliances with foreign capital were preserved, and in fact the external focus of the economy was boosted once again in the years that followed. The impulse given to export agriculture, the uncontrolled exploitation of oil and minerals in search of a positive credit balance brought with them new economic and social contradictions. The delayed break with Repsol and the conservation of the old energy system brought a severe crisis in external trade. An integrated auditing of the external debt was still pending, as was the recovery of sovereignty in the International Centre for the Settlement of Investment Disputes; profound judicial reform and reform of the police were demands still unsatisfied. After ten years the levels of poverty and indigence, although they had fallen, remained an insult in a country with an 8 percent growth rate. And, in general, the dependent economic and productive structure, based on primary exports and with no industrial strategy, remained obstacles to the creation of high-quality jobs and a structural reduction of wage inequality. But these continuities with the neoliberal policies of the past cannot conceal the transformations that have occurred across the society and the economy. These include the recovery of politics and the state as the space where expectations and militant enthusiasms are generated, as a new generation enters social and political activity. With the popular rebellion of 2001, a new ideological consensus was generated around national sovereignty and the recuperation of national resources, the rights of the citizen, and a new cultural hegemony regarding the meaning of neoliberalism and the insertion of the country into international politics, congruent with the geopolitical transformations across the continent that have made possible greater levels of independence and freedom in relation to the imperialist powers.

These changes in the relations of social forces that have found expression in a new social and economic regime distinct from its neoliberal predecessor posed the challenge of thinking through the political strategy of the anti-system forces that were part of the living process of the Argentinazo, in a different way from what had been proposed in the 1990s. Now what had to be confronted was not government and state undergoing permanent adjustment, subordinated to the IMF and indifferent to popular demands, but a wholly different one that had placed itself at the head of a relaunch of the process of capitalist accumulation, redoubling the concentration of capital and favoring business and the market economy, but which did that under new conditions, through social pacts and a new mediating role for the state that made popular and democratic demands its own. This proved to be a very difficult test, above all for the radical Left and the autonomists, who continued to press for a confrontation out of sheer inertia, without seeing that society had begun to reject it. Accustomed to the old and simpler recipes, some organizations continued to denounce adjustments and subordination and called for direct action, to which society could not respond.

7. An enduring legacy

The popular rebellion of 2001 has left a legacy that remains present in Argentine society. One subproduct of the rebellion was the recuperation of historic demands. The whole culture changed. The surprising mass character of the mobilizations in comparison with other countries, the high proportion of involvement in the various movements and collectives, the rebelliousness and the high regard in which civic rights are held, the new vision of the place the country should occupy in the world, and the radical revision of the past and its history—all these things are the inheritance left by the resistance, the tradition of struggle and the new relations of social forces generated by the popular rebellion.

The Argentina of 2001 has also left invaluable lessons for the democratic and revolutionary movements around the world, such as the role of the new social subjects in revolutionary processes. It was not a case here of a revolutionary working class leading its unstable middle-class allies. The working class either acted in a conservative manner or acted as part of the rebellion. The most creative and disruptive aspects of the movement can be attributed to these multiple sectors of the exploited who emerged during the resistance. The limits of the rebellion, in the sense that it did not advance to the point of developing anti-capitalist proposals of depth, are not the result of some fundamental social cause; they are political, ideological, and cultural in a country where the anti-capitalist forces, and all the more so after a decade of defeats, remain a minority. But beyond the debates that the rebellion has generated and will continue to generate for years to come, there is one indisputable truth, and it is embedded in the material reality of the popular, democratic, and anti-capitalist struggles that permeate the atmosphere of a new Argentina, which remains unjust, which is still a source of pain, and which will live through new crises and conflicts but will certainly never be the same again. When those new crises and conflicts erupt in the political arena, the people will not have to start from scratch. There are motorcycle vanguards of rebellion, the Kosteki and Santillán, the popular assemblies and the *piqueteros*, the empty pots and the recovered factories, and they will always be there to turn to when history next knocks on the door.

◆ ◆ ◆

This author has drawn on the following works in writing this chapter:

- "IV Relevamiento de Empresas Recuperadas por los Trabajadores," 2013, http://www.recuperadasdoc.com.ar/Presentacion_IV_relevamiento_completa.pdf.
- Manuel Barrientos and Walter Isaía, *Relatos de la Crisis que Cambió la Argentina*, Editora Patria Grande (Buenos Aires, 2011).
- Eduardo Basualdo, *Estudios de Histórica Económica Argentina desde Mediados del Siglo XX a la Actualidad* (Buenos Aires: Siglo XXI, 2010).
- Miguel Bonazo, *El Palacio y la Calle: Crónica de Insurgentes y Conspiradores*

(Buenos Aires: Siglo XXI, 2002).

- "El Estallido Social de De la Rúa es el Más Grave de la Historia Argentina desde la Semana Trágica de 1919," http://nuevamayoria.com/invest/sociolab/csola211201.htm.
- Nicolás Freibrun et al, *Qué es el Kirchnerismo: Escritos desde una Época de Cambio* (Buenos Aires: Peña Lillio y Ediciones Continente, 2011).
- Mirta Lobato and Juan Suriano, *La Protesta Social en la Argentina* (México DF: FCE, 2003).
- Marcos Novaro, *Argentina en el Fin de Siglo: Democracia, Mercado y Nación (1983–2001)* (Buenos Aires: Paidós, 2009).
- Jorge Sanmartino Orovitz, "Crisis, Acumulación y Forma de Estado en la Argentina Post-neoliberal," 2009, http://www.rebelion.org/noticias/2009/12/96377.pdf.

CHAPTER 8

The Pink Tide in Latin America: Where the Future Lay?

Mike Gonzalez

Introduction

The delight of neoliberals watching the Berlin Wall come down found its most famous and odious expression in Francis Fukuyama's declaration of "the end of history." It was the expression of a global capitalism bursting with arrogant confidence. And despite the evident contradictions of what was called, with less irony than it deserved, "actually existing socialism," the collapse of Stalinism exposed how far it had still served so many on the left as a point of reference, and not merely historically. Now the Left that had already beaten so many retreats through the 1980s—in the wake of the defeat of Popular Unity in Chile[1] and in the face of Thatcher and Reagan—could for the most part only wring its hands and search among the rubble for some souvenir of the past.[2]

In the real world, the "end of history" proved to be a second and even more ruthless phase of global capitalist expansion. It has gone by many names—"austerity," "structural adjustment" and the "anti-poverty program" were just some of the euphemisms that an international system found for the disciplining of aberrant states and governments by the World Bank and the International Monetary Fund.[3]

231

In Latin America, the process of globalization came early and with attendant violence. The first "laboratory" of neoliberalism was Chile, where in 1973 the prior conditions for the free movement of capital were created with the characteristic instruments of free trade—repression, the destruction of trade unions, the dismantling of the public sector, and the forcible reduction of living standards for the majority. It continued in Uruguay in 1973, in Argentina (1966–73 and 1976–83), and in Brazil (1968–85) under repressive military regimes. In Bolivia, what the notorious Harvard economist Jeffrey Sachs, globalization's favorite carpetbagger, described as neoliberalism's "most successful experiment" began in 1985. It was a success measured in rising rates of unemployment, disease, and hunger, as its mining industry entered into decline and the miners who had led the key struggles in the country for over thirty years were gradually dispersed.

As the negative impact of neoliberalism intensified there was resistance, both under the military regimes that oversaw its early phase and under the (guided) "return to democracy" that supplanted them. Months before the Wall fell, the "structural adjustments" imposed by Venezuela's newly elected president, Carlos Andrés Pérez, provoked an uprising among the barrios and working-class areas of Caracas and other Venezuelan cities. The Caracazo, as it was called, was brutally repressed, leaving a toll of dead and injured in the thousands. But the memory of those days of urban insurrection lasted far longer than the goods looted from shops and factories. The Caracazo can be seen as a prelude to a rising wave of mass protest and resistance to neoliberal globalization that flowed back and forth across the continent throughout the following decade.

The armed rebellion of the Zapatistas in southern Mexico, on January 1, 1994, was timed to coincide with a press conference in Mexico City at which the presidents of the United States, Canada, and Mexico were to announce the creation of the first regional coordination of their economies in the area covered by the North American Free Trade Agreement (NAFTA).[4] This formalized the progressive integration of the three economies that had been taking place through the previous ten years or so.[5]

The Zapatista rising was brief, but it captured the front pages of the world's press with dramatic pictures of indigenous people in balaclavas wielding rifles (some real, some made of wood) and seizing control, briefly, of the state capital of Chiapas, San Cristóbal de las Casas. These people were the objects of neoliberalism, its victims; they came from deeply poor communities growing maize on tiny, state-subsidized farms that could not survive once those subsidies were removed (a condition of the NAFTA agreement) and the market was flooded by the far cheaper maize coming from the vast US farms that dominated the world market. This "freedom" to overwhelm local markets was protected by neoliberalism and its administrative instrument, the World Trade Organization (WTO).

The 1990s in Latin America witnessed the most brutal phase of neoliberalism. As the land was increasingly diverted to export agriculture, small farmers and agricultural workers were driven into the cities, swelling the populations of the variously named *barrios* that surrounded the expanding megacities. The ending of protectionism opened Latin America to the cheaper imported goods that made internal production un-economic, and sent tens of thousands more into unemployment. Some of this new urban population might find a space on the crowded pavements selling the products of the low paid labor of the East, cheap imitations of the more expensive products that a shrinking but increasingly wealthy local middle class could buy. There were "Rolexes" made in Taiwan, "Lee Jeans" from Pakistan, "Cardin" made in Bangladesh. They earned a precarious living in the swelling street markets of the major cities. If they looked up, they could see the new shopping malls and office blocks that announced the booming wealth of those who represented neoliberalism. As state enterprises were sold off in a frenetic auction and at rock-bottom prices, new millionaires appeared in the society magazines. The dramatic destruction of the state sector, the privatization of public utilities and state industries not only inflated the army of the unemployed. It destroyed health provision, removed what social subsidies existed, privatized higher education, and abandoned rural populations to seek their survival as emigrants.

Foreign investments, bolstered by targeted IMF and World Bank loans, were directed by the end of the '90s into the extractive industries—oil, gas, and mining as well as the cultivation of soy and maize for foreign markets and cattle for the consumption of the developed world. And there were new actors in the field, as the Chinese construction boom exploited the copper that came from Chile, Peru, and Ecuador.

The state, meanwhile, was stripped bare. The political consequences were profound. The public sector, largely indebted to external financial agencies as a result of earlier overspending on infrastructure, was crippled by servicing the foreign debt. Neoliberalism's central consideration was the free movement of capital and the removal of any "restraints" on that freedom—be it subsidies, social security, or public sector spending on health or education. And trade unions were another of those constraints on the liberty of capital. While the trade-union movement had done little for agricultural communities, peasants, or the urban poor, it had grown among the industrial and white-collar working class and, whatever their limitations and compromises with the state, had been capable of mobilizing workers in large numbers. The devastating collapse of industry, the hemorrhaging of workers on a massive scale in the '90s, particularly in the public sector where they had traditionally been strongest, struck a powerful blow against the working class as a whole.

Neoliberalism was also winning an ideological battle. The trade-union leaders had been integrated into the machinery of the major political parties oriented on the state—indeed they were the most committed advocates of state intervention under various theoretical rubrics. The dramatic disappearance of the state now left them with a declining base and no mediating role to play. In Latin America, as in Europe and the US, these sectors very quickly collapsed in the face of neoliberalism and adopted both its analysis and its priorities. In Venezuela it was Pérez, the newly elected president from the largest of the country's official parliamentary parties, Acción Democrática, who imposed the neoliberal strategy. In Mexico, the Institutional Revolutionary Party (PRI)—the populist political expression of the state apparatus—sliced away huge areas of the state sector and served them up to multinational capital even before the NAFTA announcement. In Argentina, it was a Peronist president, Carlos Menem, who wielded the hammer for the massive auction of all Argentina's public assets in 1989–90.[6]

The examples multiply, but the key element was the destruction of the national state as an economic actor, as a guarantor of social policy, and as the representative of a shared social imaginary. It had always fulfilled these functions imperfectly, but it was nonetheless the focus of every left strategy that had evolved in previous decades. The socialist tradition in Latin America, for example, had long argued for a national program for the conquest of the state. Even Cuba, whose revolution in its brief Guevarist phase was resolutely internationalist, moved to a defense of the nation-state as its central strategy after Che's death. And Salvador Allende's Popular Unity program was a transitional reformist strategy *toward* a socialism based on a collaboration between classes. It was his commitment to a program of reform and limited state intervention that brought down the full and terrible weight of ruling-class violence in 1973 to create the appropriate social conditions for neoliberalism.

The advocates of neoliberalism were quick to ascribe the economic failures of the 1970s and 1980s, the prevailing social inequities, and the generalized corruption to earlier reform governments—Perón in Argentina, Juan Velasco Alvarado in Peru, João Goulart in Brazil, the Revolutionary Nationalist Movement (MNR) government in Bolivia among others. And the collapse of Eastern Europe left the reformist left in a state of disarray and confusion that neoliberalism exploited to the full. It was able to do so, of course, because the military regimes that enjoyed US support throughout the region in the wake of the defeat of Popular Unity did their preparatory work with savage efficiency, torturing, exiling, or murdering their revolutionary opponents.[7]

1. The rise and fall of the social movements

In its moment the Zapatista rising appeared to be an isolated event within Mexico (and in the wider context of Latin America). The Zapatista communities were immediately surrounded and besieged by sixty thousand Mexican troops. Yet the movement would have a growing influence and shape the struggles against neoliberalism far beyond Chiapas. Within weeks of the rising, the dispatches sent out on the new World Wide Web by the charismatic leader of the movement, Subcomandante Marcos, defined the enemy and illuminated the paradox at the heart of the new era of globalization.[8] His "Letter from the Lacandon Jungle" was a document as key in its moment as Fidel Castro's Second Declaration of Havana thirty-three years earlier. It was a lengthy denunciation of neoliberalism, and beyond the letter's content, its mode of distribution highlighted the contradiction between a globalizing modernity and its effect in reducing so many millions to new levels of poverty and disenfranchisement. The dramatic collapse of living standards in places like Chiapas coincided with the emergence of that apotheosis of the modern, the internet. Yet it was the World Wide Web that allowed the communities of Chiapas, half of whom had neither clean water nor electricity, to communicate with the world. Within months committees of solidarity were emerging in Europe, in Italy in particular, which took up the Zapatistas' powerful and simple slogan "Ya basta"—enough is enough.

Other movements of resistance to neoliberalism were also evolving. The indigenous movements of Bolivia and Ecuador were mobilizing, and in Brazil the Landless Workers' Movement was occupying land and defying the thugs sent by the landowners. But there was still no coordination between them. The movements arose for the most part at the margins of Latin American society—literally and figuratively. The state had everywhere failed the indigenous communities, the poor inhabitants of the *barrios*, the unemployed, and the expanding numbers engaged in the politically invisible informal economy. But while their resistance grew in intensity, it was limited to confrontations regarding specific and particular effects of the neoliberal assault: the expulsion of small farmers and agricultural workers from their land as export agriculture expanded across the region, for example. Workers who were made unemployed took their protests to the streets, like the Argentine *piqueteros*, or joined organizations fighting on local issues. Many of those forced by the same remorseless expansion of global capitalism into the rapidly growing informal sector were fighting for their own survival. And rising charges for utilities, rents, and transport were also biting into the admittedly fragile security of the lower middle-class, and particularly state employees in health, education, and other sectors.

At this critical juncture, the points of reference that had animated and informed the political debates on the left through previous decades, whatever their results or effects, were absent. The ideological assault that was a specific feature of neoliberalism's version of capitalist globalization seemed to have triumphed at a number of levels. The rising of the Venezuelan masses in February 1989 might have been a spark to light a fire across the continent had there existed a network of left organizations sufficiently embedded in the movements and with the confidence to offer a strategic alternative. But the end of that same year produced the final collapse of Eastern Europe, which, however questionable the socialist credentials of those regimes, had provided at least a historical reference for Latin America and a vocabulary of politics. Cuba, which had been responsible for generating in the 1960s a new and creative variant on the theory of revolutionary warfare, had by the early 1970s accepted the failure of the guerrilla strategy and become, at least in practice, a surrogate and a defender of "actually existing socialism."[9] It was therefore a fatal blow when *glasnost* and *perestroika* in the Soviet Union were expressed in the abandonment of Cuba. By the time neoliberalism had moved on to the post-"end of history" offensive, Cuba was reeling from the blows and entering the "special period in time of peace" (having learned the value of euphemisms) that brought the return of long-extinct diseases (like neuritis) and a catastrophic decline in the already basic standard of living of its citizens. If Cuba exemplified anything as the 1990s began, it was that the conditions of survival in the market, for every variety of competitive capital, private or state, were unrelenting. It was hard to remember, as that terrible decade began, how different the panorama seemed ten years earlier, when the Sandinista revolution overthrew the Somoza dynasty in Nicaragua in July 1979, and when, in January 1980, a quarter of a million well-organized working-class people marched through the center of San Salvador. Certainly the resurrection of the domino theory during Ronald Reagan's presidential campaign in 1981 ominously suggested that Nicaragua had stoked a fire from below that could reach into the very heart of America. Rising levels of military spending to sustain the right-wing forces in Central America, and to undermine the Nicaraguan revolution, were Washington's response.[10] At the end of the decade, in February 1990, the Sandinistas were voted out of office and replaced by a coalition of right-wing organizations, heavily financed from the North, headed by Violeta Chamorro. The Sandinistas, meanwhile, had suffered the economic consequences of a Western-financed contra war against them that claimed huge numbers of dead and wounded and sabotaged the economy.[11]

If the Sandinista victory in 1979 had seemed to vindicate the armed struggle strategy still being pursued elsewhere in Central America, its defeat was a severe strategic one.[12] The corruption and disorganization that followed on their electoral defeat only served to deepen disillusionment and to reinforce the sense that all the available strategies for the conquest of power had failed, especially coming as it did just three months after the fall of the Berlin Wall.

For the Left across Latin America, the 1990s was a time of crisis and disorientation. The combination of disappointments on both sides of the world and the failure of strategies for conquering the state produced few answers but rather an atomization of the revolutionary Left into warring fragments—always a sign of weakness. The parties who fell within the broad category of the "national popular," who had once advocated the creation of strong nation-states with a perspective of greater independence from external control, fell briefly silent across the continent before reappearing as defenders of neoliberal solutions, albeit "soft" ones. It was Peronism, after all, that sold off the Argentine economy to the highest bidder, Acción Democrática that had willingly imposed the conditions for an IMF bailout

in Venezuela, the PRI in Mexico who had abandoned the public sector beginning under the presidency of Miguel de la Madrid in 1982–88, and it was
Christian Democrats and later the Socialist Party who imposed the priorities
of global capital in Chile after the 1989 referendum that removed Pinochet
from office.[13] And it is too easy to forget that the architect of the Brazilian economic miracle, Fernando Henrique Cardoso, was himself a leading
spokesperson for dependency theory from the 1960s onward—advocating
the development of strong, protected national industries to supply the internal market and replace imports (import-substitution industrialization, or
ISI). The arguments they all offered were counsels of despair and admissions
of defeat; it was evidence, if it was needed, that the model to which they
had looked, in both economic and political terms, was Stalinism, reinforced
by the Cuban example. And Cuba's internal disaster, the object of much
gloating from the Right in the United States, was inescapable proof of the
limitations of a strategy of creating socialism in one island. The reaction of
the erstwhile democratic Left was quite simply to surrender not just to the
neoliberal economic assault but also, and perhaps most damagingly, to its
ideological hegemony, with Cardoso as a prime example.

2. Resistance without politics

The confusion and disorientation of the Left gave succor to all those who
agreed with Francis Fukuyama, and they published their versions of "I told
you so" across the continent, from Mario Vargas Llosa in Peru to ex-foreign
minister Jorge Castañeda in Mexico.[14] They insolently characterized as the
"good Left" those who had abandoned any project for radical social change
and as the "bad Left" those who held in some way or another to that out-
moded idea.

Yet resistance continued as neoliberalism's instruments of economic
freedom destroyed lives and livelihoods across the region. The Zapatistas
perhaps made the most impact outside Latin America, but the Movimento
Sem Terra (MST), the Brazilian Landless Workers' Movement, was mobilizing tens and later hundreds of thousands of the country's poorest and most
marginalized in acts of resistance that were exemplary in their creativity and
resolve. In Argentina, it was the growing movements of the unemployed, the
piqueteros, that were mounting the most militant challenges, blocking major
highways, occupying public buildings, and highlighting the lack of support

in the country for the jobless. In Colombia, teachers protested the cutbacks in public spending and the frequency of delays in paying their salaries. And in Ecuador, a decade of careful and systematic organizing by the Confederation of Indigenous Nationalities of Ecuador (CONAIE) began with a national protest in 1990 and culminated in 1999 in the first of a series of risings against "dollarization"—that is, the incorporation of the national economy into regional economic structures dominated by the United States—which brought down a president (Jamil Mahuad).

The campaigns were, in their great majority, defensive battles over the specific consequences of cutbacks and privatizations. Rural communities, small farmers, and agricultural laborers marched over the devastation that a so-called free market caused in their communities, while tariffs and protections were systematically removed in obedience to the prevailing rules of international trade as set out by the WTO. The expansion of mining and oil drilling projects threatened indigenous communities; in Bolivia the final collapse of the tin-mining industry in the High Andes sent whole populations east to the lowlands where they would begin to cultivate coca on small plots. Latin America's cities, or rather the barrios and slums surrounding them, swelled with refugees from the land as the public sector in every country was dismantled, what manufacturing there was disappeared under the wave of cheap imports from even lower-wage economies in the Far East, inflation ate into the value of local currencies, and the consequent anti-inflation policies reduced their incomes and their purchasing capacity to practically nothing.

In the absence of a strong state or trade unions, the task of offering some protection, or finding minimal funding elsewhere to pull communities back from the brink fell increasingly to nongovernmental organizations (NGOs) whose charitable impulse, in the best of cases, or whose cynical manipulation of people's needs and anxieties (especially in the case of the evangelicals proliferating at alarming speed all over Latin America), at worst, won growing influence over the resistance movements in the face of the cynicism of many erstwhile radical politicians and the disorientation of the Left. The emphasis these organizations placed on "empowerment," self-sufficiency, and independence reinforced an ideological discourse that marginalized the language of politics, offering individual solutions to collective problems. In Europe and North America it was the resurgence of anarchist or autonomist ideas, often associated with solidarity with the social movements, that reflected the growing and wholly understandable suspicion of mainstream politics of right and left. What these two very different currents shared was a refusal to engage with issues of state power.

Neoliberalism was being confronted, and the challenges spread across the world with the birth of an anti-capitalist movement. It took a number of forms in the West as the 1990s drew to its end, with demonstrations against G7, anti-militarism marches in the US, and protests over debt under the banner of Jubilee 2000 and later ATTAC in Europe. The growing awareness of unfair international trade and the burden of foreign debt were among the elements that spurred the Seattle demonstration against the WTO in November 1999, just ten years after the fall of the Wall. But the inspiration provided by the rising struggles in the South was acknowledged in the potent symbol of the red (Zapatista) bandannas that many of the Seattle demonstrators wore.

At that early stage, what was celebrated was the phenomenon of resistance itself, and as each battleground was marked on the map of Latin America there was a clear sense that a fightback had begun. The revolutionary Left, however, was slow to respond to these developments, for reasons that arose from an interpretation of the Marxist tradition that had consigned many of the forces involved to a secondary role in the class struggle. Yet it was clear that the organized working class, the historical subject of socialist revolution, was largely absent from the new movements; yet those who were increasingly taking to the streets across Latin America clearly belonged to the class of the exploited. There were clear reasons for that. Undermining the trade unions was central to the neoliberal strategies emerging out of the 1990s. The material base of the working class as a formation, the industries and workplaces where they were concentrated across Latin America, were starved of capital, replaced by competing producers both in the North and in the poorer countries of the South, and systematically closed down. There was certainly resistance, like the factory occupations that began in the late 1990s in Argentina. But the rapidly rising rates of unemployment and the massive shift of workers into the informal or services sectors, destroying the advances that had been made in previous decades, were blows struck at the very heart of the working class.

The dilemma was how to address this major and significant shift in the balance of class forces. How would organizations in the revolutionary tradition, for whom "socialism was the self-emancipation of the working class," make sense of the rise of indigenous movements, peasant mobilizations, the organizations of the landless and the unemployed who were in the vanguard of the struggle as the new century began? How would it contest the buried ideology of self-help, cooperative organization, and negotiation with neoliberalism that the majority of NGOs were advocating? And finally, what kind of coordination of struggle would the left advocate, not only because internationalism was a central tenet of the tradition, but also because struggles isolated from one another facing a highly organized and—for the moment at least—unified and centralized world capitalist class could not hope to achieve a different future. These were the urgent issues that the socialist left, in its many manifestations, must necessarily address. Unfortunately, the debates were delayed by a residual sectarianism in a fragmented and quarrelsome revolutionary Left and a Stalinist inheritance that had compromised revolutionary parties in Latin America by their commitment to alliances with social democratic and populist organizations, the very same organizations that were now, enthusiastically or otherwise, imposing the priorities of the World Bank and the IMF. The compromises that Allende offered in Chile to the "middle sectors" in the hope of winning their support had simply strengthened the bourgeois opposition and confused and disoriented the broad grassroots movement that was both beginning to defend and drive forward the process of change on the ground.[15]

The central role in that discussion would now be taken, internationally, by thinkers who, in Emir Sader's words, "instead of putting forward strategic solutions made a virtue of their absence."[16] The Zapatistas, for example, were an inspiration for the resistance movements in Latin America and beyond. Yet their leader, Subcomandante Marcos, dispensed an ambiguous message to the wider world in his declarations from the Lacandon jungle. Marcos's own background was in a softer version of Maoism, laced with anarchist notions of the autonomy of the movements. Though it was almost certainly unintended, the implication was that each struggle would generate its own forms of organization and its own language of revolution. In the real circumstances of the time the recognition that each movement found the revolutionary impulse in its own specific history and circumstances was a creative contribution to the thinking of the Left. The wider anti-capitalist movement had already recognized that in its central slogan, "Act local, think global." But it was imperative that the two aspects were connected politically if the Left was to have an impact on the unfolding struggle. By failing to engage with the specificities and addressing only the global issues, the Left effectively abandoned the key roles in the debates within the movement to those most hostile to the revolutionary tradition and to Marxism. Marxism embraces and responds to the dynamics of the living movement, or it is nothing. But the field is never left fallow. In this case the political vacuum was filled by, among others, John Holloway, a British academic living in Mexico who became the spokesman and interpreter of the Zapatistas. His book on their struggle, *Change the World without Taking Power* became the dominant analysis within the movement.[17] And it was reinforced by equally influential, though far less accessible, works by Michael Hardt and Toni Negri, *Empire* and *Multitude*.[18]

The working-class movement had suffered serious defeats at the hands of neoliberalism, but the resistance continued, mobilizing forces that had not simply arisen from nowhere. What was absent was a unifying idea that could embrace and coordinate them all, and which could address the realities of class power. While the social movements could and did successfully challenge the state in Bolivia, Ecuador, Paraguay, and elsewhere, often bringing down governments, the political problem for the Left was that their demands were limited to particular cases. Neoliberalism was the identifiable enemy, and the role of the national state in acting on its behalf was exposed too. But the broader politics of social transformation and of the role of the state within it were rarely addressed within the movements.

3. Democracy from below

The election of Hugo Chávez to the Venezuelan presidency in 1998 was a critical milestone, at least as far as external commentators were concerned. It was certainly significant that a political outsider from humble origins should have won the presidency in a country where for forty years access to power was determined by an electoral pact called *puntofijismo* between the two major political parties; the arrangement had ensured the controlled allocation of Venezuela's oil wealth and of power within the Venezuelan state. Chávez was a political outsider, a parachute regiment colonel who had led a very brief and unsuccessful coup in 1992. But he won the popular vote against an archetypal white bourgeois candidate in 1998, and in the following year announced a Constituent Assembly to write a new Bolivarian constitution. It was, in essence, a radical liberal proposal at this stage. But the election of delegates to the Assembly generated widespread political debate, and the new constitution's central clauses promised a new kind of participatory democracy, based on a "civic-military alliance."

This was an important turning point, but initially only insofar as a new occupant was entering the Miraflores presidential palace, leading the first of the new left governments. But it was events elsewhere, in Bolivia especially, that represented the beginnings of a "pink tide"—if that term is understood as the surge of a new, radically democratic movement from below rather than simply the election of new, more progressive candidates to power. The term "pink tide" was an ironic, skeptical comment on these governments coined by a *New York Times* journalist in 2005. But what was dramatically new was the rising tide of grassroots social movements posing fundamental issues, *in their practice*, about the nature of democracy itself. While the election of Chávez was significant, it seems to me that the line of continuity runs from the Caracazo through Zapatismo to the Cochabamba Water Wars, the Argentinazo of 2001, to the Gas War in the city of El Alto, Bolivia, and from there through to Oaxaca in Mexico in 2006.

The new social movements introduced a new political logic into Latin America that coincided with the emergence of new left governments. In some cases, especially Bolivia and Ecuador, the movements created the political spaces that were filled by governments. In Venezuela, the dispersed network of local community and grassroots organizations had, in many cases, common political origins in the failed guerrilla movements of the 1960s, as George Ciccariello-Maher's important "people's history," *We Created Chávez*, demonstrates.[19] Their relationship with Chávez was not organic at first, but became so in the political vacuum of the late 1990s, which Chávez came to fill with his charismatic personality and his wide-ranging nationalist discourse. He himself saw the military as playing a dominant role, until it was widened into a "civic-military alliance"—although as we shall see below the military dimension was never superseded. In the case of Bolivia it was the long history of indigenous resistance interwoven with the history of organization of the miners that shaped the extraordinary struggles of the early twenty-first century. The coca famers (*cocaleros*) of the Chapare were exemplary in building on the history of both resistance traditions when Evo Morales led their trade union. And although it is true that the profile of organized trade unions was low in many of the social movements, the collective memory of union struggles continued to play a key role, particularly in Cochabamba and El Alto.[20]

Cochabamba's battle against the privatization of water in early 2000 successfully confronted a hostile state. It was a movement that drew together trade unions, neighborhood groups, students, and indigenous communities fighting over land as well as water provision. It shared with many other movements a suspicion of traditional left organizations, who, as experience had shown, would fight for leadership of such movements only to divide them or redirect them toward struggles for power in the state. The traditions from which they emerged, however, emphasized collective decision-making, solidarity, and cooperation as well as a relationship with the natural environment summarized in the concept of *buen vivir* (the good life). This was translated in the West into a kind of "back to nature" movement, easily characterized as an anti-modern stance, a charge that would later be leveled against them by the Morales government over the TIPNIS case (discussed below).[21] It was, of course, much more profound than that and set within the framework of a clear understanding of the nature and consequences of neoliberal strategies of austerity that the movements had risen up against. Cochabamba, for example, mobilized the traditions of collective resistance against the multinational corporation Bechtel, recent purchasers of the city's water concession, and won.[22] The organization then worked to build collective instruments of water control and developed its experience in collaboration with those confronting other multinational interests in the Water and Gas Wars of El Alto.

The traditional Left, including the revolutionary Left, failed to understand the class nature of the new movements—that they were not outside the working class, but expressions of its new configurations under neoliberalism. The street traders, the coca farmers, the community activists, the indigenous communities were all fighting the same enemy (as the Zapatistas had shown) from a political perspective shaped by the forms of organization their struggles took—democratic, collective, transparent, and with social purposes. The Cochabamba Water War was not just against privatization but for collective control and administration.[23] In Ecuador the indigenous communities were mobilizing in defense of their "territorios," which meant more than just land, but also the forms of working the land and conserving it. The World Social Forums, for example, held at Porto Alegre in Brazil, took their lead from the Zapatistas and provided a space of encounter and discussion between the movements, but party political issues were explicitly excluded, as if they belonged to a different sphere, outside the struggle itself.

The movements had good cause to be skeptical. The Left of previous years—the national-popular parties like the Bolivian MNR, the Mexican People's Democratic Party (PRD) the Chilean Socialist Party, and Lula's Workers Party in Brazil—had failed to support the social movements. For that very reason, the right-wing neoliberals described them as the "good left"—the sensible compromisers, the people who accepted the inevitability of globalization and were prepared to negotiate within it. Hardt, Negri, and Holloway, however, argued that it was politics itself that was at fault—in an environment in which the absence of strategic ideas that could respond in any way to the emerging movements, their visions and their political language were dramatically exposed. In arguing the fundamental instability of social forces, their shifting location geographically and socially, and their multiple and hybrid character, which Holloway (echoing Marcos) described as "swarms of bees," they were affirming the impossibility of coordination or of acting with a coherent and consistent unity of purpose. In other words, the lack of strategic thinking was in their very nature.

In fact, the social movements *were* developing alternatives, many of them described as environmental programs or cultural projects, that were attempts to address the dominance of the capitalist model of development and production. But these were still in their early stages and unspecific on the question of state power. Their demands, nevertheless, brought them into direct conflict with existing governments, and their extremely successful mobilizations brought a number of those governments down.

4. Two logics, two futures

In each case, the governments of the pink tide took over as a result of these mass mobilizations in the context of the collapse of the previous state. But that created a fundamental tension in the processes; the demand for a radical democracy, the logic of participation and protagonism—as the Venezuelan constitution put it, the concept of *buen vivir*—that enshrined the historic demands of the indigenous communities were at the heart of these movements.

It might be argued that Venezuela was an exception, but that in my view is to misunderstand the Bolivarian process. Chávez won the presidency in 1998, but on April 12–13, 2002, a right-wing coup was launched in an attempt to bring his government down. It had been preceded by intensified confrontations between Chávez and the bourgeoisie. Chávez was kidnapped and the head of the Employers' Federation, Pedro Carmona, anointed himself president. But it was a very short-lived coup. The barrios descended into the city and surrounded the presidential palace demanding Chávez's return. At that moment, the initiative passed to the mass movement. It did so again when there was an attempt to sabotage the oil industry, during what was called the "bosses' strike" (*el paro patronal*), which lasted from December 2002 to March 2003 and which was again defeated by a mass mobilization and the critical actions of the industry's workers (though not the white-collar or managerial section that had joined the sabotage). At that moment, the mass organizations shaped the course of future events, just as they had in Bolivia and Ecuador and also briefly in Argentina.

Between 2003 and 2005, it was possible to imagine a social transformation born of this process driven from below, a change that could challenge the logic of capitalism. But there was an unresolved tension between the logic of resurgent socialism from below and the logic of occupying the state. Many years later, in the last government program he established as president (the Plan de la Patria 2013–19), Chávez would acknowledge the failure in Venezuela to seize the moment and "pulverize the bourgeoisie," transforming the state and laying the foundations of a new, democratic power. For while the social movements were building from below, the issue of control of the state fell to the traditional left forces that had played a very limited role in these new mobilizations. They had developed strategies when it came to taking state power, though they were limited to the occupation of the institutions of formal democracy and, as it would prove, to policies and strategies that could be enacted within that framework.

In Bolivia, for example, Evo Morales had worked with the previous state president, Carlos Mesa, who, while dissenting from prior levels of state violence, could not bring himself to sign a law that nationalized Bolivian gas and oil, the central demand of the social movements of El Alto. He resigned and Morales, now representing the Movimiento al Socialismo (MAS), won the presidential election of 2005. But the "nationalization" he announced on May 1, 2006, while it was a significant political moment, was in fact limited to an increase in taxes and royalties paid by foreign companies, with a limited sector taken into public ownership. In Ecuador the downfall of Lucio Gutiérrez in 2005 came as a result of a broad "civic" movement; the indigenous communities were divided and disoriented by Gutiérrez's betrayal of their cause, since it was their voting strength that had carried him to power four years earlier. The struggle of indigenous communities against mining companies on the one hand and neoliberal austerity measures on the other brought to the presidency Rafael Correa, an academic economist who had acted briefly as economics minister under the previous government before resigning after his proposals for social spending were rejected. In Argentina, the upheavals that followed the Argentinazo of December 2001, when the population of Argentina had risen up with its demand "que se vayan todos" (time to get rid of them all), produced some extremely creative forms of popular resistance, but Peronism was able to assimilate and debilitate the movements by selective subsidies and political horse trading.[24] Nestor Kirchner, who came to power there in 2003, was a second-level Peronist governor of the province of Santa Clara who won the election on promises to address the abuses of human rights under the military and to establish some limited social programs for the very poor. In Venezuela, the aftermath of the defeated bosses' strike and the Chávez victory in the subsequent recall referendum ushered in a period of radicalism—or at least so it appeared.

In each case, the response to the movements was a promise to restore the social spending so drastically reduced under earlier neoliberal governments and a recognition of indigenous *cultural* and *political* rights. These were enshrined in new constitutions written by the constituent assemblies (*constituyentes*) called in 1999 in Venezuela, in 2006 in Bolivia, and in 2007 in Ecuador. These constituent assemblies had been a central demand of the mass movements, expressions of a new and more advanced democracy based on elected and accountable delegates. They were seen as the alternative to the *constituted* (or bourgeois) democracy from which the members of the broad movements would have been in many cases excluded.

While the new governments enthusiastically adopted the discourse of radical democracy, it was significant, and alarming, that the Bolivian government of Morales excluded social movements from representation in the assembly, permitting only political parties to present candidates. It was a warning sign.

In 2005, at Porto Alegre, Chávez had declared what he called "21st century socialism" as the direction in which Venezuela was traveling. It followed in the wake of his creation of the Missions, essentially social welfare programs involving health, education, and housing for Venezuela's poor citizens. Their nature was ambiguous; while the state still remained under the control of the old functionaries, the Missions were based on local and community organization and were charged with the implementation of the programs. It would have been an error, however, to see them necessarily as forms of participatory democracy, though they were presented in rather ambiguous terms as its predecessors. The issue was how they were controlled and led. They seemed far more directed than participatory organs and their relationship with the state clientelistic. In the wake of the nationalization of oil in 2005, the Missions would be financed directly by increased oil revenues—and this at a point of high and rising world oil prices.

In terms of strategy Venezuela was by now providing some direction for the pink tide. While "sovereignty" was a key term in Venezuela, and anti-imperialism a central tenet of the developing discourse, the "socialist" nature of the process remained to be defined. No one could deny the immense popularity of Chávez, nor the support his distribution of oil revenues through the state generated. That support found expression in the overwhelming, 62 percent majority he won in the presidential elections of 2006.

At this point Chávez and his planning minister, Jorge Giordani, announced a new and more radical economic plan, which involved nationalizations—not expropriations, however, since the enterprises were bought at market prices—in telecommunications, cement, aluminum, and electricity, and the creation of social enterprises and cooperatives. The sole aluminum processing plant, Alcasa, was to be placed under workers' management directed by Carlos Lanz, an ex-guerrilla and the main advocate of workers' control. D. L. Raby described developments at this stage as the creation of "a revolutionary concept of direct popular sovereignty," in which "the conventional army has been in large part transformed into a revolutionary army."[25] This was wildly utopian and challenged by another contemporary development. Immediately after his reelection, Chávez announced the formation of a new mass party, the United Socialist Party of Venezuela (PSUV). This could by no stretch of the imagination be described in the way that Raby suggested; despite Chávez's declaration of "21st century socialism," the PSUV was the political expression of a centralized state apparatus. It was built on the Cuban model of state control, which could not be described at all as a model of socialism from below. On the contrary, it was highly centralized, and the program and conditions of membership were announced to the six million who immediately joined rather than offered for discussion and approval. Although Chávez had promised an open mass socialist party, it was not transparent or participatory in any real sense. For the Left this created an enormous dilemma. The revolutionary organizations split over the question, since to remain outside would clearly have meant isolation from the mass of working people, while entering risked co-optation or silence.

The Venezuelan government's commitment to using oil revenues to improve the lives of the majority was not in question. In many ways the perspective underpinning the project was state-led developmentalism. But the impressive growth figures during this period of unprecedently high oil prices did not indicate any change of direction or emphasis in the economy. The economic plan presented by Chávez and Giordani in 2006 appeared to point to a diversification of the economy financed by rising oil revenues. Yet the process effectively stopped in 2007 and while some enterprises were taken into state ownership when their owners deserted or threatened closure, there was no evidence of a strategy. The demands raised by the social movements had looked beyond rising state incomes toward structural transformations. That certainly could have been an escape route from the prison of the global market. And that, together with a genuine participation of the majority population in decision-making across the economy, would have justified the description of the pink tide as revolutionary and the future it promised as new and different.

While there were significant differences in the forms of organization of the movements in each country, it was clear that the Venezuelan example had encouraged and legitimized the governments of the "pink tide"—and not solely by virtue of the direct support given to them by the Bolivarian government of Hugo Chávez.

But the pink tide was not to be merely a change of personnel; it was also to be a change of the method and the content of governing. The support for the new governments was *collective* and organized; it was also provisional, as many of those organizations made clear at the outset.[26]

The election of Lula to the Brazilian presidency in 2002 might well have been seen as a new victory for the pink tide. He was after all a founder of the Workers' Party (PT), a child of poverty and a leading trade-union militant of the early 1980s. But the Lula who finally won the presidency was a different man. He had changed his clothes and his image, and his electoral propaganda in his victory year made no mention of his membership in the PT. Nevertheless the population cheered him on when he visited the World Social Forum in Porto Alegre early in 2003. Yet he went directly from there to the World Economic Forum in Davos, Switzerland, where capitalism's most powerful leaders meet to strategize. He did announce some social programs directed at the very poor, like Fome Zero (Zero Hunger) and the Bolsa de Familia (Family Basket). But these were cash transfer schemes directed at individual families and not structural changes. Thus, he refused to honor the promises made to the civil servants' union over their pensions. He had already announced, in a "Letter to Brazilians," that the neoliberal policies of his predecessor, Fernando Henrique Cardoso, would be continued.[27] For the MST, who might have hoped for action on the inequalities in land ownership, it was a disappointment, but not unexpected. It had announced before the election that its activities were only suspended, and relaunched them shortly afterward. In reality, Lula had several of its leaders arrested at the time and despite their common origins, the distance between Lula and the MST continued to widen.

Hugo Chávez's famous speech at the World Social Forum in 2005 was, of course, in tune with the demands for popular democracy coming from the social movements. But unlike Bolivia, Ecuador, and other countries in the region, there had been in Venezuela no independent expression from below from which that demand had come. In the socialist tradition, people's (or worker's power) is the expression of a new kind of state, born out of organs created in struggle by the workers themselves. In Latin America, those struggles—the Chilean *cordones* in 1972, the Bolivian *cabildos*, the Argentine *asambleas populares*, the occupation of the Mexican city of Oaxaca in 2006, and the base committees that arose in Honduras after the coup of 2009—had emerged as expressions of a different kind of power, challenging that of the bourgeois state in a transient and catastrophic equilibrium.[28] The renaming of Venezuela's ministries as Ministries of People's Power was no more than that, a change of title, since their occupants were nominated exclusively from above and without explanation. In his Plan de la Patria 2013–19, Chávez opens by acknowledging that this plan is "a program for a transition to socialism and for the radicalization of participatory democracy. Let's not fool ourselves—the socio-economic formation that prevails in Venezuela is still rentier capitalism."[29] He then went on to refer to the need to "pulverize" the bourgeois state and its "old nefarious practices." His death in March 2013 was also the death of that promise.

There was no doubt that the pink tide governments had been carried to power on a wave of popular resistance in Bolivia, Ecuador, Argentina, Venezuela, Uruguay, and briefly Paraguay too. The new governments recognized that political debt at the level of discourse, in the calling of constituent assemblies and in the plurinational nature of the new constitutions. That movement would still have to be called upon to defend the new governments in Venezuela in 2002–4 and in Bolivia in 2006–8.

But to what extent did the left governments take on, let alone "pulverize" the bourgeois state formation? The most sophisticated ideological justification of the manner in which the new states were formed comes from Bolivian vice-president Álvaro García Linera in his famous essay on "creative tensions in the Bolivian process."[30] Having described the period before Evo's accession to power as one of dual power, he then asserts that the new government was built on the "forces of insurrection." Yet he would later argue that its first phase was the construction of an "Andean Amazonian capitalism"—a formulation that Evo Morales himself would later reject and replace with "state capitalism." There was no disagreement between them, however, that it was a form of capitalism that was emerging from the "insurrectionary" phase—in direct contravention of its driving impulses. In Ecuador Rafael Correa, once his occupation of the presidency was consolidated, turned against the forces that had transformed the political landscape of Ecuador, particularly the indigenous movements fighting the mining companies ravaging their territories, denouncing them as "infantile environmentalists" and later criminalizing their struggles and arresting their leaders.[31]

It is that contradiction that García Linera refers to when he speaks of "creative tensions," claiming that they can be resolved within the process. But he himself refers to "points of bifurcation" when the options clearly conflict. In Bolivia that point came with the TIPNIS events; in Ecuador around the issue of Yasuni; and in Venezuela with the death of Chávez and the accession to power of Nicolas Maduro. On each of these occasions the strategic direction taken by the pink tide governments directly and devastatingly diverged from the promises and undertakings given to those who had carried them to power. Jeff Webber has dealt with the TIPNIS events of 2011 very thoroughly in a number of essays. In Bolivia, the government had agreed to the construction of a highway through TIPNIS (Isiboro Sécure National Park and Indigenous Territory) to facilitate access to the region for Brazilian and Argentine multinational capital, flouting its own undertaking to protect the local indigenous populations. Their march to the capital was stopped by national police sent by the interior minister, and mass protests broke out all over the country. The road construction, financed by Brazilian capital, was temporarily stopped but was resumed in 2017, after Morales withdrew the area's protected status. There was very little that was "creative" about these tensions; they were an open clash between neoliberal interests given free access to Bolivia, and those forces that fought against neoliberalism and supported a Morales government. In 2016, Evo called a referendum to support his right to stand for the presidency beyond the two terms allowed by the new constitution. He lost the vote. Two years later, in 2018, a constitutional court announced that the referendum result would be set aside and he would be allowed to stand again. "How could we manage," García Linera asked, "without our father Evo?" How quickly the collective enterprise was turned into a personalist project—*Chavismo, Correismo, Kirchnerismo, Evoismo!* The Bolivian state is now expanding the extractive sector of the economy—oil, gas, mining, and export agriculture—at the expense of local industry and small and medium agriculture.

In Ecuador it was the Amazonian region of Yasuni that fulfilled a similar revelatory role. A region of unique biodiversity, its local ecology was devastated by the presence of oil companies. The Ecuadorean Supreme Court's $9 billion fine against Chevron-Texaco for the environmental damage it caused was of course ignored in the US where the company was based. It was proposed that further oil exploration be stopped, and Correa challenged the world (and several wealthy Hollywood personalities) to provide the resources to embark on an alternative program for the region. The money failed to appear and oil production has now resumed in the region. In reality the decision to expand oil production and mining had already been taken by Correa—hence his attacks on "indigenists"—and the country has committed to an expansion of the extractive industries.

By 2018, each of the pink tide governments has reconstituted its dependence on the extractive industries, a dependency whose ending was a central plank of each of their programs. And it should be emphasized that this is not a matter of an unwise choice between economic options. Mining and oil production are global activities conducted by multinational enterprises that produce for the global market. The decisions by Bolivia and Ecuador, and similar decisions taken by Argentina and Peru, represent a reentry into the global market and the reimposition of neoliberalism. In current circumstances the return to extractivism includes a commitment from governments to provide infrastructure and guarantee profits with massive tax concessions.

5. The demise of a revolution

The most far-reaching and destructive example, at every level of this reversal of the revolutionary process, however, is Venezuela under Nicolas Maduro. Maduro was elected to the Venezuelan presidency in April 2013, immediately after the death of Chávez under circumstances which remain unexplained. He won against the right-wing candidate Henrique Capriles Radonski by less than 1 percent, and the fact that he won at all was entirely due to the relentless evocation of the dead comandante. The result was not the expression of a swing to the right but of a growing discontent and frustration among the Chavista base itself. By 2012 the public sector was deteriorating and the ineffectiveness and corruption of the state becoming increasingly obvious. A new layer of bureaucrats had taken over the state machine—the very ones that Chávez was referring to in his final message—and the PSUV, far from providing a forum for discussion and accountability, was already becoming a machinery of power devoted to protecting the bureaucracy against the mass movement. By then the leaders of the grassroots movements had largely been co-opted, just as they had in Bolivia; their role was to transmit government decisions down to the base, rather than the reverse. The Right was active and by 2014 had turned to the street violence of the *guarimbas*, organized by the far right and led by Leopoldo López and his Popular Vanguard party. Maduro's response, however, was to call elements of the Right to dialogue with the government, particularly the country's richest capitalist, Lorenzo Mendoza.

The protests escalated, and while Maduro repeated that the right to protest was sacrosanct, the numbers killed passed forty and the number of people imprisoned reached three thousand. The shortages were growing worse, especially in the poor areas, and the emptying shelves in pharmacies told their own story. The reality was that medicines were increasingly hard to find; the Barrio Adentro medical centers could only offer advice, and the public hospitals had neither medication nor equipment. The situation in the countryside was dire; agricultural production was falling and food imports, expensive and unreliable, now represented 95 percent of what was consumed. It was partly the result of insecurity on the land, lack of credits, and the rising cost of pesticides, over whose production the Chavista minister Elias Jaua had a virtual monopoly. Industrial production declined dramatically, through a lack of inputs, corruption, and mismanagement. Most importantly of all, oil production was static at 2.5 million barrels. Rafael Ramirez, president of the oil and gas company PDVSA, had promised 5 million by 2015, but lack of maintenance of plant and equipment were having the reverse effect. The bauxite to supply the Alcasa aluminum plant in Puerto Ordaz was no longer arriving because the six massive extractor machines from Belarus had ceased to function and there were no spare parts.

The most active sector of the economy continued to be currency speculation. The figures for capital flight and speculation are very hard to pin down. Ex–economic minister Jorge Giordani said in 2016 that something like $450 billion had been effectively embezzled through phantom companies. The official bolivar/dollar rate was by now around 10 to the dollar; the market rate at least a hundred times that figure. Dollars bought officially to pay for imports either made their way into foreign bank accounts or paid for goods that were priced at the unofficial rate, if and when they appeared in Venezuela. And all of this generated massive corruption. Infrastructural projects paid for with external loans, which were now increasingly high-interest, short-term loans from China, rarely reached completion—and the Odebrecht case in Brazil exposed the astronomical sums that the Brazilian construction giant paid out in bribes (or "commissions" as they were known). The state bureaucracy was complicit in all these crooked deals, and so too was the bourgeoisie. It was becoming clear that the shortages were affecting the poor, who had no access to dollars, but the 4x4s circulating in Caracas and the packed high-priced restaurants confirmed that one section of society was doing very well. Maduro would regularly announce investments that never materialized, commissions of investigation that never functioned, and regular changes of personnel at the ministerial level, which seemed to involve the relatives of other ministers.

As the December 2015 National Assembly elections approached, the Chavista media confidently predicted success, despite persistent reports to the contrary. It was as if the origins of the Maduro government were sufficient guarantee of its continuing success. The PSUV kept the social base at bay, carefully controlling the discontent that was palpable everywhere by then. There were still enough Chavista loyalists to drown out any expressions of doubt and label them fascist or tools of the international bourgeoisie waging war on the revolution. But on the ground the shortages, the mounting violence, and the arrogance of the rich in their guarded, gated communities were taking their toll. The signs were there—rising inflation, the murder of prominent independents, the killing of the indigenous leader Sabino Romero in the north leading the defense of their territories against the state coal mining company, the long queues for spare parts at the auto suppliers in search of batteries or windscreen wipers, the rise of the black economy, the *bachaqueros*, as they were called. What was happening in the social imaginary?

As the public functions of state and government ground to a halt, the frustrations grew. Long queues stretched around cash machines that only issued 300 bolivars at a time while inflation had devalued the bolivar to make it virtually useless. The whole distribution network for food and necessities had moved into the shadows, while shops yawned with empty shelves. You got your coffee from the dentist, your maize flour from the builder, your meat from a back room at the butchers. You wondered when the resignation would end.

The December 2015 election gave the opposition an absolute majority in the Assembly, the two-thirds required to block legislation—or at least it did until an Electoral Commission appointed by Maduro discovered sufficient irregularities to reduce it to a simple majority. The PSUV lost two million votes—but they did not go to the Right. No Chavista could vote for a right wing that had begun its campaign by trying to sabotage the oil industry and had continued with often lethal street barricades. They were the old Venezuela that Chávez had promised to transform. The coalition of the Right, the Democratic Unity Roundtable (MUD), entered the Assembly with no serious alternative program; their sole concern was to remove Maduro and release their martyr, Leopoldo López, from prison. Their only declared policy—to increase oil production—coincided with the Chavistas.

The Right then announced its intention to call a recall referendum to remove Maduro, as the constitution allowed. For once the regime acted quickly; it refused to recognize the Assembly elections and declared what would prove to be an almost permanent state of emergency. With hindsight it is clear that this was a definitive shift in the axis of power; the state of emergency both veiled and legitimated several processes—the militarization of the state, the use of enabling laws to supersede the constitution, the relegation of the PSUV to a supporting role while its national leadership was restricted to a group of four—Maduro, his wife Cilia Flores, Diosdado Cabello, and Vladimir Padrino López, the minister of defense and later vice-president. This inner cabal met weekly while PSUV party meetings declined in number. Flores controlled the institutional networks (she had been Assembly president), Cabello and Padrino managed the military, and Maduro dominated the public stage. But the hidden power behind them all were the Cubans, whose control of intelligence and several key state functions gave them real power, away from any public scrutiny. The democratic process, which Chávez generally had observed while seeking to control it, now became a theater of shadows. The Supreme Court and Electoral Commission were now creatures of the presidency, with no independence; their role was to provide a patina of legality to presidential decisions. It was too much for one hitherto unconditional loyalist, Luisa Ortega Díaz, attorney general under Chávez, who denounced the process and the misuse of power.

Where was the Right, the "democratic opposition" praised by European conservatives and Washington? The truth is that they were oddly silent and riven with internal division. Prices rose at gathering speed, the shortages of food and medicines became chronic. Neither the Right nor the government had any solution to offer, other than lengthy denunciations of an "economic war" waged by unnamed parties. But both the old bourgeoisie and what came to be called the "Boliburguesia" (the Chavista new bourgeoisie) continued to buy dollars at artificially low prices and speculate in the US economy, hoard goods, and resell them at hugely inflated prices, and take their bribes and commissions for public projects that simply did not happen. The Right and the "Left" denounced each other and profiteered together. Maduro meanwhile appointed a neoliberal economist, Miguel Pérez Abad, as his vice-president for the economy. As the oil price fell and there were shrinking revenues to finance state spending, the social programs began to fall apart, infrastructural projects like the new railway system ceased construction, and production—already at a low ebb—virtually ceased. Despite claims to the contrary, oil production also declined—there was a devastating fire at one of the main oil installations, and the lack of spare parts and inadequate maintenance and mismanagement did the damage at others.

In February 2016, Maduro unveiled the new economic strategy—the Arco Minero project. It should be remembered that the backdrop to this declaration was a rate of inflation that was already the highest in the world, an average weight loss among the population of around 12 kilos, or 26 pounds, the desperate daily search for food, the return of poverty, and a rising tide of violence both perpetrated by criminals and the state. Maduro's response to the privations that most ordinary Venezuelans were suffering was to invite 150 multinational companies to return to exploit the almost limitless oil and mineral reserves of the Orinoco Basin, known as the Arco Minero.

This represented the reversal of the Bolivarian Revolution. And the actions that immediately succeeded the announcement reinforced that impression. The failure to win the Assembly meant that a blanket of legitimacy could not be drawn across the project.

The Arco Minero, in Venezuela's part of the Amazon Basin, comprises 12 percent of the country's land surface. It is also one of the world's richest reserves of minerals, oil, and gas as well as the source of most of Venezuela's fresh water. Maduro announced that the region would be opened to bids from 150 multinational companies who would be granted concessions in the Arco. Edgardo Lander described the decision as a moment of civilizational crisis, and he joined with a group of the Bolivarian revolution's most respected intellectuals and analysts in denouncing it.[32] The announcement itself was a disaster on many levels, and it produced a deep internal crisis. But it also became clear that a number of earlier decisions anticipated the declaration.

In January 2015 the army was given permission to use live ammunition in controlling demonstrations. Shortly after the invitation to the multinationals, Maduro announced the formation of a new company, Cominpeg, based within the Ministry of Defense and run by the military, but independent of both ministry and government. It would take charge of the minerals sector, including oil and gas, and their extraction and distribution. The prevailing state of emergency made the region a special zone exempt from a number of constitutional provisions. In May 2016 a renewed State of Exception deepened militarization while the PSUV was given an extended public order role. A year later, in February 2017, a new rapid intervention force was created, the Rapid Deployment Force, whose task was to act quickly, especially in the barrios, to contain disorder—and to kill drug distributors and meet internal violence with violence. They would be joined by a sinister civilian equivalent, the People's Liberation Organizations (or OLPs), denounced in mid-2018 by the United Nations for the murder of at least five hundred people in the poor barrios.[33]

The campaign to collect the requisite number of signatures for a recall referendum began shortly after the Assembly elections. Although the number required was achieved, the Electoral Commission repeatedly questioned individual signatures and then blocked the referendum altogether in 2016. It is interesting to compare Chávez's own reaction to a recall referendum in 2004. He called for a political response and won. Of course that was the height of Chávez's popularity and he could be reasonably certain of victory. For Maduro it represented a danger, a risk that his key project would be derailed—and it was stopped.

The Arco Minero marked a crisis at a number of levels. It marked not simply the electoral decline of Chavismo but also its political erosion and collapse as a mass movement. The indigenous communities whose rights were guaranteed under the 1999 Constitution are now being driven from their homes. The environmental devastation that is already under way in the region need not be imagined—it can be seen throughout the Amazon Basin where multinational mining enterprises function.

Madurismo was not an ideological variation on Chávez's original purposes but the transformation of the state into a machinery of repression masked by the discourse of revolution, cynically deployed to hold the original social base, or part of it at least, in thrall. The Arco Minero project represented, very simply, a decision to re-enter the neoliberal market system as a producer of primary goods. Multinational corporations would assume direct control of the mineral deposits, the oil and gas, and produce them for a world market in exchange for royalties and taxes—that is, commissions. The arrangement was identical to the one that had prevailed under the Punto Fijo arrangements, with a new set of beneficiaries, a new state-capitalist bureaucracy that amalgamated the old bourgeoisie and the new. In 2018, Tarek El Aissami, the principal Chavista minister of the economy, announced that one-third of the public sector budget for that year would go to private interests, including such luminaries of the progressive economies as Nestlé and Santa Teresa Rum. Reelected in a delayed and highly controlled vote in June 2018, Maduro proclaimed himself president and danced on the stage with his wife. They had plenty to celebrate. They had shared among themselves the billions of dollars that oil produced. They had dismantled the structures of popular administration and replaced them with organs of repression and control masquerading as a political party. As the food crisis had intensified in the previous two years, his government introduced the CLAPs—food parcels at official prices to be delivered to individual households. For the most part they never arrived, or only in part. But the responsibility for the deliveries lay with the PSUV; they were prizes delivered to those who voted correctly. Non-members received nothing.

The economic realities are almost too painful to read about, as well as surreal. Manuel Sutherland is a young Marxist economist who has provided consistent economic analyses (the Bank of Venezuela ceased to provide data in 2011), and in a 2018 article he noted that Venezuela had the highest inflation in the world for the fourth year running—in January of that year it was at 4,520 percent and 5,065 percent for food. As Sutherland puts it, this is not socialism but a process of deindustrialization that serves the interests of a bureaucratic, commercial, and financial caste that is enriching itself on oil revenues. Here are just two of the many examples he gives: The number of dollars dispensed by the national bank for the import of meat between 2003 and 2013 increased by 17,000 percent, yet the amount of meat consumed within the country in the same period *fell* by 22 percent.[34] Also, in that same period tax revenues fell by 4.5 percent, while they rose in Argentina by 15.8 percent and in Bolivia by 20.6 percent.

In the immediate aftermath of the 2018 presidential elections, Maduro issued a call to invite capital to negotiate. He did not suggest an open dialogue with the millions who gave Chávez their undivided support and suffered for it while Maduro played his fiddle—though in his case it would be more appropriate to say that Venezuela burned while he danced. Demonstrating staggering cynicism, the presidential couple danced the salsa at his election rally while his majority fell to slightly over 30 percent. In the arithmetic of Venezuelan politics, Maduro had lost 30 percent of the electorate— that is, some seven million people in five years. For an electoral statistician, that must constitute a record of some sort.

The Arco Minero project, however, was not simply a surrender of the economy to global capital. Chávez himself had proposed the project before his death and then withdrew the proposal. Although these extraordinary reserves would have guaranteed financial survival, the project would have signified the end of the Bolivarian revolution. In the first place, the recognition of indigenous rights in the constitution would be the first to be swept away by the proposals. Their rights would be buried under the bulldozers of Exxon-Mobil or Goldcrest International or their Chinese or Russian or Belarussian or Canadian equivalents. The communities would be swept aside. It has to be said that the existing conditions in the area are in many ways inhuman. The mining towns are more like encampments, to which miners return on the weekend to brothels and bars and gaming joints where they spend everything they earn. They return as the week begins to the unregulated, dangerous, and murderous conditions of the artisan mines. The government and the multinationals argue that their plan would change the conditions of small-scale, artisan mining; of course it would—by creating the conditions of large-scale mining, the pollution of rivers that will carry their poison into the river system of the Amazon Basin, the contamination of Venezuela's main source of drinking water, the enslavement of local populations in appalling conditions—they can be seen in Peru, in Ecuador, in Brazil, and in the Orinoco itself. For all his contradictions, Chávez understood that the consequence of the project would be social and environmental devastation. Clearly that is of no significance to the Maduro regime. Its concern is power, and the enduring possession of it.

The militarization of government and society occurred by internal manipulation between Cabello, Padrino, and Maduro, with the able assistance of Cuba. Today eleven of thirty-two ministers are military and occupy the key ministries; twenty-three of thirty-two state governors are military; the key organizers in the PSUV are military. What has been called "economic war" was the justification for repression under the guise of social control. Most importantly the military took key positions in the economy too, just as it had in Raul Castro's Cuba. In a bureaucratic state-capitalist regime, the fusion of repression and economic control are essential—hence the military enterprises and the ubiquity of high-level military officers.

It was a parody of Chávez's civic-military alliance. Whereas he envisaged an integration of the army into a revolutionary social project, Maduro's version is, so to speak, a subordination of the civic to the military as servants of neoliberalism. If the core strategy of Chavismo was to divert oil revenues to stimulate and diversify the productive national economy (though it was never fully implemented, and where it was attempted it failed), Maduro's plan works in the opposite way, abandoning the productive sector to depend wholly on extractive revenues. But this is not a debate about economic strategies. There can be no participatory democracy in a neoliberal extractive strategy, no economic democracy to reflect a political democracy. A glance at the current situation reveals the contrary: the ideal conditions for an oil economy are autocracy or at least an extreme concentration of power.

This was the final condition. Having abandoned and postponed elections for governors as well as for the president, Maduro called a constituent assembly of handpicked delegates early in 2018, having excluded some five million voters from the election of delegates. The constitution will be changed as a result, though there will be no prior warning of how and in what direction. It would confirm the current logic if Maduro were to anoint himself president for life, following the lead of his friend Daniel Ortega in Nicaragua. The hunger protests and the lootings will be silenced in various ways: by direct state violence, or by the manipulation of people's hunger through the distribution of the CLAPs. This leaves in place a level of corruption that is scarcely imaginable—except that the level of oil revenues that have reached the country and disappeared can be calculated in the tens of billions of dollars. Little wonder Maduro danced!

Conclusion

Though Venezuela is the most damning example, the other pink tide regimes have adopted neoliberal strategies, subordinated the economies to the extractive multinationals and accepted the dependence that that implies. Some new elements have been added to the bourgeoisie, some others have left for greener pastures. Rafael Correa drove the Ecuadoran economy back into the arms of the IMF and then withdrew to Belgium. His nominated successor, Lenín Moreno, has brought a number of corporate executives into his government, confirmed the extractive strategy, and announced that his government will no longer "stigmatize" the international financial agencies. Bolivia, a country where what were correctly described as "struggles for life" placed the concept of democracy from below on the political agenda, has now placed its mineral deposits back in the hands of multinational capital. The destruction of the beautiful Salt Lake of Uyuni will be the consequence of the sale of the lithium beneath. In Argentina the open neoliberalism of Mauricio Macri, elected in 2015, was indistinguishable from the strategy of his Peronist opponent Scioli, who represented the continuity of the policies of Cristina Kirchner, delivering Argentina to export agriculture and mining. The regime of Daniel Ortega, the murderous autocrat who still waves the Sandinista banner, is still included among the left governments, as he mows down his own people in defense of austerity.

But the most poignant is Venezuela. And not simply because its leaders still claim that hunger, repression, and corruption are somehow compatible with socialism. What is most tragic is that many on the left outside Latin America still defend what is happening there and, still remain silent on the simplistic grounds that the "enemy of my enemy is my friend."

It is the obligation of socialists to speak the truth to power, whatever the color of their flags. Silence is complicity. Speaking the truth about what is happening, however painful it may be, is the indispensable first step toward a future worthy of those who fought their way into the twenty-first century, and who practiced, however briefly, a new kind of socialist democracy.

Postscript

The year 2019 began and ended with two events that confirmed the grave challenges faced by any revolutionary project in Latin America. In January Juan Guaido, the incumbent of the rotating presidency of the National Assembly, announced that he was assuming power on behalf of the Assembly and withdrawing recognition of Nicolas Maduro as the president of Venezuela. It was the culmination of three years of mutual denunciation and disputed elections. Guaido's political coup occurred against a background of deepening economic crisis, runaway inflation, and extreme hardship for a majority for whom obtaining food and medicines was more difficult by the day. Unsurprisingly, support for Guaido came immediately from the US government and the Lima Group of Latin American nations mainly hostile to the governments of the pink tide. By the end of the year, parallel diplomatic representation and a continuing argument over who was the legitimate power simply aggravated the enormous difficulties faced by ordinary people, while the leaders of both factions appeared to have no difficulty in obtaining their luxury goods or in gaining access to food, medicines, or imported luxury goods.

As the year ended, in Bolivia Evo Morales was removed from power, together with his cabinet, by a military coup. His replacement, Jeanine Añez, a deputy president of the Bolivian National Assembly, took the oath beside a crucifix and an enormous bible, while her supporters burned the *wiphala*, the indigenous flag, in the streets. Morales is currently in Mexico, under the protection of the government of President López Obrador. It is clear that the coup was moved by the forces of the Media Luna, the eastern provinces of the country that have been the base of right-wing opposition to Morales since his inauguration in 2005. Again, the coup arose out of a disputed election result. Two years earlier Morales had put to a referendum a proposal to extend the limit of presidential terms (under the 2009 constitution) from two to three (he had only served two full terms previously), which would effectively allow him a fourth presidential term. The referendum rejected the proposal and Morales turned to a constitutional court to overturn the referendum result. In 2019 he won with a vote 20 percent lower than his previous election. The dispute then was whether he had gained a 10 percent advantage over his opponent, the ubiquitous Carlos Mesa, which would have enabled him to assume power.

The two "political coups" follow a pattern of right-wing mobilizations over the previous decade and a half. What is most significant here, however, is that the impact of Morales's rejection of the referendum result, and the increasing personalism of his government, weakened the very forces that had beaten back previous right-wing attacks. In presidential elections on October 20, from which Morales was barred from standing, Luis Arce of his party, the MAS, was elected. Morales himself returned from exile, in the midst of the Covid crisis. In Venezuela the attempted coup of 2002 and the subsequent bosses' strike had been stopped by the mass mobilization of the barrios. The movements that carried both Morales and Maduro to power rested on concepts of participatory democracy and transparency; the discourse is still deployed, but it serves now not to advance the revolutionary project but to veil its abandonment.

CHAPTER 9

The Tragedy of
the Egyptian Revolution

Sameh Naguib

Introduction

The inauguration ceremony for President Abdel Fattah al-Sisi, which took place on June 8, 2014, was filled with symbols of restoration. The event took place in the garden of one of King Farouk's palaces. The audience included all the top generals of the army and police, the top businessmen, judges, ex-ministers from the Mubarak era, and an assortment of Gulf sheikhs and leaders. In the front row sat Mohamed Hassanein Heikal, the journalist and writer who advised Nasser in the 1950s and 1960s, Sadat in the early 1970s and General Sisi both before and after the 2013 coup. The new first lady made a theatrical entrance coming down the palace steps together with Jihan Al-Sadat, who herself was first lady in the 1970s. What was on show was a celebration of continuity, from the kings of the first half of the twentieth century to the officers of the second half of the twentieth century and beyond. After the "turbulence" of 2011–13, the state and the ruling class were firmly back in power.

But what actually happened during those "turbulent" years? The complex ensemble of events and processes that began in January 2011 and continues to shape the Egyptian polity and society today have been a source of inspi-

265

ration, demoralization and, perhaps above all, confusion to observers internationally. Was January 2011 an actual revolution? What were the structural causes for such an upheaval? Why did the revolutionary process lead to a Muslim Brotherhood presidency and Islamist-dominated parliament? What was the role of the working class and the Left? How was the army leadership capable of both overthrowing the Muslim Brotherhood presidency and reversing the whole revolutionary process? What are the prospects for revolution in Egypt today? Has the revolutionary process ended, or will the structural crises that led to 2011 and the political experiences gained by wide layers of young Egyptians during and since that historic event lead to further revolutionary upheavals?

These are obviously not just questions of academic and general historical interest. The series of events that started in Tunisia and Egypt seven years ago have irreversibly changed the political and social landscape of the whole Middle East. Wars, civil wars, collapsed states, sectarian strife, further revolutionary upheavals and counterrevolutionary waves all seem to be on the agenda for the foreseeable future. The effects of this turbulence and the outcomes of the current struggles will reverberate far beyond the Arab world. Understanding the events and processes of those fateful years, of which the Egyptian revolution is at the very epicenter, remains a fundamental task for all those who were inspired by those eighteen days at the center of Cairo. This chapter will attempt to provide an analysis of this unprecedented cycle of revolutionary and counterrevolutionary mobilizations, focusing on the abovementioned questions.

In regard to the events of 2011, perhaps it would be best to start with the question of *what* before delving into the questions of *why* and *how*. The *what* question has triggered all kinds of academic and political debates. The year 2011 has been described as a "refolution," a "coup-volution," and even simply as a coup.[1] For many of the participants in the events of 2011, it was not only a revolution but one that has yet to be completely defeated. In everyday conversations in Egypt, there is "before" the January revolution and "after" the January revolution.

So, do the events that began in January 2011 in Egypt constitute a revolution? What started as a promising revolutionary situation in 2011 did not lead to any revolutionary consequences, but rather to a military coup and counterrevolutionary regime. In fact, if we take a "before" and "after" approach, it would be safe to say that the regime that emerged after the coup of July 2013 was far more authoritarian and neoliberal than the Mubarak regime in power before 2011.

However, if we take a more dynamic approach to the question of revolution, examining the processes that took place "during" that period between January 25, 2011, and the coup of July 2013, focusing on the active participation of the masses and the unprecedented levels of mobilization, and the effects of the initial waves of mass protest on the state structure, particularly the police, then we can go beyond the question of definitions to the more important task of understanding what happened and why it failed. The fact that it has taken a brutal and ongoing counterrevolutionary mobilization to halt and reverse that process is in itself an indication that the events of 2011 involved an unprecedented "interference of the masses in the course of history" that was ultimately defeated.[2]

How does one understand such a failed revolutionary attempt? On a social level, there was no transfer of power, even temporarily from one class to another. On a political level, there was a transition to formal democracy and free elections in 2012. That transition, however, constitutionally ensured that real power remained in the hands of the army and the old Mubarak security apparatus. It was also ephemeral as the storm of counterrevolution rapidly put an end to the experiment. Perhaps the events of 2011 in Egypt are best captured by focusing on the concept of a "revolutionary situation," involving a challenge to the existing state rule that gained the support of a significant part of the population, and the inability of the state to prevent that process from unfolding.[3]

The revolutionary situation of 2011 involved an unprecedented and audacious attempt by millions of Egyptians to create a different world. The story of that attempt and how it was defeated is the subject of the rest of this chapter.

1. Legacies of the past

The millions who burst into the streets and squares of Egypt's cities in 2011 had inherited a history that in many ways shaped the course of events during and after that momentous year. That history included a process of capitalist development with many peculiarities that had transformed the country but failed to turn Egypt into a successful center of capital accumulation; a colonial legacy that set the stage for a modern politics dominated by nationalism and Islamism; a postcolonial authoritarian state dominated by the army and security apparatus, whose main political features have not changed fundamentally since Nasser; a militant working class; and a history of resistance, protest, and violent repression.

1.1 Capitalism, violence, and cotton

The nineteenth century saw the violent and rapid integration of Egypt into the world capitalist economy. The shock of the Napoleonic invasion of 1798 and the ease with which the French army was able to crush the Mamluks shaped the reforms of Muhammad Ali (1805–48). The most important reforms included introducing cash crops for exports, particularly cotton in the Delta and sugarcane in the south, transforming the irrigation systems, overturning the old Ottoman system of tax farming (Iltizam), first by replacing it by direct state control of agriculture and then through reforms that slowly introduced private property in land, following then-common mercantilist trade policies, and starting a local textile industry. All these reforms, based as they were on corvée Egyptian labor and Sudanese slave labor, were a variation on what has been called "defensive modernization": the attempt to borrow some of the technical aspects of industrial capitalism in order to maintain what was a predominantly pre-capitalist social formation.[4] Although the early industrialization project failed, Egypt began to be integrated into world trade through cotton exports. During the 1820s and 1830s between 10 and 25 percent of the revenues of the Egyptian state derived from the sale of cotton.[5]

The reforms of Muhammad Ali triggered mass resistance and revolts throughout the country as they depended on a rapid increase in *corvée* labor, raising taxes and introducing the then-novel institution of forced army conscription. The resistance did not only involve army desertions and flight from villages to avoid both taxes and conscription, but also a series of rural revolts. There were two major peasant uprisings between 1820 and 1823 in the southern province of Qena. Another larger revolt took place in the Delta region of Menoufiah. These uprisings were all led by religious Sufi leaders claiming to be descendants of the prophet Muhammad. Only through brutal and deadly campaigns carried out by special army forces was the regime able to crush them.[6]

The American Civil War and the ensuing cotton famine (1861–65) attracted large-scale capitalist investments to Egypt mainly from Britain and

France, with the military and political backing of their states.[7] The transformation of Egypt during that period, brilliantly summarized by Rosa Luxemburg in *The Accumulation of Capital*, involved the digging of major irrigation canals, the creation of a new class of landowners, during which most peasants became landless, the completion of the move from subsistence farming to cash crops, mainly cotton and sugarcane, the digging of the Suez Canal, and the building and expansion of a modern railway network. The financing of all these projects was achieved through debts incurred by the Egyptian state to the banks and governments of Europe.[8] The actual price was ultimately paid by the majority of Egyptian peasants through the loss of land and subsistence, forced labor, increased taxation, and army conscription. Through violent seizures and foreclosures for nonpayment of debts or taxes, peasants lost their land to large landowners made up of the royal family, army and state officials, rich Egyptian peasants, and merchants and the increasingly powerful European money lenders.[9] The *kurbaj*, the buffalo-hide whip, stood as symbol of the tax collector, the large landowner, and the monarch.

One of the consequences of these rapid developments was the emergence of an educated Egyptian intelligentsia. New schools fed institutions of higher education, including military academies, that taught a range of modern secular subjects. Between 1863 and 1881 these new schools graduated about ten thousand students.[10] The only other source of learning was Al-Azhar and the Quranic schools. This growing intelligentsia, in both its religiously and secularly educated wings, exerted a disproportionate political and cultural influence despite making up a small share of the population.

1.2 British colonialism and resistance

The British military bombarded its way into Egypt, crushing the beginnings of a national revolt led by Egyptian army officers and occupying the country. British colonial rule accelerated Egypt's capitalist transformation, consolidating private property in land and propping up a weak monarchy that was also the largest land-owning family. Cities and urban centers, including major ports, transport junctions, and trading and service areas, began attracting foreign capital into industries mainly for the processing of cotton, but also for the production of consumer goods for the local market. The economy continued to be geared to the production of cotton, which represented 93 percent of exports just before the First World War.[11]

The year 1919 saw the first nationwide revolt in Egypt. Although it was an anti-colonial uprising, led by bourgeois nationalists, it also involved peasant movements for land and an urban working-class movement demanding higher wages and unionization. Despite being crushed by the British occupation forces, the revolt resulted in negotiations over independence and led in 1923 to some formal concessions. These however did not solve the land problem or get rid of the British occupation forces or their control over both the economy and polity. The reluctant bourgeois leadership of the nationalist movement preferred negotiations to mass mobilizations.[12]

Another major cycle of both economic and political protest started in 1946 after the end of the Second World War and only ended with the 1952 Nasserist coup.[13] The Wafd Party[14] had failed to achieve full independence or end the stranglehold of the large landowners and foreign capital over the economy. Its bourgeois leadership feared a revolution by the workers and peasants far more than they aspired to national independence.

This failure of bourgeois nationalism pushed many to seek alternatives. One of these alternatives was the Islamism of the Muslim Brotherhood. Founded in the late 1920s by Hassan Al-Banna, it had grown rapidly during the 1930s and early 1940s to become the largest political force in the country. Its message was a simple one: the Wafd leaders had failed to achieve independence because they had abandoned Islam. They had embraced the culture and language of the West. Only through a return to the teachings of Islam would Egyptians be able to achieve independence. The more the Wafd leaders became bogged down in endless negotiations with the British, the more Al-Banna's message resonated with significant sections of the population, particularly sections of both the traditional and modern petty bourgeoisie.[15]

The second alternative was the Communist movement. After being outlawed and heavily repressed by the Wafd government in the early 1920s, it was re-established in the late 1930s. The movement grew rapidly, particularly in the universities and in the workers' movement. Heavily influenced by Stalinism, the movement embraced "national front" politics and continued to support and ally itself with the Wafd.

The cycle of protests that started in 1946 was both anti-colonial and social. A militant workers' movement organized a series of strikes demanding higher wages and unionization, peasants demanded land and an end to the dominance of the large landowners, and students demonstrated to demand national independence. What seemed to be an ideal revolutionary opportunity, however, was squandered. The Wafd, as a bourgeois nationalist movement, was discredited and practically paralyzed; the Communists failed to establish an independent revolutionary working-class base and instead continued to support the Wafd; the Muslim Brothers, with their petty bourgeois conservatism, were unable and unwilling to lead a revolution or even support the social demands of the workers and peasants. In fact, it was army officers who seized the moment by taking power in 1952.

1.3 The failed developmental state

Under Nasser's leadership, the "Free Officers" established a developmental state with the aims of solving the land problem, achieving complete independence and industrializing the country.[16] Major land reforms broke the hold of the old land-owning ruling class, and the state embarked on a state-capitalist industrialization program based on import substitution and modeled on the Soviet five-year plans (as happened in India and China and many other Third World countries during that period of decolonization and national liberation regimes).[17] However, Egypt's economy, although sustaining relatively high growth in GDP and manufacturing output in the 1950s and 1960s, continued to rely very heavily on imports, hampering the state's ability to make the necessary investments in fixed capital.

It is important to note that those Third World countries that were able to industrialize rapidly during that period (e.g., Brazil, Mexico, Taiwan, Singapore, South Korea) did so through a combination of import substitution and selective export promotion, thus accumulating the necessary financial means to invest in transforming their economies into significant centers of manufacturing.[18] In absolute terms, there was substantial industrialization during the Nasser era and some major transformations in fixed capital such as the building of the Aswan High Dam. But in relative terms Egypt was already falling far behind some of the other newly industrializing countries and continued to be plagued by financial crises.[19] The economy, despite achieving a relatively high growth rate in the 1950s and 1960s, continued to rely very heavily on imports and made very little headway in the export of manufacturing goods. Politically, the regime established a one-party authoritarian system. The Muslim Brothers were banned and their cadres imprisoned. The Communists were also repressed and jailed until they dissolved their organization in the mid-1960s and joined Nasser's ruling party. By the late 1960s, however, it was clear that Nasser's developmental state had failed to achieve the leap in industrialization and modernization it had promised. Defeated militarily and economically bankrupt, it did not even attempt a second five-year plan.

1.4 Neoliberalism

Neoliberalism came early to Egypt. Plans to liberalize the economy, dismantle the large public sector, and encourage both local and foreign private capital were put in place in the mid-1970s. The attempts of the Sadat regime to impose an IMF austerity plan in 1977 led to the largest strikes and mass demonstrations in the country's history. The army was deployed to crush the revolt and Sadat canceled the austerity measures. Although confrontations only lasted two days, dozens were killed and all liberalization programs were put on hold. The next two decades saw a very cautious and slow process of economic neoliberal reform, with increasing repression, mounting government debts, and sporadic but limited outbreaks of strikes and other social movements.

Politically, Islamism re-emerged as a major player on the political and cultural scene in the 1980s.[20] By the 1990s, the Muslim Brotherhood had become by far the largest opposition movement, with an estimated membership of between seven hundred thousand and one million.[21] The rise and fall of fringe Islamist armed groups using individual terrorism to attack security forces, local Christians, and tourists only reinforced the position of the Muslim Brotherhood as a reformist and nonviolent opposition. And although a new communist movement emerged in the universities in the early 1970s, it was unable to compete with the Islamists and slowly disintegrated. By the time of the collapse of the Soviet Union, the Egyptian left had shrunk to insignificance.

The big neoliberal push came in the 1990s during the reign of Hosni Mubarak. The policy aimed, through privatization and market reforms, to encourage foreign direct investment, radically increase and diversify exports, and hence increase both private and public investment in fixed capital, transforming Egypt in the process. In reality, the reforms carried out were to increase poverty and unemployment, concentrate wealth far beyond the dreams of the monarchy and landowners of the nineteenth and early twentieth century, and continue the long-term relative decline of capital accumulation in Egypt. By the early twenty-first century, Egypt had truly become one of the weakest links in the chain of newly industrializing countries.[22]

2. Mubarak's last decade

The last ten years of Mubarak's rule saw the acceleration of several processes. There was an unprecedented speeding up of neoliberal reforms. Although neoliberal policies had been implemented in collaboration with the International Monetary Fund and the World Bank since the early 1990s, the pace of the reforms was dramatically accelerated with the appointment of Mubarak's last government, that of Prime Minister Ahmed Nazif in 2004.[23] In the succeeding four years an unprecedented wave of privatization affected all vital sectors of the economy including telecommunications and banking. As Adam Hanieh notes, "Buyers were generally international firms, Gulf-based conglomerates, or large domestic capital—often acting in joint partnership."[24]

This rapid and extensive process of privatization was coupled with deep cuts in benefits and subsidies for the poor. As a result, large numbers of public sector workers lost their jobs due to privatization, and there was a rapid decline in living standards. The conditions for workers and the poor took an added hit on account of the price instability and general economic turbulence caused by the world recession, as global prices rose sharply in 2007 and early 2008, and as exports, flows of remittances, and foreign direct investment all declined by 14.5 percent, 17.7 percent, and 29.3 percent, respectively, between 2007 and 2009.[25]

Thus, a major feature of Mubarak's last decade was a rapid process of what David Harvey has called "accumulation by dispossession," as the final remnants of the Nasserist-era social provisions were dismantled and as capital was concentrated in the hands of an alliance of state and security officials, army generals, local capitalists, gulf sheikhs, and multinational corporations.[26] The cumulative effect of the neoliberal onslaught was that the number of Egyptians living on two dollars a day or less—the international poverty line—more than doubled, from 20 to 44 percent.[27]

2.1 Cycles of protest

Mubarak's last decade was also marked by the development of two distinct but related cycles of protest. The first of these was political and was sparked initially by the second Palestinian Intifada in 2000. Mass protests in solidarity with the Palestinians took place in all major Egyptian cities, starting in the universities but quickly spreading to include secondary schools and popular neighborhoods. This gave a major boost both to the secular leftist opposition and to the Muslim Brotherhood, as both rushed to organize the solidarity movement and attract the newly politicized youth. The Palestinian Intifada galvanized the whole political spectrum of opposition. This did not only involve demonstrations but also petition campaigns calling on Mubarak to end diplomatic relations with the Israelis, to open the borders with Gaza, and to allow people to get aid into Gaza. A new revolutionary Left, represented mainly by the Revolutionary Socialists, began to play a growing role in the new mobilizations.[28]

In 2003 there was another wave of protest, this time against the U.S. invasion and occupation of Iraq. There were major demonstrations in nearly every Egyptian city, and this time there was also the first serious occupation of Tahrir Square. The demonstrations began in February, and in March activists called for people to assemble at Tahrir Square as soon as the invasion started. The demonstrations at Tahrir Square only lasted for two days. But in comparison with what had happened before, it was a significant development—some twenty thousand to twenty-five thousand people in pitched battles with the police for two days. It was the first time that pictures of Mubarak were torn down and burnt, and people made a direct link between opposition to the US war and opposition to the Mubarak regime. This was the first of several small-scale dress rehearsals for 2011.

Then again in 2004, the same players—the radical left and reformist organizations on the one hand, and Islamist organizations on the other—participated in initiating a movement for democracy. A very broad alliance of opposition forces was formed and named itself Kefaya.[29] This alliance included Nasserists, liberals, and several left-wing organizations, including the Egyptian Communist Party, the Revolutionary Socialists, and others. It also brought together many significant independent figures who signed onto the Kefaya movement, including prominent journalists, artists, and writers. The Kefaya demonstrations in late 2004 had three main demands. The first was that Mubarak would not nominate himself again in the upcoming presidential elections and that his son would never "inherit" the presidency. The second was to lift Egypt's emergency laws. And the third was to have free and fair presidential and parliamentary elections.

Despite the fact that the early demonstrations against Mubarak, organized by the Kefaya movement, were very small, the general support on the streets was very wide.[30] It resonated so much in fact that the Muslim Brotherhood was under extreme pressure to start moving in the same direction. So, early in 2005 the Muslim Brotherhood organized mass demonstrations for exactly the same democratic demands. They were able to organize much bigger demonstrations, both on university campuses and on the streets. As always there was reluctance among Brotherhood leaders. Before staging their first rally in Cairo on March 27, they attempted to obtain a government permit and only moved without one after their request was denied.[31]

A parallel and even more significant development to the growing political opposition was the rapid and unprecedented surge in workers' strikes. This surge started in one of Egypt's largest industrial establishments, the Misr Spinning and Weaving Company in the Delta town of Al-Mahalla Al-Kubra. The strike that began there on December 4, 2006, was to spark the widest and most militant worker's movement in Egypt since the 1940s.[32]

Four significant features of the Mahalla strike are worth mentioning. The first was the central role played by women in the strike. Women workers in the company's garment factory actually began the strike with the chant that later became famous: "Here are the women, where are the men?"[33] The second feature was that it was an actual strike rather than the usual work-in that characterized workers' collective action, particularly in the large public-sector establishments. The third feature was the duration of the strike, which lasted for two weeks. Previously, strikes would rarely last more than a day.[34] The fourth related feature was the police response. The usual response to stoppages in such vital industrial establishments was violent and swift, with police forces using all means including live ammunition and mass arrests to break up the strike. The response this time was an offer of prolonged negotiations with strike representatives.

All four features were to become the norm during the strike wave of 2007 and 2008. The strikes spread across the different industries and the service sector, concentrated in the civil and public sector, but then spread beyond that, both to the private sector and to sectors that had no history of militant strikes, including doctors, nurses, teachers, tax collectors, and many others.

Splits and cracks began to appear among the ruling circles. Should they continue with their accelerated neoliberal program and crush workers' resistance? Or should they slow down and try to contain the movement? Should they go ahead with the planned succession plan for Mubarak's son, Gamal? Or should they choose a more acceptable figure, perhaps from the military, as Egypt's next president and thus appease the growing opposition to the ruling family? Massive coercion or attempted containment? Containment would be seen as a concession to the growing movements from below and might embolden them even more against the regime. Coercion could risk an uncontrollable explosion. Neither side within the ruling circles had any real confidence that their strategy would save the regime. The confusion at the top became apparent during the 2005 parliamentary elections. The elections were carried out in three stages. In the first stage, it seemed that the containment faction had the upper hand. Ballot rigging was minimal and the Muslim Brotherhood, the largest opposition force, was able to get eighty-eight seats (20 percent). This frightened the coercion faction, and the next two stages were violently rigged, thereby maintaining a large majority for the ruling National Democratic Party (NDP).[35]

A planned strike by the Mahalla workers on April 6, 2008, was forcefully prevented by the police, leading to mass demonstrations throughout the town. This was the second and more menacing dress rehearsal for the 2011 revolution. Police cars, ruling party headquarters, and police stations were attacked and pictures of Hosni Mubarak torn down. It is estimated that tens of thousands of workers took part in the uprising. At this point the regime reverted to violent suppression. A youth movement naming itself after that strike (the Sixth of April Movement) grew rapidly in the last two years of Mubarak's rule. Utilizing social media, it was able to recruit thousands of young Egyptians on a program of democratic change through peaceful means. Inspired by the East European color revolutions, they wished for a similar transition to democracy in Egypt.

The regime had reached an impasse. A neoliberal policy carried out by a corrupt state run by military and police generals led to an unprecedented concentration of wealth and power, in which the boundaries between the state and capital, generals and billionaires became blurred. The same policy led to a sharp rise in unemployment and poverty. There was no significant transformation in the performance of the Egyptian economy, no "tiger on the Nile" as Boutros Ghali, the then finance minister and engineer of the neoliberal reforms, had promised.

The growing opposition to Mubarak took many forms. The regime was rattled by a cycle of political protest starting with solidarity with the Palestinian Intifada and against the occupation of Iraq and morphing into a more generalized democratic opposition to the regime. The growing political opposition resonated with a rising tide of workers' strikes. Although the two movements remained relatively isolated from each other, the two sides of the opposition, the political and the economic, the democratic and the social, were part of the same process deepening the political crisis. The more these two movements grew, the more divisions within the regime began to appear. The policies of the regime echoed that confusion, swinging between containment and coercion, between reform and paralysis.

3. Eighteen days

The events of 2011 represented, on the one hand, a continuation and deepening of the patterns of social and political protest of the previous decade, and, on the other, a significant qualitative and quantitative change. All the previous cycles of political protest involved demonstrations and sometimes occupations, but with few exceptions, most significantly the Mahalla demonstrations of 2008, they would not involve major confrontations with the police or develop on a national scale.

The main direct triggers for what unfolded starting on January 25 were, first, the unprecedented rigging of the November 2010 parliamentary elections in which not a single opposition candidate won. The Muslim Brothers, who had eighty-eight seats in the previous parliament, did not get a single seat in 2010. The extent of direct police control and rigging was extreme even by Egyptian democratic standards. Second, in December details of the police torture and murder of a young Alexandrian blogger, Khaled Said, spread rapidly on social media, with hundreds of thousands signing up to a special website called "We are all Khaled Said." The third triggering event came in early January with the bombing of a Coptic church, which led to major demonstrations by Copts in central Cairo. Finally, there was Tunisia. The example of ordinary people being able to topple a corrupt, authoritarian neoliberal dictator and force him to flee the country had an electrifying effect.

What started on January 25, 2011, as a day of demonstrations called for by leftist and liberal activists, raising demands against police brutality and dictatorship, rapidly developed into the largest mass demonstrations in Egyptian history. As the numbers swelled the chants began to unify around what was by then the famous slogan of the Tunisian revolution: "The people want to overthrow the regime."[36] The activists who had started the demonstrations had rapidly become a tiny minority. The attempts by the police and riot forces to stop the growing movement using tear gas, rubber bullets, and then live ammunition failed dramatically as the sheer numbers of the demonstrators completely overwhelmed the police, forcing them to retreat from one barrier to the next. This contrasted sharply with the previous patterns of protest, where the police would mobilize thousands of soldiers to lay siege to a few hundred protesters. Now the thousands of soldiers were surrounded by far larger numbers, forcing them to retreat and eventually leading to the disintegration of the whole police force. The leadership of the Muslim Brotherhood, the largest opposition force in the country, issued statements against participation in the January 25th demonstrations. This did not stop thousands of their youth taking part on the day. It also did not stop the police blaming them anyway. The minister of the interior issued a statement blaming the Muslim Brotherhood for the unrest.[37]

Opposition forces, this time including the Muslim Brotherhood, called for a "Day of Rage" after Friday prayers on January 28. The state had shut down both the internet and mobile networks in a desperate attempt to prevent activists and organizers from communicating. The shutdown backfired as people gathered in mosques and coffee shops and main streets on the 28th. In Cairo the destination of the demonstrations, far bigger and angrier than those on the 25th, was Tahrir Square, the largest square and transport junction in the city. Major battles took place at all major roads and bridges leading to Tahrir. Similar battles were taking place on the main streets in Suez, Mahalla, Alexandria, and several other cities and towns. Large numbers of police cars, armored vehicles, and police stations were set on fire, with police officers, once the main source of fear on Egyptian streets, fleeing for their lives. NDP buildings were torched and signs, portraits, and pictures of the hated dictator were torn down. In fact, the scale of violence in these confrontations showed that what was happening across the country was more than a peaceful revolution led by middle-class youth. Over 50 percent of police stations in Greater Cairo and over 60 percent of police stations in Alexandria were attacked, the majority of them burnt down, and over four thousand police vehicles were destroyed.[38]

By nightfall the police forces had been withdrawn, with the exception of those still protecting the notorious Interior Ministry. Naturally, many of the demonstrators attempted to storm the building. Well-positioned snipers shot to kill. Over a dozen protesters died and hundreds were injured.[39] As they withdrew from the streets, the Ministry of the Interior opened up prisons and let out thousands of seasoned criminals in order to create a sense of fear and chaos among the wider population. Yet their plan failed. Popular committees sprang up to defend neighborhoods, to organize traffic, and even to clean the streets. The president ordered the army into the cities to crush the uprising and to restore "order."

The occupation of Tahrir Square started that night. The scale of the occupation was unprecedented. Although the Muslim Brotherhood mobilized for and participated in the occupation and the defense of the square, the secular and democratic nature of the event was clear. The participation of thousands of women, both veiled and unveiled, and the central role played by Coptic youth gathering in the square, together with the mass participation of the "ultras"—non-religious soccer club fans—eliminated the likelihood of any attempt to give an Islamic or religious framing to the event.[40]

The atmosphere was already one of cautious celebration. Ordinary men and women had defeated the hated police and, numbering in the millions, were occupying the center of Cairo. Everybody knew that there would be many battles to come and that many had died and many more were yet to die. But there was a newfound sense of confidence and solidarity that in itself was cause for celebration.

Organizers, representing all political groups and participating forces, formed committees to organize the occupation, defend the square, distribute food and water, and discuss the formulation of demands. Discussion circles, public meetings, and the shouting down or applauding of speakers made the politics of the square an example of collective solidarity and democratic self-organization. The demands that came out of the square were centered on the themes of freedom, social justice, and human dignity. Although these were rather vague slogans, a set of concrete demands were also put forward. These included the demand that those responsible for the hundreds of deaths and thousands of injuries since January 25 be put on trial; an end to the Mubarak presidency; the indictment and trial of the president and his inner circle for crimes committed against the Egyptian people; an end to emergency laws; new, free presidential and parliamentary elections; and new social and economic policies that would end corruption and monopoly and redistribute wealth.

On the night of that Friday of Rage, Mubarak made his first speech blaming the government as inept and promising to appoint a new cabinet.

There were no apologies for the dead and injured and no mention of the people's demands. By the following day he appointed two generals to executive positions, selecting his Chief of Intelligence, General Omar Suleiman, as his first ever vice-president and General Ahmad Shafiq as prime minister. These two men were both hated figures from Mubarak's immediate entourage. Suleiman was known as "Dr. Torture" for his leading role in the US-led extraordinary renditions program, which transported prisoners to Egypt and other Arab countries for torture. He was also known as a particularly close ally of Israel in its wars on Gaza. On Monday, January 31, in an address to the nation the new vice-president Suleiman said that Mubarak had asked him to open a dialogue with all opposition groups and to ask the judiciary to overturn the disputed election results of last November. It was a tactical retreat by the regime to gain time and exhaust the protesters.

New protests were called for Tuesday, February 1, in all major cities. The reaction of the army generals was one of the major turning points in the revolution. Military spokesman General Ismail Othman declared on national television that the army recognized the legitimate demands of the people and would not shoot at them. The army command was positioning itself as belonging to the "people" and being above politics. It presented itself as separate from and independent of Mubarak and the police. The aim was both to try to contain the revolutionary crisis and to protect its own institution from the revolutionary fever. On the square, however, people felt they were winning this historic battle. An explosion of individual and group creativity was taking place. Thousands of banners and placards with the people's demands, expressed with poetry, jokes, and personal stories, filled the square. Graffiti, murals, and slogans covered every building wall.

By Tuesday evening, Mubarak gave his second speech in response to the massive demonstrations of the day. He pledged to complete his term and that he would not leave under pressure. This time he seemed to have been better advised as he recalled his service to his country for over six decades while pledging to oversee major reforms. In the speech, he promised not to seek reelection but to leave in September and made a well-choreographed emotional pledge to die in Egypt.

The speech did have an effect as some considered his pledges as serious concessions. It also encouraged those opposed to the revolution to campaign openly in the media for an end of the demonstrations and occupations. However, the regime had no intention of making any concessions and was already planning the storming of Tahrir Square. A number of prominent pro-Mubarak businessmen, leaders of the ruling NDP, and state security officers devised a plan for a full-blown attack on the demonstrators. A small army of paid thugs was assembled to violently break up the occupation on Wednesday, February 2.

The attack came in two main waves. The first involved thugs on camels and horses, armed with knives and swords storming into the square, in what looked like a scene from a medieval battle. Although they were able to reach the center of the square, they underestimated both the numbers and the fighting spirit of the occupation as groups of revolutionary youth were able to force them out of the square. The expected next attack came in the evening when thousands of thugs, plain-clothed policemen and snipers started gathering, particularly at the entrance closest to the Egyptian Museum and on the roofs of several buildings. A nearby bridge gave the thugs an elevated position and therefore a tactical advantage at that entrance. The barricades were reinforced with burnt-out police cars and trucks and thousands of fighters prepared for battle. After a long night of street fighting, in which dozens were killed and wounded, the police and thugs were defeated. By daybreak, hundreds of thousands joined their fellow demonstrators in a show of support and solidarity. The leaders of the protests had already called for massive demonstrations on Friday, February 4, across Egypt after congregational prayers, calling the event "Departure Day," in a reference to their hopes to force Mubarak to resign and leave the country.[41]

Omar Suleiman had earlier called for a national dialogue with the opposition. This dialogue actually took place on Sunday, February 6. It included not only the tame and loyal opposition of discredited figures from the supposedly left-wing Tagammu Party[42] and the liberal Wafd Party, but also several key leaders of the Muslim Brotherhood (including Mohamed Mursi, later to become president), Naguib Sawiris, head of the richest family in Egypt, and some members of youth coalitions that had been lured into Suleiman's trap.

The meetings took place in a major government hall with a huge portrait of Mubarak hanging on the wall. But the reaction on the streets and squares was one of anger at the supposed opposition figures that took part in the talks. The Muslim Brotherhood youth openly attacked their leadership on a decision they saw, rightly, as a betrayal of the revolution and its martyrs. At the end of the meeting government representatives issued a communiqué that thanked Mubarak and reiterated the regime's perspective and interpretation of events. It claimed, inaccurately, that all participants agreed on the road map toward finding a solution to the "crisis." This was supposedly based on limited reforms to the constitution and new elections. It did not promise the immediate lifting of the emergency laws. Ironically, a day after the dialogue Suleiman declared on national TV that "Egypt is not ready for democracy."[43]

Under pressure from their youth, the Brotherhood leadership announced that the talks had failed and that Suleiman had not offered anything substantial. The failed negotiations coincided with the start of a wave of workers' strikes that was to seal Mubarak's fate. The first wave started on February 6 and within three days spread across the country, involving more than three hundred thousand workers.[44] The strikes resonated with the revolution on the squares in several ways. First, in a sense it carried the revolution into state institutions, paralyzing them and therefore indirectly strengthening the revolution in the squares. The strike wave included public transport workers, government hospital workers, postal workers, sanitation workers, and workers in state-owned enterprises including six thousand workers servicing the Suez Canal. Second, many of the strikes targeted the corrupt functionaries of Mubarak's ruling party with demands that institutions be "cleansed" or purged of all corrupt officials. This played a further role in paralyzing the once powerful networks and resources of the ruling NDP.[45] The strike wave continued to spread to vital sectors of the state and economy as Telecom Egypt workers demonstrated in front of many telephone exchanges in Cairo and the provinces. Railway workers paralyzed the rail network and public transport workers shut down the bus garages. Strikes and sit-ins spread to the petroleum sector, major textile mills, and even public hospitals.

Even the *New York Times* had to admit to the important role this intervention by the working class played in changing the shape of Egypt after Mubarak, writing a few days after the dictator's fall: "The labor unrest this week at textile mills, pharmaceutical plants, chemical industries, the Cairo airport, the transportation sector and banks has emerged as one of the most powerful dynamics in a country navigating the military-led transition that followed an 18-day popular uprising and the end of Mr. Mubarak's three decades of rule."[46] The strike waves made the occupations stronger and brought many more people to the squares and streets. The resonance between strikes in the workplaces and occupations in the squares and streets, although not organizationally linked, proved fatal to the regime. As fresh, even larger demonstrations were being planned, Vice-President Omar Suleiman made a short televised speech: "Citizens, during these very difficult circumstances Egypt is going through, President Hosni Mubarak has decided to step down from the office of president of the republic and has charged the Supreme Council of the Armed Forces to administer the affairs of the country. May God help everybody."[47]

The dictator was ousted, but the state he represented remained largely intact. The police forces had crumbled, but the army had survived after very little internal dissent. Workers had shaken the country with strikes and occupations, but did not form an alternative center of power. The occupied squares and streets were an inspiring show of self-organization and direct democracy, but their power proved ephemeral. Eighteen days of demonstrations, occupations, and strikes had forced the resignation of the hated dictator. Yet despite the carnival atmosphere that engulfed the square in celebration of the victory, it was to prove just the beginning of a long and complicated struggle.[48]

4. The reign of SCAF

On February 13, the Supreme Council of the Armed Forces (SCAF) dissolved parliament and suspended the constitution, but it kept the hated Mubarak-appointed government in place. It promised to investigate the old regime's corruption and the police crimes committed against the people. On February 17, Habib Al-Adly, minister of the interior, and his aides were arrested. Also arrested that day were the regime's three billionaire ministers—Ahmed Al-Maghrabi, Zoheir Garana, and Ahmed Ezz, the steel tycoon and organizational head of the NDP.[49] Massive demonstrations again took place on Friday, February 18, as a celebration of the ousting of Mubarak and to demand changing the government and trials for the president and his men.

There were three main pillars to the SCAF strategy after Mubarak. The first was to end the waves of strikes and demonstrations that continued to spread throughout the country. SCAF initiated a propaganda campaign claiming that the revolution had already succeeded and therefore there was no need for further protests. Mubarak had been ousted, a new political road map would be put forward, the army had stood by the people, and therefore the people had to go back to work and law and order had to be restored, and those that continued to demonstrate and strike were part of a conspiracy against Egypt.[50] A statement put out by SCAF asserted that "the Supreme Council of the Armed Forces is aware of plans to harm the country . . . these included protests and strikes . . . that negatively affect citizens and stop the wheels of production from turning."[51] The second pillar was to actually put forward a feasible political roadmap with a minimum of procedural democracy that would both ensure that the revolutionary situation would end and the main levers of state power would remain firmly in the hands of the military. The third pillar was to create the right political alliance that would make the first two tasks possible. The new road map would not have been possible without the willing participation of the Muslim Brotherhood, the largest political mass movement in the country. In fact, the Muslim Brotherhood began from the week after Mubarak fell to mobilize against strikes and further demonstrations and in support of SCAF's new road map.

SCAF appointed a panel of judges to prepare a set of constitutional amendments to organize parliamentary elections, a constitutional assembly, and presidential elections. These amendments would be put to a referendum on March 19. The panel was headed by a Muslim Brotherhood sympathizer and had another MB conservative member on its board. The proposed amendments secured the position of SCAF and the military not only in the sense of their sustained immunity from any civilian supervision or oversight, but also in ensuring that any future democratic reforms would not affect their control over foreign policy and security issues and would keep in place the right of the army leadership to transfer civilians for trial in military courts.

Both Salafist and Brotherhood activists used religious slogans to support the SCAF road map and constitutional amendments. They also continued to defend the role of the army in relation to the revolution. A statement by the Brotherhood leadership made this assertion: "The Muslim Brotherhood wants to see the success of the revolution, and we are fully aware that the position of our great army in relation to the revolution is one of the principal factors in its success."[52]

Both SCAF and the Muslim Brotherhood, together with several liberal parties and most of the private and public media, carried out a campaign against the continuing strike waves. The Brotherhood issued a statement making that explicit:

> The Muslim Brotherhood calls on all sections of the Egyptian people to keep the wheels of production and development turning. Demonstrations for sectional demands, albeit a fundamental right, are detrimental to production and damage the economy, particularly as the revolution is linked to keeping the motor of the economy turning.[53]

The alliance of the Muslim Brotherhood and many of the Salafist groups with SCAF, although it ended the sense of unity between Islamist and secular opposition that characterized Tahrir, did not succeed in ending the revolutionary process. It did however split the opposition. The radical Left, together with left nationalists and the plethora of youth movements that had emerged from Tahrir, continued to mobilize on the streets and squares. The fall of Mubarak encouraged larger segments of the working class and the poor to demonstrate, strike, and occupy. It is important to note that hundreds of thousands would join new "days of action" during the months following the removal of Mubarak. And these days of action, coupled with strikes and occupations, continued to force concessions from SCAF, despite its alliance with the Muslim Brotherhood.

The Revolutionary Socialists had grown rapidly during the eighteen days. By taking an early position against SCAF and by being at the center of organizing further occupations and demonstrations, they were able to become an important focal point for the growing anger against the army command and against the betrayals of the Muslim Brotherhood.

A major demand of the continuing weekly Friday demonstrations was the dismissal of the Mubarak-appointed government of Ahmed Shafiq. On March 3, SCAF conceded and appointed Essam Sharaf, an independent technocrat, to form a new transitional government. But Sharaf not only held on to some of Mubarak's appointees; he also added others that were either big businessmen or connected in one way or another to the old regime. Major revolutionary initiatives continued. On March 4 and 5, angry young protesters stormed the hated state security offices, for decades centers for torture, illegal detention, and murder. The SCAF–Muslim Brotherhood alliance, however, did succeed in winning a majority in the March 19 referendum for the constitutional amendments.

SCAF faced the growing protests with unprecedented waves of repression and attempted legal restrictions. On March 23 the government put forward a law criminalizing strikes and protests that disrupt the normal function of institutions or services, whether private or public. The sentences for breaking this new law were one year in jail and a fine of 500,000 Egyptian pounds.[54] But strikes continued to spread, obviously and intentionally "disrupting the normal function of institutions," yet the government and SCAF did not at first make any attempts to actually enforce the law.

On Friday, April 1, new mass demonstrations took place in Tahrir Square, Alexandria, Suez, and other major cities in what was called the "Friday to

Save the Revolution." The protesters called for the banning of the NDP and for speeding up the process of investigating corruption and putting Mubarak, his sons, and other top officials on trial. The new wave of demonstrations forced SCAF into making more concessions. Thus on April 7, Zakariya Azmi, Mubarak's chief of staff and most trusted aide, was arrested. This was followed by the arrests of Ahmed Nazif, Mubarak's last prime minister (April 10); Safwat El-Sherif, the president of the Shura Council and NDP general secretary (April 11); and Fathi Sorour, the parliamentary speaker (April 13). The arrest of Mubarak and his two sons, Gamal and Alaa, was ordered on April 13. The two sons were transferred to Tora prison in Cairo while Mubarak was transferred to a hospital in Sharm El Sheikh as he allegedly suffered a heart attack.

On April 8 hundreds of thousands gathered in Tahrir Square for a "Friday of Cleansing and Trial." This was to turn into the first major confrontation between demonstrators and the military police. Several army officers took part in the demonstrations in their uniforms. They chanted slogans against Field Marshal Mohammed Hussein Tantawi and against corruption in the army. Several demonstrators, including the officers, staged a sit-in at the center of the square, deciding to continue the demonstration throughout the night. This fraternization between protesters and uniformed officers and the new tone of anger against SCAF became intolerable for the army leadership. Military police were ordered to break up the sit-in. They shot into the crowds, killing at least one person and injuring dozens. All the protesting officers were arrested. Throughout all these confrontations the Muslim Brotherhood leadership maintained its support of SCAF, yet would also occasionally mobilize to put pressure on it.

The summer of 2011 would reveal the extent of contention over the ownership of the revolution. The Muslim Brotherhood would mobilize hundreds of thousands on the squares and streets in support of the road map, but also in opposition to some of the measures of the army leadership. The Left and youth movements, together with the newly emerging women's movement and Coptic youth, would mobilize hundreds of thousands against SCAF and military trials and call for a much deeper reckoning with the old regime's businessmen, politicians, and generals, together with a more direct and inclusive form of democracy and social justice. The strike waves would continue to deepen, with demands for "cleansing" and management accountability coupled with more immediate social and economic demands.[55] Oppressed sections of society began expressing their own demands and organizing against discrimination and oppression. Women, the Coptic minority, the Nubian community in the South, and Egyptians of the Sinai Peninsula all came out to express their anger and their demands against a state that had systematically oppressed them, discriminated against them, and silenced their voices for generations.

However, it was not only the oppressed and exploited who would emerge during those tumultuous months. Counterrevolutionary mobilizations would carry on, on a small scale at first, but slowly gaining confidence and momentum. Demands for law and order, for stability, for the return to normality, for saving the nation from chaos, for avoiding civil war were slowly gaining wider influence. The fall of Mubarak was not the end but rather the beginning of a widening and deepening range of revolutionary and counterrevolutionary mobilizations.

5. The autumn of anger

5.1 October days

As mentioned above, Coptic youth played a central role in the demonstrations and occupations during the early phase of the revolution.[56] After Mubarak was removed, there were regular demonstrations and sit-ins in front of the State Television Broadcasting building, one of the main symbols of the Mubarak state, just off Tahrir Square. These centered on demands specific to the Coptic community, against discrimination and against the growing wave of attacks on Coptic churches, which occurred either in collusion with the state or resulted in no legal reckoning for those involved. The fall of Mubarak had encouraged all oppressed sections of society to start mobilizing for equality and freedom. The significance of the emerging Coptic movement was that, for the first time in the modern history of the Coptic question, the movement was independent and critical of the Coptic Church hierarchy, which continued to side with the state and the military.

On October 9, thousands of Copts organized a demonstration in front of the State Television building to protest against the burning of a church in Upper Egypt. The march to the building was first attacked by thugs but once it reached its destination the army unit used live ammunition and drove into the crowd with armored tanks. Twenty-eight people were killed, including several prominent youth leaders, and hundreds were injured. The massacre was an important turning point, not only for the Coptic community but also for the broader sentiment toward SCAF and the military. The military itself denied any wrongdoing and blamed the Coptic youth or "infiltrators" for the violence. State television even announced that the army was being attacked by Christians and called on loyal citizens to "come and protect your armed forces."[57] The revolutionary youth saw this as further evidence that SCAF had no intention of retreating from the scene and that the old regime was still in power. "Down with SCAF" and "The people want to execute the field marshal" became the slogans of that moment. More concretely, the demand for the end of military rule and the formation of a civilian transitional ruling body took center stage. The Muslim Brotherhood and their Salafi allies, however, continued to support SCAF. They condemned the violence but were critical of the Copts for organizing the mass demonstrations in the first place.

5.2 November days

The Muslim Brotherhood played an important role in the revolutionary mobilizations that toppled Mubarak, yet part of its leadership was already negotiating with the regime even before his fall. It quickly entered an alliance with SCAF once it was in power, announcing the revolution was over and that the SCAF-proposed road map was the only way forward. But it was still a mass organization, and many of its young members had taken part in the revolution and expected their leadership to keep their promises and truly put an end to the corrupt old regime and its security and military apparatus.

The alliance between the Muslim Brotherhood and SCAF was therefore neither particularly stable nor long-lived, as subsequent events would prove. In November, the government and SCAF put forward a document containing "constitutional amendments" that would severely curtail the power of parliament (for which elections were set to start on November 28) and would again further insulate the army and its leadership and keep the levers of power firmly in their hands, describing them as "protectors of the constitution." The Muslim Brotherhood and its newly formed political arm, the Freedom and Justice Party, threatened that unless the government withdrew its constitutional proposals, there would be "widespread popular protests" culminating in a new "million people march" on November 18. It was liberal parties such as the newly formed Egyptian Democratic Party and the Stalinist pro-government Tagammu Party that actually endorsed the document.

A new mass occupation of Tahrir started on Friday, November 18. This time the Muslim Brotherhood and their Salafist allies joined the opposition again, calling for an end to military rule. The mobilization involved hundreds of thousands from all over the country and spread to other cities such as Suez and Alexandria. On that Friday one person was killed and over seven hundred were injured as police used teargas and rubber bullets in their attempt to disperse the demonstrators. Despite the crackdown, by the end of the day Tahrir Square was occupied by demonstrators as more and more people joined this new anti-SCAF mobilization. However, this time there were deep divisions on the streets. The Islamists, despite their mobilization, were limited to demanding the complete withdrawal of the constitutional proposals and to move on with the elections. The radical left and youth movements wanted to continue and deepen the mobilization and turn it into a new wave of demonstrations and occupations until there were concrete concessions by SCAF. The police continued to push into the square from the main road leading to the Interior Ministry (Mohamed Mahmoud Street). Protesters, however, pushed them back toward the ministry. The clashes continued for several days. By Monday thirty-three protesters had been shot dead with live ammunition and thousands were injured, many losing an eye as police snipers would aim buckshot at protester's eyes.

On Tuesday SCAF held an emergency meeting and announced several concessions, including the withdrawal of the constitutional proposals and the transfer of power to an elected president by the middle of 2012, a year ahead of what was announced previously. This was enough for the Muslim Brotherhood and its allies to demobilize their supporters and withdraw from the square. The occupation and confrontations would continue without them, however, with at least twenty more dead and several thousand more injured as wave after wave of protesters tried to push back the armed police forces toward the Ministry of Interior.[58]

By the following Friday there were three separate mobilizations, a three-way division that would become deeper and more complicated in the coming months and years. A revolutionary rally in Tahrir, mirrored in other towns and cities across the country, called for an immediate end to military rule and justice for the martyrs of the revolution, including fair and open trials for all those responsible for the massacres starting with Field Marshal Tantawi and the whole membership of SCAF. A second separate mobilization, waged in support of Palestine and calling for the elections to take place as scheduled, was organized by the Muslim Brotherhood and its allies in another area of central Cairo near the Al-Azhar mosque. And, ominously, a third mobilization, organized by supporters of SCAF, took place close to the main army command headquarters.

5.3 Parliamentary elections

As the parliamentary elections started on November 28 and stretched to January 11, 2012, the political center of gravity moved away from the squares and streets and toward the polling stations. The hopes and aspirations of large sections of the masses became concentrated in the first free democratic parliamentary elections. This was not seen as a step back from Tahrir but rather the culmination of the battles and struggles and sacrifices since January 25. For many, participating in the elections represented a dual perspective in which strikes, demonstrations, and occupations would interact with the more formal, restricted struggles of elections and parliamentary politics. That continued to be the rhetoric of the Muslim Brotherhood and its allies, but also of many of the liberal, leftist, and nationalist parties and leaders. However, the issue would split the revolutionary youth as a significant segment advocated boycotting the elections and focusing on street mobilizations.[59]

About 28 million people representing 54 percent of eligible voters participated in the elections. The Muslim Brotherhood organized an electoral alliance with several secular liberal and nationalist parties, called the Democratic Coalition for Egypt, but in reality the Muslim Brotherhood was by far the dominant electoral force. In total, this Brotherhood-led Democratic alliance won 10,138,134 votes, over a third of the total.[60] However, the more surprising result was that of the Islamic Alliance, which included the main Salafist parties, coming in second with 7,534,266 votes. Once votes were converted into seats, the Freedom and Justice Party became the largest bloc with 216 (representing 43.4 percent of the seats), followed by the Islamic Alliance, with 125 (about 25 percent of the seats).[61]

Salafism had a long history in Egypt. Before the revolution there were three main trends. The first was an apolitical religious movement advocating a puritan version of Islam through proselytizing in mosques and Islamic charities, but accepting the existing political regime. This trend has historically been supported and encouraged by the Mubarak regime as an antidote to the challenge both of the Muslim Brotherhood and other oppositional Islamist movements. The second was a far more militant political Salafism that advocated the use of violence against what they considered infidel rulers. And the third was a Salafist trend that advocated peaceful political action against "infidel" rulers together with revivalist proselytizing. The revolution forced a major regroupment among Salafist movements as political space opened up and newly radicalized youth looked to religious leaders for political answers. Three new political parties were formed: the Authenticity Party, the Building and Development Party, and the largest in the group, the Al-Nour Party.[62] The Islamic bloc was the electoral alliance of these three Salafist parties.[63] The Salafist tendency was critical of the Muslim Brotherhood for being too pragmatic and opportunist and for making too many concessions to secular political forces.

It is important to note that within the wider Salafist movement, there was a variety of different attitudes to the revolution. Criticism of the Muslim Brotherhood was not exclusively on conservative religious grounds. A grass-roots Salafist movement led by charismatic lawyer and religious preacher Hazem Salah Abu Ismail was critical of the Muslim Brotherhood leadership for making too many concessions to the old regime and SCAF, whereas Al-Nour Party leaders opposed the MB leadership for being too oppositional. So, despite what seemed to be a unified tendency of revivalist religious groups, we find a whole range of positions on the revolution, on economic policies, on attitudes toward remnants of the Mubarak regime, the security apparatus, and SCAF. However, the Islamic alliance that took part in the elections was composed mainly of the ultra-conservative Nour Party that would later support the military coup of 2013. Its success posed a serious challenge for the Muslim Brotherhood leadership, as the latter tried to balance between concessions and confrontations with the old regime and the military, and also between their pragmatic politics and their Islamist conservative agenda.

The liberal alliance and the Left did exceptionally badly in the elections. The former won only thirty-four seats whereas the Left, both Stalinist (the Revolution Continues Alliance) and left-Nasserist (Al-Karama Party), gained seven and six seats, respectively.[64] Neither liberals nor leftists had organizations large enough to electorally challenge the Muslim Brotherhood, and many of their young supporters remained on the streets and in the occupations and refused to participate in what they regarded as an attempt to contain the revolution. These results would eventually push many in the secular opposition into a catastrophic alliance with the military. For them, such an alliance seemed the only way to resist the rising power of the Islamists.

5.4 Presidential elections

The period between the end of the parliamentary elections in January 2012 and the beginning of the presidential elections in May of the same year saw growing disillusionment with "the parliament of the revolution," as it was not able or willing to legislate significant reforms on questions of corruption, repression, or transitional justice. Neither was it prepared to challenge the continuing dominance of the security and military apparatuses of the old Mubarak state.

The presidential elections of May 2012 would dominate the political scene. The Muslim Brotherhood reneged on its promise not to put forward a candidate from its ranks and eventually settled on Mohamed Mursi. And as for the military and the old Mubarak state, they felt confident enough to put forward a candidate of their own, the ex-General and last Mubarak-appointed prime minister and a major player in Mubarak's inner circle, Ahmed Shafiq. The revolutionary camp was broadly represented by the left-Nasserist Hamdin Sabahi, running under the slogan "One of us," and a progressive Islamist, Abd al-Munim Abu al-Futuh, who had broken his ties with the Muslim Brotherhood the previous year.[65]

The results of the first round were significant and indicative of future trends. Mohamed Mursi, the Muslim Brotherhood candidate, came first with 24.7 percent of the vote. This represented a serious drop in support for the Brotherhood since the parliamentary elections. Ahmed Shafiq, the pro-Mubarak, openly counterrevolutionary candidate, came a very close second with 23.6 percent. This reflected the ability of the old state apparatus to rebuild a base since the shock of January 2011, as the police, the military, and the old ruling party were able to mobilize sections of the middle class-es and the peasantry, on an openly counterrevolutionary "law and order" campaign. Shafiq promised to return the country to order and stability after eighteen months of constant turmoil and disruption and what he identified as chaos. In addition, he presented himself as the last barrier against an Islamist takeover, warning that a Mursi victory would create an Islamic theocratic state, taking Egypt back to the Middle Ages. In what was to become one of the main strategies of the unfolding counterrevolution, he urged Coptic Christian and women voters to support him in order to safe-guard their civil and political liberties.[66]

The left-Nasserist Hamdin Sabahi came a surprising close third with 20.7 percent of the vote. Using the 2011 revolution slogans that demanded "bread, freedom, and social justice" and relating those to the still popular re-forms of the Nasserism of the 1950s and 1960s, he was able to galvanize both youth voters and significant sectors of urban working-class voters, particular-ly in the main urban centers of Cairo, Alexandria, and Port Said, which were also the main foci of the revolution. He gained the largest numbers of votes in all three cities—in Cairo, where he came in first, he won 27.8 percent of the vote; in Alexandria, 31.6 percent; and in Port Said, 40.4 percent.

Part of the explanation for these results lies in the historical memory of the Nasserist era, particularly in urban working-class areas. The contrast be-tween Nasser's attempted redistribution of wealth through land reforms and nationalizations and what was seen as a constant attack on the poor by the Mubarak regime through privatization and other neoliberal reforms meant that those voting for Sabahi were actually seeking a left-wing alternative. However, the fact that Abd al-Munim Abu al-Futuh, the ex-Brotherhood leader who had split and moved to the left, got 17 percent of the votes, focusing his campaign on similar themes to those of Sabahi, was another significant development. It meant first that Abu al-Futuh was not able to differentiate himself enough from the Brotherhood to represent a viable al-ternative to sections of Brotherhood supporters that were radicalized by the revolution and angered by the concessions of their leadership to the military, so they ended up sticking with the Brotherhood candidate despite their crit-icisms. Second, it represented a split in the "revolutionary camp" between those from an Islamist background and those from a secularist background. This secular-Islamist divide would later prove fatal to the revolution.

The second round, between Mursi and Shafiq, the Brotherhood can-didate and the old regime candidate, created a serious political crisis. The military and the old regime put all their resources and mobilized all their old networks throughout the country. The Brotherhood did its best, not only to utilize its considerable organizational and mobilizing strength but also to present Mursi as the candidate of the January 2011 revolution against what was truly a full-fledged attempt by the old regime to return to power.

According to official figures, Mursi won with 13.2 million votes against Shafiq's 12.3 million votes.[67] Although this was seen by many as a victory against the old regime, the situation was complicated. An open candidate of the overthrown Mubarak regime had nearly won in presidential elections only eighteen months after the revolution. At the same time Mursi, although the only choice for many revolutionaries, was far from a revolutionary figure himself. He had, together with his organization, already chosen compromise over confrontation with the old regime and already betrayed many of the hopes and aspirations of the revolution, even before coming to power. Yet despite his concessions to SCAF and the military and despite the alliance between the latter and the Muslim Brotherhood and the old regime, he had no real intention of sharing power with the Muslim Brotherhood.

In ensuring the Brotherhood would be paralyzed in power, the military leadership relied on another part of the state apparatus that would prove instrumental in the following months and years. The Supreme Constitutional Court, the highest judicial body in Egypt, had already made it possible for Shafiq to stand in the runoff by ruling unconstitutional the parliamentary Political Isolation Law, which barred leading members of the old regime from running for office.[68] Its second move, on June 14, was to rule the parliamentary elections themselves unconstitutional on technicalities, thus paving the way for SCAF to dissolve parliament, which it promptly did just days before Mursi became president. SCAF also announced that it would assume all legislative powers until a new parliament was elected. On June 17, the second day of the runoff elections, SCAF produced a new "supplement" to the Constitutional Declaration of March 2011. This practically stripped the president of his authority over matters of national defense and security. The supplement noted that SCAF would retain complete authority over the armed forces, including control of the Ministry of Defense and all military appointments and promotions.[69] So Mursi was being stripped of his powers even before becoming president. A leading Muslim Brotherhood official, Mohamed al-Biltagi, described these moves as a "full-fledged coup."

6. The Muslim Brotherhood in power?

On June 29, Mursi gave his first public speech as president in Tahrir Square, in front of hundreds of thousands that had gathered for the momentous occasion. He promised to continue the road of the January revolution and that the real source of his power came from the masses on the squares and streets of Egypt. Needless to say, he did not keep his promise and did everything possible to isolate himself from those squares and streets. The old regime had remained intact, not only in the army command and security apparatuses but also in all state institutions, particularly the judiciary, and in the entrenched interests of local, regional, and global capital. This situation could only have been challenged by further mass mobilizations and revolutionary measures against the main pillars of the old regime. Instead, Mursi and the Brotherhood chose a policy of appeasement and concessions to those forces of the old regime, opposing all forms of further revolutionary mobilizations and practically paving the way for counterrevolution.

In terms of economic policy, the government formed by Mursi went out of its way to assure both foreign and local capital that it would continue with the same neoliberal policies of Mubarak. Khayrat al-Shatir, the leading Brotherhood member and one of the main architects of Mursi's economic policy, described politics as "the art of the possible" and stressed that the priority at that moment was to develop and sustain the strategic partnership with the United States.[70] Hassan Malek, another leading Brotherhood member and businessman, organized Mursi's business trip to China in August 2012, to which he was accompanied by eighty major businessmen, among whom were some of the same billionaires that were part of Mubarak's inner circle and leading members of the old ruling party.[71] Mursi even backed a SCAF decree giving immunity from criminal prosecution to businessmen accused of corruption under Mubarak.[72] The first government formed by Mursi was made up of strong supporters of neoliberalism, including those that held positions of power during the Mubarak era.[73]

In terms of the balance of power between the newly elected president and SCAF and the old state institutions, Mursi was to confine himself to half-hearted declarations and decisions that were rapidly retracted. For example, on July 8, Mursi issued a decree reinstating the dissolved parliament. On July 9, a sharply worded statement signed by most senior figures of the judicial establishment, including the Supreme Constitutional Court, the State Council, and the Judges Club, forced Mursi to annul the decree a few days later.

On August 12, in a move that seemed to show that Mursi was at last challenging SCAF and the Mubarak state, he announced the retirement of Field Marshal Tantawi, the minister of defense and head of SCAF, together with army chief of staff Sami Anan and several other top military generals. But it was soon revealed that not only had the army leadership previously approved even that seemingly bold move, it actually proposed the move as part of its own plan for generational renewal. Perhaps nothing expresses the emptiness of that gesture more than the fact that the new Mursi-appointed minister of defense was none other than General Abdel Fattah al-Sisi.[74] In fact Mursi continued to take steps to ensure and even enhance the political and economic privileges of the military. Even the police would be protected from any serious reforms or reconstruction or "transitional justice." In fact, in January 2013 Mursi would appoint police general Mohamed Ibrahim, previously in charge of Egypt's notorious prison system, as his new interior minister.[75]

Yet the more concessions Mursi and the Brotherhood made to the military and the old regime, the more untenable their situation became. The Brotherhood's plan was to become accepted as a partner in power in return for containing the revolution and keeping intact the privileges and wealth of Mubarak's generals and businessmen and their regional and global allies. Instead of relying on mass mobilizations and a return to the squares to force concessions from Mubarak's men, they went in the opposite direction. Their rhetoric became that of law and order and the need for social peace.

The generals, however, could only accept complete surrender. It was the generals that understood the nature and threat of the revolution. They understood that the Brotherhood, despite playing a role as a necessary temporary ally, which gave the generals the time and space to regain their strength after the January 2011 shock, would not be able to contain the revolution and crush the energy and confidence that it had given to millions of young people across the country. There was no compromise solution. Although the revolution had achieved very little in terms of concrete political and economic transformations, it had created a near-permanent state of protest. The country was brimming with occupations of public space, workplace mobilizations, and demonstrations by all those sectors of society that had been silenced for decades. This was a situation neither the Brotherhood nor the institutions of procedural democracy could contain.

7. Revolutionary and counterrevolutionary mobilizations

The opposition that emerged during the Mursi presidency expressed the complexity of the continuing revolutionary crisis. In the first few months after the inauguration, there was on the one hand a more confident and vocal representation of supporters of the old regime blaming Mursi and the Brotherhood for food and energy shortages, for the continuing perceived lack of security, and for supposed foreign conspiracies against the unity and very existence of the Egyptian nation and state. The Brotherhood, according to this narrative, was taking Egypt toward a mixture of civil war and religious extremism. What was needed was a return to the relative stability and law and order of the Mubarak era. Although the opposition was concentrated explicitly on the Mursi presidency and the supposed control and power of the Muslim Brotherhood leadership, the implicit argument was against the revolution itself: it was only because of the revolution that the Brotherhood came to power, and therefore the revolution was the root of all evil.

The second oppositional tendency began independently of the first but would later merge with it. Secular opposition movements and parties that had participated in the January revolution and had a history of opposition against the Mubarak regime saw the Mursi presidency and the perceived rising power of the Muslim Brotherhood as an existential threat to the very possibility of a liberal or democratic Egypt. The Mursi presidency, according to this group of liberal, left-wing, and secular nationalist forces, was the first step in turning Egypt into a theocratic dictatorship in which individual freedoms, women's rights, and the rights of religious minorities would be crushed and, as in the Iranian case, an Islamist dictatorship would take Egypt into the abyss. According to this group, the Muslim Brotherhood had highjacked the Egyptian revolution, and therefore all groups must unite to get rid of the Mursi presidency and bring back the political process to the secular democratic road map they preferred.

The third type of opposition was based in the revolutionary movements that had opposed both Mubarak and the rule of SCAF that followed. This included the radical left and the revolutionary youth movements together with the considerable sections of workers and urban poor that were radicalized by the revolution. For these movements, Mursi had betrayed the revolution, not because of his or the Brotherhood's Islamist agenda, but rather because of his concessions to the army leadership, the state institutions, and the old ruling class. For this revolutionary opposition, the Brotherhood was practically shielding the old regime and allowing the forces of counter-revolution to regroup and rebuild. This opposition wanted to develop the revolutionary process, both socially and politically, and saw Mursi and the Brotherhood as an obstacle in its path.

The situation was further complicated by the separation between social and political struggles. On the one hand, there were economic and social struggles against both state institutions and private capital, steered by demands for wage increases, social security, health care, permanent contracts, and price controls; on the other hand, there were the rising political movements against the Mursi presidency. In April 2013 a new wave of workers' strikes shook the country as hundreds of thousands of workers again took strike action against what they saw as the betrayal of the promises for social justice and reforms.

During the same month, a political campaign that named itself Tamarud (Rebellion) was formed. This campaign, composed mainly of youth connected to the second trend of opposition, was initiated with a grassroots petition calling for early presidential elections. It was able to link together the different contradictory and separate forms of opposition, both social and political, and focus them against the Mursi presidency. The intentional focus on Mursi, leaving out completely any mention of SCAF, the old regime, or the capitalist class, proved to be particularly useful to the counterrevolutionary opposition. A grassroots movement with the seemingly revolutionary aim of removing another president was tapping into the growing social anger while mobilizing all those opposed to the Islamic agenda of the Brotherhood. This created a level of ambiguity and ideological indeterminacy that would prove vital for the counterrevolutionary project.

Instead of Mursi and the Brotherhood organizing a broad-based democratic front bringing together all those opposed to the old regime and the military to protect democracy against any attempted coup or return of the old regime, we get a situation where the old regime and the military were able to become part of a contradictory alliance of forces, all focused on ending the Mursi presidency, by any means necessary. The two sections of the opposition, one representing the old regime and its military and security forces, and the other a wide section of the secular opposition fiercely opposed to Islamism, were coalescing into one "national front" calling for an end to the Mursi presidency.

On November 22, Mursi issued a new constitutional declaration, shielding presidential decrees signed since June 2012 from any legal challenges and appointing a new prosecutor general. Although this was a move against a judiciary that was clearly part of the old regime and was coordinating its stranglehold of the presidency with the military command, it was perceived as an attempt to establish a dictatorship. Again, one of the reasons Mursi's move was not seen as part of a struggle against the old regime was the fact that it did not involve any mass mobilization against SCAF and its allies in the judiciary and that it came after months of trying to appease those same forces.

The move triggered mass protests, called for by the newly formed National Salvation Front. This front openly declared the alliance between the secular opposition and an increasingly confident section of the old regime against Muslim Brotherhood "dictatorship." The front openly coordinated with the military command in the person of the then-minister of defense Abdel Fattah al-Sisi. It included the main liberal, leftist, and Nasserist parties, together with ex-ministers, ruling party members, and billionaire businessmen from the Mubarak era.

The mass protests that started in late November and continued through the coming months, culminating in the mass demonstrations and occupations of June 30, seemed on the surface to be a second wave of the 2011 revolution. However, even if some of the participants in that new wave of protests perceived it that way, it was in fact mainly a counterrevolutionary mobilization. The Right has always been able to mobilize using the tools of the Left. In Chile in 1973, there were mass demonstrations and strikes against Allende. In Thailand, during the past two decades, right-wing forces in alliance with the military and the monarchy organized demonstrations and occupations (the Yellow Shirt movement) to undermine elected governments.[76] In fact it would be strange if counterrevolutions did not utilize tools of the revolution. If Mubarak fell as a result of a mass movement utilizing demonstrations, strikes, and occupations, then a restoration would surely require an impressive mass mobilization using the same tools. In addition, it sows confusion in the enemy camp (the revolutionary camp) by muddying the ideological waters, by projecting the same appearance on a qualitatively different and opposite phenomenon. The Tamarud movement that organized itself as a grassroots mass mobilization was in fact coordinated and funded by military intelligence and other security agencies. It was later revealed that the Gulf state of the United Arab Emirates had established a fund to finance the movement.[77]

The mobilization against the Mursi presidency was carefully planned to demonize the Muslim Brotherhood and isolate it, using many of the methods, slogans, and symbols of the 2011 revolution. But the Muslim Brotherhood itself helped this process, first by being practically paralyzed and incapable of building any wide mass support against the counterrevolutionary mass mobilization. It also helped the process by trying to form an Islamist front instead, isolating itself even further and making it easier for the military and its allies to represent the Brotherhood as an existential threat.

The shifting allegiances of sections of the Coptic minority are a good example of that process. Copts were a major component of the first wave of revolution in 2011 against the Mubarak regime. They were also a prominent part of the movement against military rule during the SCAF's reign. Large numbers of Coptic youth were radicalized by the revolution, both against the state and against the Church hierarchy historically linked to the state. However, during the Mursi presidency, the inability of the Muslim Brotherhood to connect in any way with the demands of the Coptic minority and its shift to an even more Islamic agenda in its alliance with the Salafists made it relatively easy for the military and its new secular allies to mobilize the Copts, this time through the traditional Church hierarchy against the Mursi presidency and the danger of an Islamist state that would relegate them to second-class citizens. This was particularly clear as the final votes on the draft constitution were pushed through the Constituent Assembly, which had lost, not only all Coptic representation, but also almost all representation from non-Islamist political forces. As more and more Copts joined the anti-Mursi mobilization, the Brotherhood condemned the movement as predominantly Christian and anti-Muslim, thus pushing even more Copts into the counterrevolutionary camp.

A similar process occurred around the question of women's rights. Again, women were a major component of the revolution of 2011. That year saw the emergence of a new women's movement and the largest demonstrations in modern Egyptian history against sexual harassment and discrimination. The conservative agenda of the Muslim Brotherhood and its Salafi allies encumbered them from addressing the women's question. The members of the military-secular alliance again posed themselves as defenders of women's rights and freedoms against the reactionary Islamist agenda.

The military-secular mobilization, even more subtle and complex in terms of the Coptic and women's questions, engaged in a discourse based on the following logic discourse: Coptic youth should not have opposed the state and Church hierarchy during the 2011 revolution, because that is what helped the Muslim Brotherhood to come to power and pose this existential problem. Copts should flock back to their churches and support the historical alliance with the state to protect themselves from the ravages of Islamism and the fate of other Middle Eastern Christian minorities. Women should not have joined the revolution of 2011 as it ended up with a regime opposed to their rights and freedoms and even safety. Only the state and its military could protect women. Honest, respectable mothers, wives, and daughters should participate in this new "revolution" to restore the state and remove the Islamists from power.

The process of co-optation also took hold of the worker's movement. As mentioned above, the revolution of 2011 had accelerated the creation of independent trade unions, challenging the old state-controlled unions that had been dominant since the 1960s. Many of the major strikes between 2011 and 2013 seriously challenged the old union structures and created new ones based on the strike committees that emerged in all major sections of the working class. Many of the leaders of these unions, coming together under the newly formed Independent Trade Union Federation, were linked, first to the National Salvation Front, then to the military-secular mobilization against Mursi.

The counterrevolutionary mobilization was heavily financed by Saudi Arabia and other Gulf states. These were not only major partners and investors in Mubarak's neoliberal Egypt, but also wanted above all to end the revolutionary turbulence that had destabilized their own thrones.[78] All privately owned newspapers and television channels were used in a coordinated fashion to mobilize for the end of the Mursi regime and for the mass mobilization of June 30, 2013.

June 30 itself turned out to be the largest mass mobilization since January 2011. However, the contrast between the two mobilizations could not be more extreme. It was the ideological ambiguity of many of the 2011 slogans and symbols that made it possible to utilize them for what was ultimately the opposite purpose. The Egyptian national flag, for example, was a major symbol in both 2011 and 2013. In the former it was taken over from the state by the revolutionary masses in an act of defiance. In the latter, it was once more the flag of the Egyptian state against the threat of chaos and anarchy.

In 2011 the police, as direct representatives and protectors of Mubarak's state, were major targets of the revolutionary masses. In 2013 police officers took part in the demonstrations and protected them. Women participated in 2011 as citizens fighting for democracy and equality and against discrimination and harassment. In 2013 women participated in support of a return to law and order and stability. In 2011 the army took a direct stance of neutrality, as it indirectly supported every counterrevolutionary attempt. In 2013 the army was at the very core of the demonstrations, celebrating and being celebrated, and again together with the police playing a crucial role in protecting the demonstrations.

Perhaps the greatest myth and ambiguity of all was that of "the people." The Egyptian "people" supposedly carried out the 2011 revolution, and the same Egyptian "people" were carrying out a second "revolution" in 2013. Despite both events and processes involving millions of people, the claim that somehow they were the same seems in retrospect simply untrue. Only relatively small sections of the population were involved in both cases. However, many of the "people" that were opposed to the 2011 revolution or decided not to take part were a major part of the mobilizations of 2013. Even Egyptian media reported and commented on the unprecedented participation of upper- and middle-class Egyptians in 2013 in contrast to 2011. Both revolutions and counterrevolutions involve mass mobilizations; however, they mobilize different classes and sections of the population, at different moments and toward different goals. The fact that the counterrevolutionary mobilization utilized the real growing anger of sections of the working class and youth against the paralysis of the Mursi regime, and used ambiguous slogans and symbols similar to those of the 2011 revolution, meant that there was inevitable overlap in who participated in the two events.

For the Revolutionary Socialists, there was clarity concerning the nature of the National Salvation Front mobilizations and their alliance with the military. However, June 30 at the time represented to them an opportunity to challenge the military-secular mobilization with a counter-mobilization against the Mursi presidency as well as SCAF and the remnants of the old regime. In retrospect that was a mistake, as the balance of forces had already shifted decisively in favor of the counterrevolutionary camp and as the participation of the Revolutionary Socialists in that day of demonstrations was to cause considerable confusion among the wider movement as to the nature of the event.[79] All attempts during that day to march separately from the pro-army demonstrations failed. The heavy presence of the police and army in and around the major demonstrations meant practically that only anti-Brotherhood and anti-Mursi slogans would be allowed.

8. More than a restoration: Sisi's coup

As events unfolded, it became clear that the June 30th mobilization was the popular prelude to the military coup of July 3, 2013.[80] The coup was swift and brutal. The Brotherhood had already organized mass occupations to resist the coup. The main ones were in Rabaa al-Adaweya Square in Cairo and Al-Nahda Square in Giza. These would be the final mass occupations of public space in Egypt.

General Abdel Fattah al-Sisi,[81] the minister of defense, announced the annulment of the constitution, a transitional presidency to be represented by the head of the Supreme Constitutional Court, and a government that was to include left-wing, Nasserist, and liberal ministers. In perhaps one of the most vulgar examples of the capitulation of former opposition activists to military dictatorship, Kamal Abu Eita—former head of the Independent Trade Union Federation, leader of one of the largest national strikes in the 2006–8 strike wave, and seasoned Nasserist opposition figure during the Mubarak era—was appointed minister of labor in the first postcoup cabinet.[82] Mohamed Al-Baradei, a major liberal opposition figure, was appointed vice-president. In fact, most of the parties and figures of the National Salvation Front would go on to support the General and his violent coup. The Egyptian Communist Party, for example, fully endorsed the coup, calling it the "second Egyptian revolution" and that it liberated the country from Islamic fascism.[83] Major Egyptian left-wing intellectuals would come out in support of the coup, even after any confusion about the intention of its leaders had been long dispelled.

The General's first major repressive move was to carry out the bloodiest massacres in modern Egyptian history as he sent in military and police troops to storm and end the Muslim Brotherhood occupations in the Rabaa and Nahda squares. On August 14, 2013, an estimated one thousand people were killed as live ammunition was used to clear the squares.[84] During the first year of the coup, over fifty thousand people would be imprisoned and hundreds would receive death sentences. What started as a campaign to eradicate the Muslim Brotherhood developed into a full reign of terror as demonstrations became illegal and many activists connected to the 2011 revolution that had not openly capitulated to the generals would be killed, disappeared, imprisoned, or forced into exile.

Paradoxically, the revenge of the generals has involved the utilization of the tools of revolution, mass mobilizations, occupations, and demonstrations to build support for the "regrouping" of the state—a state that is going on the offensive, not only to eradicate the Muslim Brotherhood or even to restore the Mubarak regime, but to learn from the mistakes and weaknesses of the old regime and to utilize the fears and lessons of the revolution to carry out the class aims that the old regime had shied away from. The logic is simple:

the old regime would not have fallen if it was not weak and had not been strategically flawed.[85] If there was a chance to rebuild the class power that the old regime nearly lost, then new radical policies and strategies need to be put in place. If the old regime was too scared to carry out radical neoliberal reforms, then the new regime must be bold and go ahead even if it means major class battles.[86] If the old regime relied on an implicit balance with the opposition led by the Muslim Brotherhood, now is the time to destroy that organization and that balance. If the old regime was authoritarian but had its limits in terms of risking the use of violence, the new regime must not hesitate even if that means massacres. Many of the features of the new regime are shaped by that logic. The Egyptian military has always been at the center of power, but usually operated from behind the scenes.[87] Now it openly plays a leading role in security, economic and infrastructural projects, the major media outlets, and all forms of diplomacy and foreign relations.

Although economic policies have been guided by neoliberalism since the 1990s, the neoliberal onslaught since the coup has been unprecedented. The military, in partnership with both local and multinational capital, has embarked on a series of extreme neoliberal reforms that make the Mubarak regime seem relatively benign. Ever since the 1950s the regime has relied on a delicate balance between state institutions, particularly the military and the other security agencies such as the police. That balance has been thrown aside and the military is in full control of all aspects of security, with the police serving as subordinate tool. The Mubarak regime relied on a political machine, the National Democratic Party, to mobilize and control. The Sisi regime relies totally on the security and intelligence apparatus. For the first time since the 1960s, Egypt has neither a ruling party nor a significant opposition party.

What has been happening is not simply a restoration but rather a qualitative shift to a new model of authoritarian neoliberalism. This model relies on a permanent state of emergency, not only in the legal sense, but more importantly in the coupling of long-term austerity with intense repression. Capitalism with a monstrous military face.

Conclusion

The failed revolution of 2011 represents the most significant "intervention" by the masses in the course of modern Egyptian history. Looked at from the perspective of the previous century, the revolutionary crisis of 2011 reveals the relative failure of the postcolonial developmental state established in the 1950s to "develop" Egypt into a successful center of capital accumulation. If one takes the perspective of the previous decade, the 2011 revolutionary crisis was the culmination of both accelerated neoliberal reforms, accompanied by growing state repression, and the maturing of both a democracy movement against the Mubarak regime and a related but separate workers' movement against the accumulated social effects of neoliberalism. If one takes an even closer perspective, the 2011 revolutionary events reveal several peculiarities, some related to Egypt's specific social and political landscape and others perhaps to the global historical period we are all living through.

First, the revolution was urban both in terms of where it was centered and in terms of the specific shape the protests took. Cairo, Alexandria, and Suez were its main focal points. Mass demonstrations, strikes, and occupations of public space were its main features.

Second, the ideological map of the revolution was dominated by reformist Islamism and, to a much lesser extent, by relatively new secular youth movements calling for peaceful democratic transition. The influence of the revolutionary Left grew rapidly during the events, but from a much smaller base and was therefore unable to seriously contend for hegemony in the movement.

Third, although the revolution involved the rise of a militant workers' movement clearly resonating with the democratic movement of the squares, it remained separate from that movement. The divide between politics and economics remained largely intact.

Fourth, the revolution was betrayed twice—first by the Muslim Brotherhood who, after the fall of Mubarak, allied themselves with the military; then by the secular opposition who entered an alliance with the same military and remnants of the old regime, paving the way for counterrevolution.

Fifth, the failure of the revolution also meant the success of the counterrevolution. This involved a comparable mass mobilization, utilizing the same tools and methods of the revolution, exploiting the ideological indeterminacy of many of its slogans and symbols.

Egypt after the storm of 2011–14 is not simply a restored version of the Egypt of Mubarak. History is not repeating itself. One should think of the cycle of events between 2011 and 2014 not in terms of a circle, but rather a spiral. Despite the defeat, millions of people had a glimpse of a different world and not only experienced the euphoria of the occupations but also the hard-earned lessons of revolutionary strategy and tactics. If the coup leaders had a learning curve and were able to learn from their class's mistakes, then it should also be true for revolutionaries.

The inauguration celebrations of General Sisi took place behind the electrified walls of a palace protected by hundreds of tanks, armored cars, and thousands of soldiers and officers. The ghost of Tahrir will continue to haunt them and should continue to inspire us.

PART 3:
THEORETICAL IMPLICATIONS

CHAPTER 10

The Actuality of the Revolution[1]

Neil Davidson

Introduction

Now that the centenary of the Russian Revolution is behind us, we might be forgiven for wondering whether the promise of global socialism that it temporarily held out is ever going to be fulfilled. Indeed, anyone who has never entertained doubts on this score must be not only worryingly insensitive to the experience of defeat, but also to have misunderstood what Marxism teaches on the subject. For Marx and Engels, the working class had the capacity to achieve socialism; but that outcome was certainly not inevitable, and only in rhetorical flourishes toward the end of otherwise scientific works did they suggest otherwise.[2] The only inevitability was class *conflict*, in all its myriad forms, as workers sought to resist the process of exploitation constitutive of the capitalist mode of production, and the way in which this conflict would from time to time find more or less conscious expression in class *struggle*, which opened the possibility of bringing capitalism to an end.

Yet the founders of historical materialism did not believe that the class struggle would continue *indefinitely* without a permanent working-class victory, since they saw the anarchic, self-destructive nature of capitalism propelling humanity toward a variety of unhappy outcomes, all of which involved at least temporary social retrogression. In 1848 they drew on earlier historical examples—most obviously the fate of the Roman Empire—to identify

309

"the common ruin of the contending classes" as one possibility should the exploited fail to overthrow their exploiters.[3] In 1878 Engels added a second possibility, that of economic collapse brought about by the way in which the productive forces had grown beyond the control of the bourgeoisie, "a class under whose leadership society is racing to ruin like a locomotive whose jammed safety-valve the driver is too weak to open," so that "if the whole of modern society was not to perish," control of the economy would have to be wrested from its grasp—a quite different use of the railway metaphor from that of Marx, nearly thirty years earlier.[4] In 1887 Engels envisaged a third and final version of the apocalypse, in the form of "a world war, moreover of an extent the violence hitherto unimagined."[5] Paradoxically, however, of the three possible ways that might lead to the collapse of capitalist society—stalemated class struggle, irrecoverable economic crisis, inter-imperialist war—it was the last, the most immediately catastrophic in terms of destroying life and property, that Engels regarded as producing the most immediate conditions for revolution.

With the outbreak of the Russian Revolution in 1917 and its sequels in Central and Eastern Europe, it appeared that Engels had been correct. Writing in her prison cell in Berlin, during the cataclysm but before the revolutionary wave began, Luxemburg expanded on the alternatives of socialism or barbarism implicit in Engels's work, without however his assumption that war would necessarily lead to the former. Indeed, perhaps her most important argument was that barbarism was not only the terminus of capitalist development but, in the era of imperialism, an ongoing reality:

> *This world war* means a reversion to barbarism. The triumph of imperialism leads to the destruction of culture, sporadically during a modern war, and forever, if the period of world wars that has just begun is allowed to take its damnable course to the last ultimate consequence.[6]

There is a sense, however, in which the barbarism of which Luxemburg spoke was not new in the capitalist world, but simply in its European heartlands; beyond them, as she was perfectly aware, it was nothing so novel. And today, in parts of Central Africa and the Middle East in particular, generalized social collapse is the everyday lived experience of millions. "Barbarism," Mike Davis rightly observes, "is all around us."[7]

Yet the three possible triggers of global retrogression identified by Engels are less applicable today—although not, alas, for positive reasons. Far from involving a destructive stalemate, the class struggle has been an overwhelmingly one-sided affair in which ruling classes have largely continued to emerge victorious since the working-class defeats of the 1970s and 1980s signaled the onset of the neoliberal era. And, although maintaining the rate of profit certainly becomes more difficult for the system as it ages, as I will argue below, capitalism will not simply collapse of its own accord—a process that would in any case be unlikely to benefit the working class. Finally, the possession of nuclear weapons threatens not just barbarism but actual annihilation; however, without being in any way complacent about current rivalries between the dominant nation-states, the end of the Cold War has diminished the prospect of their use—for the time being at any rate these rivalries have been displaced onto proxy conflicts over control of resources and geo-strategic advantage in the global South, one of the reasons for the regional descent into barbarism mentioned in the preceding paragraph.

Nor do we have the luxury of a slow decline. For we are faced with a prospect even more somber than even those that Marx, Engels, or Luxemburg imagined: that of human civilization being brought to an end through environmental collapse before victory can be achieved. "The choice, said Rosa Luxemburg in 1918, is between socialism or barbarism," writes Michael Mann, "though climate socialism would be very different to the socialism she envisaged, closer to the reformism she denounced."[8] But the extremity of the situation is such that "climate socialism" cannot be restricted to reformism. As Adrian Parr has noted, the problem is not simply human-made climate change—in other words the concentration of CO_2 in the atmosphere—but human-made environmental change more generally, including "the privatization of the commons, landfills, freshwater scarcity, floods, desertification, landslides, coastal and soil erosion, drought, crop failures, extreme storm activity, land degradation and conversion for agriculture and live-stock farming, urban heat-island effect, polluted waterways, ocean acidification, and many other problems on a growing list."[9] Nevertheless, as she points out, climate change is the most immediately urgent issue. Parr argued in 2013 that we were in the last decade when it would be possible to reduce warming to less than one degree; higher than two degrees of warming, which was expected by 2050 on then-current projections, and the situation would be irreversible.[10] David Wallace-Wells has given some indication of what warming by two degrees will involve:

> At 2C, the ice-sheets will begin their collapse, bringing, over centuries, 50 meters of sea-level rise. An additional 400 million people will suffer from water scarcity, major cities in the equatorial band of the planet will become

unlivable, and even in the northern latitudes heatwaves will kill thousands each summer. There would be 32 times as many extreme heatwaves in India, and each would last five times as long, exposing 93 times more people.

He then adds, in a final twist of the knife: "This is our best-case scenario."[11] A growing consensus, however, suggests that point has already been passed, with some authorities predicting that global warming will rise by 3.2 degrees before 2100, regardless of whether or not the 2015 Paris Accord is put into effect.[12] In other words, there will be severe consequences regardless of what we do now, and any realistic assessment of our chances of avoiding the full extent of the coming disaster would have to conclude that the odds of success are not high. Nevertheless, there are two reasons why it is important not to indulge in what is sometimes described as "catastrophism," a sensibility that holds that the full extent of the disaster is unavoidable, no matter what we do.

The first is that it is conducive to a politics of fear. There have of course been historical situations in which collective fear has galvanized revolutionary activity, most notably *"le grande peur"* that preceded the French Revolution.[13] In our current circumstances, however, it tends to benefit the enemies of socialism:

> From a rhetorical standpoint, catastrophism is a win/win for the right, as there is no accountability for false prophesy. On the one hand, it rallies the troops and creates a sense of urgency. On the other hand, though, fear and paranoia serve a rightist political disposition more than a left or liberal one. Authoritarian politics benefits more than left politics from fear.[14]

As if to demonstrate the truth of this contention, the authoritarian politics of fear dominated the campaign for the Republican Party presidential nomination in 2015–16 and the subsequent election. "Fear is the essence of Trumpism," wrote one US journalist during the nomination campaign, adding: "Trump isn't simply reflecting fear; he's conjuring it—both among his followers and among those he demonizes."[15] The fear that Donald Trump evokes and provokes is not, of course, of global environmental collapse—since man-made climate change is obviously an invention of politically correct liberals seeking to put more power in the hands of incompetent government elites—but the collapsing American Way of Life under pressure from a long list of threatening groups, including criminal Mexicans, homicidal Muslims, unscrupulous Chinese, and disrespectful Iranians.

The second reason to avoid catastrophism is that it can lead to passivity, as capitalism's supposedly helpless plunge toward self-destruction compensates us for the lack of an agency capable of consciously overthrowing it. Here, as Razmig Keucheyan points out,

> the weakness of the left ceases to be a problem. The end of capitalism takes the form of suicide rather than murder. So the absence of a murderer—that is, an organized revolutionary movement—doesn't really matter anymore.

However, as Keucheyan goes on to argue, this is to seriously underestimate the adaptability of the system, even in conditions of extremity:

> Capitalism might well be capable not only of adapting to climate change but of profiting from it. One hears that the capitalist system is confronted with a double crisis: an economic one that started in 2008, and an ecological one, rendering the situation doubly perilous. But one crisis can sometimes serve to solve another. Capitalism is responding to the challenge of the ecological crisis with two of its favorite weapons: financialization and militarization. . . . Nothing in the system's logic will make it go away. A world of environmental desolation and conflict will work for capitalism, as long as the conditions for investment and profit are guaranteed. And, for this, good old finance and the military are ready to serve. Building a revolutionary movement that will put a stop to this insane logic is therefore not optional. Because, if the system can survive, it doesn't mean that lives worth living will.[16]

The adaptations that Keucheyan describes here cannot of course be sustained indefinitely, as eventually the material conditions for sustaining human life will cease, even for the ruling class. His central point nevertheless remains valid: even the unfolding catastrophe will not be enough to force the bourgeoisie into voluntarily abandoning capitalism.

As the capitalist system ages, then, the revolutionary stakes actually become higher: not only an end to exploitation and oppression—momentous and difficult enough goals in themselves—but the very survival of our species. However, the aging of the system also affects the role of revolutionaries in ways other than simply making their task more urgent: it transforms the conditions under which future revolutions will have to be made. The question that socialists have to address is whether these conditions have been transformed to such an extent that they make revolution more difficult than at earlier points in the history of capitalism, perhaps to the point of making it impossible. One way of answering this question might be to start from another, namely, whether there are general conditions of possibility for the socialist revolution, *irrespective* of the historical period, but which take specific forms *depending* on the historical period. The first ("general conditions") I will treat as a question of theory, the second ("specific forms") as one of history—although there is and can be no absolute distinction between them, as theory is at least partly abstracted from concrete historical instances, and history is only comprehensible within a theoretical framework.

1. Three aspects of actuality

I will begin with the concept that gives this chapter its title: "the actuality of the revolution," first used by Lukács in his book on Lenin, published shortly after the death of his subject in 1924.[17] This extraordinary work did not merely distill or condense Lenin's thought, but developed it in several ways, of which "the actuality of the revolution" itself is one of the most important. For Lukács it had three aspects.

Actuality 1: Material preconditions

First, "the actuality of the revolution" meant that the *material preconditions* for the socialist revolution existed in two respects: one was the expansion of the productive forces, to the point where the outcome of the revolution could meet human needs on the basis of equality; the other was the associated growth of the working class, to the point where it could act as the social force capable of bringing about the revolution. When were these conditions met?

Engels himself thought the material conditions for socialism had arrived as early as the mid-1870s: "The possibility of securing for every member of society, by means of socialized production, an existence not only fully sufficient materially, and becoming day-by-day more full, but an existence guaranteeing to all the free development and exercise of their physical and mental faculties—this possibility is now, for the first time, here, but *it is here*."[18] A working class large and militant enough to overthrow the new capitalist world only emerged after the consolidation of bourgeois states in Central and Southern Europe, North America, and Japan during the 1860s—an exact date is obviously impossible to identify, but at any rate it lies between the Paris Commune of 1871 and the Russian Revolution of 1905. If we require a symbolic year by which both conditions were met, however, then we might settle on 1889, the year during which the Second International was launched. Confirmation might also be found in the left-wing literature of the time. William Morris's *News from Nowhere*, first published in 1890, a year after the International was re-established, is perhaps the first novel to imagine a socialist future not as a miraculous or unexplained event, but as the result of a revolutionary process possible at the time the book was written.[19]

Not coincidentally, these decades also saw the opening of the era of imperialism, which Lenin in particular saw as the geopolitical order expressive of the monopoly stage of capitalism. In 1918 he claimed it was coincident with "the era of socialist revolution," his assumption being that it would continue until either the revolution is successful or the world is destroyed by the clash of rival imperialisms—a prospect now more capable of total realization than in Lenin's day.[20] Yet this periodization elides a central issue: the material conditions for socialist revolution might have existed in Western and Central Europe, North America, Australasia, Japan, perhaps some parts of Latin America; they did not in the most individual states of the colonial and semi-colonial world—that is to say, across most of world.

Around the time of the Russian "Great Rehearsal" of 1905, Trotsky tried to resolve the question of individual socioeconomic backwardness through his initial formulations of the strategy of permanent revolution. He was of course aware of the problem that would face any Social Democratic government on the day after seizing power:

> The revolutionary authorities will be confronted with the objective problems of socialism, but the solution of these problems will, at a certain stage, be prevented by the country's economic backwardness. There is no way out from this contradiction within the framework of a national revolution.[21]

The solution therefore lay outside this framework, since "the objective pre-requisites for a socialist revolution have already been created by the economic development of the advanced capitalist countries."[22] The socialist revolution in the West was therefore necessary for the Russian Revolution to survive on a socialist basis, not only as a source of class solidarity in the struggle against counterrevolution—although this would be the most immediate requirement—but also as the mechanism that would make available to the new regime the financial, technological, and scientific resources that would enable it to overcome the inheritance of Tsarist backwardness.

In 1917 Lenin's thought converged with that of Trotsky over the significance of the international setting in which the Russian Revolution had taken place.[23] This represented a shift in Lenin's position. Although always insistent on the need for proletarian internationalism, he had not previously seen the Russian Revolution as being dependent on support from other revolutions, so long as it remained within the parameters of bourgeois revolution. Ever the realist, Lenin understood that a socialist revolution was a different matter: a bourgeois republic in Russia might be acceptable to the global ruling class, a socialist republic would not be. No matter how important the soviets were as examples of proletarian self-emancipation, they, and the revolution that rested upon them, would not survive the combination of internal bourgeois opposition and external imperialist intervention. A recurrent theme of Lenin's writings, from October 25, 1917, on, was that without revolutions in the West—whether caused by the wartime crisis, or undertaken in emulation of the Russian example, or some mixture of the two—the Russian republic could not survive.[24] One example, taken from early in the revolution, will suffice here:

> We are far from having completed even the transitional period from capitalism to socialism. We have never cherished the hope that we could finish it without the aid of the international proletariat. We never had any illusions on that score. . . . The final victory of socialism in a single country is of course impossible.[25]

This dependency on the rapid development of the world revolution meant that the Russian Revolution always involved a "wager" on success that could never be guaranteed, but that was precisely why Lenin and Trotsky insisted on identifying the right moment at which to act, as we shall see when considering Actuality 3.[26]

The condemnation that the Bolsheviks received from the reformist and centrist wings of the socialist movement was not, however, because of the risks involved in launching a bid for power on the expectation of external support; in most cases the international context was simply ignored, and the internal lack of development in Russia given as sufficient reason for it being unprepared for socialist revolution.[27] Thus, Lukács remarks, "Kautsky explains to Bernstein that the question of the dictatorship of the proletariat can quite easily be left to the future—to a very distant future."[28] Lukács refers to Kautsky since the latter argued precisely that the attempt to establish socialism in Russia was premature: in the absence of both capitalist development and democratic institutions the revolution could only ever have been bourgeois in nature. On this basis socialist revolution should, however, have been possible in Germany, since it was both highly industrialized and had a tradition of parliamentary democracy that had seen hundreds of Social

Democratic representatives elected to the Reichstag; but no—if socialist revolution was impossible in Russia because it was too *backward*, it was unnecessary in Germany because it was too *advanced*: elections would suffice.[29] As this sophistry suggests, his objective was to avoid revolutionary conclusions whatever the situation.

Given that over a hundred years have elapsed since these debates took place, one might expect them to be of purely historical interest. Even if the material conditions for socialism had not matured by 1917, surely they must have done by now? Apparently not. The argument to the contrary tends to take three forms.

One is where left-reformist politicians argue that particular local conditions need to be overcome before socialism can be a realistic possibility. Before the December 2009 elections in Bolivia, Jeffery Webber interviewed Edgar Torres Mosqueira, the country's ambassador to Canada. Invited by Webber to comment on the apparent contradiction between the attitudes of President Morales and Vice-President García Linera concerning the possibilities for socialism in the foreseeable future, Mosquiera responded by invoking a theory of phases:

> In this first phase, first and foremost, we are emphasizing the inclusion of these social actors that have never benefitted from the way the state has been run. We have to overcome the social exclusion, marginality, illiteracy, malnutrition, [high levels of] mortality. These are fundamental stages if we are going to be able to advance. If in this first phase we do not fulfill this historic role we will be running against the mandate of the indigenous peoples and the social movements. Therefore, it's very premature to launch a call for twenty-first century socialism if we haven't fulfilled this first phase.[30]

The problem here is obviously not Mosqueira's desire to improve the condition of Bolivia's indigenous population, but his retreat to Second International assumptions that every country had to achieve a certain level of internal development before socialism can be feasible. There are two problems with this. On the one hand, while reforms are certainly possible within capitalism, the system is inherently uneven, which manifests itself in a series of structured inequalities; countries may rise or fall within the hierarchical order, particularly between the two extremes, but there will never be an even distribution of both wealth and power either within or between them—overcoming these inequalities is, after all, one of the arguments for socialism in the first place. On the other hand, the socialist revolution, if it happens at all, will not take the form of a series of self-contained transitions within the boundaries of individual nation-states, but will rather be an international process in which those that inherit greater resources from the capitalist era will come to the aid of those, like Bolivia, that inherit less.

The second case for stages might be that the necessary material conditions had previously existed but no longer do because of the economic retrogression that followed the return of economic crisis in 2007. Before the Greek situation reached its moment of truth in 2015, for example, former finance minister Yanis Varoufakis "confessed" that he had been "campaigning on an agenda founded on the assumption that the Left was, and remains, squarely defeated": "So, yes, in this sense, I feel compelled to acknowledge that I wish my campaigning were of a different ilk; that I would much rather be promoting a radical agenda whose *raison d'*être is about replacing European capitalism with a different, more rational, system—rather than merely campaigning to stabilize a European capitalism at odds with my definition of the Good Society." For Varoufakis then, we are faced with a situation in which, paradoxically, "a crisis-ridden, deeply irrational, repugnant European capitalism whose implosion, despite its many ills, should be avoided at all cost." Radicals consequently have "a contradictory mission": "to arrest European capitalism's free-fall *in order* to buy the time we need to formulate its alternative."[31] This type of argument assumes that the neoliberal era represents an aberration, rather than a stage in capitalist development, and that its crisis is an exceptional event, rather than being exactly what Marxist theory (and historical experience) would lead us to expect. And while Varoufakis and those who think like him are busy trying to restore the pre-crash neoliberal *status quo ante*, right-wing populists take the opportunity of the massive economic distress it has caused to build their social movements.

There is, however, a third and more fundamental argument about the lack of developmental readiness for socialism, which refers back to the Russian Revolution itself. The late Samir Amin once mocked Marxists in the West for allegedly believing that

> we must wait until the level of development of the productive forces at the centre is capable of spreading to the entire world before the question of the abolition of classes can really be put on the agenda. Europeans should thus allow the creation of a supranational Europe so that the state superstructure can be adjusted to the productive forces. It will doubtless be necessary to await the establishment of a planetary state corresponding to the level of

the productive forces on the world scale, before the objective conditions for superseding it will obtain.[32]

I doubt there were many Marxists who seriously held the position caricatured by Amin when his words were published in 1980; by the end of the decade, however, the situation had radically changed.

Shortly after the USSR collapsed in 1991, Peter Wollen wrote admiringly of Kautsky that "he had learned that socialism could only be achieved when capitalism had provided the economic preconditions through the development of the productive forces." The "inner logic" of this position, according to Wollen, is that "the full potential of socialism is itself problematic until capitalism has expanded to the point where it has created the possibility of *global* change." His conclusion: "Socialists should accept that it may be better to have a realistic hope, however distant, than a false hope based on a deformed foreshortening, however immediate and close at hand it may seem to be."[33] The notion of "false hope" was also invoked by Meghnad Desai in the light of the collapse of the Stalinist regimes: "After a brief and stormy seventy-five-year life, the Russian socialist venture, the attempt to speed up the pace of history, the weak link that Marx failed to see, came to an abrupt but complete end." The entire experiment had failed because the Bolsheviks did not understand what Marx had apparently understood, namely that:

> Capitalism would not go away until after it has exhausted its potential. The information technology has just begun. What more may come we do not know—biotechnology, new materials, outer space as colonizable land. The whole world is not yet integrated into world capitalism.

So we still have to wait until "full integration" takes place: "The limits of capitalism will be reached when it is no longer capable of progress." For Lord Desai, that outcome is evidently a long way off: "The continued dynamism of capitalism at the beginning of the twenty-first century is Marx's revenge on the Marxists—all those who, in his name, lied and cheated and murdered, and offered false hope."[34] This obviously raises the question of why the Russian Revolution offered only "false hope" to humanity: "The October Revolution was a peasant revolution led by a Marxist party which could see revolutionary potential only in the working class." On this reading, the Bolsheviks simply misunderstood the nature of the revolution they were leading. Desai rejects Trotskyist interpretations (of any sort) that emphasize the degeneration of the revolution through isolation and the external pressure of the world system. Instead, he claims that there was no degeneration because there was never a working-class revolution in the first place:

> The importance of characterizing the October Revolution as a peasant revolution with the ostensible leadership of a Marxist party is that one need not agonize about the worker's state being corrupted or becoming degenerate. From the beginning it was not a worker's state in any material sense. ... Nobody betrayed it.[35]

Wollen and Desai are of course correct to highlight that capitalism remains what it has always been—the most dynamic system in human history that, even in conditions of recession, continues to innovate, generate new technologies, and deepen its penetration into territories where it has only relatively recently been introduced. But they seem unable to draw the necessary conclusion from this: capitalism will never "exhaust its potential," the arrival of the "final crisis" remains the compensatory illusion it has always been. But even if this were not the case, as I pointed out in the introduction, *the onset of catastrophic climate change means that we do not have the time to wait for capitalism to exhaust itself.* Indeed, as Benjamin Kunkel has argued, if the overthrow of capitalism is too long delayed we may in any case inherit an environment in which the vision of a fully communist society is simply impossible to realize: "Capitalism will only have a more or less badly despoiled world to bequeath to its successor, whether—updating Rosa Luxemburg—that turns out to be ecosocialism or ethnobarbarism."[36]

Actuality 2: Revolutionary preparedness

The second meaning of actuality relates not to objectively determined levels of global development, but to a subjective attitude of *revolutionary preparedness*. Only months after the defeat of the revolutionary movements of 1848–49, which the "Manifesto of the Communist Party" had heralded, Marx was warning his comrades against imagining that the world could simply be bent to their political desires:

> The materialist standpoint of the *Manifesto* has given way to idealism. The revolution is seen not as the product of realities of the situation but as the result of an effort of will. Whereas we say to the workers: You have 15, 20, 50 years of civil war to go through in order to alter the situation and to train yourselves for the exercise of power, it is said: We must take power at once, or else we may as well take to our beds.[37]

But Marx had come to realize that the material conditions for socialist revolution did not yet exist on a global scale. Once they had, did this mean that revolution was possible—as the old television advert for Martini used to have it—"any time, any place, anywhere"?

Che Guevara certainly drew this lesson from the Cuban guerrilla war that brought him and his comrades into power: "It is not necessary to wait until all conditions for making revolution exist; the insurrection can create them."[38] This was a common theme among Cuban revolutionary leaders. "The duty of every revolutionary is to make the revolution," announced Fidel Castro—in a phrase often wrongly ascribed to Guevara—at the Second General Assembly of the Cuban People in 1962.[39] He subsequently added, in a speech that acknowledged revolutionaries might not always be able to "make the revolution": "We prefer . . . to make mistakes trying to make revolution without the right conditions than to . . . make the mistake of never making revolution."[40] As Samuel Farber argues in a sympathetic but critical study of Guevara, this is a species of voluntarism, which Guevara carried forward into his economic policies after coming to power.[41] Here, the backwardness of a particular state is not to be overcome by the assistance of more advanced allies, but by an effort of will and moral commitment on the part of population. Writing of the Cuban Revolution, Guevara asked: "How can we produce the transition to socialism in a country colonized by imperialism, without any development of its basic industries, in a situation of monopoly production and dependent on a single market?" How indeed? After rejecting arguments that it was premature and that, in developmental terms, other Latin American countries were in a better position to make the revolutionary transition, Guevara concludes with his interpretation of what happened:

> Taking advantage of unusual historical circumstances and following the skillful leadership of their vanguard, the revolutionary forces take over at a particular moment. Then, assuming that the necessary objective conditions already exist for the socialization of labor, they skip stages, declare the socialist nature of the revolution, and begin to build socialism.[42]

Whatever his subjective aspirations and beliefs—which seem to have been entirely sincere—Guevara was not attempting to lead a socialist revolution but to establish a developmental state capitalism. Guevara was genuinely repelled by many aspects of the Stalinist regime in Russia, but his own belief that socialism could be constructed in isolation and under any set of conditions led him to recreate it in all essentials. As Alasdair MacIntyre pointed out in the late 1960s, this was a problem that extended beyond Cuba:

> One paradox of post-Stalin Stalinism is that it may be those who are most repelled by the surviving Stalinist features of the Soviet Union who therefore try to build a socialist revolution in isolation from the Soviet camp or at least in the minimum of contact with it. But in so doing they revive the very thesis of "socialism in one country" on which Stalinism was founded.[43]

Yet even this endeavor cannot be carried out under simply any conditions—a fact which was to cost Guevara his life while trying to do so in Bolivia.

I refer to Guevara, not because his particular strategic conception of guerrilla struggle continues to have any purchase on the Left, but because his voluntarism, especially filtered through the fantasies of his Western admirers—above all those of Régis Debray—was so often confused with Lenin's strategic approach. In an admiring introduction to Debray from 1967, the editors of *New Left Review* made this claim:

> What above all distinguishes Debray's writings is their relentlessly Leninist focus on *making the revolution*, as a political, technical and military problem.... Revolution is on the order of the day *here and now*, even if a prodigious and costly effort will be needed to achieve it.[44]

As we shall see in relation to Actuality 3, there are situations where the revolution is *genuinely* "on the order of the day, here and now"; these are not in the power of revolutionaries to create, however, but emerge from the multiple contradictions of capitalism—although revolutionaries should of course attempt to heighten these.

Romantic but doomed guerrilla strategies may have thankfully ceased to be fashionable; moralizing exhortation is, however, unfortunately alive and well. Revolutionaries whose hatred of pseudo-socialism and bureaucratic impediments to the self-activity of the masses cannot be doubted can still be found calling for immediate insurrection, regardless of particular local conditions, as the only possible response to the disastrous conditions of our times, as in this breathless invocation by the Invisible Committee:

> We can no longer even see how an insurrection might begin. Sixty years of pacification and containment of historical upheavals, sixty years of democratic anesthesia and the management of events, have dulled our perception of the real, our sense of the war in progress. We need to start by recovering this perception. . . . It is useless *to wait*—for a breakthrough, for the revolution,

the nuclear apocalypse or a social movement. To go on waiting is madness. The catastrophe is not coming, it is here. We are already situated within the collapse of a civilization. It is within this reality that we must choose sides.[45]

This is not an isolated example. John Holloway has also identified the moment of insurrection as here and now. His is possibly the most extreme case for revolution as an expression of daily collective refusal of capitalism:

> History in this view acquires a revered importance. History is the building up towards the future event. It tells us of the heroic struggles of the past, helps us to understand what went wrong, shows us how the objective conditions are maturing. Sometimes this history goes hand in hand with an analysis of the long-term cycles of capitalism, encouraging us to think that the pendulum of history will again swing our way, that however ridiculous it may seem to dream today of communism, the tide will turn in our direction. The other conception of revolution says *no*: no to capitalism, revolution now. Revolution is already taking place. This may seem silly, immature, unrealistic, but it is not. *Revolution now* means that we think of the death of capitalism not in terms of a dagger-blow to the heart, but rather in terms of death by a million bee-stings, or a million pin-pricks to a credit-inflated balloon, or (better) a million rents, gashes, fissures, cracks. Since the issue is not when to strike at the heart, it makes no sense to think of waiting until the objective conditions are right. At all times it is necessary to tear the texture of capitalist domination, to refuse, to push against-and-beyond. Revolution is now: a cumulative process, certainly, a process of cracks spreading and joining up, but revolution is not in the future, it is already under way.[46]

This passage is a good example of Holloway's rhetorical trickery. He sets up, in heroically iconoclastic tones, a set of left-wing positions that he then dismisses on the grounds that to hold them is to indulge in a consolatory practice that, in effect, colludes with the reproduction of capitalism itself; but at no point does he provide instances or an actual argument. It is not clear to me why he thinks that attempting to learn from the historical past is necessarily always debilitating—it might, for example, be worthwhile trying to discover why the strategy of the Zapatists, much-vaunted by Holloway and others, remains harmlessly confined to Chiapas and has generated no successors anywhere else. For Holloway, there is no need to waste time on tedious historical reflection, however, because new exciting developments—revolutions, now!—are "already under way." The renting and gashing and fissuring and cracking that Holloway mistakes for "the revolution" is, however, more properly understood as the day-to-day process of resistance to the demands of capital that working-class people carry out on a daily basis—and have *always* carried out: it is this which prevents capital assuming complete dominance over our lives even now. It is not in itself revolutionary—or rather, can only become so under particular circumstances, but to identify these circumstances would involve all the tedious participant analysis that Holloway finds both impossible and pointless.[47]

What then should revolutionaries be doing, if not demanding the immediate construction of the barricades? In fact, Actuality 2 involves revolutionaries treating all the activities they undertake, no matter how "unrevolutionary" in themselves, *as preparation for the arrival of the revolutionary moment,* the precise timing of which they cannot predict. As Lukács pointed out, the ability to make these connections between everyday activity and the ultimate goal is one of the key tests of revolutionary organization: "The actuality of the revolution therefore implies study of each individual daily problem in concrete association with the socio-historic whole, as moments in the liberation of the proletariat."[48]

When Lukács wrote these words in 1924, it still seemed feasible that the Communist Parties could play this role. By the end of the following decade, Walter Benjamin implied that Stalinism, like Social Democracy before it, was characterized by a refusal to contemplate that "the revolutionary situation" would *ever* arrive:

> In reality, there is not a moment that would not carry with it its own revolutionary chance—provided only that it is defined in a specific way, namely as the chance for a completely new resolution of a completely new problem. For the revolutionary thinker, the peculiar revolutionary chance offered by every historical moment gets its warrant from the political situation.[49]

Benjamin's language is so far removed from that of everyday activism that it is easy to misunderstand. Neither he nor Lukács are saying that revolutionaries should be declaring a state of permanent insurrection, which would indeed be voluntarism, or even that revolutionaries should make a fetish about proclaiming what needs to be done in order to win, when such a demand has no purchase in the actual situation ("Call a general strike to kick out the Tories!" etc., etc.). They are saying rather that revolutionaries should behave in the knowledge that we are in the period in which revolution is historically possible and necessary. At certain places and times the overall contradictions of the era will—as we shall see—lead to crises, to genuine "revolutionary situations"; the task of the revolutionary is not, however, to passively wait for these to arise but to help bring them about and then take the opportunities they present, as Gramsci observed from his fascist prison:

> In reality one can "scientifically" foresee only the struggle, but not the concrete moments of the struggle, which cannot but be the results of opposing forces in continuous movement.... In reality one can "foresee" to the extent that one acts, to the extent that one applies a voluntary effort and therefore contributes concretely to creating the result "foreseen."[50]

He had earlier expressed the same point in more concrete terms in a document co-written with Palmiro Togliatti during the mid-1920s: "The Communist Party links every demand to a revolutionary objective; makes use of every partial struggle to teach the masses the need for general action and for insurrection against the reactionary rule of capital; and seeks to ensure that every struggle of a limited character is prepared and led in such a way as to be able to lead to the mobilization and unification of the proletarian forces, and not to their dispersal."[51]

Lenin once quoted the Prussian minister of the interior, Von Puttkamer, as saying: "Behind every strike lies the hydra [monster] of revolution."[52] This is sometimes misinterpreted as meaning that every strike can develop into a revolution—a Holloway-style assumption that suggests rather limited personal experience of this most elementary form of the class struggle. Of course, there have been occasions when mass strikes have either led or had the potential to lead to revolutionary situations, but this is not what either Puttkamer or Lenin meant. From their very different perspectives they understood that strike activity was one of the means by which workers came to realize the extent of their own power, to develop their organizational capacities, to distinguish between friends and enemies, to test strategies and tactics—so that when the hour of revolution did strike, they would be a class capable of taking and holding power. As this suggests, there can come a point when the *immediate situation* is revolutionary—in other words, socialism is not just theoretically possible, but actually emerging from the struggles of the day.

Actuality 3: Revolutionary situations

These occasions are the third meaning of actuality, when the general levels of development that make socialism conceivable are joined by a set of more immediate conditions, including those created by the preparatory work of revolutionaries, to produce a *revolutionary situation* in which taking power is an imminent possibility. Lukács described these situations as being when "the actuality of the proletarian revolution is no longer only a world historical horizon arching above the self-liberating working class, *but that revolution is already on its agenda.*"[53] But agendas, alas, are not always implemented. "Many potential revolutions fail for want of attempt," writes Andrew Abbott, "just as many attempted revolutions fail for want of structural opportunity."[54] If the latter type of failure occurs because of voluntarism associated with Guevara, where revolutionaries refuse to take account of actual circumstances, the former occurs for the opposite reason, where revolutionaries insist on waiting for a perfect set of circumstances that may never arrive, while missing the most favorable circumstances when they do. Lenin was acutely conscious of the latter problem, writing in 1915, "Not every revolutionary situation . . . gives rise to a revolution; revolution arises only out of a situation in which . . . objective changes are accompanied by a subjective change, namely, the ability of the revolutionary *class* to take revolutionary mass action *strong* enough to break (or dislocate) the old government, which never, not even in a period of crisis, 'falls,' if it is not toppled over."[55] Trotsky later made the same point:

> A mass uprising is no isolated undertaking, which can be conjured up any time one pleases. . . . But if the necessary conditions for the uprising exist, one must not simply wait passively, with open mouth. As Shakespeare says, "there is a tide in the affairs of men which, taken at the flood, leads on to fortune."[56]

In September 1917, Lenin was faced with the actual dilemma of identifying the right moment to act, and in doing so, making a sharp turn away from his previous stance of supporting cooperation with the other left parties. As China Miéville explains:

> Lenin grew fretful about what would happen if the party did *not* act on its own. He feared revolutionary energies might dissipate, or the country slide on into anarchy—or that brutal counterrevolution might arise. . . . The party had been right, he repeated, not to move in July, without the masses behind it. But now it had them. Here again was one of those switchbacks that so discombobulated his comrades. It was not mere caprice, however, but the results of minute attention to shifts in politics. Now, he insisted, with the masses behind it, the party must move.[57]

The question of the *party* needing to act raises the question of who or what precisely takes the decision to challenge for power. "The working class," let alone its allies among other classes ("the popular masses"), cannot act as a unified entity—there can never be a point where every single member of that class arrives at precisely the same conclusion—and consequently it can only act through forms of representative institution; this was why Lenin was so insistent that the Bolsheviks had to have majority working-class support before attempting to overthrow the Provisional Government and why it was the Congress of Soviets that ultimately took the decision. Once the decision is taken, the insurrection itself has to be conducted in a manner that Lenin termed an "art." Lukács notes the way in which Lenin emphasizes "moments that are consciously *made*, that is to say brought into by the subjective side (by the conscious acting subject—groupings of forces, surprise attacks, etc.)": "Insurrection as an art is, then, one moment in the revolutionary process where *the subjective moment has a decisive predominance.*"[58]

What are the immediate objective conditions within which decisions have to be made? Lenin himself gave what is probably the most famous description of the three "symptoms of a revolutionary situation":

(1) when it is impossible for the ruling classes to maintain their rule without any change; when there is a crisis, in one form or another, among the "upper classes," a crisis in the policy of the ruling class, leading to a fissure through which the discontent and indignation of the oppressed classes burst forth. For a revolution to take place, it is usually insufficient for "the lower classes not to want" to live in the old way; it is also necessary that "the upper classes should be unable" to live in the old way; (2) when the suffering and want of the oppressed classes have grown more acute than usual; (3) when, as a consequence of the above causes, there is a considerable increase in the activity of the masses.[59]

Of the three "symptoms," it is the second which is most questionable, for it is not clear that revolutionary situations *necessarily* involve increased "suffering and want," although they may do. On some occasions Trotsky concurred with Lenin's diagnosis, writing: "The economic and social prerequisites for a revolutionary situation take hold, generally speaking, when the productive powers of the country are declining; when the specific weight of a capitalist country on the world market is systematically lessened and the incomes of the classes are likewise systematically reduced; when unemployment is not merely the result of a conjunctural fluctuation but a permanent social evil with a tendency to increase." Beyond these objective factors are of course the subjective responses to them by members of the different social classes, "mainly of course, of the proletariat and its party."[60] And this is the key point, for, as Trotsky pointed out elsewhere, economic crises are *inde-*

terminate in their impact on the working class.[61] Indeed, it may be the polar opposite situation that causes the working class to move into revolutionary activity. One of the last ruling-class thinkers to seriously consider the dynamics of revolution, Alexis de Tocqueville, made precisely this point in his famous "paradox":

> It is not always when things are going from bad to worse that revolutions break out. On the contrary, it oftener happens that when a people which has put up with an oppressive rule over a long period without protest suddenly finds the government relaxing its pressure, it takes up arms against it. Thus the social order overthrown by a revolution is almost always better than the one immediately preceding it, and experience teaches us that, generally speaking, the most perilous moment for a bad government is one when it seeks to mend its ways.[62]

Tocqueville is generalizing here from the French Revolution and consequently is not specifically referring to workers; the argument can, however, also be relevant to them. As Trotsky was to highlight, long-term unemployment is rarely conducive to worker militancy: "In contrast, the industrial revival is bound, first of all, to raise the self-confidence of the working class, undermined by failures and by the disunity in its own ranks; it is bound to fuse the working class together in the factories and plants and heighten the desire for unanimity in militant actions." But Trotsky also warned against over-generalizing *this* into an absolute law, since "there exists not a mechanical but a complex dialectical interdependence between the economic conjuncture and the character of the class struggle."[63]

Finally, Gramsci partially supported Lenin's argument about the impact of worsening conditions, but added a further variant: "A rupture can occur either because a prosperous situation is threatened or because the economic malaise has become unbearable and the old society seems bereft of any force capable of mitigating it."[64]

In the classical Marxist tradition there are therefore three possible economic contexts in which workers might move toward revolutionary action: first, where an economic revival gives workers confidence to organize and take action; second, where, at the beginnings of an economic downturn, an already confident and organized working class mobilizes to resist state and employer attempts to reduce pay and conditions; and third, where a temporarily defeated working class has been subjected to such an assault that it is finally driven to resist. Any of these responses, at least in a situation where the ruling class is divided, can potentially be the basis of a revolutionary situation. But to these three contexts can be added a fourth, implicit in Trotsky's work, which is less concerned with impact of boom and slump, crisis and recovery within the established structures of industrial capitalism, and more with the actual *experience* of industrialization itself.

The explanatory framework that Trotsky subsequently used to explain the possibility of his version of permanent revolution—the "law" of uneven and combined development—focused on the consequences of attempts on the part of the Tsarist state to overcome its historical backwardness:

> Historical backwardness does not imply a simple reproduction of the development of advanced countries, England or France, with a delay of one, two, or three centuries. It engenders an entirely new "combined" social formation in which the latest conquests of capitalist technique and structure root themselves into relations of feudal or pre-feudal barbarism, transforming and subjecting them and creating peculiar relations of classes.[65]

The former levels of stability typical of feudal or tributary societies are disrupted by the irruption of capitalist industrialization and all that it brings in its wake: rapid population growth, uncoordinated urban expansion, dramatic ideological shifts. "When English or French capital, the historical coagulate of many centuries, appears in the steppes of the Donets Basin, it cannot release the same social forces, relations, and passions which once went into its own formation."[66] Trotsky was particularly interested in the process by which these forms were *fused*, the result permeating every aspect of society, ideology as much as economy. The "uneven" aspect of uneven and combined development is demonstrated by the partial nature of its adoptions from the advanced countries:

> Russia was so far behind the other countries that she was compelled, *at least in certain spheres*, to outstrip them. ... The absence of firmly established social forms and traditions makes the backward country—*at least within certain limits*—extremely hospitable to the last word in international technique and international thought. Backwardness does not, however, for this reason cease to be backwardness.[67]

Within these spheres and limits, however, backward societies could attain *higher* levels of development than in their established rivals.[68]

Trotsky was writing specifically about Russia, but almost every capitalist society that has undergone the introduction of factories and the expansion of cities has experienced uneven and combined development to *some* degree, with the important exceptions of the Netherlands, England, and Catalonia, which completed the transition to capitalism before these processes began. Why then have they had such different outcomes, above all with respect to their propensity for revolution? There are obviously a number of factors involved, but the two most important seem to be the existence or otherwise of a revolutionary party and the class nature of the state. In the case of Russia, the Bolshevik Party formed a nucleus capable of becoming the mass organization that emerged in the course of the revolution, but which was missing elsewhere at the relevant time. But in relation to the state, the degree of development is reversed. The states to the west of Russia were essentially capitalist in nature and thus, even if they did not conform to bourgeois-democratic norms, had sufficient flexibility and adaptability to exercise hegemonic rule, a point to which I will return in Section 4. For the feudal-absolutist state in Russia, this kind of malleability was impossible, not least because of the partial adoptions it made from the West: "The [backward] nation . . . not infrequently debases the achievements borrowed from outside in the process of adapting them to its own more primitive culture."[69] Initially at least, "debased adaptation" helped *preserve* the pre-capitalist state in Russia. From 1861, Tsarism established factories using the manufacturing technology characteristic of monopoly capitalism in order to produce arms with which to defend feudal absolutism. The danger for the state lay in what these factories required in order to run, namely workers—and workers more skilled, more politically conscious than any previous absolutist or early capitalist state had ever faced. "Debased adaptation" was intended to preserve the existence of the undemocratic state; but to the extent that the former was successful it helped provoke the working class into destroying the latter.

For Trotsky then, the most important consequence of uneven and combined development was the enhanced capacity it potentially gave the working classes for political and industrial organization, theoretical understanding, and revolutionary activity: "When the economic factors burst in a revolutionary manner, breaking up the old order; when development is no longer gradual and 'organic' but assumes the form of terrible convulsions and drastic changes of former conceptions, then it becomes easier for critical thought to find revolutionary expression, provided that the necessary theoretical prerequisites exist in the given country."[70]

But the type of explosiveness associated with uneven and combined development is not restricted to it, or the less-developed countries, but is a characteristic of the types of recurrent transformation associated with changes to established regimes of accumulation, even in the more advanced countries. Writing in the early 1950s, Hobsbawm attempted to explain the periodically "explosive" growth in "size, strength and activity" of what he called "social movements" in Britain through the nineteenth and early twentieth centuries. The "explosive" moments to which he refers were characterized by "qualitative as well as quantitative changes": "They are, in fact, generally expansions of the movement into new industries, new regions, new classes of the population: they coincide with the clustering of new organizations, and the adoption of new ideas and policies by both new and existing units." Partly for these reasons, the specifics of each case will be different.[71] Extending this mode of analysis to the US working class, Kim Moody has more recently identified similar conditions that, coming together in our time, might lead to results of the sort described by Hobsbawm.[72] Is it possible to extend the notion of "explosiveness" or "inflammability" beyond episodes in the history of British or American trade unionism, or even the labor movement more generally? When does a social explosion have the potential to turn into something more far-reaching, a "revolutionary situation"?

Lenin's schema for a revolutionary situation was oversimplified, as he was well aware, since on several other occasions he argued that revolutions were never simple events in which the working class confronts the capitalist class, or rather its state. The most famous of these arguments occurs in his defense of the Irish Easter Rising of 1916 from accusations that it had merely been an attempted putsch.[73] Less than a year later, Lenin could be found commenting on the unfolding of the February Revolution (still "from afar" at this stage), and claiming that the type of unavoidable complexity he had detected in Ireland was not only visible in Russia but had contributed directly to the overthrow of the autocracy: "That the revolution succeeded so quickly and—seemingly, at the first superficial glance—so radically, is only due to the fact that, as a result of an extremely unique historical situation, *absolutely dissimilar currents, absolutely heterogeneous* class interests, *absolutely contrary* political and social strivings have *merged*, and in a strikingly 'harmonious' manner."[74] Trotsky made a similar point shortly after Lenin's death in a speech warning Bolshevik cadres about the inescapable complexity of the revolutionary process: "For a revolution the *coinciding* of necessary conditions is required."[75]

Louis Althusser later attempted to construct a general theory out of Lenin's writings on this subject. His main contention was that "the general contradiction" between the forces and relations of production (which Althusser saw as being embodied in the struggle between workers and capitalists) cannot by itself lead either to a revolutionary situation or its transformation into revolutionary victory:

> If this contradiction is to become "*active*" in the strongest sense, to become a ruptural principle, there must be an accumulation of "circumstances" and "currents" so that whatever their origin and sense (and many of them will *necessarily* be paradoxically foreign to the revolution in origin and sense, or even its "direct opponents"), they "*fuse*" into a *ruptural unity*: when they produce the result of the immense majority of the popular masses *grouped* in an assault on a regime which its ruling classes are *unable to defend*. Such a situation presupposes not only the "fusion" of the two basic conditions into a "single national crisis," but each condition considered (abstractly) by itself presupposes the "fusion" of an "accumulation" of contradictions.[76]

As is quite often the case in Althusser's work, this passage is written at an extraordinary high level of abstraction, but it is possible to render the essential point in more concrete terms. Here, for example, Rex Wade sets out "the series of concurrent and overlapping revolutions" that characterized the Russian Revolution of 1917:

> The popular revolt against the old regime; the workers' revolution against the hardships of the old industrial and social order; the revolt of the soldiers against the old system of military service and then against the war itself; the peasants' revolution for land and for control of their own lives; the striving of middle-class elements for civil rights and a constitutional parliamentary system; the revolution of the non-Russian nationalities for rights and self-determination; the revolt of most of the population against the war and the seemingly endless slaughter. People also struggled over differing cultural visions, over woman's rights, between nationalities, for domination within ethnic or religious groups and among and within political parties, and for the fulfillment of a multitude of aspirations large and small.[77]

Listing these different components of the revolutionary process does not—or at any rate *should* not—involve reducing the role of the working class to being simply one among many, for although workers were a minority of the Russian population, insofar as the revolution had the potential to have a socialist rather than "bourgeois-democratic" outcome, they were in the forefront because only they had the power to halt and ultimately transform the process of capitalist production.

Emphasizing the multiplicity of social forces involved in the Russian Revolution is important because, in the debates over communist strategy that followed the formation of the Third International, the revolutionary forces were often reduced to being only the proletariat and the peasantry—the problem being that in the West, the peasantry had been either destroyed "as a class" (as in England) or, more frequently, integrated into the capitalist system and consequently no longer revolutionary (as in Germany). In his response to Lenin's "'Left-Wing' Communism," Hermann Gorter correctly observed that the absence of a revolutionary peasantry meant that the strategies deployed by the Bolsheviks in Russia could not simply be transplanted from East to West with any hope of success.[78] Gorter was wrong, however, to repeatedly argue that the Western proletariat was "alone." This was only true on the assumption that allies had to belong to another exploited class and not to groups (whose membership might in any case overlap with that of the working class) defined by other characteristics (nation, sex, religion) for which they are subject to oppression. The actual compatibility of struggles to end the exploitation of the working class and the oppression of identity-based groups was demonstrated during the Russian Revolution, but the potential *tension* between them only became fully declared in the second half of the twentieth century. Since these issues are unavoidable when discussing revolutionary situations, particularly from the mid-twentieth century on, and when envisaging any which may occur in the future, I will address them here as a way of concluding my discussion of Actuality 3.

2. Exploitation and oppression(s)

There is no such thing as an undifferentiated "oppression": there are several types, all of which take different forms and involve different experiences. Is it nevertheless still possible to establish a relationship between exploitation and oppression "in general"? In a book by socialist-feminist Juliet Mitchell published in 1971, early in the emergence of what is now usually called "second-wave" feminism, the author asks:

> Is the feminist concept of women as the most fundamentally oppressed people and hence potentially the most revolutionary to be counterposed to the Marxist position of the working class as *the* revolutionary class under capitalism? If so, with what consequences? What is the relationship between class struggle and the struggles of the oppressed? What *are* the politics of oppression?[79]

These are good questions, but the assumption underlying them is that the class struggle against exploitation occurs in one place, and the struggle of oppressed groups against their oppression occurs in a series of other places; but as we shall see, this involves a misunderstanding, or at least a very restricted definition of what exploitation involves. Tithi Bhattacharya has rightly asked whether "the relationship between exploitation (normally tethered to class) and oppression (normally understood through gender, race, etc.) . . . adequately expresses the complications of an abstract level of analysis where we forge our conceptual equipment, and a concrete level of analysis, i.e., the historical reality where we apply those tools."[80] I agree with Bhattacharya that the answer is "no." In searching for a more adequate analytic framework, Lukács may once again be a useful starting point, in particular his discussion of totality in *History and Class Consciousness*:

> The dialectical method is distinguished from bourgeois thought not only by the fact that it alone can lead to a knowledge of totality; it is also significant that such knowledge is only attainable because the relationship between parts and whole has become fundamentally different from what it is in thought based on the categories of reflection. In brief, from this point of view, *the essence of the dialectical method lies in the fact that in every aspect correctly grasped by the dialectic the whole totality is comprehended and that the whole method can be unraveled from every single aspect.*[81]

Of all subsequent writers on the subject of totality, Bertell Ollman has perhaps done most to develop these insights and—for those not schooled in the categories of German Idealist philosophy—present them in slightly more comprehensible terms:

> Few people would deny that everything in the world is related to everything else—directly or indirectly—as causes, conditions, and results; and many insist that the world is unintelligible save in terms of such relations. Marx goes a step further in interiorizing this interdependence within each element, so that the conditions of existence are taken to be part of what it is.[82]

What does this mean for the relationship between exploitation and oppression? Do they constitute different aspects of capitalist totality or, on the contrary, do the various forms of the latter have a purely contingent relationship to capitalism? The problem is not a new one and can be traced back to Marx's own lifetime. Angela Davis once noted of the early feminists in the US immediately before the Civil War: "The leaders of the women's rights movement did not suspect that the enslavement of Black people in the South, the economic exploitation of Northern workers and the social oppression of women might be systematically related."[83] Davis found this incomprehension regrettable, although it was perhaps understandable in the context of the time; it is less so over 150 years later but is nevertheless considerably more widespread.

In contemporary discussions, Marxist emphasis on the role of the working class—"privileging" it, so to speak—is criticized on the grounds that doing so either ignores struggles against oppression, or at least relegates them to a secondary level of importance. It is important to understand what is being criticized here. It is perfectly legitimate to point out, for example, that *Capital* itself does not encompass all aspects of human experience in capitalist society. Edward Thompson famously argued that this was because Marx was to an extent still trapped in the categories of his adversary, Political Economy—the problem being that "the whole society comprises many activities and relations (of power, of consciousness, sexual, cultural, normative) which are not the concern of Political Economy, which have been *defined out* of political economy, and for which it has no terms."[84] Thompson may have been correct in this assessment, or, as I believe, he may have been expecting *Capital* to do more than Marx ever intended it to do; or, it may simply be that *Capital* would have dealt with the absent "activities and relations" had Marx actually succeeded in completing it.[85] But the critiques to which I refer here do *not* argue that Marx omitted discussion of oppression because of his particular focus in *Capital* or for contingent reasons connected with its composition; they argue instead that Marx, and subsequent Marxists, do not regard oppression as particularly important compared to working-class exploitation. For some of these critics, Marxists supposedly think that working-class exploitation trumps separate and autonomous forms of group oppression.[86] For others, Marxists apparently regard oppressed groups as subsets of the working class, which has priority for that reason.[87] Neither position corresponds to what either Marx or his genuine followers actually believed or believe.

First, the central category for Marxists is *not* class, but mode of production. Marx was far from being the first person to identify the existence of social classes, nor to understand that they had antagonistic relationships; he was, however, the first to discover that historically specific ways of organizing material production determined the nature of these classes through the exploitation of one by another.[88] There is, in other words, a difference between saying that, on the one hand, various oppressions are produced within the concrete expressions (societies or social formations) of specific modes of production and, on the other, saying that they are "really" forms of class oppression. Some forms of oppression, like those based on gender, seem to have existed for as long as exploitative modes of production have done; others, like those based on "race," have been much more restricted to the capitalist era. Neither is directly based on class relations: the question is whether or not they are now necessary for the maintenance of the existing capitalist order.

Second, as the previous paragraph suggests, Marx did not "reduce" all forms of oppression to class, although some vulgar Marxists have done so; for one thing, he did not think of human beings as being solely defined by their relationship to production. To be a worker is to occupy a social role, but the occupants do not exist solely in relation to the means of production, even though that relationship suffuses all others. To imagine otherwise is precisely to adopt the perspective *of the capitalist*, for whom people only exist as workers, or possibly as consumers. In his discussion of rights, for example, Marx dismisses an approach in which workers "are grasped from one *particular* side, e.g., if . . . they are regarded *only as workers* and nothing else is seen in them, everything else is ignored."[89] Workers also belong to national groups, subscribe to religious beliefs, and have particular sexual orientations: there are of course working-class ways of fighting for the rights associated with these aspects of social being, but they themselves are not products of the workplace, nor can they necessarily be resolved there. Moreover, the experience of being a worker is channeled and filtered through these other social identities. As Stuart Hall wrote of race, it is "the modality in which class is 'lived,'" the medium through which class relations are experienced, the form in which it is appropriated and "fought through."[90] It is also true that the majority of people who belong to national groups, subscribe to religious beliefs, or have particular sexual orientations will also be members of the working class, since it now constitutes the majority of the global population.

Third, workers are not, however, only oppressed because they happen to belong to groups who are oppressed for other reasons; their oppression is an integral part of the process of exploitation. Part of the difficulty here is that "exploitation" is a category of political economy that describes a process undergone and resisted by slaves, peasants, and workers; but whatever was the case for the first two of these classes, no one experiences *capitalist* exploitation any more than they experience the tendency of the rate of profit to fall. *They experience instead the oppression which exploitation involves.* Marx suggested this at various points throughout his career, starting in the mid-1840s:

What constitutes the alienation of labor? Firstly, the fact that labor is *external* to the worker, i.e. does not belong to his essential being; that he therefore does not confirm himself in his work, but denies himself, feels miserable and not happy, does not develop free mental and physical energy, but mortifies his flesh and ruins his mind. Hence the worker feels himself only when he is not working; when he is working he does not feel himself.... His labor is therefore not voluntary but forced, *it is forced labor*. It is therefore not the satisfaction of a need but a mere *means* to satisfy needs outside of itself.[91]

By the publication of Volume 1 of *Capital*, over twenty years later, his language had if anything grown even more extreme. Capitalist manufacture proper "converts the laborer into a crippled monstrosity by furthering his particular skill as in a forcing-house, through the suppression of a whole world of productive drives and inclination.... It mutilates the worker, turning him into a fragment of himself."[92]

One of the difficulties we face in relation to the last point is that neither Marx nor other figures of the classical Marxist tradition used the concepts of exploitation and oppression in the way that became established in the 1960s. Indeed, on some occasions they suggested that exploitation not only *involved* oppression but was an *example* of it; in effect, they use the terms "exploitation" and "oppression" interchangeably, except where the former is being used in a technical sense, as in calculations of the rate of exploitation.[93] Thus, in *Capital* Marx described piece-wages as involving "a hierarchically organized system of exploitation and oppression."[94] On the eve of 1848 Engels looked forward to working-class organizations achieving "the freeing of labor from the oppression of capital."[95] In 1899 Lenin wrote of how strikes brought "thoughts of the struggle of the entire working class for emancipation from the oppression of capital."[96] And during the 1905 revolution he argued: "The economic oppression of the workers inevitably calls forth and engenders every kind of political oppression and social humiliation, the coarsening and darkening of the spiritual and moral life of the masses."[97] But here Lenin seems to be thinking of the workplace supervision, police repression, and alcoholic self-medication involved in keeping workers under control rather than specific oppressions based on identity with which we are now familiar.[98]

Marx, Engels, and Lenin were specifically referring to the experience of factory manufacture, now shrinking in the West, but growing to embrace millions of new workers in China and other areas of the global South, often under conditions equal in their horror to those Marx observed during his exile in Britain.[99] But different forms of "mutilation" also occur today in the original sites of capitalist development, where the old collieries and factories have been replaced by the new call centers and dispatch warehouses. James Bloodworth has recounted his experiences working in one of the latter, Amazon in Rugely, Staffordshire. The oppression suffered by Bloodworth and his fellow workers did not simply involve the body searches at the beginning and end of a shift, or the electronic surveillance of how quickly they were performing their tasks, but the way it penetrated every aspect of their lives:

> You get up each morning at eleven, you have breakfast, shower and prepare your feet for the day ahead—several sticking plasters, two pairs of socks—and then you drag your body out of the door by twelve thirty. You return home at midnight and you are usually in bed by one. Wash, rinse, repeat. Fastidiousness goes out the window. You have two meals a day and it is incumbent on you to get as much food inside you as possible at each sitting because it is impossible to know when you will next get the chance to eat a proper meal. Some snare-up in the security line on your lunch break could easily result in you missing out on a hot meal that day. . . . The need to offset the physical and emotional drain of manual work is one thing—fags, booze and junk food are some of the few pleasures left to you. But time is another. The speedy efficiency which characterizes middle-class life is non-existent in many working-class homes. Poverty is the thief of time. You wait around for buses and landlords. You are forced to do overtime at the drop of a hat. You hang around for an eternity waiting for the person who has told you they will sort out the administrative error in your pay slip. You go searching for a shop to print the wad of documents you need to start work. You must traipse around the supermarket looking for special offers with the diligence of a librarian searching for that rare first edition. You have to walk home afterwards.[100]

Two points need to be added here.

First, as in the case of Amazon employees, not every worker employed by capital is involved in producing surplus-value ("productive labor")—in fact it is only a minority who have ever done so; others ("unproductive labor") are involved in *realizing* value by, for example, transporting commodities or selling them; others still maintain the functioning of capitalist society as a whole by policing or educating the working class. But as the case of Amazon also shows, they are still subject to oppression.

Second, that oppression does not necessarily involve the kind of physically draining or damaging workplace conditions that the term immediately suggests. Arlie Russell Hochschild compares the seven-year-old child working sixteen hours a day in a wallpaper factory described by Marx in *Capital* with a twenty-year-old flight attendant today. The latter is paid far more, works far fewer hours, and will almost certainly live longer, and yet, as Hochschild writes, "a close examination of the differences between the two can led us to some unexpected common ground," for both are under the domination of an alien power:

> The work done by the boy in the wallpaper factory called for a coordination of mind and arm, mind and finger, and mind and shoulder. We refer to it simply as physical labor. The flight attendant does physical labor when she pushes heavy meal carts through the aisles, but she does mental work when she prepares for and actually organizes emergency landings and evacuations. But in the course of doing this physical and mental labor, she is also doing something more, something I define as *emotional labor*. . . . The reason for comparing these dissimilar jobs is that the modern assembly-line worker has for some time been an outmoded symbol of modern industrial labor; fewer than 6 percent of workers now work on assembly lines. Another kind of labor has now come into symbolic prominence—the voice-to-voice or face-to-face delivery of service—and the flight attendant is an appropriate model for it. . . . Though the flight attendant's job is no worse and in many ways better than other service jobs, it makes the worker more vulnerable to the social engineering of her emotional labor and reduces her control over that labor. Her problems, therefore, may be a sign of what is to come in other such jobs.[101]

A flight attendant does at least perform a necessary function, assuming that flying is going to be undertaken at all. But what of those occupations, christened by David Graeber as "bullshit jobs," which have no real purpose and whose occupants are aware of this fact? As Graeber points out: "There is a profound psychological violence here. How can one even begin to speak of the dignity of labor when one secretly feels one's job should not exist?" Such knowledge will tend to produce "a sense of deep rage and resentment."[102]

Treating the experience of the working class as *primarily* one of oppression, however, does *not* mean that it can be treated on the same basis as racism or sexism. For Chuck Barone: "Like other forms of oppression, classism at the intergroup (meso) level consists of prejudice based on negative attitudes toward and classist stereotypes of working-class people, and discrimination based on overt behaviors that distance, avoid, and/or exclude on the basis of class distinctions."[103] There are, however, a number of reasons for being suspicious of this concept of classism, not least because it seems to have been first used by Friedrich von Hayek.[104] The main substantive objection to it is, however, that belonging to a social class is *not* primarily about having an "identity" that can be subject to prejudice or discrimination. The point has been well made by Eagleton:

On the surface, the class-race-gender triplet appears convincing enough. Some people are oppressed because of their gender, some on account of their race, and others by virtue of their class. But this is a deeply misleading formulation. For it is not as though some individuals display certain characteristics known as "class," which then result in their oppression. On the contrary, Marxists have considered that to belong to a class just *is* to be oppressed, or to be an oppressor. Class is in this sense a wholly social category, as being female or having a certain skin pigmentation is not. These things, which are not to be mistaken for being feminine or African American, are a matter of the kind of body you have rather than the sort of culture you belong to.... There can be liberated women, in the sense of individuals who are both female and emancipated, but there cannot be liberated wage-slaves in the sense of people who are both at the same time.[105]

And there is a further, related reason why Marxists regards class exploitation as different in kind from non-economic forms of oppression: the implications of ending them, as Ellen Meiksins Wood has pointed out. Clearly, she writes:

> class equality means something different and requires different conditions from gender or racial equality. In particular, the abolition of class inequality would by definition mean the end of capitalism. But is the same necessarily true about the abolition of gender or racial inequality? Gender and racial inequality are not in principle incompatible with capitalism. The disappearance of class inequalities, on the other hand, by definition *is* incompatible with capitalism. At the same time, although class exploitation is *constitutive* of capitalism as gender or racial inequality are not, capitalism subjects *all* social relations to its requirements. It can co-opt and reinforce inequalities and oppressions which it did not create and use them in the interests of class exploitation.[106]

It is possible to imagine a capitalist world in which women are not oppressed, but it is not possible to imagine a capitalist world in which workers are not exploited or, since it flows from their exploitation, oppressed.

At this point, however, some care is required because, from this correct starting point, some Marxists, including Wood herself, have pushed the argument to conclusions which by no means follow, as in this case when writing specifically about the oppression of women:

> Capitalism could survive the eradication of all oppressions specific to women as women—while it would not, by definition, survive the eradication of class exploitation. This does not mean that capitalism has made the liberation of women necessary or inevitable. But it does mean that there is no

specific structural necessity for, or even a strong systemic disposition to, gender oppression in capitalism.[107]

Wendy Brown, a thinker in many respects quite different from Wood, nevertheless agrees on this point, writing that "the feminist ambition to eliminate gender as a site of subordination could technically be met within a capitalist life form—that is, there is nothing in sexed bodies or even in gender subordination that capitalism cannot live without." Her conclusion: "Capitalism neither loves nor hates social differences. Rather it exploits them in the short run and erodes them in the long run."[108]

In purely abstract terms, Wood and Brown are right, but I wrote "*imagine* a capitalist world in which women are not oppressed" above because, although it is theoretically possible to conceive of capitalism without non-class oppressions, and the ideology of social neoliberalism is essentially based on such a vision, in reality it would be impossible to achieve as these are integral to the maintenance of ruling-class power, as social reproduction theorists rightly remind us. David McNally notes in the specific case of racism that it is pointless to engage in abstract debates about whether or not it is *theoretically* necessary to capitalism: "What we can say is that the actual historical process by which capitalism emerged in our world integrally involved social relations of race and racial domination."[109] And the argument can be generalized, as Alexander Anievas and Kerem Nişancioğlu have done in their account of the historical origins of Western dominance:

> The conquest, ecological ruin, slavery, state terrorism, patriarchal subjugation, racism, mass exploitation and immiseration upon which capitalism was built continue unabated today. The violent past ... was therefore not merely a historical contingency, external to the "pure" operation of capital, or a phase of "incompleteness" out of which capitalism emerged or will emerge. Rather, these practices and processes are "constitutive" in the sense that they remain crucial to capital's ongoing reproduction as a historical social structure.[110]

The difference between Wood and Brown's position and that of McNally, Anievas, and Nişancioğlu is essentially the difference between the abstract economic model presented by Marx in *Capital* and the concrete historical process on which he drew to illustrate it: the former theory does not require racism, sexism, or any form of non-economic oppression, but the latter reality did, and still does.[111] The difference is sometimes presented in other ways, as in David Harvey's distinction between *capital* and *capital-*

ism, which is helpful here: "From the standpoint of capitalism, this central and foundational contradiction within the economic engine constituted by capital clearly has a vital role to play, but its tangible manifestations are mediated and tangled up through the filters of other forms of social distinction, such as race, ethnicity, gender and religious affiliation so as to make the actual politics of struggle within capitalism a far more complicated affair than would appear to be the case from the standpoint of the labor-capital relation alone."[112] Yet Harvey does not extend his understanding of this distinction into struggles that have erupted from outside the capital-labor relation. In response to one critic of his book, *Seventeen Contradictions and the End of Capitalism*, he writes:

> Obviously, the racial discriminations that have animated political struggles in the United States are important because the outcome of such struggles will define the future conditionalities of other transformations of that social formation. But we should be clear that such struggles are anti-racist and not necessarily anti-capitalist.

More specifically, Harvey writes that he did not regard the demonstrations that took place in Ferguson, Missouri, after the police murder of Mike Brown "as dealing very much with anti-capitalism."[113] But as David Roediger points out, while he wishes that "the people in Ferguson talked explicitly about ending capitalism . . . to assume that their struggles are therefore not anti-capitalist ones seems formalistic in the extreme."[114]

Recent discussions of oppression have been more concerned with establishing links between its different manifestations under capitalism, mainly through the concept of intersectionality, than with establishing the connection between all forms of oppression and capitalist exploitation.[115] Intersectionality is in many respects the equivalent in social movements to "interdisciplinarity" in academic subject areas: both are attempts to compensate for the absence of the concept of totality, in the case of the former in strategic rather than theoretical terms. There are two central problems with it. One is that intersectionality has become what Edward Said once described as a "travelling theory."[116] In this case it is one that has travelled from its origins in Black Feminism to one that can be accommodated by neoliberalism, with its emphasis on individual roles: the personal is political reduced to the political *is* the personal—and nothing else.[117] But even where this accommodation has been resisted, there is a second and more fundamental difficulty. As one critical supporter of the intersectional critique of capitalism points out, powerful though it is in many respects, "to say that oppressions inter-sect, interact and mutually reinforce one another is still to pose them as separate."[118] In fact, as McNally points out, intersectionality is an example of what he calls "Social Newtonianism," in which different relations collide but do not interact. In a social system, however, the connections between different forms of oppression are not random but systematic, and "to be *systematically* related involves considerably more than mere intersection": "they constitute an integral system."[119]

Holly Lewis makes a similar argument in more concrete terms:

> Race, gender, religion, and nation are not "things that happen to individ-uals": they are social relations conditioned by capitalism *and conditioned by one another*. Each relation is defined by all other relations with which it in-teracts. Just as the experience of maleness is always inflected by gender and sexuality. This is because what happens in the world happens all at once.

And just because particular Marxists have failed to treat oppression as anything other than a contingent aspect of capitalism does not mean that Marxism itself is incapable of providing a better explanation:

> The universalism of Marxism . . . is not the reduction of human experience to a model but the acknowledgement that we all exist in one world. . . . Op-pressions cannot be pinned to the wall like so many dead butterflies. They do not come at us like bolts from distinct and unrelated points.[120]

This discussion may appear to have taken us some distance from the nature of revolutionary situations, but it is in fact central to it. If exploitation and other forms of oppression are linked by the process of capitalist histori-cal development, then the "merger" of movements hailed by Lenin remains a possibility, albeit one that will still have to be fought for and organized. Marx himself argued that this should be an objective for the trade unions: "They must convince the world at large that their efforts, far from being narrow and selfish, aim at the emancipation of the downtrodden millions."[121] Lenin himself doubted that the unions could play this role and saw it instead as falling to revolutionaries, as he argued in a famous passage from "What Is to Be Done?": "The Social-Democrat's ideal should not be the trade-union secretary, but the tribune of the people, who is able to react to every manifes-tation of tyranny and oppression, no matter where it appears, no matter what stratum or class of the people it affects."[122] In fact, one task of revolutionaries must surely be to convince "the trade union secretary" of the need for workers' organizations to become "tribunes of the oppressed," as a step on the road to Marx's "complete emancipation."

The Russian Revolution provides a powerful demonstration of the two propositions argued in this section. The first is that Marxism is capable of uniting the struggles against exploitation and oppression. There was a fundamental difference between Bolshevik conceptions of female liberation and those associated with the mainstream of Western feminism:

> After acquiring [the vote], no feminist movement in the West, until recent years, made any further steps towards realizing economic or sexual liberation; even less did it engage in any mass movement for the liberation of women of the working class or minorities. Bolshevik "feminism" reversed the social timetable of Western feminism. For the latter, political emancipation was the goal; for the former, it was only the beginning.[123]

There is no need to downplay the divisions and debates between revolutionaries in Russia after 1917 concerning issues of sex and gender; and there were also undoubtedly tensions, gaps, and contradictions in what was done, but in relation to these issues, the Bolshevik regime was one of the first to give all women the vote and was alone at the time in legalizing abortion and making divorce accessible; indeed, this aspect of the revolutionary achievement lasted longer than most others—including soviet democracy itself.[124]

The second proposition demonstrated by the Russian Revolution is the relationship between women's oppression and capitalism. The Stalinist counterrevolution of 1928 is in many ways a test case: the regime constructed a then-novel form of integral state capitalism, compressing all the horrors of "normal" capitalist industrialization into decades, rather than centuries. Part of this process—unsurprisingly, in the light of our earlier discussion—involved removing most of the rights that women had won regarding their sexuality and control over their own bodies until, by 1936, they were being celebrated as breeding machines for the production of workers and soldiers.[125]

3. A fourth actuality: International revolutionary conjunctures

It is part of the tragedy of the twentieth century that Russia in 1917 remains the only occasion in which the moment was even temporarily seized, although there have been many more when it *could* have been during the "revolutionary situations" discussed above. The type of relatively compressed moment in which subjectivity acquires such decisive importance does not, however, arise instantaneously, but in the context of longer periods of development; this suggests a further type of actuality in addition to the three I have already discussed and summarize here. Actuality 1, the material conditions for socialism on a global scale, was established by the last decades of the nineteenth century and, if anything, the continuing uncontrolled growth of the productive forces since then has rendered the world overripe for revolution, to the point of threatening environmental destruction in its continued absence. Actuality 2, preparedness for revolution as the underlying assumption behind even quite routine socialist activity, remains the most effective general guide to revolutionary practice, although it has only ever been put into effect intermittently and unevenly. Actuality 3 is where the objective conditions produced by capitalism create the imminent possibility of victory in the struggle for power (a "revolutionary situation"), involving movements of both the exploited and oppressed, in which the subjective agency of revolutionaries can potentially lead to a successful outcome.

There is, however, a fourth form of actuality, only implied in Lukács's book, lying between Actuality 1 and Actuality 3 in temporal terms. Actuality 4 is neither a global era of developmental readiness nor a local episode of political decision, but a period that occurs *after* the former has been achieved and *within which* the latter becomes possible. I refer to such periods as "revolutionary conjunctures," when revolution moves from being an abstract hypothesis to a concrete possibility, but where the question of state power is not yet directly posed.[126] I would argue that there have been three actual examples of these, all in the twentieth century: 1917–23, 1943–49, and 1968–76.[127] As this periodization suggests, these conjunctures are relatively rare and differ from "revolutionary situations" in three respects.

First, *revolutionary conjunctures are extended processes*. Revolutionary situations are decisive turning points lasting days or weeks—perhaps months at most—in which the moment ("of truth") is either seized or allowed to pass; but revolutionary conjunctures can last for years, in which a set of global conditions and responses take place under varying local circumstances.

Second, *revolutionary conjunctures are, by definition, international*. Revolutionary situations necessarily arise within individual states, even if several of them occur more or less simultaneously; but revolutionary conjunctures encompass "many states" (if not always the entire states system) from the very start, in a common if uneven pattern of crises and resistance. As Harvey writes, "Simultaneity of revolutionary upsurges in different location, as in

1948 or 1968, strikes fear into any ruling class precisely because its superior command over space is threatened."[128] External intervention by one capitalist power into the affairs of another in order to prevent revolutionary contagion is scarcely unknown, whether this takes a passive form—as in the Prussian military allowing the Versailles troops free access to suppress the Paris Commune in 1871—or an active one, as in the South African intervention in former Portuguese colonies from the mid-1970s; but where potentially interventionist powers are all facing their own challenges, even if these have different intensities, their ability to do so is greatly diminished.

Third, *revolutionary conjunctures can give rise to revolutionary situations, not the other way around.* The Russian Revolution inspired other revolutionary movements, but it was only able to do so in a way that had any effect because it was part of the conjuncture that arose during the First World War, which as Trotsky noted, "drew into its maelstrom countries of *different* stages of development, but made the same *claims* on all the participants."[129] No other state in Europe was exactly like the Tsarist autocracy, of course, but there were enough common features with other states—the importance of heavy engineering, often associated with arms manufacture, and the existence of a skilled and highly militant workforce in the plants, for example—for relevant lessons to be learned. This point is of paramount importance, as revolutionary situations, even the temporary establishments of revolutionary regimes, have arisen in *individual* territories, but failed at least in part because they were unable to extend the local transformation beyond their borders: Paris in 1871 to the rest of France; Catalonia in 1936–37 to the rest of Spain; Hungary in 1956–57 or Poland in 1980–81 to the rest of Eastern Europe. Russia in 1917–23 also experienced this isolation, but unlike these other examples it occurred in a context where this was the outcome of international revolutionary defeat, not the absence of international revolutionary opportunity.

So much for what distinguishes revolutionary conjunctures from revolutionary situations; what general characteristics do they have in common with each other? We should first note what these do *not* share, namely a direct connection to the outbreak of economic crisis. The periods beginning in 1917 and 1943 were in both cases responses to the increasingly intolerable pressures of inter-imperialist war and occupation, that of the latter exacerbated by the—in Europe at least—unprecedented brutality of the fascist regimes. In the period beginning in 1968, imperialism also played a role, although in this case the context was not the direct experience of inter-imperialist conflict, but the example of Vietnamese resistance to the US. The period beginning in 1968 certainly took place against the backdrop of a gradual decline in the rate of profit, but one that would only lead to the return of crisis toward its end. The crises of 1929 and 1973 did not lead to revolutionary conjunctures, but rather to the triumph of fascism in Germany in the case of the former and the more prolonged imposition of neoliberalism in the case of the latter. Most recently, the crisis of 2007/8 did not lead to a generalized revolutionary conjuncture, although it did—after the elapse of several years—set the context for several cross-border manifestations that combined demonstration and prefiguration (the English student revolt of 2010; "the movement of the squares" in Greece and Spain in 2011; the emergence of Occupy, mainly in the US and UK, during the same year; the radicalization of the "Yes" movement during the Scottish independence referendum in 2013–14) and one major regional revolutionary upheaval in the form of the Arab Spring. What these periods of revolutionary conjuncture *did* share were the following:

First, they have all involved a combination of different but overlapping movements (using this term in its broadest sense) that were—in Lenin's terms—"dissimilar," "heterogeneous" and "contrary," and, while they may not always have "merged," or even been capable of "merging," were simultaneously ranged against the existing order, making it possible (as in 1968) to simply refer—not always accurately—to "the" movement. Crucially, these movements occurred both *within* individual nation-states and *across* the international states system.

Second, participants in each conjuncture were, to varying degrees, aware that they were part of a historical moment that extended beyond their own particular issue or geographical location, and that the different movements of which it was constituted could and should influence each other—a recognition of the interconnected nature of global capitalism. This consciously international nature of the conjuncture provided the possibility of success in one place being extended to others, not artificially, at the end of a bayonet (as in the case of the English and French bourgeois revolutions), but organically, out of comparable conditions present in each.

Third, the conjunctures were time-limited. Without success *somewhere*, they could not be indefinitely sustained. So in a sense both "1917" (outside of Russia) and "1968" involved a race against time to build effective revolutionary parties capable of leading the movement to victory, before it retreated, exhausted, or the bourgeoisie were able to restore order, which, by 1923 and 1976, respectively, they had succeeded in doing. (In my view, the dominance of Stalinism and Social Democracy meant that there was no realistic possibility of achieving this in "1943.") Revolutions that begin with socialist potential can end as merely political in nature (Germany in 1918–19, Italy in 1943–45, Portugal in 1974–75)—or, if they do succeed as social revolutions, it is as the contemporary form of the bourgeois revolution (Turkey in 1923, China in 1949, Ethiopia in 1974). Struggles for the liberation of oppressed groups can achieve legal equality, but thereafter adapt in ways that are compatible with the continued existence of capitalism and that may even strengthen it; or movements simply carry on, but in increasing isolation from each other. Then one day revolutionaries wake up and realize that it is no longer 1919 or 1945 or 1972—or whichever year successful international revolution seemed the most likely occur. Whether or not they recognize the nature of the changed period has historically been a major factor in determining how politically effective or otherwise they have been from that point on.

4. Toward a new revolutionary conjuncture?

Perry Anderson has referred to the conjuncture of '68 as "the last hour of what Lukács, in his tribute to Lenin in 1923, had called the actuality of the revolution."[130] Is this pessimism justified? It is certainly true that the twentieth-century revolutionary conjunctures occurred at surprisingly regular intervals of around two decades. The closures of 1922–23 were followed twenty years later by the openings of 1943; the closures of 1948–49 were followed twenty years later by the openings of 1968. We might therefore have expected the closures of 1975–76 to have been followed by further openings around the mid-1990s—but, over a hundred years after the opening of the first revolutionary conjuncture of the twentieth century, and fifty years after the opening of the last, we still await their successor.

Are we then in what Alain Badiou calls an "intervallic moment"? He describes such a moment in the following way:

> It is what comes *after* a period in which the revolutionary conception of political action has been sufficiently clarified that, notwithstanding the ferocious internal struggles punctuating its development, it is explicitly presented as an alternative to the dominant world, and on that basis has secured massive, disciplined support. In an intervallic period, by contrast, the revolutionary idea of the previous period, which naturally encountered

formidable obstacles—relentless enemies without and a provisional inability to resolve important problems within—is dormant. It has not yet been taken up by a new sequence in its development.

In these periods, reactionaries always claim "that things have resumed their *natural* course." According to Badiou such a "period of reaction" can be dated from "the late 1970s."[131] His periodization is correct, but fifty years is a very long interval and one is entitled to wonder if the performance is ever going to resume.[132]

It is not, of course, that movements have ceased to arise or that struggles, and even revolutions, have ceased to take place—indeed, some of these have been on a far larger scale and of far greater intensity than those of "1968": it is rather that, unlike the latter, they tended to take place in relative isolation from each other, or at best as regional groupings like those discussed in earlier chapters of this book. The revolutions of 1989–91 in Eastern Europe occurred well within the previous twenty-year timescale. These were not, however, part of a new global conjuncture, but rather more geographically focused, less widespread than even the events of 1848–49, let alone those that followed in the twentieth century. More importantly, the events themselves were primarily regarded—not least by many of the participants—as being about overthrowing the impediment posed by the Stalinist regimes to joining the ranks of democratic capitalism represented by the West, rather than a contribution to overthrowing the system in all its forms, East and West. Two subsequent regional upheavals discussed in this book—the "pink tide" in South America from 1998 and the "Arab Spring" in the Middle East and North Africa from 2010—had far more potential for socialist revolution, but in the end their national components either succumbed to inherent reformist limitations (in the case of the first) or were defeated by the more powerful and better organized forces of counterrevolution (in the case of the second): the contrasting agonies of Venezuela and Syria illustrating their respective paths to defeat in sharpest relief.

Let us assume, however, that a new revolutionary conjuncture, comparable to the three that defined the twentieth century, is being prepared by the multiple contradictions of capitalism. But a new period of this sort is unlikely to resemble its predecessors in any respect other than that it will involve the only struggles that cannot be accommodated within capitalism: the abolition of exploitation and oppression, and the prevention (or at least minimization) of catastrophic climate change. Why? I began this chapter by reflecting on the distance between our situation and that of "1917"; but perhaps it is more pertinent to establish the distance between our situation and that of "1968."

Even in "1968," the components always included struggles against not only pre-capitalist state forms, but also the remaining formal colonies, colonial-settler states, and authoritarian regimes claiming justification from religious tradition. These no longer exist in anything like the numbers that they did fifty years ago. Fredric Jameson has gone so far as to claim that everything associated with "pre-modernity" had "finally been swept away without a trace."[133] Anderson agrees with this general analysis while rejecting the more extreme conclusions that he claims are often improperly drawn from it, pointing out that Jameson's argument "does not depend on any contention—obviously absurd—that contemporary capitalism has created a homogenous set of social circumstances round the world."[134] Actually, that is *exactly* what Jameson says, but Anderson is nevertheless right to reject claims for homogeneity; one can easily identify exceptions that fall into one or other of the four categories I listed above, many of them in North Africa and the Middle East (respectively, Saudi Arabia, Western Sahara, Israel, and Iran). The point, however, is that these types of archaic or exceptional states are in numerical decline. Why does this matter?

Shortly after the fall of the Stalinist regimes, Fred Halliday comforted himself with the thought that, even though revolutions in the advanced capitalist countries were unlikely under conditions of liberal democracy, there were only "two dozen countries in the world which meet this criterion": "In other words, for the great majority of the 169 states in the world, the conditions under which revolutions can occur still prevail."[135] Ten years later, Jeff Goodwin essentially accepted the same argument, but concluded—logically enough—that the subsequent expansion of representative democracy meant revolutionary conditions were now much rarer.[136] As far as representative democracy is concerned, this assessment involves two claims: one is that attempts to establish representative democracy have the potential for socialist revolutionary outcomes; but the other is that if representative democracy *is* established, it then becomes an obstacle to socialist revolution in the future. This, however, is only one of two obstacles. As Anderson notes in his commentary on Gramsci's *Prison Notebooks*, the other is the capacity of capitalist democracies for violence, which is greater than that of Tsarism:

> Firstly, because the Western social formations are much more industrially advanced, and this technology is reflected in the apparatus of violence itself.

Secondly, because the masses typically consent to this State in the belief that they exercise government over it. It therefore possesses a popular legitimacy of a far more reliable character for the exercise of this repression than did Tsarism in its decline.[137]

As we shall see, Anderson was right to draw attention to the *extent* of the differences between capitalist and pre-capitalist states (and "Tsarism" can stand here as a synonym for all the different varieties of the latter); but he is at least partly wrong about the *nature* of those differences.

First, capitalist states do indeed have greater repressive powers than their pre-capitalist forerunners or contemporaries; but equally important is their flexibility, which enables them to make gradual structural reforms in ways that pre-capitalist states, of the sort that existed in Trotsky's lifetime and for several decades after his death, could not; the latter consequently had to be either overthrown by popular revolution, "transformed" by passive revolution, or destroyed in war. The same type of flexibility is also constitutive of contemporary capitalist states, even those in the global South or former "East." However backward they may be in many other respects, they have a far greater capacity for absorption and renovation under pressure. Goodwin's "state-centered" approach identifies a number of "practices" or "characteristics" that can make the emergence of revolutionary movements or situations less likely. The most relevant to our discussion is "political inclusion," which

> discourages the sense that the state is unreformable or an instrument of a narrow class or clique and, accordingly, needs to be fundamentally overhauled. . . . Accordingly, neither liberal populist polities nor authoritarian yet inclusionary (for example) "populist" regimes have generally been challenged by powerful revolutionary movements.[138]

If the states in question need not be "democratic," then this suggests a second difficulty with Anderson's argument, namely his claim that representative institutions in and of themselves form a second "bulwark" against overthrow. It is true that mass suffrage has not proved as dangerous to capitalism as the bourgeoisie initially feared (and Marx and Engels originally thought) it would be; but recognizing this does not involve accepting the much more sweeping claim that it is the main source of popular legitimacy for the capitalist state. Most capitalist states in the West and the system over which they presided were afforded legitimacy by their working classes *before* the vote was extended to them. The key factor in securing the adherence of the subaltern is surely not democracy, but the concept most closely associated with Gramsci, hegemony, which may include democratic institutions, but not necessarily so. Above all, it is not exercised solely through the state, as Peter Thomas explains:

> A class's hegemonic apparatus is the wide-ranging series of articulated institutions (understood in the broadest sense) and practices—from newspapers to educational organizations to political parties—by means of which a class and its allies engage their opponents in a struggle for political power. This concept traverses the boundaries of the so-called public (pertaining to the state) and the private (civil society), to include all initiatives by which a class concretizes its hegemonic project in an integral sense.[139]

These are some of the mechanisms through which hegemony is maintained; its content need not be wholehearted endorsement of capitalism. Jeremy Lester notes: "Capitalism is not maintained by a mass popular affirmation or affection for what the system objectively produces for society as a whole; it is maintained by the way it has hitherto marginalized alternatives against it, a 'better the devil you know' kind of common-sense attitude, which in turn promotes a notion of apathy and disinterestedness in the very possibility of change." In this context all that capitalism requires is to maintain a majority of the working class in circumstances that are bearable compared to the imaginable alternatives. And, as Lester points out, those for whom it is not bearable "often lack the conceptual and linguistic tools to understand their position in this system, let alone do anything about it."[140]

The attitude that Lester describes has always existed under capitalism, at least once the initial traumas of industrialization had passed. During the neoliberal era, however, we have seen it develop in another, even darker direction, toward what the late Mark Fisher called "capitalist realism." In his view this was "never really necessarily about the idea that capitalism was a particularly good system," but unlike what might be called the traditional operation of hegemony, this does *not* depend on the system being bearable for a majority; instead, it is

> more about persuading people that it is the only viable system and the building of an alternative is impossible. That discontent is practically universal does not change the fact that there appears to be no workable alternative to capitalism. It does not change the belief that capitalism holds all the cards and that there is nothing we can do about it—that capitalism is almost like a force of nature, which cannot be resisted. There is nothing that has happened since 2008 that has done anything to change that, and that is why capitalist realism still persists.

The result, argued Fisher, was "an attitude of resignation, defeatism and depression."[141] The practical implications of such an attitude are often supposed to be a retreat into personal consumption. "At a time when never before have so many been so deeply cynical about the possibility of fundamental socio-economic and political change, denying their own subjective agency and rejecting any notions of collective emancipation as dangerous, abstract utopianism, there is a depressing truth in the fact that, for many people, the consumer power of the individual is all that remains in our late capitalist society," writes Phillipe Le Goff.[142] In fact, another response is also possible, the implications of which are even more ominous.

Historically, revolutionary conjunctures have offered alternative paths out of particular crises, which need not be absolutely polarized; but the extent of the current crisis means that this is unlikely to be the case in any future occasion. "Crisis brings out on one side deep reactionary forces that want to prevent necessary change, and it calls forth revolutionaries on the other side who want to overthrow entire systems," writes Daniel Chirot, but above all: "It produces masses who do not know which way to turn."[143] What would pull people, often themselves victims of the crisis, to embrace the reactionary side? Writing of Trump's supporters in Louisiana, Hochschild observed that he "allowed them both to feel like a good moral American and to feel superior to those they considered 'other' or beneath them":

> This giddy, validating release produces a kind of "high" that felt good. And of course people wanted to feel good. The desire to hold on to this elation became a matter of emotional self-interest.

She rightly notes that "economic self-interest is never entirely absent," but it is less significant than the "release from the feeling of being a stranger in one's own land": "Having once experienced the elation—the 'high'—of being part of a powerful, like-minded majority, released from politically correct rules of feeling, many wanted to hold on to that elation."[144] To understand what underlies this emotion, I want to draw on two thinkers who, in most respects, are as different from each other as it is possible to be: W. E. B. Du Bois and Friedrich Nietzsche.

Reflecting on social relations in the southern US states after the final defeat of Radical Reconstruction in 1877, Du Bois argued that receipt of a "public and psychological wage" could explain why the poor whites refused to ally with the former slaves.[145] The typical situation of the white Southern petty bourgeoisie and working class was that in relation to their black neighbors, they enjoyed marginally superior material conditions, and this therefore acquired a quite disproportionate social significance compared with its economic value, allied as it was to the non-economic psycho-social compensation whites received from occupying a position of absolute ascendancy over the blacks. The majority of Southern whites, most of the time, appear not to have considered that superior conditions existed elsewhere or how their own might be raised to that level, let alone surpass it. As Roediger writes in his discussion of Du Bois, "Status and privileges conferred by race could be used to compensate for alienating and exploitative class relationship, North and South. White workers could, and did, define and accept their class position by fashioning identities as 'not slaves' and 'not Blacks.'"[146]

Du Bois was discussing a highly specific historical situation; Nietzsche, on the other hand, claimed to have discovered an attitude that was a universal aspect of human nature—the satisfaction that the "creditor" (meaning anyone who has been injured by another in any way) gains from seeing the "ower" suffer hurt or humiliation:

> Instead of an advantage directly compensatory of his injury (that is, instead of an equalization in money, lands, or some kind of chattel), the creditor is granted by way of repayment and compensation a certain *sensation of satisfaction*—the satisfaction of being able to vent, without any trouble, his power on one who is powerless, the delight *"de faire le mal pour le plaisir de le faire"* [doing wrong for the pleasure of doing it], the joy in sheer violence: and this joy will be relished in proportion to the lowness and humbleness of the creditor in the social scale, and is quite apt to have the effect of the most delicious dainty, and even seem the foretaste of a higher social position. Thanks to the punishment of the "ower," the creditor participates in the rights of the masters. At last he too, for once in a way, attains the edifying consciousness of being able to despise and ill-treat a creature—as an "inferior"—or at any rate of *seeing* him being despised and ill-treated, in case the actual power of punishment, the administration of punishment, has already become transferred to the "authorities." The compensation consequently consists in a claim on cruelty and a right to draw thereon.[147]

But as Miéville notes, although conceived as a "timeless truth about the human psyche," today it reads more like "advice for the culture industry and their paymasters on how to dole out a public and psychological wage, the 'aspirationalism' and 'entrepreneurialism' channeled into spectacular sadisms. Extending to the lower orders a small share in domination."[148] This passage by Nietzsche has also been noted by Philip Mirowski, another writer concerned with what he calls the "everyday sadism" of the neoliberal order, in which anyone not actually among the indigent can experience "a kind of guilty pleasure in the thousand unkind cuts administered by the enforcers of top-down austerity": "Through this guilty pleasure, people of modest means are ushered into the vicarious experience of what it feels like to be extravagantly rich in a period of decline."[149]

What we may be seeing is a fusion of the attitudes identified by Du Bois and Nietzsche. In relation to the former, it does not take a great deal of difficulty to recognize new forms of psychological compensation currently being offered—and not only to the white population—in relation to migrants. And, to an even lesser extent than in the case of the South, it is not the preservation of marginal—and not-so-marginal—differences in material conditions which is most important: it is rather the emotional satisfaction of allowing free rein to feelings of hatred toward groups who can be identified as alien, "other," and the imaginary source of otherwise inexplicable economic decline or unwanted cultural change. And here is where Nietzsche's dark joy enters. For migrants, unlike the black population of the South, are not a potential threat requiring to be kept in their place, but one actively engaged, however unwillingly, in transforming the host societies: this is the crime for which they "owe" their persecutors. For the latter, it is almost as if, having given up, not only on abolishing or reforming capitalism ("capitalist realism"), but even the possibility that material conditions might improve, all that remains to make the despair bearable is the expression of misdirected anger, *even if it injures the person expressing that anger*. In the context of Brexit, Fintan O'Toole argues that what is often simply referred to as "populism" is in fact what he, following Timothy Snyder, calls "sadopopulism," "in which people are willing to inflict pain on themselves so long as they can believe that in the same moment, they are making their enemies hurt more."[150]

Sadopopulism does not of course affect all social classes equally. Liberal myths to the contrary, it is not a majority of working-class people who have to date succumbed to it. Even if we assume that everyone who voted Leave in the EU referendum did so for racist and anti-migrant reasons, and that those who voted Remain did so in opposition to those views—and this would be a gross over-simplification—in the case of the former, nearly 59 percent of those doing so belonged to the middle classes and only 24 percent belonged to the poorest sections of the working class. The percentage breakdown in class terms is virtually identical in relation to who voted for Trump.

In both cases, the ballot saw large-scale abstention by those who were most likely to vote for the nominally more progressive alternative, and a radicalization of those who actually did vote for the nominally more reactionary one.[151] But just because sadopopulism has hitherto mainly expressed the economic and social insecurities of the petty bourgeoisie, that is no reason to assume that it might not spread more widely among demoralized or unorganized working-class people. As Moody writes, "capitalism offers opportunities, not certainties," but it offers opportunities to more than one social force.[152]

What then will be the components of a future global revolutionary conjuncture? And, more specifically, which are likely to act as triggers? Before turning to some possibilities, two points are important to note.

First, we need to distinguish the possible triggers of a future revolutionary conjuncture from what might be called the everyday activities of the revolutionary Left. In other words, I take it for granted that revolutionaries should be, for example, opposing imperialist interventions in the global South, resisting the rise of the populist hard right, and attempting to unionize pseudo-"self-employed" gig economy workers—in other words maintaining the revolutionary preparedness that constitutes Actuality 2; but the trigger will not necessarily come from any of these areas, even though they will certainly be components of the conjuncture once it begins. There are any number of reasons why, for example, a general strike of public sector workers may not be the starting point for a new upheaval. Daniel Bensaïd's gloss on Lenin is alert to the possibility of surprise:

> If one of the outlets is blocked with particular care, then the contagion will find another, sometimes the most unexpected. That is why we cannot know which spark will ignite the fire.

In this conception, which I endorse, the watchword is: "'Be ready!' Ready for the improbable, for the unexpected, for what happens."[153] Moody too is right to observe that "it is impossible to fully gauge the subjective factor needed to set things in motion," consequently: "Predictions of an upsurge are almost always a futile pursuit. . . . What is needed now is not crystal ball gazing but preparation."[154] As we shall see, these warnings do not mean that it is impossible to make a series of educated guesses about where the sparks are likely to fly, only that it is likely to be done successfully if we do not assume it will accord with our preferences (because revolutionaries have experience in one particular area) or what we find convenient (because they already have resources deployed in another). Making this kind of adjustment requires revolutionary organizations to be genuinely of their time, rather than of an earlier time when they were first built, still less the even earlier time when their historical models were new.[155]

Second, the trigger may not be, as it were, a positive event. Benjamin was undoubtedly right to say that "'status quo' is the catastrophe," but unfortunately this does not mean that matters cannot get sharply worse, even in terms of the existing barbarism that I identified in this chapter's introduction.[156] After all, the first two revolutionary conjunctures of the twentieth century occurred in the context of world wars, aspects of which either indirectly ("1917") or directly ("1943") triggered them. Yet in 1914, even where socialists did not rush to support "their" state in the inter-imperialist war, many still regarded it as a murderous diversion from real politics that had to be endured until they could be resumed in the aftermath. Initially, only a handful of revolutionaries regarded the war as both a catastrophe *and* an opportunity for socialists that had to be seized if it was to be brought to an end in such a way—i.e., through socialist revolution—as would prevent future catastrophes taking place. When crisis breaks out, the task of revolutionaries is not to aid the bourgeoisie by aiding them in restoring the *status quo ante*—which is usually impossible in any event—but to try to turn it to the advantage of the exploited and oppressed. One of the problems with the response of many on the British radical left to Brexit was that in the crisis they saw only catastrophe and not opportunity.

As in earlier revolutionary conjunctures, the "trigger-components" will almost certainly develop out of existing issues, campaigns, and movements, rather than taking completely novel forms. Of course, fifty years ago some of these were either only in their formative stages (e.g., environmentalism) or had not yet emerged (e.g., transgender rights), but most would be familiar in one form or another. But it is also possible to imagine, for example, new age-defined groups taking shape in the way that Further and Higher Education students did in the 1960s, but in this case involving school students, perhaps in opposition to testing in the UK or—to pick two campaigns that have already begun—for gun control in the US and the School Strike for Climate internationally. In what follows I will highlight three areas that have the potential, either singly or jointly, to act as catalysts and make some suggestions as to their character.

The first dates back to the origins of the capitalist world system, but may now be about to play a novel role: *economic crisis*. I noted earlier that, historically, revolutionary conjunctures have not emerged out of economic crises, but that hitherto absent connection may now be made. All previous crises—1873, 1929, 1973—have, after a greater or lesser time lag, resulted in the transition to a new period of capitalism. And, while some aspects of capitalism are obviously definitional and therefore feature in all periods (e.g., the exploitation of wage labor) and others may emerge in one period and continue into another (e.g., imperialism), these periods have their own distinct characteristics, usually connected to the dominant countervailing tendency of the rate of profit to fall. But 2007/8 has *not* seen the transition from neoliberalism to a new period, only its continuation under crisis conditions, with some attempts by right-wing populists, of whom Trump is obviously the most important, to deploy aspects the 1930s protectionist handbook.

The failure to reorient from neoliberalism suggests that, as the system ages, the options available for the restoration of the rate of profit become fewer and less effective. The weakness of the recovery after 2008 has led to the widespread fear that another crisis—and not simply a regular cyclical downturn—is all but inevitable. In his account of the financial crash of 2008 and its consequences, Adam Tooze compares that year to 1914, which—pursuing the analogy—implies that 1939 is looming ahead.[157] But this would take place in circumstances where wages have been stagnant or falling for over a decade. In other words, for workers there has been no recovery, and a second wave of global crisis would see their conditions decline still further. We may therefore be about to witness the third of the economic contexts in which workers might move toward revolutionary action, the one which has until now been largely hypothetical: where a temporarily defeated working class has been subjected to such an assault that it is finally driven to resist.

I have already argued that the notion of a "final (economic) crisis" is a chimera; *catastrophic climate change*, however, will eventually prove final, not only for capitalism, but for the planet, or at least those aspects that sustain human life. Naomi Klein is therefore right to observe that the rise of climate-change denial among right-wingers is rational at one level, for "they have come to understand that as soon as they admit that climate change is real, they will lose the central ideological battle of our time":

> Climate change detonates the ideological scaffolding on which contemporary conservatism rests. A belief system that vilifies collective action and declares war on all corporate regulation and all things public simply cannot be reconciled with a problem that demands collective action on an unprec-

edented scale and a dramatic reining in of the market forces that are largely responsible for creating and deepening the crisis.[158]

Whether climate-change-denying sections of the ruling class actually believe their own claims or simply think that they will be able to protect themselves from the consequences is less important than the possibility of their fears being realized: that a movement will emerge that understands the connection between climate change and capitalism. Such an understanding will not, however, automatically produce revolutionary consciousness, and this is in part precisely because, although climate change has hitherto mainly affected the global South, it is not restricted to there and its impact is beginning to be felt in the metropolitan heartlands of the system, including the port cities that are central to the world economy.[159] Nor is it only coastal areas that are threatened. In Southern California during December 2017, in what is supposed to be the rainy season, "the Thomas fire, the worst of those that roiled the region that year, grew 50,000 acres in one day, eventually burning 440 square miles and forcing the evacuations of more than 100,000 Californians," reports Wallace-Wells: "Five of the 20 worst fires in California history hit the state in the autumn of 2017, a year in which more than 9,000 separate ones broke out, burning through almost 1.25m acres—nearly 2,000 square miles made soot."[160]

These types of outbreak make it likely that a serious movement to stop carbon emissions will emerge, of which Extinction Rebellion in the UK is one manifestation; but precisely because they are happening in Southern California as well as in Bangladesh, it is also likely to be divided into pro- and anti- capitalist wings, pitching those who think the environment can be saved within the system—the Green New Deal in the US is an example of this kind of thinking—and those who understand that it cannot—and of course there are representatives of the first position in the global South, just as there are representatives of the second in the West. For this reason a mass movement against catastrophic climate change will contain similar class divisions as were present in the movements against oppression that characterized "1968." Nevertheless, what gives climate change revolutionary potential is that its consequences are *not* subject to partial reformist intervention: people can be rescued from catastrophic events involving flooding or bush fires, but the events cannot be prevented from re-occurring, nor can their effects be easily reversed. Consequently, the task of stopping, let alone reversing, climate change can either appear too vast to be accomplished—leading to either despair or magical thinking—or to open up the possibility of a total transformation as the only realistic response.

One effect of climate change is *mass migration*, as populations flee, for example, from rising water levels or the loss of arable land. It is not, of course, their only motivation, as mass movement is also propelled by the desire to escape from war, criminal gangs, or simply to seek better material conditions—and of course "economic migration" occurs within nation-states as well as between them, primarily in the classic movement of peasants from rural to urban environments currently occurring more spectacularly in China. Migration is useful for capital: it provides a labor force for whom social reproduction has been, as it were, outsourced, and because migrant labor is usually cheap, it can render unnecessary, or at least postpone, the need to invest in labor-saving technologies. But it should also be disposable. Ferguson and McNally call this "deportability," in relation to the US: "Notwithstanding the growing number of deportations, the purpose of inhumane and punitive border enforcement is not primarily to deport undocumented workers, but to deepen their condition of *deportability*." Deportation is "a means to intensify the profound vulnerability of workers who live with the knowledge that they are inherently deportable."[161] It is not the fact of migration that means it may act as a conjunctural trigger, but two responses to it. One is a scenario where sections of the host population mobilize in solidarity with migrants against either state or vigilante oppression.[162] Even more important, however, is the self-activity of migrants themselves, whatever their point of origin.

An illustration of how internal migration can stimulate the class struggle can be found in recent developments in the city of Guangzhou, regional capital of Guangdong Province. Guangzhou is one of the major car-manufacturing centers in South China. The majority of workers in the industry are male rural migrants on short-term (usually three-year) contracts, living in employer-provided dormitories outside the factory compounds. Yet, because the employers do not actually run the dormitories, they are not subject to the type of disciplinary rules that hinder workers in other industries subject to stricter after-work supervision. Partly because of this, organizing is easier and Guangzhou has become one of the centers of auto-worker strike activity in China, where—to pick only one year—two waves of strikes in 2010 succeeded in winning wage rises of between 300 and 800 yuan.[163] The historical experience of uneven and combined development suggests that internal migrants are eventually absorbed into workplaces and communities, their initial exceptional militancy dissipating in the process, but this may not always be the case, particularly in a situation of unresolved economic crisis.

The situation of external migrants is obviously different, since unlike internal migrants they tend to be subjected to oppression on racial or ethnic grounds, or to less specific forms of "othering," yet in spite of this they have displayed levels of agency often in advance of those in similar class positions among the host population. The various "A Day Without Us" strikes, particularly in 2017 and 2018, emphasized the centrality of migrant labor to Western economies, but a specific example of militancy can be found in the struggle of the cleaning workers at the London School of Oriental and African Studies (SOAS) between 2006 and 2017. Perhaps as many as 90 percent of cleaning workers in the UK are migrants, in the case of SOAS mainly from Latin America (principally Colombia and Ecuador). Their jobs were outsourced to a private company, ISS, which did not recognize unions; they were paid the minimum wage but—despite SOAS being situated in Bloomsbury—not the London Living Wage; and they were denied the most basic benefits. A campaign across 2006–7 saw them win pension rights, the minimum wage at London levels, and holiday pay based on that wage. Union recognition followed in 2009, but so did attempts by ISS to bring in the UK Border Agency to check the residential status of the workforce, leading to nine deportations. Despite this, the cleaners were not cowed and, with support from the students and academic staff, finally forced the school to take cleaning and other functions like catering back in-house.[164] The vanguard role of migrants is not new. A succession of what Satnam Virdee calls "racialized outsiders" in Britain—"Irish Catholic, Jewish, Indian, Caribbean and African"—have consistently acted as a radicalizing force:

> Their attachment to the British nation tended to be less firm, whilst their participation in subaltern conflicts gave them a unique capacity to see through the fog of blood, soil and belonging so as to universalize the militant yet often particularist fights of the working class. In this sense, they acted as a leavening agent nourishing the struggles of all, informed by their unique perspective on society.[165]

The recurrence of economic crisis in the absence of recovery; the spread of climate chaos into the core of the system; the demands of migrant labor for the same rights as host populations—will these be the triggers for a new revolutionary conjuncture? To claim that this is inevitable would be to commit the same dogmatic error that I have criticized earlier in this chapter. They are plausible contenders, but the very argument I have made here involves understanding that the triggers may be completely unexpected: the task is to recognize them when they occur and respond appropriately.

The success of any future revolutionary conjuncture will depend on overcoming the exploitation/oppression distinction in new forms of unity against the totality of capitalism. One reason for optimism may be that this is already beginning to take place. I have already mentioned the School Strike for Climate movement, in which school students are deploying the tactics of the labor movement to intervene in one of the central issues of our time, but so too are a new generation of feminists. The feminist strike movement started in Poland in October 2016, spread across the Americas and southern Europe, and became a global phenomenon on March 8, 2017. As Cinzia Arruzza and her comrades point out:

> The movement has invented new ways to strike, while infusing the strike form itself with a new kind of politics. By combining the withdrawal of labor with marches, small-business closures, blockades and boycotts, it is replenishing the repertoire of the general strike as a mode of protest—once large, but shrunk by decades of neoliberal aggression. At the same time, it is democratizing the strike and broadening its scope by redefining what counts as "labor." Beyond waged work, women's strike activism is also withdrawing domestic labor, sex and "smiles"—making visible the indispensable role played by gendered, unpaid work in capitalist society by valorizing activities from which capital benefits but for which it does not pay. With respect to paid work, too, the feminist strike is redefining what counts as a labor issue—targeting not just wages and hours, but sexual harassment and assault, barriers to reproductive justice and curbs on the right to strike.

As these authors argue: "This new feminist militancy thus has the potential to overcome the stubborn and divisive opposition between 'identity politics' and 'class politics.'"[166] But overcoming this division will not *only* depend on the oppressed adopting "class struggle" methods, but on working-class organizations making themselves central to overcoming oppression. And, as we saw in the section "Exploitation and Oppression(s)," this is not a fashionable new idea but one that was insisted on in some of the iconic texts of classical Marxism.

Conclusion: From rehearsal to performance

I began the previous section by wondering whether Badiou's "interval" would ever again be interrupted by a resumption of the actual "performance" of revolution. A related theatrical metaphor was perhaps the most evocative of all those used to encapsulate the meaning of "1968": *rehearsal*. "The theoretical practical conclusion was that May 1968 was just a beginning, a 'dress rehearsal,' a pale copy of February 1917 in Russia," wrote Bensaïd, recalling the conclusion that he and his comrades reached: "We had to harness ourselves without delay for the preparations for October."[167] Similar perspectives were adopted well beyond the ranks of Trotskyism and outside the borders of France. Prisca Bachelet, for example, recalled: "I thought we were in 1905. France wasn't our frame of reference; for me it was 1905 in relation to 1917."[168] Mark Elbaum observes that virtually *all* revolutionary groups in the US, whatever their particular provenance, used the same highly specific historical analogy to comprehend their own situation: "The extent of social upheaval in the 1960s—and the obvious fact that it was not led by a strong left party—made it fairly easy for activists to think of 1968–73 as the American 1905." But 1905 would be followed by 1917: "Most of them realized that there would be periods of ebb ahead, though in their youthful exuberance some couldn't imagine an ebb lasting as long as the 12 years between 1905 and 1917."[169] And it is unlikely that *any* of them imagined one that would in reality last for over forty years after the conjuncture of '68 came to an end.

The real problem, however, is with the notion of rehearsal itself, at least in the sense that it was used during 1968. For, as Mitchell Abidor points out, Russian revolutionaries in 1905 did not regard themselves as taking part in a rehearsal, "great" or otherwise: "In 1905 the Russians thought they were living in 1917, i.e., they were engaged in a fight that was not a preparation for something greater than would occur later: they intended to seize power at that moment."[170] In fact, 1905 only became a "dress rehearsal" in retrospect. But there is another sense in which we *can* properly speak of rehearsal. The title of this volume's predecessor, *Revolutionary Rehearsals*, identified a series of revolutionary situations between France in 1968 and Poland in 1981 as events of that type.[171] But the work of preparation need not take so dramatic or potentially decisive a form. During 1968 itself, John Berger wrote that that year's mass demonstrations possessed "prophetic, rehearsing possibilities":

> Demonstrations express political ambitions before the political means necessary to realize them have been created. Demonstrations predict the realization of their own ambitions and thus may contribute to that realization, but they cannot themselves achieve them. The question which revolutionaries must decide in any given historical situation is whether or not further symbolic rehearsals are necessary. The next stage is training in tactics and strategy for the performance itself.[172]

We return then to Actuality 2, "revolutionary preparedness," the understanding that, not only demonstrations, but all forms of mass self-activity can be preparations for some greater moment of social transformation, if they are treated as such. We can in this way try to hasten the onset of the next conjuncture, but it is not in our gift to initiate it: the key thing is to recognize the conjuncture when it finally opens and to act accordingly.

NOTES

Introduction

1. Versions of this introduction have been presented by Colin Barker at various conferences and by Gareth Dale at Alternative Futures and Popular Protest (University of Manchester) in April 2019. We are grateful to contributions from the floor, and to Laurence Cox and Jeff Goodwin, for helping us to develop the argument. Neil Davidson was involved in its drafting and revising from the outset, providing invaluable advice.

2. A translation of the whole work into Korean with a new editor's preface appeared in 2011 (Seoul: Chaekgalpi Publishing Co.). The preface appeared in English as Colin Barker, "Twenty-Five Years of Revolution," *International Socialism* 135 (2012): 147–56.

3. Charles Tilly, *European Revolutions: 1492–1992* (London: Wiley, 1996).

4. Mark Beissinger, *The Urban Advantage in Revolution* (forthcoming).

5. Benjamin Constant, "The Liberty of Ancients Compared with That of Moderns," 1819, https://oll.libertyfund.org/pages/constant-the-liberty-of-ancients-compared-with-that-of-moderns-1819.

6. Neil Davidson, *How Revolutionary Were the Bourgeois Revolutions?* (Chicago: Haymarket, 2012), 578.

7. See Ellen Kay Trimberger, *Revolution from Above: Military Bureaucrats and Development in Japan, Turkey, Egypt and Peru* (New Brunswick, NJ: Transaction Books, 1978).

8. Theda Skocpol and Ellen Kay Trimberger, "Revolutions and the World-Historical Development of Capitalism," *Berkeley Journal of Sociology* 22 (1977–78): 101–13.

9. Antonio Gramsci, *Selections from the Prison Notebooks* (London: Lawrence & Wishart, 1971).

10. Beissinger, *The Urban Advantage in Revolution*.

11. Stolen elections, of course, do not necessarily bring about a revolutionary situation, as Americans discovered in 2000. See Mark Thompson, *Democratic Revolutions: Asia and Eastern Europe* (London: Routledge, 2004).

12. Beissinger, *The Urban Advantage in Revolution*. From chapter 2, "The Growth and Urbanisation of Revolution."

13. Timothy Garton Ash, *We the People: The Revolution of '89 Witnessed in Warsaw, Budapest, Berlin and Prague* (New York: Penguin, 1990).

14. Judy Batt, "The End of Communist Rule in East-Central Europe: A Four-Country Comparison," *Government and Opposition* 26, no.3 (1991): 368–90; Gareth Dale, "'A Very Orderly Retreat': Democratic Transition in East Germany, 1989–90," *Journal of Contemporary Central and Eastern Europe* 14, no. 1 (2006): 7–35.

15. Colin Barker and Colin Mooers, "Theories of Revolution in the Light of 1989 in Eastern Europe," *Cultural Dynamics* 9 no.1 (1997): 17–43; Gareth Dale, *The East German Revolution of 1989* (Manchester: Manchester University Press, 2006).

16. Paul Almeida, "Social Movement Partyism: Collective Action and Oppositional Political Parties," in Nella Van Dyke and Holly McCammon, eds., *Strategic Alliances: Coalition Building and Social Movements* (Minneapolis: University of Minnesota Press, 2010), 170–96.

17. Peter Alexander, Thapelo Lekgowa, Botsang Mmope, Luke Sinwell, and Bongazi Xezwi, *Marikana: A View from the Mountain and a Case to Answer* (Aukland Park, South Africa: Jacana Media, 2012).

18. David Potter, David Goldblatt, Margaret Kiloh, and Paul Lewis, *Democratization* (Milton Keynes: Open University Press, 1997), Table 1.2, p. 9. The proportion of states reckoned to be "partial democracies" rose from 7 percent to 26 percent over the same period. In another estimate, "the number of states that qualify empirically as democracies has grown steadily from forty-two in 1972, to fifty-two in 1980, to seventy-six in 1994, and to ninety in 2007." Sangmook Lee, "Democratic Transition and the Consolidation of Democracy in South Korea," *Taiwan Journal of Democracy* 3, no.1 (2007): 102.

19. This is in line with research showing workers' movements to be the most solid base of democratization. See Sirianne Dahlum et al., "Who Revolts? Empirically Revisiting the Social Origins of Democracy," *Journal of Politics* 81, no. 4 (2019): 1494–99; Ruth Berins Collier and James Mahoney, "Labor and Democratization: Comparing the First and Third Waves in Europe and Latin America," IRLE Working Paper No. 62-95, 1995, http://irle.berkeley.edu/files/1995/Labor-and-Democratization.pdf; also Ruth Berins Collier, *Paths Toward Democracy: The Working Class and Elites in Western Europe and South America* (Cambridge: Cambridge University Press, 1999).

20. Sebastian Balfour, *Dictatorship, Workers, and the City: Labour in Barcelona since 1939* (Oxford: Clarendon Press, 1989), 221.

21. Quoted in Manuel Fernandez, "Spain: The Gathering Storm," Marxists Internet Archive, https://www.marxists.org/history/etol/newspape/isj/1975/no080/fernandez.htm (accessed October 25, 2018).

22. Balfour, *Dictatorship, Workers, and the City*, 231.

23. One author who sees labor movements in particular as partly shaping the transition in Brazil is Salvador Sandoval, "Social Movements and Democratization: The Case of Brazil and the Latin Countries," in Marco C. Guigni, Doug McAdam, and Charles Tilly, eds., *From Contention to Democracy* (Lanham, MD: Rowman and Littlefield, 1998), 169–201. He makes no mention of the Landless Workers' Movement (MST), organized nationally since 1984.

24. Neil Davidson, "Is Social Revolution Still Possible in the Twenty-First Century?," *Journal of Contemporary Central and Eastern Europe* 23, no. 2–3 (2015): 136.

25. Colin Barker and Gareth Dale, "Protest Waves in Western Europe: A Critique of 'New Social Movement' Theory," *Critical Sociology* 24, nos. 1–2 (1998): 65–104.

26. Barker and Dale, "Protest Waves in Western Europe."

27. Neil Davidson, Patricia McCafferty, and David Miller, eds., *Neoliberal Scotland: Class and Society in a Stateless Nation* (Newcastle: Cambridge Scholars, 2010).

28. Quinn Slobodian, *Globalists: The End of Empire and the Birth of Neoliberalism* (Cambridge, MA: Harvard University Press, 2018), 5.

29. Amartya Sen, "Democracy as a Universal Value," *Journal of Democracy* 10, no. 3 (1999): 3–17.

30. Dietrich Rueschemeyer, Evelyne Huber Stephens, and John Stephens, *Capitalist Development and Democracy* (Chicago: Chicago University Press, 1992).

31. Claude Ake, "Dangerous Liaisons: The Interface of Globalization and Democracy," in *Democracy's Victory and Crisis*, Axel Hadenius, ed. (Cambridge: Cambridge University Press, 1997), 282–96.

32. Snehal Shingavi, "Austerity, Neoliberalism, and the Indian Working Class," *International Socialist Review*, no. 103 (2016–17), https://isreview.org/issue/103/austerity-neo-liberalism-and-indian-working-class-0.

33. John Walton and David Seddon, *Free Markets and Food Riots: The Politics of Global Adjustment* (Oxford: Blackwell, 1994), 39–40.

34. Others might point to the short-lived "Caracazo" in Venezuela in 1989, the 1990 indigenous uprisings in Ecuador, or the growth of MST land occupations in Brazil. What marked the Zapatista uprising was the international response it generated, thanks to its leaders' eye for publicity.

35. Elizabeth Humphrys, "Global Justice Organising in Australia: Crisis and Realignment after 9/11," *Globalizations* 10, no. 3 (2013): 451–64.

36. Michael Hardt, "An Interview with Michael Hardt," *Historical Materialism* 11, no. 3 (2003): 129–30.

37. Elizabeth Humphrys, "Organic Intellectuals and the Australian Global Justice Movement: The Weight of 9/11," in *Marxism and Social Movements*, Colin Barker, Laurence Cox, John Krinsky, and Alf Nielsen, eds. (Leiden: Brill, 2013).

38. See also Lesley J. Wood, *Direct Action, Deliberation, and Diffusion: Collective Action after the WTO Protests in Seattle* (Cambridge: Cambridge University Press, 2012), chap. 11.

39. "'Infrastructures' of resistance" is from Alan Sears, *The Next New Left: A History of the Future* (Halifax, Canada: Fernwood, 2014), 1–2.

40. This draws on materials assembled in Jeffery Webber, *The Last Day of Oppression, and the First Day of the Same* (Chicago: Haymarket, 2017).

41. Miguel Angel Martínez López, "Democracy and Capitalism from the Viewpoint, Practice and Context of Social Movements: The Case of the Umbrella Movement in Hong Kong, 2014," Paper for the 23rd International Conference on Alternative Futures and Popular Protest, Manchester, March 2018.

42. Some of these—and others—are documented in Cristina Flesher Fominaya, *Social Movements and Globalization: How Protests, Occupations and Uprisings Are Changing the World* (London: Palgrave, 2014), and in Margit Mayer, Catharina Thörn, and Håkan

Thörn, eds., *Urban Uprisings: Challenging Neoliberal Urbanism in Europe* (London: Palgrave, 2016); see also Sean Purdy, "Brazil's June Days of 2013: Mass Protest, Class, and the Left," *Latin American Perspectives* 46, no. 4 (2019): 1–22.

43. That broad question also came into prominence, in different but interconnected fashion, in three movements in the USA: #BlackLivesMatter, #MeToo, and, most recently, the 2018 school student movement against gun violence—all of them paralleling and echoing movements in other countries.

44. Francis Fukuyama, *The End of History and the Last Man* (New York: Free Press, 1992).

45. Mark Beissinger, *The Urban Advantage in Revolution* (forthcoming), chap. 2.

46. Ben Ehrenreich, "Welcome to the Global Rebellion against Neoliberalism," *The Nation*, November 25, 2019, www.thenation.com/article/global-rebellions-inequality/.

47. Jorge Enrique Forero, "A Not So 'Passive' Tide: A Critical Review of the Neo-Gramscian Readings of the Latest Latin American Leftist Turn," paper presented at the July 2017 postgraduate colloquium, Kassel University.

48. Panagiotis Sotiris, "The Realism of Audacity: Rethinking Revolutionary Strategy Today," *Salvage*, 2015, https://salvage.zone/online-exclusive/the-realism-of-audacity-rethinking-revolutionary-strategy-today/.

Chapter 1: Social Movements and the Possibility of Socialist Revolution

1. Thanks for comments on an earlier draft to Anne Alexander, Ian Allinson, Ian Birchall, Jack Bloom, Laurence Cox, Gareth Dale, Anne Englehardt, Cristina Flesher Fominaya, Mike Gonzalez, John Krinsky, Jane McAlevey, Brian McDougall, David McNally, Madelaine Moore, Annie Nehmad, and David Renton. All responsibility remains mine. [Colin was working on this chapter when he died early in 2019. He might have revised it further if he had been given the opportunity, but he felt it was close to what he wanted to say. In any event, we have included it here in the form Colin left it, with only minimal editing, so as to allow his authorial voice to be heard on this last occasion, without external amendment.—Gareth Dale and Neil Davidson]

2. Cinzia Arruzza, "Capitalism and the Conflict over Universality: A Feminist Perspective," *Philosophy Today* 61, no. 4 (2017): 847–61.

3. A friend asked why I make no mention here of the movements in Chiapas, Mexico, and in Rojava (Western Kurdistan), both reportedly characterized by high levels of democratic popular participation. The answer is that I lack adequate information.

4. Mark Fisher, *Capitalist Realism: Is There No Alternative?* (Winchester, UK: Zero Books, 2009), 2.

5. Karl Marx, "Letter to J. Weydemeyer, March 5, 1852," in Karl Marx and Friedrich Engels, *Selected Correspondence* (Moscow: Progress Publishers, 1965), 69.

6. Karl Marx and Friedrich Engels [1845–46], *The German Ideology*, C. J. Arthur, ed. (London: Lawrence and Wishart, 1965), 86.

7. In 1879 Marx and Engels felt it necessary to repeat this as a founding principle: see "Circular Letter to Bebel, Liebknecht, Brache et al.," in *The First International and*

After, David Fernbach, ed. (Harmondsworth: Penguin Books, 1975), 360–75.

8. I first read this in "The Two Souls of Socialism," *International Socialism*, first series, 11 (Winter 1962): 12–19, https://www.marxists.org/archive/draper/1966/twosouls/.

9. Marcus E. Green, "Rethinking the Subaltern and the Question of Censorship in Gramsci's Prison Notebooks," *Postcolonial Studies* 14, no. 4 (2011).

10. Antonio Gramsci, *Prison Notebooks*, vol. 2, Joseph Buttigieg, ed. and trans. (New York: Columbia University Press, 2012), 21; see also Marcus Green, "Gramsci Cannot Speak: Presentations and Interpretations of Gramsci's Concept of the Subaltern," *Rethinking Marxism* 14, no. 3 (2002): 2.

11. Javier Auyero and Débora Alejandra Swistun, *Flammable: Environmental Suffering in an Argentine Shantytown* (Oxford: Oxford University Press, 2009); Javier Auyero, *Patients of the State: The Politics of Waiting in Argentina* (Durham, NC: Duke University Press, 2012).

12. Antonio Gramsci, *Selections from the Prison Notebooks,* Quintin Hoare and Geoffrey Nowell-Smith, eds. (London: Lawrence and Wishart, 1971), 327–28, Q11§12.

13. Gramsci, *Selections from the Prison Notebooks*, 324, 333, Q11§12. The translation has been modified to remove its gendered stresses.

14. Gramsci, *Selections from the Prison Notebooks*, 337, Q11§12.

15. This practical-judgmental aspect of ideology is rightly stressed by Göran Therborn, *The Power of Ideology and the Ideology of Power* (London: Verso, 1980).

16. V. N. Voloshinov [1929], *Marxism and the Theory of Language* (Cambridge, MA: Harvard University Press, 1986).

17. Therborn, *The Power of Ideology and the Ideology of Power*, 77.

18. For Antonio Gramsci, a key notion is the "contradictory" aspect of consciousness, seen for example in the simultaneous combination of the most advanced and the most backward thought in the same "active man-in-the-mass." Alex Callinicos locates a source of such contradictions in the effects of different structural positions on individuals' "interpellations of subjectivity." I would, myself, stress more the shifting and uncertain sense of possibilities for action in the "man (or woman)-in-the-mass" experiences. See Alex Callinicos, *Making History: Agency, Structure and Change in Social Theory* (London: Polity, 1987), 156–57.

19. James C. Scott, *Weapons of the Weak: Everyday Forms of Peasant Resistance* (New Haven, CT: Yale University Press, 1987).

20. Marc Steinberg offers an especially useful review of theories of ideology, in "The Dialogue of Struggle: The Contest over Ideological Boundaries in the Case of the London Silk Weavers in the Early Nineteenth Century," *Social Science History* 18 (1994): 505–42.

21. Michael Lebowitz poses the same question slightly differently: "To struggle against a situation in which workers 'by education, tradition and habit' look upon capital's needs 'as self-evident natural laws,' we must struggle for an *alternative* common sense." "If You're So Smart, Why Aren't You Rich?," *Monthly Review* (April 2015), http://monthlyreview.org/2015/04/01/if-youre-so-smart-why-arent-you-rich/.

22. Contrary to the tendency in sociology in the 1980s to distinguish between "trade unions" and "labor movements" on one side and "social movements" on the other (a dis-

tinction even given institutional expression in US academia), we treat the term "social movements" as *including* workers' organizations and movements.

23. Gerald Marwell and Pamela Oliver, "Collective Action Theory and Social Movements Research," in *Research in Social Movements, Conflict and Change*, vol. 7, Louis Kriesberg, ed. (Greenwich, CT: JAI Press, 1984).

24. A similar logic is applied by E. P. Thompson with respect to the definition of "classes": "To put it bluntly: classes do not exist as separate entities, look around, find an enemy class, and then start to struggle. On the contrary, people find themselves in a society structured in determined ways (crucially, but not exclusively, in productive relations), they experience exploitation (or the need to maintain power over those whom they exploit), they identify points of antagonistic interest, they commence to struggle around these issues and in the process of struggling they discover themselves as classes, they come to know this discovery as class-consciousness. Class and class-consciousness are always the last, not the first, stage in the real historical process." E. P. Thompson, "Eighteenth-Century English Society: Class Struggle without Class?," *Social History* 3, no. 2 (1978): 165.

25. Alf Nilsen and Laurence Cox center their discussion of Marxist accounts of social movements on these differences in scaling and the processes by which movements expand or limit their scope; see "What Would a Marxist Theory of Social Movements look like?" in *Marxism and Social Movements*, Colin Barker, Laurence Cox, John Krinsky, and Alf Gunvald Nilsen, eds. (Chicago: Haymarket Books, 2014).

26. I take the term "cycles of learning" from Michael Vester [1970], *Die Entstehung des Proletariat als Lernprozes: Die Entstehung Antikapitalistischer Theorie und Praxis in England, 1792–1848* (The Emergence of the Working Class as a Learning Process: Development of Anti-capitalist Theory and Practice in England, 1792–1848), 3rd ed. (Europäische Verlagsanstalt: Frankfurt am Main, 1975). I am grateful to Jairus Banaji for providing a partial translation of this classic work: "The Emergence of the Working Class as a Learning Process," *Historical Materialism*, September 20, 2017, http://www. historicalmaterialism.org/blog/emergence-working-class-learning-process.

27. Alan Sears, *The Next New Left: A History of the Future* (Halifax, Canada: Fernwood, 2014), 1–2; see also Jeffery R. Webber, *Red October: Left-Indigenous Struggles in Modern Bolivia* (Leiden: E. J. Brill, 2011), where the concept is put to powerful analytic use. *The Next New Left* explores the challenge of activist renewal in the age of austerity. Over the past few decades, state policy-makers and employers have engaged in a massive process of neo-liberal restructuring that has undermined the basis for social and labor movements. In this book, Alan Sears seeks to understand the social environment that made activist mobilization possible—and was largely taken for granted—during the twentieth century. Just as the neoliberal era has restructured the very foundations of our lives, so too has it undermined the previously existing infrastructure of dissent, meaning that renewal in social movements will depend on the development of new forms of activist capacity-building. The low frequency of social struggles and mass protests in today's society exposes the need for new work by activists and theorists to confront neoliberalism and austerity head-on, and to understand the basis of activ-

ism and the possibilities of its renewal. By examining social movements of the past, Sears's analysis focuses on the means through which activists develop the capacity for solidarity, communication and demonstration and provides readers with possibilities for a renewal of activism in response to the deteriorating living conditions caused by the ongoing austerity offensive. https://github.com/citation-style-language/schema/raw/master/csl-citation.json.

28. Rodrigo Nunes, *Organization of the Organizationless: Collective Action after Networks*, a collaboration between the Post-Media Lab & Mute Books (2014), http://www.meta-mute.org/editorial/books/organisation-organisationless-collective-action-after-networks.

29. Suspicion of "leadership" is a recurring feature of contemporary movements, but seems partly misplaced. For an argument that, properly understood, leadership is an inherent and vital part of democracy, see Colin Barker, Alan Johnson, and Michael Lavalette, "Leadership Matters: An Introduction," in *Leadership in Social Movements*, Colin Barker, Alan Johnson, and Michael Lavalette, eds. (Manchester: Manchester University Press, 2001).

30. For the period before 1970, see George Kolankiewicz, "The Polish Industrial Manual Working Class," in *Social Groups in Polish Society*, David Lane and George Kolank-iewicz, eds. (London: Macmillan, 1973). For the period after 1976, see Colin Barker, *Festival of the Oppressed: Solidarity, Reform and Revolution in Poland 1980–81* (London: Bookmarks, 1986); Jan Jozef Lipski, *KOR: A History of the Workers' Defense Committee in Poland, 1976–1981* (Berkeley: University of California Press, 1985); Lawrence Goodwyn, *Breaking the Barrier: The Rise of Solidarity in Poland* (New York: Oxford University Press, 1991); Roman Laba, *The Roots of Solidarity: A Political Sociology of Poland's Working-Class Democratization* (Princeton, NJ: Princeton University Press, 1991); Michael H. Bernhard, *The Origins of Democratization in Poland: Workers, Intellectuals and Oppositional Politics, 1976–1980* (New York: Columbia University Press, 1993).

31. See Gareth Dale's chapter on Eastern Europe in this volume and Colin Barker and Colin Mooers, "Theories of Revolution in the Light of 1989 in Eastern Europe," *Cultural Dynamics* 9, no. 1 (March 1997): 17–43.

32. Neil Davidson, "The Neoliberal Era in Britain: Historical Developments and Current Perspectives," *International Socialism*, second series, 139 (July 2013): 182–93. For a cogent reminder, see Sam Gindin's comment on the 1950s and 1960s: "It wasn't the subsequent set of policies, summarized as neoliberalism, that created working-class weakness. Rather, those policies exposed the already existing limits of the labor movement and increased the confidence of elites in further exploiting the movement's long-standing weaknesses." "Unmaking Global Capitalism" *Jacobin*, June 1, 2014, https://jacobinmag.com/2014/06/unmaking-global-capitalism.

33. See, for instance, Colin Barker, "The British Labor Movement: Aspects of Current Experience," *International Socialism*, first series, 28 (1967): 13–21; Tony Cliff, "The Balance of Class Forces in Recent Years," *International Socialism*, second series, 6 (1979): 1–50; Chris Harman, *The Fire Last Time: 1968 and After* (London: Bookmarks, 1988); Steve Wright, *Storming Heaven: Class Composition and Struggle in Italian Autonomist Marxism* (London: Pluto Press, 2002); Dan Surkin and Marvin Georgakis, *Detroit,*

I Do Mind Dying: A Study in Urban Revolution (New York: St. Martin's Press, 1975);
James A. Geschwender, *Class, Race, and Worker Insurgency: The League of Revolutionary
Black Workers* (Cambridge: Cambridge University Press, 1977).

34. Peter Alexander and Peter Pfaffe, "Social Relationships to the Means and Ends of
     Protest in South Africa's Ongoing Rebellion of the Poor: The Balfour Insurrections,"
     Social Movement Studies 13, no. 2 (2014): 204–21.

35. Ira Katznelson, *City Trenches: Urban Politics and the Patterning of Class in the United
     States* (New York: Pantheon Books, 1982); Manuel Castells, *The City and Grassroots: A
     Cross-Cultural Theory of Urban Social Movements* (London: Edward Arnold, 1983), 268.

36. Omar G. Encarnación, "Democratizing Spain: Lessons for American Democratic
     Promotion," in *The Politics and Memory of Democratic Transition: The Spanish Model*,
     Gregorio Alonso and Diego Muro, eds. (London: Routledge, 2011), 246.

37. Rosa Luxemburg [1905], *The Mass Strike, the Political Party and the Trade Unions* (London: Bookmarks, 1986), 32.

38. Charles Tilly, "Social Movements as Historically Specific Clusters of Political Per-
     formances," *Berkeley Journal of Sociology* 38 (1993–94): 1–30 (my emphasis, CB); for a
     similar view, see Alan Scott, *Ideology and the New Social Movements* (London: Unwin
     Hyman, 1990). Francesca Polletta suggests that this risks reducing social movements
     to the status of "proto-interest groups." That means conflating a variety of actual or
     potential aspirations of movement adherents to a monolithic group identity, obscuring
     the ways that goals are themselves shaped during actual struggles, and missing the pos-
     sibility that movement goals may include the development of new social and political
     identities. The same structural inequalities may indeed provide the starting point for
     very different collective identities and purposes. See Francesca Polletta, "Strategy and
     Identity in 1960s Black Protest," *Research in Social Movements, Conflict and Change* 17
     (1984): 85–114.

39. It is fairly remarkable how little theoretical attention is paid to internal disagreements
     ("discord") within movements, even though these are part of the everyday experience
     of every significant movement. One writer who proves an exception to this generaliza-
     tion is Cyrus Ernesto Zirakzadeh, *Social Movements in Politics: A Comparative Study*,
     2nd ed. (Harlow: Longman, 1997; London: Palgrave Macmillan, 2006); see also Judith
     Stepan-Norris and Maurice Zeitlin, *LEFT OUT: Reds and America's Industrial Unions*
     (Cambridge: Cambridge University Press, 2003).

40. Leon Trotsky [1932–33], *The History of the Russian Revolution* (London: Pluto Press,
     1977), 17. As Neil Davidson points out, Trotsky's generalization is partly mistaken:
     there have been many revolutions—notably the "revolutions from above" in Europe
     after 1848—which have been "conducted from above" precisely to *forestall* "the forcible
     entrance of the masses." Neil Davidson, "History from Below," *Jacobin*, January 2018,
     https://jacobinmag.com/2018/01/leon-trotsky-russian-revolution-stalin-lenin. These
     "revolutions from above"—notably the unifications of Italy and Germany—provided
     the models for Gramsci's theorizing of "passive revolution."

41. Goodwyn, *Breaking the Barrier*, xxxi.

42. Alan Shandro, "'Consciousness from Without': Marxism, Lenin and the Proletariat,"

Science and Society 59, no. 3 (1995): 268–97.

43. Gramsci, *Selections*, 353, Q10II§54 (translation modified)

44. Cited in Chris Harman [1973], *Class Struggles in Eastern Europe, 1945–83*, 2nd ed. (London: Pluto Press, 1983), 262.

45. Martin Luther King Jr., "Our Struggle," *Liberation*, April 1956, in *The Papers of Martin Luther King Jr.*, vol. 3, Clayborne Carson, ed. (Berkeley: University of California Press, 1997), 238, and at https://kinginstitute.stanford.edu/king-papers/documents/our-struggle.

46. Sidney Tarrow, *Democracy and Disorder: Protest and Politics in Italy, 1965–1975* (Oxford: Clarendon, 1989), 20.

47. Raquel Varela and Joana Alcântara, "Social Conflicts in the Portuguese Revolution, 1974–1975," *Labour/Le Travail* 74 (Fall 2014): 151–177; Colin Barker, *Festival of the Oppressed*; Anne Alexander and Mostafa Bassiouny, *Bread, Freedom, Social Justice: Workers and the Egyptian Revolution* (London: Zed Books, 2014), especially 285–318; Philip Marfleet, *Egypt: Contested Revolution* (London: Pluto Press, 2016), 8, 31, 59, 118.

48. No serious general strike movement can avoid dealing with the food question, without risk of being starved back to work.

49. Jeremy Brecher, *Strike!* (Boston: South End Press, 1978).

50. Chris Ealham, *Class, Culture and Conflict in Barcelona* (London: Routledge, 2005), 154, 160–62; Andy Durgan, "Workers' Democracy in the Spanish Revolution, 1936–1939," in *Ours to Master and Own: Workers Control from the Commune to the Present*, Immanuel Ness and Dario Azzellini, eds. (Chicago: Haymarket Books, 2011), 157–61.

51. Diana Denham and CASA Collective, *Teaching Rebellion: Stories from the Grassroots Mobilization in Oaxaca* (Oakland, CA: PM Press, 2008); Richard Roman and Edur Velasco Arregui, "Mexico's Oaxaca Commune," in *Socialist Register 2008: Global Flashpoints*, Leo Panitch and Colin Ley, eds. (London: Merlin Press, 2008).

52. Kevin Ovenden, *Syriza: Inside the Labyrinth* (London: Pluto Press, 2015), 61–62.

53. One strike delegate from a Gdansk-area factory recorded that the occupation-strike went badly in his workplace precisely because they didn't pay attention to these matters. See Jan Szylak, "My Reminiscences of August 1980," in *Sisyphus Sociological Studies*, vol. 3, *Crises and Conflicts, The Case of Poland 1980–1981*, Wladyslaw W. Adamski, ed. (Warsaw: PWN–Polish Scientific Publishers, 1982).

54. Jan Gajda, "August 1980 as I Saw It," in *Sisyphus Sociological Studies* 3; see also earlier examples of worker justice in Boaventura de Sousa Santos, "Popular Justice, Dual Power and Socialist Strategy," in *Capitalism and the Rule of Law*, Bod Fine, ed. (London: Hutchinson, 1979).

55. David McNally, "'Unity of the Diverse': Working Class Formations and Popular Uprisings from Cochabamba to Cairo," in *Marxism and Social Movements*.

56. Raúl Zibechi, "Counter-Power and Self-Defense in Latin America," *ROAR Magazine*, January 29, 2018, https://roarmag.org/essays/raul-zibechi-counterpower-self-defense/.

57. Ricky J. Pope, and Shawn T. Flanigan, "Revolution for Breakfast: Intersections of Activism, Service, and Violence in the Black Panther Party's Community Service Programs," *Social Justice Research* 28, no. 3 (2013): 445–70.

58. Raúl Zibechi, "From Social Movements to 'Other' Societies in Movement," *Upside Down World*, October 9, 2017, http://upsidedownworld.org/archives/international/social-movements-societies-movement-part-1/.

59. Luxemburg, *The Mass Strike*, 39–41.

60. Luxemburg, *The Mass Strike*, 32.

61. Pamela E. Oliver, "Bringing the Crowd Back In: The Non-organizational Elements of Social Movements," *Research in Social Movements, Conflict and Change* 11 (1989): 1–30.

62. Webber, *Red October*; see also McNally, "'Unity of the Diverse.'"

63. Aristide L. Zolberg, "Moments of Madness," *Politics and Society* 2 (1972): 183–207. Frances Fox Piven and Richard Cloward doubt that workers generalize: "People experience deprivation and oppression within a concrete setting, not as the end product of large and abstract processes, and it is the concrete experience that molds their discontent into specific grievances against specific targets. Workers experience the factory, the speeding rhythm of the assembly line, the foreman, the spies and the guards, the owner and the paycheck. They do not experience monopoly capitalism." See *Poor People's Movements: Why They Succeed, How They Fail* (New York: Pantheon, 1977), 20–21. This quite misses the *compulsion* to "philosophize" that arises in mass movements.

64. Moira Birss, "The Piquetero Movement: Organizing for Democracy and Social Change in Argentina's Informal Sector," *Journal of the International Institute* 12, no. 2, (2005): https://quod.lib.umich.edu/j/jii/4750978.0012.206/--piquetero-movement-organizing-for-democracy-and-social?rgn=main;view=fulltext; see also Javier Auyero, *Contentious Lives: Two Argentine Women, Two Protests, and the Quest for Recognition* (Durham, NC: Duke University Press, 2003).

65. Colin Barker, *Festival of the Oppressed*; Jadwiga Staniszkis, *Poland's Self-Limiting Revolution* (Princeton, NJ: Princeton University Press, 1984); Colin Barker, "Crises and Turning Points in Revolutionary Development: Emotion, Organization and Strategy in Solidarność, 1980–81," *Interface: A Journal for and about Social Movements* 2, no. 1 (2010): http://interfacejournal.nuim.ie/wordpress/wp-content/uploads/2010/11/Interface-2-1-pp79-117-Barker.pdf.

66. Kevin Ovenden, *Syriza: Inside the Labyrinth* (London: Pluto Press, 2015), 19, 54.

67. Oskar Anweiler, *The Soviets: The Russian Workers, Peasants, and Soldiers Councils, 1905–1921* (New York: Pantheon Books, 1974), 168–78.

68. Mike Gonzalez, "Chile 1972–3: The Workers United," in *Revolutionary Rehearsals*, Colin Barker, ed. (London: Bookmarks, 1987); Marina Adler, "Collective Identity Formation and Collective Action Framing in a Mexican 'Movement of Movements,'" *Interface: A Journal for and about Social Movements* 4, no.1 (2012): 287–315. See also Peter Saxtrup Nielsen, "The Strategic Role of the Soviets in the Class Struggle," *International Viewpoint*, January 22, 2018, http://internationalviewpoint.org/spip.php?article5343&utm.

69. Barker, *Festival of the Oppressed*; David Ost, *Solidarity and the Politics of Anti-politics: Opposition and Reform in Poland since 1968* (Philadelphia: Temple University Press, 1990).

70. See the discussion among leading activists from the KOR network, notably Jacek

Kuroń and Bogdan Borusewicz, in *Labor Focus on Eastern Europe* 4, nos. 4–6 (1981): 15, and the discussion in Barker, *Festival of the Oppressed.*

71. For one general survey, see Neil Davidson, "Right-Wing Social Movements: The Political Indeterminacy of Mass Mobilization," in *Marxism and Social Movements.*

72. See Philip Marfleet, *Egypt: Contested Revolution* (London: Pluto Press, 2016), 154–56.

73. Pierre Broué [1971], *The German Revolution 1917–1923* (Leiden: E. J. Brill, 2006); Chris Harman, *The Lost Revolution: Germany 1918–1923* (London: Bookmarks, 1982).

74. We have to thank John Riddell for the volumes of Comintern debates he has translated and edited. See especially *Toward the United Front: Proceedings of the Fourth Congress of the Communist International, 1922* (Chicago: Haymarket Books, 2012).

75. Gramsci, *Selections from the Prison Notebooks*, 260, Q6§137.

76. Peter Thomas, *The Gramscian Moment: Philosophy, Hegemony, and Marxism* (Leiden: E. J. Brill, 2010).

77. According to the International Labor Organization, the global labor force grew between 1980 and 2007 from 1.9 billion to 3.1 billion, a rise of 63 percent—with 73 percent of the labor force located in the developing world, and 40 percent in China and India alone. The South's share of industrial employment rose from 51 percent in 1980 to 73 percent in 2008. See John Bellamy Foster, Robert W. McChesney, and R. Jamil Jonna, "The Global Reserve Army of Labor and the New Imperialism," *Monthly Review* 63, no. 6 (November 2011).

78. According to the British Office for National Statistics, the service sector includes "retail, hotels, restaurants, transport, storage, IT, finance, insurance, real estate, administration and support services, professional, scientific and technical services, education, health, social work, arts, entertainment, recreation, public administration, defense, etc."; it employs 80 percent of Britain's labor force and 91 percent of London's. (Thanks to Mike Haynes for this information.)

79. "If we take the categories of the unemployed, the vulnerably employed, and the economically inactive population in prime working ages (25–54) and add them together, we come up with what might be called the *maximum size of the global reserve army* in 2011: some 2.4 billion people, compared to 1.4 billion in the active labor army. It is the existence of a reserve army that in its maximum extent is more than 70 percent larger than the active labor army that serves to restrain wages globally, and particularly in the poorer countries." See Bellamy Foster et al., "The Global Reserve Army of Labor."

80. Sara Farris notes that women now constitute the majority of migrants to Europe, above all to work in the care and domestic sectors. Work in these sectors is not easily mechanized, which has had two consequences: "Not only [has] domestic-care work . . . been mostly redistributed onto the shoulders of migrant women or partly commercialized, but also . . . it is one of those sectors where Marx's analysis of the reserve army of labor cannot be easily applied. . . . The female migrant workforce thus seems to amount not to a reserve army, constantly threatened with unemployment and deportation and used in order to maintain wage discipline, but to a regular army of extremely cheap labor." See "Femonationalism and the 'Regular' Army of Labor Called Migrant Women," *History of the Present* 2, no. 2 (2012). See also Ewa Jasiewicz, "At Your Service? Migrant

Women Workers in the UK Hospitality Sector," Novara Media, March 10, 2017, http://novaramedia.com/2017/03/10/at-your-service-migrant-women-workers-in-the-uk-hospitality-sector/.

81. For an interesting view from China, see Chris Smith and Pun Ngai, "Class and Precarity in China: A Contested Relationship," *Chinoiresie*, http://www.chinoiresie.info/class-precarity-in-china/.

82. In the UK, the numbers of workers on "zero hours contracts" quadrupled from 225,000 in 2000 to 900,000 in 2016. Georgina Lee, "The Number of People on Zero Hours Contracts Has Quadrupled since Records Began," Channel 4, August 7, 2017, https://www.channel4.com/news/factcheck/the-number-of-people-on-zero-hours-contracts-has-quadrupled-since-records-began.

83. Susan Ferguson and David McNally, "Precarious Migrants: Gender, Race and the Social Reproduction of a Global Working Class," *Socialist Register 2015*: *Transforming Classes*, Leo Panitch and Greg Albo, eds. (London: Merlin Press, 2014).

84. Heide Gerstenberger, "State, Capital, Crisis," *ACME: An International E-Journal for Critical Geographies* 12, no. 2 (2013): 349–65.

85. Gerstenberger, "State, Capital, Crisis."

86. Paul D. Almeida, "Defensive Mobilization: Popular Movements against Economic Adjustment Measures in Latin America," *Latin American Perspectives* 34, no. 3 (May 2007): 123–39; see also Jerome Roos, "The New Debt Colonies," *Viewpoint*, February 2018, https://www.viewpointmag.com/2018/02/01/new-debt-colonies/.

87. Jerome Roos, *Why Not Default? The Political Economy of Sovereign Debt* (Princeton, NJ: Princeton University Press, 2019); see also Roos, "The New Debt Colonies."

88. Adam Bott, "Sweden's Great Welfare Heist," *Red Pepper*, April 2014.

89. Allyson M. Pollock, *NHS Plc: The Privatization of Our Health Care* (London: Verso, 2015).

90. Ovenden, *Syriza*.

91. Patrick Bond, Ashwin Desai, and Trevor Ngwane, "Uneven and Combined Marxisms within South Africa's Urban Social Movements," in *Marxism and Social Movements*; Edmund Amann and Werner Baer, "Neoliberalism and Its Consequences in Brazil," *Journal of Latin American Studies* 34, no. 2 (2002); Jeffery R. Webber, *From Rebellion to Reform in Bolivia: Class Struggle, Indigenous Liberation, and the Politics of Evo Morales* (Chicago: Haymarket Books, 2011).

92. Kim Moody, *In Solidarity: Essays on Working-Class Organization and Strategy in the United States* (Chicago: Haymarket Books, 2014).

93. Paul Kellogg, personal communication.

94. Dan Clawson and Mary Anne Clawson, "What Has Happened to the US Labor Movement? Union Decline and Renewal," *Annual Review of Sociology* 25 (1999): 97.

95. Kim Moody and Charles Post, "The Politics of US Labor: Paralysis and Possibilities," *Socialist Register 2015*, 2.

96. Jeffery R. Webber et al., "Return of the Strike: A Forum on the Teachers' Rebellion in the United States," *Historical Materialism* 26, no. 4 (2018).

97. In Britain, major unions have similarly argued for short-term "job-saving" strategies in

support of fracking, nuclear power, and the Trident missile system.

98. Jane McAlevey, *No Shortcuts: Organizing for Power in the New Gilded Age* (Oxford: Oxford University Press, 2016).

99. Colin Barker and Gareth Dale, "Protest Waves in Western Europe: A Critique of 'New Social Movement' Theory," *Critical Sociology* 24, nos. 1–2 (1998).

100. Cristina Flesher, "Fominaya: European Anti-austerity and Pro-democracy Protests in the Wake of the Global Financial Crisis," *Social Movement Studies* 16, no. 1 (2017).

101. Paul Almeida, "Defensive Mobilization."

102. Raúl Zibechi, "Progressive Fatigue? Coming to Terms with the Latin American Left's New 'Coyuntura,'" *NACLA Report on the Americas* 48, no. 1 (2016): 22–27; see also Jeffery R. Webber, "Assessing the Pink Tide," *Jacobin*, April 11, 2017; Jeffery R. Webber, *The Last Day of Oppression, and the First Day of the Same: The Politics and Economics of the New Latin American Left* (Chicago: Haymarket Books, 2017).

103. David J. Bailey, "Contending the Crisis: What Role for Extra-parliamentary British Politics?," *British Politics* 9, no. 1 (2014); see also David J. Bailey, "Hard Evidence: This Is the Age of Dissent—and There's Much More to Come," The Conversation, January 11, 2016, https://theconversation.com/hard-evidence-this-is-the-age-of-dissent-and-theres-much-more-to-come-52871.

104. See, for example, Tithi Bhattacharya, ed., *Social Reproduction Theory: Remapping Class, Recentering Oppression* (London: Pluto Pres, 2017); Notes from Below editors, "The Workers' Inquiry and Social Composition," *Notes from Below*, January 29, 2018, http://www.notesfrombelow.org/article/workers-inquiry-and-social-composition.

105. Miguel A. Martínez López, "Between Autonomy and Hybridity: Urban Struggles within the 15M Movement in Spain," in *Urban Uprisings: Challenging Neoliberal Urbanism in Europe*, Margit Mayer, Catharina Thörn, and Håkan Thörn, eds. (London: Macmillan, 2016).

106. Commentary on the "indignados" and Occupy movements of 2016 seemed to be especially prone to this kind of exaggeration. What was forgotten is how often former "breakthroughs" also get forgotten: blogging about his visit to Occupy Wall Street in the autumn of 2011, Benjamin Junge recorded, "The whole time I'm there, I only see one instance where someone has used rhetoric from the World Social Forum (a la 'Another World Is Possible'). This is rather striking to me. I mention the WSF (and the two US Social Forums, Atlanta and Detroit) to everyone I meet and without exception no one's heard of it or them. How can this be?" Who in a new generation of protesters will recall "Occupy"? Benjamin Junge, Notes from Visit to "Occupy Wall Street," October 10, 2011.

107. Alan Sears, *The Next New Left: A History of the Future* (Halifax: Fernwood Publishing, 2014).

108. Kim Moody, "Labor's New Sources of Leverage," interview by Chris Brooks, *Labor Notes*, August 12, 2016, http://labornotes.org/MoodyInterview.

109. McAlevey, *No Shortcuts*, chap. 4.

110. Black American scholar Cedric Johnson offers some cogent arguments in "The Panthers Can't Save Us Now," *Catalyst* 1, no. 1 (2017): https://catalyst-journal.com/vol1/

no1/panthers-cant-save-us-cedric-johnson.

111. That argument appears in Jeff Goodwin, *No Other Way Out: States and Revolutionary Movements, 1945–1991* (Cambridge: Cambridge University Press, 2001).

112. Webber, "Assessing the Pink Tide"; Webber, *The Last Day of Oppression*, chap. 9; Mike Gonzalez, *The Ebb of the Pink Tide: The Decline of the Left in Latin America* (London: Pluto Press, 2018), and his chapter in this volume.

113. Raúl Zibechi, in an interview in early 2019, summarized: "I believe that the politics of the progressive governments, specifically the politics of subsidies or the monetary transfers to popular sectors to integrate leaders of the movement into the governments have produced a great debilitation, the movements have been demobilized to a certain extent." See "The State of Social Movements in Latin America: An Interview with Raúl Zibechi," Black Rose Anarchist Federation, January 17, 2019, http://blackrosefed. org/social-movements-latin-america-zibechi/.

114. Cited in Webber, "Assessing the Pink Tide."

Chapter 2: 1989: Revolution and Regime Change in Central and Eastern Europe

1. Jürgen Habermas, *Die Nachholende Revolution* (Frankfurt/Main: Suhrkamp, 1990).

2. Richard Wilkinson, *The Impact of Inequality: How to Make Sick Societies Healthier* (London: Routledge, 2005), 113–14.

3. World Wildlife Fund, "Living Planet Report," 2012, http://wwf.panda.org/about_our_ earth/all_publications/living_planet_report/.

4. Jana Juráňová, "How Our Past Is Still in Our Present," in *Women in Times of Change, 1989–2009*, Agnieszka Grzybek, ed. (Warsaw: Heinrich Böll Stiftung, 2009).

5. Nikolai Genov, *Global Trends in Eastern Europe* (Aldershot, UK: Ashgate, 2010), 17.

6. See, for example, Peter Gowan, *Global Gamble: Washington's Faustian Bid for World Dominance* (London: Verso, 1999). Gowan underestimated the degree to which the Council for Mutual Economic Assistance was fragmenting and reorienting toward the global economy, independently of US blandishments.

7. Georgi Derluguian, "What Communism Was," in *Does Capitalism Have a Future?* Immanuel Wallerstein et al., eds. (Oxford: Oxford University Press, 2013).

8. Peter Haslinger, "Gewaltoptionen und Handlungslogiken im Revolutionsjahr 1989 in Ostmitteleuropa," in *1989 und die Rolle der Gewalt*, Martin Sabrow, ed. (Göttingen: Wallstein, 2012), 259.

9. Eduard Rudolf Roth, "The Romanian Revolution of 1989 and the Veracity of the External Subversion Theory," *Journal of Contemporary Central and Eastern Europe* 24, no. 1 (2016).

10. Claus Offe, "Wohlstand, Nation, Republik. Aspekte des deutschen Sonderweges vom Sozialismus zum Kapitalismus," in *Der Zusammenbruch der DDR* (Frankfurt/Main: Suhrkamp, 1993), 293–94; Claus Offe, *Varieties of Transition: The East European and East German Experience* (Cambridge: Polity, 1996), 21; Robert Kurz, *Honecker's Rache* (Berlin: Edition TIAMAT, 1991), 48; Wolfgang Haug, *Das Perestrojka-Journal* (Ham-

burg: Argument, 1990), 31.

11. Charles Maier, *Dissolution: The Crisis of Communism and the End of East Germany* (Princeton, NJ: Princeton University Press, 1997), xiv, 119.

12. Nigel Swain, "Negotiated Revolution in Poland and Hungary, 1989," in *Revolution and Resistance in Eastern Europe: Challenges to Communist Rule*, Kevin McDermott and Matthew Stibbe, eds. (Dorset: Berg, 2006), 152.

13. Maier, *Dissolution*, xiv.

14. Detlef Pollack, "Die Friedlichkeit der Herbstakteure 1989," in *1989 und die Rolle der Gewalt*.

15. Edward Hamelrath, "Zwischen Gewalteskalation und Sicherheitspartnerschaft: Der Fall Dresden," in *1989 und die Rolle der Gewalt*, 209.

16. Heiner Bröckermann, "Die Nationale Volksarmee und die Gewaltfrage im Herbst 1989," in *1989 und die Rolle der Gewalt*.

17. Pollack, "Die Friedlichkeit der Herbstakteure 1989."

18. Armin Mitter and Stefan Wolle, *"Ich liebe euch doch alle . . .": Befehle und Lageberichte des MfS* (Berlin: BasisDruck, 1990), 248.

19. James Krapfl, *Revolution with a Human Face, Politics, Culture, and Community in Czechoslovakia, 1989–1992* (Ithaca, NY: Cornell University Press, 2013).

20. Lawrence Goodwyn, *Breaking the Barrier: The Rise of Solidarity in Poland* (Oxford: Oxford University Press, 1991).

21. David Stefancic, *Robotnik: A Short History of the Struggle for Worker Self-Management and Free Trade Unions in Poland* (New York: Columbia University Press, 1992), 2–7.

22. Cyrus Zirakzadeh, *Social Movements in Politics* (London: Longman, 1997), 114.

23. David Ost, *Solidarity and the Politics of Anti-Politics: Opposition and Reform in Poland since 1968* (Philadelphia: Temple University Press, 1990); Colin Barker, *Festival of the Oppressed: Solidarity, Reform and Revolution in Poland* (London: Bookmarks, 1986).

24. Linda Fuller, *Where Was the Working Class? Revolution in Eastern Germany* (Chicago: University of Illinois Press, 1999).164.

25. Goodwyn, *Breaking the Barrier*, 205 and passim.

26. Goodwyn, *Breaking the Barrier*, 83.

27. Goodwyn, *Breaking the Barrier*, 245.

28. Zirakzadeh, *Social Movements in Politics*, 115–16.

29. Fuller, *Where Was the Working Class?*, 160–61.

30. Axel Bust-Bartels, *Herrschaft und Widerstand in den DDR-Betrieben* (Frankfurt/Main: Campus, 1980), 28.

31. Renate Hürtgen, "Keiner hatte Ahnung von Demokratie, im Betrieb sowieso nicht.' Vom kollektiven Widerstand Zur Eingabe oder Warum die Belegschaften 1989 am Anfang eines Neubeginns standen," in *Der betriebliche Aufbruch im Herbst 1989. Die unbekannte Seite der DDR Revolution*, Bernd Gehrke and Renate Hürtgen, eds. (Berlin: Bildungswerk, 2001).

32. Jörg Roesler, "Die Produktionsbrigaden in der Industrie der DDR," in *Sozialgeschichte der DDR*, Hartmut Kaelble et al., eds. (Stuttgart: Klett-Cotta; Peter Hübner, 1994); "Stagnation or Change? Transformations of the Workplace in the GDR," in *Dictator-*

ship as Experience: Towards a Socio-Cultural History of the GDR, Konrad Jarausch, ed. (Oxford: Berghahn, 1999).

33. Jeffrey Kopstein, *The Politics of Economic Decline in East Germany, 1945–1989* (Chapel Hill: University of North Carolina Press, 1997), 12.

34. Axel Bust-Bartels, "Humanisierung der Arbeit," *Aus Politik und Zeitgeschichte*, October 29, 1977, p. 54.

35. *Zurück zu Deutschland* (Bonn: Bouvier, 1990), 261ff.

36. Satnam Virdee, "Racism and Resistance in the British Trade Unions, 1948–79," paper presented at Racializing Identity, Classifying Race conference, St. Antony's College, Oxford, 1997.

37. See especially Franz Walter, "Freital: Das 'Rote Wien Sachsens,'" in Franz Walter, Tobias Dürr, and Klaus Schmidtke, *Die SPD in Sachsen und Thüringen zwischen Hochburg und Diaspora* (Bonn: Dietz, 1993).

38. Bernd Gehrke and Renate Hürtgen, eds., *Der Betriebliche Aufbruch im Herbst 1989*, 280.

39. Bernd Gehrke, "Demokratiebewegung und Betriebe in der 'Wende.' Plädoyer für einen längst fälligen Perspektivwechsel?," in *Der betriebliche Aufbruch im Herbst 1989*, 211.

40. Gehrke, "Demokratiebewegung und Betriebe," 37.

41. Fuller, *Where Was the Working Class?*, 19.

42. Fuller, *Where Was the Working Class?*, 33.

43. Ehrhart Neubert, *Eine protestantische Revolution* (Berlin: Kontext, 1990), 66.

44. Krapfl, *Revolution with a Human Face*.

45. Jan Wielgohs and Helmut Müller-Enbergs, "Die Bürgerbewegung Demokratie Jetzt," in Helmut Müller-Enbergs et al., *Von der Illegalität ins Parlament* (Berlin: Links, 1991), 137.

46. Marianne Schulz, "Neues Forum," in *Von der Illegalität ins Parlament*, Helmut Müller-Enbergs et al., eds. (Berlin: Links, 1991), 20–21.

47. Fuller, *Where Was the Working Class?*, 98–100.

48. Fuller, *Where Was the Working Class?*, 84.

49. Francesca Weil, "Wirtschafliche, politische und soziale Veränderungen in einem Leipziger Betrieb 1989/90," in *Revolution und Transformation in der DDR*, Günther Heydemann et al., eds. (Berlin: Duncker and Humblot, 1999), 536.

50. Fuller, *Where Was the Working Class?*, 37.

51. Karl-Dieter Opp et al., *Die volkseigene Revolution* (Stuttgart: Klett-Cotta, 1993), 214, emphasis added; Karl-Dieter Opp et al., *Origins of a Spontaneous Revolution: East Germany, 1989* (Ann Arbor: University of Michigan Press, 1995), 164.

52. According to a survey of some five thousand demonstrators conducted by Kurt Mühler, Steffen Wilsdorf, and Leipzig students, members of the intelligentsia made up between 17 and 33 percent of Leipzig demonstrators between November 1989 and February 1990. (Kurt Mühler and Steffen Wilsdorf, "Die Leipziger Montagsdemonstration – Aufstieg und Wandel einer basisdemokratischen Institution des friedlichen Umbruchs im Spiegel empirischer Meinungsforschung," *Berliner Journal der Soziologie*, 1991, 1.) While the former figure is low relative to the intelligentsia's weight in society, the latter is not and would appear to contradict the findings of Opp et al. Alternatively, it may

signify a greater willingness of graduates to return questionnaires.

53. In Wayne Bartee's survey of Leipzig demonstrators, most were clearly in working-class occupations (30 percent blue collar; 15 percent teachers, nurses, technicians, museum, and clerical workers). Some categories cannot clearly be identified in class terms, e.g., "salaried employees" in industries such as publishing (30 percent), or those in church-related jobs other than clergy (5 percent). But in such cases it is fair to assume that the bulk of occupations covered were working class (e.g., copy editor, secretary, cleaner) rather than middle class (e.g., bookshop manager). See Wayne C. Bartee, *A Time to Speak Out: The Leipzig Citizen Protests and the Fall of East Germany* (Santa Barbara, CA: Praeger, 2000), 125.

54. Bernd Lindner, "Die Politische Kultur der Straße als Medium der Veränderung," *Aus Politik und Zeitgeschichte*, 27 (1990), 23.

55. Steven Pfaff, "From Revolution to Reunification: Popular Protests, Social Movements and the Transformation of East Germany" (PhD thesis, New York University, 1999), 506; Gehrke, "Demokratiebewegung und Betriebe in der 'Wende' 1989," 215.

56. Susanne Lohmann, "The Dynamics of Informational Cascades: The Monday Demonstrations in Leipzig, East Germany, 1989–91," *World Politics* 47 (1994): 62.

57. Uwe Bastian, "'Auf zum letzten Gefecht . . .' Dokumentation über die Vorbereitungen des MfS auf den Zusammenbruch der DDR Wirtschaft," Arbeitspapiere des Forschungsverbundes SED-Staat, 9, Berlin: Freie Universität, 33–34.

58. Armin Mitter and Stefan Wolle, *Ich liebe euch doch alle . . .* (Berlin: BasisDruck, 1990), 226.

59. See, e.g. Lutz Rathenow, "Nachdenken über Deutschland," in Hubertus Knabe, ed., *Aufbruch in eine andere DDR* (Reinbek: Rowohlt, 1989), 286.

60. Dresden Region Stasi files (my thanks are due Hans-Jochen Vogel for supplying copies of files from the Dresden Stasi archives); *Telegraph* (dissident GDR periodical), no. 4; Ehrhart Neubert, *Geschichte der Opposition in der DDR, 1949–1989* (Berlin: Links, 1998), 851.

61. Gehrke, "Die 'Wende'-Streiks. Eine erste Skizze," in *Der betriebliche Aufbruch im Herbst 1989*, 253.

62. Igor Maximytschew and Hans-Hermann Hertle, "Die Maueröffnung," *Deutschland Archiv* 27 (1994): 1143.

63. Otto König, speaking to the SED Central Committee on November 9, BA-SAPMO, Parteiarchiv, IV 2/1/709.

64. Hartmut Zwahr, *Ende einer Selbstzerstörung* (Göttingen: Vandenhoek & Ruprecht, 1993), 60.

65. Krapfl, *Revolution with a Human Face*.

66. Donatella Della Porta, "Cycles of Protest and the Consolidation of Democracy," *Partecipazione e Conflitto: Open Journal of Sociopolitical Studies* 7, no. 3 (2014): 447–68.

67. Krapfl, *Revolution with a Human Face*.

68. Krapfl, *Revolution with a Human Face*.

69. Rita Pawlowski, "No State Can Exist without Women! German 'Turning Point' Experiences 1989/90 and Afterwards," in *Women in Times of Change, 1989–2009*, Agnieszka

Grzybek, ed. (Warsaw: Heinrich Böll Stiftung, 2009); Eva Schäfer, "Die fröhliche Revolution der Frauen," in *Wir Wollen Mehr als ein "Vaterland": DDR-Frauen im Aufbruch*, Gislinde Schwarz and Christine Zenner, eds. (Reinbek: Rowohlt, 1990), 28.

70. Cordula Kahlau, ed., *Aufbruch! Frauenbewegung in der DDR* (München: Verlag Frauenoffensive, 1990), 168.

71. Stefan Troebst, "Bulgarien 1989: Gewaltarmer Regimewandel in Gewaltträchtigem Umfeld," in *1989 und die Rolle der Gewalt*.

72. Jake Lowinger, *Economic Reform and the "Double Movement" in Yugoslavia: An Analysis of Labor Unrest and Ethno-Nationalism in the 1980s* (Ann Arbor, MI: ProQuest, 2011).

73. Jaruzelski, quoted in Włodzimierz Borodziej, "Vom Warschauer Aufstand zum Runden Tisch: Politik und Gewalt in Polen 1944–1989," in *1989 und die Rolle der Gewalt*, 297.

74. Document archived in BA SAPMO, SED-Parteiarchiv, and cited in Gareth Dale, *Between State Capitalism and Globalisation: The Collapse of the East German Economy* (Oxford: Peter Lang, 2004).

75. Borodziej, "Vom Warschauer Aufstand zum Runden Tisch," in *1989 und die Rolle der Gewalt*.

76. Jack Bloom, *Seeing through the Eyes of the Polish Revolution: Solidarity and the Struggle against Communism in Poland* (Leiden: E. J. Brill, 2013), 275.

77. David Ost, *The Defeat of Solidarity: Anger and Politics in Postcommunist Europe* (Ithaca, NY: Cornell University Press, 2005), 41.

78. Padraic Kenney, *A Carnival of Revolution: Central Europe, 1989* (Princeton, NJ: Princeton University Press, 2002).

79. Ost, *The Defeat of Solidarity*, 46.

80. Ost, *The Defeat of Solidarity*, 46.

81. Nigel Swain, "Negotiated Revolution in Poland and Hungary, 1989," in *Revolution and Resistance in Eastern Europe: Challenges to Communist Rule*, Kevin McDermott and Matthew Stibbe, eds. (London: Berg, 2006), 142.

82. Pollack, "Die Friedlichkeit der Herbstakteure 1989."

83. Jochen Lässig, quoted in Pfaff, "From Revolution to Reunification," 508.

84. Hamelrath, "Zwischen Gewalteskalation und Sicherheitspartnerschaft," 222.

85. Krapfl, *Revolution with a Human Face*.

86. Krapfl, *Revolution with a Human Face*.

87. Nina Bandelj, *From Communists to Foreign Capitalists: The Social Foundations of Foreign Direct Investment in Postsocialist Europe* (Princeton, NJ: Princeton University Press, 2011), 63–64; Cornel Ban, *Ruling Ideas: How Global Neoliberalism Goes Local* (Oxford: Oxford University Press, 2016).

88. Ost, *The Defeat of Solidarity*, 20.

89. Ost, *The Defeat of Solidarity*, 35.

90. Colin Barker, "Empowerment and Resistance: 'Collective Effervescence' and Other Accounts," in *Transforming Politics: Explorations in Sociology*, Paul Bagguley and Jeff Hearn, eds. (Palgrave Macmillan: London, 1999).

91. Donnacha Ó Beacháin and Abel Polese, "Introduction," in *The Color Revolutions in the Former Soviet Republics*, Donnacha Ó Beacháin and Abel Polese, eds. (London: Rout-

ledge, 2010), 7.

92. Francoise Companjen, "Georgia," in *The Color Revolutions in the Former Soviet Republics*, 15.
93. Nathaniel Copsey, "Ukraine," in *The Color Revolutions in the Former Soviet Republics*, 41.
94. David Lewis, "Kyrgyzstan," in *The Color Revolutions in the Former Soviet Republics*, 47–56.
95. Vladimir Ilyich Lenin, "Two Tactics of Social-Democracy in the Democratic Revolution," 1905, www.marxists.org/archive/lenin/works/1905/tactics/ch13.htm.
96. Andrew Wilson, *Ukraine's Orange Revolution* (New Haven, CT: Yale University Press, 2005), 75, 199.
97. Copsey, "Ukraine," 36.
98. Brian Grodsky, *Social Movements and the New State: The Fate of Pro-democracy Organizations When Democracy Is Won* (Redwood City, CA: Stanford University Press, 2012); Lincoln Mitchell, *The Color Revolutions* (Philadelphia: University of Pennsylvania Press, 2012), 173; Companjen, "Georgia," 24.
99. Copsey, "Ukraine," 43.
100. Lewis, "Kyrgyzstan," 46.
101. Mitchell, *The Color Revolutions*, 170.

Chapter 3: The End of Apartheid in South Africa

1. In 2012, police murdered thirty-four strikers at a Lonmin platinum mine, where Ramaphosa was a director.
2. John S. Saul, "The Transition in South Africa: Choice, Fate . . . or Recolonisation?," *Critical Arts* 26, no. 4 (September 2012): 592, https://doi.org/10.1080/02560046.2012.723850.
3. Saul, "The Transition in South Africa," 591–92.
4. Pallo Jordan, "The African National Congress: From Illegality to the Corridors of Power," *Review of African Political Economy* 31, no. 100 (June 2004): 204, https://doi.org/10.1080/0305624042000262248. It argues that radical policy shifts have from the party's birth in 1912 been part of its political reality so that heterodoxy has often become the new orthodoxy. This tradition of change has been accelerated by local and global realities since 1994—an assumption of office with virtually no power over the civil service and upper reaches of the security forces and a post-Cold War environment which generated a demonised state intervention. Being in office has also changed the character of the ANC with the party now attracting those seeking a career and the perks of office, a consequence of which has been repeated allegations of the misuse of state funds levelled against ANC representatives. Finally, the paper notes that the ANC's second term has been marked by growing tensions with the Communist Party and a foreign policy with, as its central pillar, the creating of space for Africa to define its own future.
5. Claire Ceruti, "How and Why the ANC's Nationalization Policy Changed: Economic Nationalism and the Changing State-Capital Relation" (master's diss., University of the Witwatersrand, 1995), 230–31.
6. David Webster and Maggie Friedman, "Repression and the State of Emergency: June

1987–March 1989," in *South African Review* 5, Glen Moss and Ingrid Obery, eds. (Johannesburg: Ravan Press and South African Research Services, 1989), 17.

7. Webster and Friedman, "Repression and the State of Emergency," 22.

8. Webster and Friedman, "Repression and the State of Emergency," 18–23.

9. Webster and Friedman, "Repression and the State of Emergency," 35ff.

10. Liz Abrahams, *Married to the Struggle: "Nanna" Liz Abrahams Tells Her Life Story*, Yusuf Patel and Philip Hirschsohn, eds. (Bellville, South Africa: UWC with Diana Ferrus Publishers, 2005), 62.

11. Abrahams, *Married to the Struggle*, 61.

12. David Niddrie, "Negotiations: Another Site of Struggle," *Work in Progress* 60 (August 1989).

13. Tom Lodge, "People's War or Negotiations? African National Congress Strategies in the 1980s," in *South African Review* 5.

14. Christopher S. Wren, "Botha, Rebuffed by His Party, Quits South Africa Presidency," *New York Times*, August 15, 1989, http://www.nytimes.com/1989/08/15/world/botha-rebuffed-by-his-party-quits-south-africa-presidency.html

15. Jo-Anne Collinge, "Defiance: A Measure of Expectations," *Work in Progress* 61 (September 1989): 6.

16. SAHO, "Congress of South African Trade Unions (COSATU)," South African History Online, December 8, 2011, http://www.sahistory.org.za/topic/congress-south-african-trade-unions-COSATU.

17. "Purple Rain Protest," Wikipedia, https://en.wikipedia.org/w/index.php?title=Purple_Rain_Protest&oldid=723787362; SAHA, "The Purple Shall Govern—the Beginning of the End; September 2 1989," Sunday Times Heritage Project, September 2, 1989, sthp.saha.org.za/memorial/the_purple_shall_govern.htm.

18. Hamish McIndoe, Kurt Swart, and Allan Duggan, "Demo Chaos—1000 Held," *Sunday Times*, September 3, 1989, sthp.saha.org.za/memorial/articles/demo_chaos_1000_held.htm.

19. Leander, "South African Major Mass Killings Timeline 1900–2012," South African History Online, January 8, 2013, http://www.sahistory.org.za/topic/south-african-major-mass-killings-timeline-1900-2012; SAHA, "Crushing the Labor Relations Act," South African History Archive, http://www.saha.org.za/workers/one_and_many_workers_unite_for_a_living_wage.htm.

20. Niddrie, "Negotiations," 9.

21. Collinge, "Defiance."

22. WiP, "Editorial," *Work in Progress* 61 (September 1989): 1.

23. Alex Duval Smith, "Why FW de Klerk Let Nelson Mandela Out of Prison," *The Guardian*, January 31, 2010, http://www.theguardian.com/world/2010/jan/31/nelson-mandela-de-klerk-apartheid.

24. Smith, "Why FW de Klerk Let Nelson Mandela Out of Prison."

25. Owen Crankshaw, "The Changing Structure of the Workforce 1965–1985," *South African Labor Bulletin* 15, no. 1 (June 1990): 28.

26. Crankshaw, "The Changing Structure," 29.

27. Sheena Duncan, "Riekert Commission Report," *The Black Sash*, August 1979.

28. Anthony Lemon, *Homes Apart: South Africa's Segregated Cities* (Bloomington: Indiana University Press, 1991); Thomas S. Szayna, "Annex: Demographic Characteristics of South Africa in the Late 1980s," in *Identifying Potential Ethnic Conflict: Application of a Process Model* (Santa Monica: Rand Corporation, 2000), http://www.rand.org/pubs/monograph_reports/MR1188.html.

29. Duncan, "Riekert Commission Report"; Lemon, *Homes Apart*.

30. Harold Wolpe, "On the Articulation of Modes of Production: Review Article," *Journal of Southern African Studies* 8, no. 1 (October 1981), 123–38.

31. Jaqueline Beck, "Border Industries," *The Black Sash*, February 1968.

32. Szayna, "Annex: Demographic Characteristics," 5.

33. Noor Nieftagodien, "The Township Uprising, September–November 1984," in *Book 5: People, Places and Apartheid* (Pretoria: Department of Education, 2012), http://www.sahistory.org.za/archive/book-5-people-places-and-apartheid-chapter-4-township-uprising-september-november-1984-noor.

34. Lemon, *Homes Apart*.

35. The Vaal Triangle is a highly industrialized and urbanized area about 60 kilometers south of Johannesburg. It is delineated by three industrial towns that host a petrochemical facility and a giant steel company, which were established and controlled by the state during Apartheid, and partly privatized to raise funds in 1979 and 1989, respectively.

36. Diana E. H. Russell, *Lives of Courage: Women for a New South Africa* (Bloomington, IN: iUniverse, 1989), 49; Nieftagodien, "The Township Uprising."

37. Nieftagodien, "The Township Uprising."

38. Lord E.R. MacConnel, "Vaal Civic Association Report to the UDF," January 14, 1984, http://hpra-atom.wits.ac.za/atom-2.1.0/index.php/vaal-civic-association-report.

39. K. Van Dijkhorst and W.F. Krugel, "Judgement in the Delmas Treason Trial 1985–1989: General 730-740," Historical Papers, University of the Witwatersrand, November 15, 1988, http://www.historicalpapers.wits.ac.za/inventories/inv_pdfo/AK2117/AK2117-L12-01-01-jpeg.pdf.

40. Mark Phillips et al., "Municipal Elections: Success or Failure for Government Strategy?," *South African Labor Bulletin* 13, no. 7 (November 1988).

41. Jo-Anne Collinge, "Sanctions Loop Hole," *Work in Progress* 61 (September 1989): 42.

42. Abrahams, *Married to the Struggle*, 59.

43. Labor Research Services, "Inflation," *South African Labor Bulletin* 14, no. 4 (October 1989): 140.

44. Ipsa Research, "The Stayaway from the LRA," *Indicator SA* 5, no. 4 (Spring 1988), http://reference.sabinet.co.za/webx/access/journal_archive/0259188X/884.pdf.

45. Kehla Shubane, "Emzabalazweni: There Is Politics in the Trains," *South African Labor Bulletin* 13, no. 7 (November 1988).

46. SALB, "Shop Stewards Speak about Action against the Bill," *South African Labor Bulletin* 13, no. 3 (April 1988): 16.

47. SALB, "Shop Stewards," 17.

48. SALB, "Interview: 'You Cannot Operate in an Unrest Situation . . .'," *South African*

Labor Bulletin 13, no. 3 (April 1988): 25.

49. SALB, "Interview," 30.

50. Lodge, "People's War or Negotiations?," 47.

51. Lodge, "People's War or Negotiations?," 53, 43, 54.

52. ANC, "Second National Consultative Conference: Report of the Commission on Cadre Policy, Political and Ideological Work," June 1985, http://www.anc.org.za/content/second-national-consultative-conference-report-commission-cadre-policy-political-and-ideological-work; Martin Legassick, *Armed Struggle and Democracy: The Case of South Africa* (Uppsala: Nordiska Afrikainstitutet, 2002).

53. Tripartite Alliance Co-ordinating Committee, "Minutes of the Meeting of the Tripartite Alliance Co-Ordinating Committee Held on 15 November 1990 at the ANC Head Office," November 15, 1990, http://www.sahistory.org.za/archive/minutes-of-the-meeting-of-the-tripartite-alliance-co-ordinating-committee-held-on-15-november-1990-at-the-anc-head-office.

54. Jonathan Hyslop, "Introduction: The State and Politics," in *South African Review* 5, 9ff.

55. Mark Swilling and M. Phillips, "The Emergency State: Its Structure, Power and Limits," in *South African Review* 5.

56. Thanks to John Rose for reminding me about this.

57. Jeremy Seekings, *The UDF: A History of the United Democratic Front in South Africa, 1983–1991* (Cape Town: New Africa Books, 2000).

58. Tripartite Alliance Co-ordinating Committee, "Minutes," 2–3.

59. Alex Callinicos, "Marxism and Imperialism Today," *International Socialism*, second series, 50 (1991): 127.

60. Mike Morris, "Who's In? Who's Out? Trying to Sidestep a 50% Solution," *Work in Progress* 87 (1993): 41.

61. Nicholas Haysom, "Negotiating a Political Settlement in South Africa," in *South African Review* 6, Glen Moss and Ingrid Obery, eds. (Johannesburg: Raven Press, 1992), 28.

62. S. Johns and R. Hunt Davis, eds., *Mandela, Tambo, and the African National Congress: The Struggle against Apartheid, 1948–1990: A Documentary Survey* (New York: Oxford University Press, 1991), 228.

63. Umsebenzi, "No Retreat Now!," *South African History Online* 6, no. 4 (1990): 1.

64. National Conference, "Resolution on Negotiations and the Suspension of Armed Struggle," *Mayibuye*, February 1991, 24, http://disa.ukzn.ac.za/sites/default/files/pdf_files/MaFeb91.pdf.

65. Jo-Anne Collinge, "Launched on a Bloody Tide: Negotiating the New South Africa," *South African Review* 6, p. 9.

66. Mayibuye, "Towards an All Party Conference: Interview with Walter Sisulu," *Mayibuye*, February 1991, 17.

67. Haysom, "Negotiating a Political Settlement," 35.

68. Collinge, "A Bloody Tide," 15.

69. Glenda Daniels, "The Great VAT Strike," *Work in Progress* 79 (December 1991): 19.

70. Tom Lodge, "The African National Congress in the 1990s," *South African Review-SARS*, no. 6 (1992): 62.

71. Quoted in Ceruti, "How and Why the ANC's Nationalization Policy Changed," 195.
72. "Codesa II: Blowing Hot and Cold. Interview with Thabo Mbeki," *Mayibuye* 3, no. 5 (June 1992): 11.
73. Quoted in Ceruti, "How and Why the ANC's Nationalization Policy Changed," and "CODESA II," 12.
74. Monako Dibetle, "Boipatong: Ghosts of a Massacre," *M&G Online*, June 14, 2012, http://mg.co.za/article/2012-06-14-ghosts-of-a-massacre-drove-my-father-to-an-early-grave/.
75. Mayibuye, "A Year of Decisive Progress: Interview with Nelson Mandela," *Mayibuye* 4, no. 1 (February 1993), 10.
76. Mayibuye, "Codesa II," 9.
77. Mayibuye, "Millions Act in Unity," *Mayibuye* 3, no. 7 (August 1992), 10.
78. Joe Slovo, "Negotiations: What Room for Compromise?" *African Communist*, no. 130 (1992): 36.
79. Slovo, "Negotiations," 37.
80. Pallo Jordan, "Strategic Debate: A Response to Joe Slovo," *African Communist*, no. 131 (1992): 8; ANC Youth League, "Summary of Ideas on Negotiations and the Way Forward," *African Communist*, no. 131 (1992): 48–50; Jeremy Cronin, "The Boat, the Tap and the Liepzig Way," *African Communist*, no. 130 (1992): 45.
81. Karl Von Holdt, "The Challenge of Participation," *South African Labor Bulletin* 17, no. 3 (June 1993): 48–52.
82. Jeremy Cronin, "We Need More Than Group Therapy," *Work in Progress* 89 (June 1993): 14.

Chapter 4: Uprisings and Revolutions in Sub-Saharan Africa, 1985–2014

1. Philippe de Dorlodot, *Marche d'espoir: Kinshasa 16 Février 1992 Non-violence pour la Démocratie au Zaire* (Paris: l'Harmattan, 1994), 100–102.
2. Dorlodot, *Marche d'espoir*, 102.
3. Dorlodot, *Marche d'espoir*, 25–26.
4. Dorlodot, *Marche d'espoir*, 28.
5. Dorlodot, *Marche d'espoir*, 30.
6. Dorlodot, *Marche d'espoir*, 36–37.
7. Dorlodot, *Marche d'espoir*, 50.
8. Dorlodot, *Marche d'espoir*, 38–39.
9. G. de Villers and J. M. Tshonda, "When Kinois Take to the Street," in *Reinventing Order in the Congo*, Theodore Trefon, ed. (London: Zed Books, 2004), 144.
10. Blaine Harden, *Africa: Dispatches from a Fragile Continent* (London: HarperCollins, 1993), 53.
11. Harden, *Africa*, 54.
12. Robert Giraudon, "Un Scandale Géologique?," *Afrique Contemporaine* 183 (1997): 44–54.

13. Vincent de Paul Lunda-Bululu, *Conduire la Premiere Transition au Congo-Zaire* (Paris: L'Harmattan, 2003), 278–84.

14. Janet MacGaffey and Rémy Bazenguissa-Ganga, *Congo-Paris: Transnational Traders on the Margins of the Law* (London, James Currey, 2000), 30.

15. MacGaffey and Bazenguissa-Ganga, *Congo-Paris*, 30.

16. MacGaffey and Bazenguissa-Ganga, *Congo-Paris*, 30.

17. Claude Sumata "Migradollars and Poverty Alleviation Strategy Issues in Congo (DRC)," *Review of African Political Economy* 29, nos. 93–94 (2002): 619–28.

18. Cited in Ludo Martins, *Kabila et la Révolution Congolaise* (Anvers: Editions EPO, 2002), 115.

19. Michael Bratton and Nicolas van de Walle, *Democratic Experiments in Africa: Regime Transitions in Comparative Perspective* (Cambridge: Cambridge University Press, 1997), 5.

20. See Eddie Webster and Glen Adler, "Towards a Class Compromise in South Africa's 'Double Transition': Bargained Liberalisation and the Consolidation of Democracy," *Politics and Society* 27, no. 3 (1999): 347–85.

21. Neil Davidson, "From Deflected Permanent Revolution to the Law of Uneven and Combined Development," *International Socialism*, second series, 128 (2010), uk/from-deflected-permanent-revolution-to-the-law-of-uneven-and-combined-development.

22. See John Walton and David Seddon, *Free Markets and Food Riots: The Politics of Global Adjustment* (Oxford: Blackwell, 1994).

23. Phil Marfleet, "Globalisation and the Third World," *International Socialism*, second series, 81 (1997): 104.

24. See Leo Zeilig and David Seddon, "Marxism, Class and Resistance in Africa," in *Class Struggle and Resistance in Africa*, Leo Zeilig, ed. (Chicago: Haymarket Books, 2009).

25. A. K. Zghal, "The 'Bread Riot' and the Crisis of the One-Party System in Tunisia," in *African Studies in Social Movements and Democracy*, M. Mamdani and E. Wamba-dia-Wamba, eds. (Dakar: CODESRIA, 1995), 99–129.

26. See Miles Larmer, *Mineworkers in Zambia* (London: Tauris Academic Studies, 2007).

27. Christopher Colclough, *The Labor Market and Economic Stabilization in Zambia*, World Bank Working Papers, Policy Planning and Research (Washington, DC: Country Economics Department, 1989), 1.

28. See Munyaradzi Gwisai, *Revolutionaries, Resistance and Crisis in Zimbabwe: Anti-neoliberal Struggles in Periphery Capitalism* (Harare: I.S.O. Pamphlet, 2002).

29. See Zeilig and Seddon, "Marxism, Class and Resistance in Africa."

30. Silvia Federici, "The New Student Movement," in *A Thousand Flowers: Social Struggles against Structural Adjustment in African Universities*, Ousseina Alidou, George Caffentzis, and Silvia Federici, eds. (New York: Africa World Press, 2000), 88.

31. J. I. Dibua, "Students and the Struggle against Authoritarianism in University Governance in Nigeria," in *African Universities in the 21st Century*, vol. 2, P. T. Zeleza and A. Olukosh, eds. (Dakar: Codesria, 2004), 473.

32. No doubt the influence of events in South Africa also played a role; after all, the entrenched, racist government in Pretoria had been forced to the negotiating table by anti-Apartheid forces. A sense of a continent (and world) in flux, both north and south,

with no regime insulated from the rising tide of protest, was *the* overwhelming political mood at the time.

33. Bratton and Van de Walle, *Democratic Experiments in Africa*, 5.

34. David Seddon and Leo Zeilig, "Class and Protest in Africa: New Waves," *Review of African Political Economy* 32, no. 103 (2005): 9–27.

35. John A. Wiseman, *The New Struggle for Democracy in Africa* (Aldershot: Avebury, 1996), 49.

36. See Chris Harman, "The Prophet and the Proletariat," *International Socialism*, second series, 64 (1994), https://www.marxists.org/archive/harman/1994/xx/islam.htm.

37. See Thomas Hodgson, "The Revolutionary Tradition in Islam," *Race and Class* 21, no. 3 (1980).

38. A "curtailed revolution" refers to the limited scope of the new, postrevolutionary government and transition in this period. Instead of seeing a full revolutionary transformation in the countries discussed in this chapter, what issued from these uprisings was the resumption of the structural adjustment that had generated the revolutionary movements in the first place! An apparent paradox that we discuss below.

39. See Miles Larmer, Peter Dwyer, and Leo Zeilig, "Southern African Social Movements at the 2007 Nairobi World Social Forum," *Global Networks* 9, no. 1 (2009).

40. Zachariah Mampilly, "Burkina Faso's Uprising Part of an Ongoing Wave of African Protests," *Washington Post*, November 2, 2014, www.washingtonpost.com/news/monkey-cage/wp/2014/11/02/burkina-fasos-uprising-part-of-an-ongoing-wave-of-african-protests.

41. Interview with Leo Zeilig, Harare (Zimbabwe), March 20, 2010.

42. Interview (Harare), July 31, 2003.

43. Interview (Harare), August 14, 2003.

44. See Gwisai, *Revolutionaries, Resistance and Crisis in Zimbabwe*.

45. *Etude Nationale Prospective "Burkina 2025": Rapport General* (Ouagadougou: Direction Générale de L'économie et de la Planification, 2005), vii–141.

46. Andy Wynne, "What's Next in Burkina Faso," *Socialist Worker*, November 6, 2014, https://socialistworker.org/2014/11/06/whats-next-in-burkina-faso.

47. Marianne Saddier, "The Upright Citizens of Burkina Faso," *Africa Is a Country*, October 2014, https://africasacountry.com/2014/10/the-citizens-of-burkina-faso/.

48. Javier Blas, "Pressure Mounts on Burkina Faso Military to Relinquish Power," *Financial Times*, November 2, 2014, https://www.ft.com/content/6b-10da28-629d-11e4-aa14-00144feabdc0.

49. Jean-Claude Kongo, interview (Ouagadougou), March 14, 2016. See also Kongo, "Remembering Sankara: The Past in the Present," in Kongo and Zeilig, *Voices of Liberation: Thomas Sankara* (Cape Town: HSRC Press, 2017), 177–98.

50. See "A Barefoot Revolution—Burkina Faso's October Revolution and Its Aftermath," DW English, https://www.dw.com/en/a-barefoot-revolution-burkina-fasos-october-revolution-and-its-aftermath/a-18677984.

51. We are aware that SAPs did not lead automatically or uniformly to the revolutionary situations and certainly not in a straightforward way. There were complicated, mediat-

ing links in different parts of the continent, which had a profound impact on the extent and nature of these revolutions.

52. See Chris Harman, "The Clash of Fundamentals," *Socialist Review* 285 (May 2004), http://socialistreview.org.uk/285/clash-fundamentals.

53. Zachariah Mampilly, "Burkina Faso's Uprising Part of an Ongoing Wave of African Protests," *Washington Post*, November 2, 2014.

54. Interview (Harare), June 23, 2003.

55. Interview (Dakar), February 12, 2004.

56. See Frantz Fanon [1961], *The Wretched of the Earth* (Harmondsworth: Penguin Books, 1963), 134–35.

57. Mampilly, "Burkina Faso's Uprising Part of an Ongoing Wave"; see also Adam Branch and Zachariah Mampilly, *Africa Uprising: Popular Protest and Political Change* (London: Zed Books, 2014).

58. Andy Wynne, "Burkinabes Say: 'Enough Is Enough!,'" *Pambazuka News*, November 4, 2014, www.pambazuka.org/governance/burkinabes-say-%E2%80%98enough-enough%E2%80%99.

59. Antonio Gramsci, *Further Selections from the Prison Notebooks*, Derek Boothman, ed. (London: Lawrence and Wishart, 1996), 395–96, Q10II.

Chapter 5: "Reformasi": Indonesians Bring Down Suharto

1   I am thankful to Mohamad Zaki Hussein and Max Lane for significant insights, and to Janey Stone for assistance in preparation of the manuscript. For an important discussion of Indonesian politics today, including the role of Danial Indrakusuma, see Lane's "Indonesia: Trade Unions and the Regeneration of Radical Politics," *Marxist Left Review* 7 (Summer 2014).

2. By "indigenous" I don't mean Aboriginal peoples, but rather the Indonesian term *pribumi*, signifying the Malay peoples "close to the earth." The function of such language is mainly to exclude the Chinese.

3. See Richard Robison, *Indonesia: The Rise of Capital* (Sydney: Allen and Unwin, 1986).

4. On the role of the CIA, see John Roosa and Joseph Nevins, "The Mass Killings in Indonesia," *CounterPunch*, June 2, 2012.

5. Suharto and Sukarno are Javanese names. The "su" is an honorific which can be replaced by others, e.g., Pak Harto or Bung Karno. They can also be spelled *Soeharto* or *Soekarno*, which is the old Dutch spelling.

6. Another telling line from Iwan Fals: "Setan-setan politik, yang dating mencekik" (Political devils come to choke us).

7. Eyewitness report from Steven Miller.

8. Eyewitness report from Abraham Fanggidae.

9. "Surat kawan-kawan dari dalam Rumah Tahanan Kejaksanaan Agung," received by e-mail, September 20, 1996.

10. I was caught up in three election cavalcades. During the most dramatic, marchers danced on the roof of my bus.

11. Known locally as the monetary crisis—*krisis moneter*, or *krismon*.

12. Jeffrey Sachs, "The Wrong Medicine for Asia," The Earth Institute, Columba University, 1997, http://www.earth.columbia.edu/sitefiles/file/Sachs%20Writing/1997/NY-Times_1997_TheWrongMedicineforAsia_11_03_97.pdf.

13. The national currency, the Rupiah (abbreviation Rp), has inflated so much since 1998 that direct comparisons with its value today would add little to the story.

14. See Muhammad Cohen, "Happy to Be Chinese in Indonesia," *Asia Times*, October 20, 2011.

15. This is the correct name of the factory. P.T is the equivalent of "Ltd." or "Inc." Famous is the company name. P.T. goes before Famous.

16. What follows is my own eyewitness account.

17. The poem was reproduced in *Kompas* by Kwik Kian Gie; see his "Kesenjangan Sosial, Ekonomi, dan Politik," in *Kompas Online*, May 18, 1998, http://www.seasite.niu.edu/indonesian/Reformasi/Chronicle/Kompas/May18/kkg01.htm. It's my translation, but there are others.

18. Vedi R. Hadiz, e-mail 1998, re-confirmed by e-mail, June 8, 2013.

19. On race riots and the security forces' behavior, see Cohen, "Happy to Be Chinese in Indonesia."

20. Quoted in Loren Ryter, "The Morning After," *Inside Indonesia*, no. 56 (October–December 1998).

21. E-mail from Dicky Pelupessy, November 4, 2013.

22. PRD leaders insisted they did not actually back Abdurrahman Wahid or support a decree to dissolve parliament. They acknowledged, however, that many of their members had interpreted party statements as meaning just that and had acted accordingly. Conversation at the Asia Pacific People's Solidarity Conference, Sawangan, June 6, 2001.

23. For example, there was significant interest in the Australian writers Doug Lorimer and Max Lane, and the *Suara Sosialis* internet newsletter, produced by Setiabudi and the present author. The story of *Suara Sosialis* is recounted in Tom O'Lincoln, *The Highway Is for Gamblers* (Melbourne: Interventions, 2017).

24. Foreign participants in the debates at this time included me, Max Lane, Doug Lorimer, and a Belgian, Jean Duval. In 1999 I circulated what was apparently the first-ever Indonesian language edition of Lenin's *April Theses*.

25. For more information about Danial Indrakusuma, see Max Lane, "Indonesia: Trade Unions and the Regeneration of Radical Politics," *Marxist Left Review* 7 (Summer 2014).

26. Jun Honna, *Military Realities and Democratisation in Indonesia* (London: Routledge-Curzon, 2003), 176.

27. On the PRD's recent trajectory, see Max Lane, "Green Left Weekly and the Indonesian Left," August 12, 2009, maxlaneonline.com/on-indonesian-positics/green-left-weekly-and-the-indonesian-left/. I visited the PRD on April 17, 2013, in Tebet, Jakarta; they graciously explained their position in a long discussion, but I was not convinced.

28. Report on May Day 2002: Tom O'Lincoln, "May Day in Jakarta," *Counter Action*, June 2002, http://redsites.info/mayday.htm.

Chapter 6: Bolivia's Cycle of Revolt:
Left-Indigenous Struggle, 2000–2005

1. This chapter draws from my book, *Red October: Left-Indigenous Struggles in Modern Bolivia* (Chicago: Haymarket, 2012).

2. Pablo Stefanoni and Hervé Do Alto, *Evo Morales de la Coca al Palacio: Una Oportunidad para la Izquierda Indígena* (La Paz: Malatesta, 2006), 17.

3. Salvador Romero Ballivián, *El Tablero Reordenado: Análisis de la Elección Presidencial de 2005* (La Paz: Corte Nacional Electoral, 2006), 49–50.

4. INE, *Anuario Estadístico* (La Paz: Instituto Nacional de Estatística, 2001).

5. Kenneth M. Roberts, *Deepening Democracy? The Modern Left and Social Movements in Chile and Peru* (Redwood City, CA: Stanford University Press, 1998), 59–67.

6. Karl Marx and Friedrich Engels [1848], *The Communist Manifesto* (New York: Penguin, 1985), 93–94.

7. Xavier Albó, "El Alto, la Vorágine de una Ciudad Unica," *Journal of Latin American Anthropology* 11, no. 2 (2006): 333.

8. Lesley Gill, *Teetering on the Rim: Global Restructuring, Daily Life, and the Armed Retreat of the Bolivian State* (New York: Columbia University Press, 2000), 35–6.

9. If the formal working class enjoys greater opportunities than most informal workers to interrupt the process of capital accumulation through disruption at the point of production—through strikes and other methods—informal workers are still able at times to break down accumulation in the sphere of circulation—particularly through roadblocks. Commodities can no longer reach their destinations in internal and external markets when key roads are shut down.

10. Juan Arbona and Benjamin Kohl, "La Paz–El Alto: City Profile," *Cities* 21, no. 3 (2004): 261.

11. Susan Spronk, "Roots of Resistance to Urban Water Privatization in Bolivia: The 'New Working Class,'" *International Labor and Working-Class History* 71, no. 1 (2007): 20.

12. Nina Laurie and Carlos Crespo, "Deconstructing the Best Case Scenario: Lessons from Water Politics in La Paz–El Alto, Bolivia," *Geoforum*, 38 (2007): 841–54.

13. Godofredo Sandoval Z. and M. Fernanda Sostres, *La Ciudad Prometida: Pobladores y Organizaciones Sociales en El Alto* (La Paz: ILDIS-Systema, 1989), 22. El Alto became an independent municipality in 1988.

14. The accelerated urbanization in Bolivia in the second half of the twentieth century largely followed wider trends in the global South; see Mike Davis, *Planet of Slums* (London: Verso, 2006).

15. Benjamin Kohl and Linda Farthing, *Impasse in Bolivia: Neoliberal Hegemony and Popular Resistance* (London: Zed Books, 2006).

16. Albó, "El Alto, la Vorágine," 332; Arbona and Kohl, "La Paz–El Alto," 258.

17. "El 66,9% de los Habitantes Viven en la pobreza," *La Razón*, March 6, 2005.

18. Pablo Rossell Arce and Bruno Rojas Callejas, *Ser productor en El Alto: Una Aproximación a la Dinámica Productive y el Desarrollo Local en El Alto* (La Paz: CEDLA, 2000), vi.

19. Rossell Arce and Rojas Callejas, *Ser productor*, vii.

20. Lesley Gill describes the "heterogeneous mix of street vendors, petty merchants, and artisans" in the streets of El Alto. "Women sell fruits, vegetables, and a variety of trinkets on the streets . . . frequently accompanied by small children," she observes, while others commute to La Paz each morning as "domestic servants, gardeners, shoeshine boys, and part-time handymen." Teenage daughters and elderly women are often tasked, meanwhile, with the unpaid reproductive work of caring for younger siblings or grandchildren. Gill, *Teetering on the Rim*, 68, 1, 41.

21. Gill, *Teetering on the Rim*, 2.

22. Rossell Arce and Rojas Callejas, *Ser Productor*, 29.

23. Perhaps the most extensive study contains information on five large enterprises: a Coca–Cola bottling plant, a tannery, a wooden-door factory, a weaving factory, and a plastics factory. Rossell Arce and Rojas Callejas, *Ser Productor*.

24. PNUD/UNDP, *La Economía Más allá del Gas: Informe Temático Sobre Desarrollo Humano* (Second edition, La Paz: PNUD/UNDP, 2005), 88–115; Rossell Arce and Rojas Callejas, *Ser Productor*, 14.

25. Victor Agadjanian, "Competition and Cooperation among Working Women in the Context of Structural Adjustment: The Case of Street Vendors in La Paz–El Alto, Bolivia," *Journal of Development Studies* 18, nos. 2–3 (2002): 259–85; Rossell Arce and Rojas Callejas, *Ser Productor*, 24–36.

26. Rossell Arce and Rojas Callejas, *Ser Productor*, 24–36.

27. Roberto de la Cruz, interviews, El Alto, May 12 and June 30, 2005.

28. Sian Lazar, "Personalist Politics, Clientelism and Citizenship: Local Elections in El Alto, Bolivia," *Bulletin of Latin American Research* 23, no. 2 (2004): 229–43; Fernando Mayorga, *Neopopulismo y Democracia: Compadres y Padrinos en la Política Boliviana (1989–1999)* (La Paz: Plural Editores, 2002); Máximo Quisbert Quispe, *FEJUVE El Alto 1990–1998: Dilemas del Clientelismo Colectivo en un Mercado Político en Expansión* (La Paz: TOHA/Ediciones Aruwiyiri, 2003); Sandoval Z. and Sostres, *La Ciudad Prometida*.

29. Magdalena Cajías de la Vega, "El Poder de la Memoria: Articulaciones Ideológico-culturales en los Movimientos Sociales Bolivianos," *Barataria* 1, no.1 (2004): 22.

30. Juan Arbona, "'Sangre de Minero, Semilla de Guerrillero': Histories and Memories in the Organization and Struggles of the Santiago II Neighourhood of El Alto, Bolivia," *Bulletin of Latin American Research* 27, no. 1 (2008): 25; Félix Choque, interview, La Paz, May 3, 2005.

31. Cajías de la Vega, "El Poder de la Memoria," 22; Sinclair Thomson and Forrest Hylton, *Revolutionary Horizons: Past and Present in Bolivian Politics* (London: Verso, 2004), 18.

32. INE, *Anuario Estadístico*.

33. Gonzalo Gosálvez, interview, La Paz, April 9, 2005.

34. Félix Patzi, interview, La Paz, May 2005.

35. Patricia Costas Monje, Public Lecture, Comuna Collective, La Paz, 2005.

36. Albó, "El Alto, la Vorágine," 335–36.

37. Pablo Mamani Ramírez, *Microgobiernos Barriales: Levantamiento de la Ciudad de El Alto (Octubre 2003)* (La Paz: Centro Andino de Estudios Estratégicos, 2005), 52.

38. Mamani Ramírez, *Microgobiernos barriales*, 83.
39. Juan Manuel Arbona, "Los Límites de los Márgenes: Organizaciones Políticas Locales y las Jornadas de Octubre," *Nueva Sociedad*, 197 (2005): 7; Juan Manuel Arbona, "Neo-liberal Ruptures: Local Political Entities and Neighborhood Networks in El Alto, Bolivia," *Geoforum* 38 (2007): 128–29.
40. Alan Sears, *The Next New Left: A History of the Future* (Halifax: Fernwood, 2014).
41. Sian Lazar, "Ciudad Rebelde: Organizational Bases for Revolt," *Bulletin of Latin American Research* 25, no. 2 (2006): 186–87.
42. Álvaro García Linera, "Los Movimientos Indígenas en Bolivia," in *Movimiento Indígena en América Latina: Resistencia y Proyecto Alternativo*, Fabiola Escárzaga and Raquél Gutiérrez, eds. (Puebla: Benemérita Universidad Autónoma de Puebla, 2005), 896.
43. García Linera, "Los Movimientos Indígenas en Bolivia," 598.
44. García Linera, "Los Movimientos Indígenas en Bolivia."
45. García Linera, "Los Movimientos Indígenas en Bolivia," 599.
46. Álvaro García Linera, Marxa Chávez León, and Patricia Costas Monje, *Sociología de los Movimientos Sociales en Bolivia: Estructuras de Movilización, Repertorios Culturales y Acción Política* (Second edition, La Paz: Oxfam and Diakonia, 2005), 599–600.
47. García Linera, et al., *Sociología de los Movimientos*, 595.
48. García Linera, "Los Movimientos Indígenas en Bolivia," 594.
49. Lazar, "Ciudad Rebelde," 187.
50. Beimar Josué Montoya Villa and Rosa Rojas García, *El Despertar de un Pueblo Oprimido: Estructuras de Movilización y Construcciones Discursivas en La Ciudad de El Alto, en el Mes de Octubre de 2003* (La Paz: Musux Wayra, 2004), 50–51.
51. Mauricio Cori, interview, El Alto, May 4, 2005; De la Cruz, interviews; Luis Gómez, *El Alto de Pie: Una Insurrección Aymara en Bolivia* (La Paz: HdP, La Comuna, Indymedia Qollasuyu Ivi Iyambae Bolivia, 2004); Henry Merida Gutiérrez, interview, El Alto, April 1, 2005; Julio Pabón Chávez, interview, El Alto, March 30, 2005; Edgar Patana, interviews, El Alto, May 10 and 17, 2005.
52. Mamani Ramírez, *Microgobiernos Barriales*, 69.
53. Mamani Ramírez, *Microgobiernos Barriales*, 72.
54. Mamani Ramírez, *Microgobiernos Barriales*, 82–83.
55. Marxa Chávez, Public Lecture, Comuna Collective, La Paz, 2005; Cori, interview.
56. De la Cruz, interview; Jorge Solares Barrientos, interview, La Paz, April 5, 2005.
57. FSTMB, "Comunicado a los trabajadores y al pueblo boliviano" (La Paz: FSTMB archives, 2003).
58. "El 70% de la Población de 4 Ciudades no cree en Goni," *Los Tiempos*, September 8, 2003.
59. "Exportación de Gas Detona el Descontento," *La Prensa*, September 9, 2003.
60. Forrest Hylton and Sinclair Thomson, 'the Roots of Rebellion: Insurgent Bolivia," *NACLA Report on the Americas* 38, no. 3 (2004): 18; "Chronology of Events Leading to the Bolivian President's Resignation," *Associated Press* October 18, 2003.
61. Álvaro García Linera, interview, La Paz, April 10, 2005.
62. Hylton and Thomson, "The Roots of Rebellion," 16.

63. FUDTCLP–TK is affiliated to but often acts autonomously from the CSUTCB.

64. Hylton and Thomson, *Revolutionary Horizons*, 111; "Exportación de Gas Detona el Descontento"; "DosMarchas y un Paro Cívico Bloquearon El Alto y Parte de La Paz," *La Razón*, September 9, 2003.

65. "Dos Mil Campesinos Ayunan, Hoy se Decide si Hay Bloqueo," *La Prensa*, September 11, 2003.

66. "El Mallku Prepara Bloqueo y Anuncia ana 'Guerra Civil,'" *La Prensa*, September 12, 2003; "Bloqueo de Caminos en el Norte de La Paz," *El Diario*, September 13, 2003; "Bloqueo de Yungas Inicia la Guerra del Gas," *La Prensa*, September 15, 2003; "Los Colonizadores Inician hoy Bloqueos en Yungas," *La Razón*, September 15, 2003.

67. "Campesinos en Huelga de Hambre Instruyen el Bloqueo de Caminos," *La Patria*, September 12, 2003; "Presidente Instruye Imponer Orden Ante la Ola de Protestas," *La Prensa*, September 12, 2003; "El Gobierno Prepara a las FFAA para Evitar Bloqueos," *Los Tiempos*, September 12, 2003.

68. "La Policía y las FFAA Toman las Carreteras en el Altiplano," *La Prensa*, September 13, 2003.

69. "Ante los Conflictos el Gobierno Asegura que Hará Cumplir la Ley," *Opinión*, September 15, 2003.

70. "Bloqueos preceden una 'protesta nacional' contra la venta del gas," *La Patria*, September 16, 2003.

71. The EMP had been an on-again, off-again rocky alliance since its inception in early 2003 that encompassed the *cocaleros* of the Chapare and the Movimiento al Socialismo (Movement Toward Socialism, MAS), both led by Evo Morales; the COB, led by Jaime Solares; and the newly formed Coordinadora de Defensa del Gas (Coordinator in Defense of Gas), led by Oscar Olivera, and other groups.

72. "El Alto Levanta el Paro, en Caranavi hay Bloqueos," *El Deber*, September 17, 2003.

73. "El Diálogo en Yungas se Rompió y los Bloqueos Cobran más Fuerza," *La Razón*, September 19, 2003; "Varios Sectores Unirán Mañana sus Protestas en Torno al Gas," *La Razón*, September 18, 2003.

74. "'Guerra del Gas' Provoca Tensión Social en El País," *Opinión*, September 19, 2003; "El MAS y al Menos Diez Sectores Marcharán Contra la Venta del Gas," *La Razón*, September 19, 2003.

75. "El Gobierno Libra la Primera Batalla del Gas," *Los Tiempos*, September 19, 2003.

76. "'Guerra del Gas.'"

77. "Una Precisión de Evo Morales, 'La marcha fue una consulta,'" *Vóz*, September 20, 2003.

78. García Linera, interview. García Linera later became vice-president under Evo Morales, from 2006 to 2019.

79. Susan Spronk and Jeffery R. Webber, "Struggles against Accumulation by Dispossession in Bolivia: The Political Economy of Natural Resource Contention," *Latin American Perspectives* 34, no. 3 (2007): 33–38.

80. Claudia Espinoza, "19 de Septiembre ¿Comienza otro Ciclo?," *Pulso*, September 19, 2003.

81. Espinoza, "19 de Septiembre."

82. "Multitudinaria Marcha Paralizó el Centro Paceño al Mediodía," *El Diario*, September 20, 2003; "Multitudinaria Marcha la Paralizó Anoche La Paz," *La Prensa*, September 20, 2003; "El Temor a los Saqueos Paralizó por Completo a la Urbe Alteña," *La Razón*, September 20, 2003.

83. "La COB Apuesta al Paro General," *La Razón*, September 20, 2003.

84. Álvaro García Linera, "La Crisis de Estado y las Sublevaciones Indígena-Plebeyas," in *Memorias de Octubre*, Álvaro García Linera, Raúl Prada, and Luis Tapia, eds. (La Paz: Muela del Diablo, 2004), 62.

85. Hugo José Suárez, *Una Semana Fundamental: 10–13 Octubre 2003* (La Paz: Muela del Diablo, 2003), 17.

86. "Vuelve el Luto al País: Operativo de Rescate Deja Seis Muertos," *Los Tiempos*, September 21, 2003.

87. "Goni: No hay Diálogo con Bloqueos," *La Prensa*, September 22, 2003.

88. "Vuelve el Luto."

89. "Matanza de Warisata extiende los Bloqueos y Sube la Tensión," *Los Tiempos*, September 22, 2003.

90. García Linera, "La Crisis de Estado," 62.

91. Claudia Espinoza, "Plan Añutaya: La Respuesta Comunal," *Pulso*, September 26, 2003.

92. Cori, interview.

93. De la Cruz, interview.

94. "Comité Ejecutivo de la Central Obrera Boliviana–Gobierno Desarrolla Campaña de Amedrentamiento y Amenazas" (La Paz: COB Archives, 2003); "Instructivo, Comité Ejecutivo de la Central Obrera Boliviana" (La Paz: COB Archives, 2003); "Resoluciones del Ampliado Extraordinario de la COB" (La Paz: COB Archives, 2003); "Comunicado de la Federación de Mineros" (La Paz: FSTMB Archives, 2003); "Muera la Represión Militar del Gonismo–communique" (La Paz: FSTMB Archives, 2003).

95. "Resoluciones del Ampliado Extraordinario de la COB."

96. "Humillación a Campesinos Aumenta Rechazo al Presidente más Impopular," *La Patria*, September 24, 2003.

97. "Programa de Lucha de la COB" (La Paz: COB Archives, 2003).

98. "Programa de Lucha."

99. "Programa de Lucha."

100. "Resoluciones del Ampliado Extraordinario de la COB."

101. Gómez, *El Alto de Pie*, 68.

102. Hylton and Thomson, *Revolutionary Horizons*, 113.

103. "Una Jornada de Violencia en El Alto Provocó una Veintena de Hridos," *La Razón*, October 9, 2003.

104. "Comunicado a la Opinión Pública" (La Paz: FSTMB Archives, 2003); "Los Mineros llegan a La Paz; Advierten de una Convulsión," *La Prensa*, October 9, 2003.

105. "El Presidente Deslegitima las Protestas que Crecen," *La Prensa*, October 10, 2003; "Dos Muertos y 20 Heridos por Enfrentamientos en Ventilla," *Opinión*, October 10, 2003; "Goni Asegura que Pequeña Minoría Pretende Destruir la Democracia," *Opin-*

ión, October 10, 2003.

106. Suárez, *Una Semana Fundamental*, 41.

107. "Protestas se Intensifican, Cocaleros a los Bloqueos," *El Deber*, October 11, 2003.

108. "COB y CSUTCB Acordaron no Negociar por Separado," *El Diario*, October 11, 2003; "El Alto Rechaza el Diálogo y Evita la Circulación hasta Bicicletas," *La Razón*, October 11, 2003.

109. "COB y CSUTCB."

110. García Linera, "La Crisis de Estado," 7; Mamani Ramírez, *Microgobiernos Barriales*, 61–63.

111. Mamani Ramírez, *Microgobiernos Barriales*, 68; Suárez, *Una Semana Fundamental*, 45. It is important to note that the circumstances leading to the death of the soldier, Cigmar García, are disputed. The official version of García's death is that he was kidnapped, beaten, and then assassinated by protesters. The version offered by witnesses from the El Alto neighborhood in which he died, Villa Ingenio, is quite different. They claim that the soldier refused to shoot on the civilian protesters and was consequently executed by a military captain. Gómez, *El Alto de Pie*, 97. The plausibility of the latter account is heightened by the fact that flowers appeared at the site of the soldier's death as well as a letter recording the events surrounding his death as told by the neighborhood witnesses. Given the political and social context of El Alto during these days, the neighborhood residents would have been in no mood to honor the death of just any soldier.

112. Suárez, *Una Semana Fundamental*, 47.

113. García Linera, "Crisis de Estado," 63.

114. Gómez, *El Alto de Pie*, 101–6; "Vecinos Piden la Dimisión de Goni," *La Prensa*, October 14, 2003.

115. "Vecinos Piden."

116. Gómez, *El Alto de Pie*, 111.

117. "Alistan sus Armas para que Goni Renuncie," *La Prensa*, October 14, 2003.

118. Gómez, *El Alto de Pie*, 120. On October 14, the fissures in the ruling class deepened. Juan del Granado, the mayor of La Paz, began calling for the president's resignation, as did the millionaire businessperson and leading member of the MIR, Samuel Doria Medina. A number of members of the Nueva Fuerza Republicana (New Republican Force, NFR) also joined the opposition against Sánchez de Lozada. Finally, dozens of artists and intellectuals from La Paz united behind María Romero and demanded an end to the reign of Sánchez de Lozada.

119. Gómez, *El Alto de Pie*, 103; Suárez, *Una Semana Fundamental*, 49.

120. "EEUU apoya a Goni y dice que no Reconocerá Otro Gobierno," *La Razón*, October 14, 2003.

121. Mamani Ramírez, *Microgobiernos Barriales*, 69.

122. Mamani Ramírez, *Microgobiernos Barriales*, 71.

123. Michael A. Lebowitz, *Build It Now: Socialism for the Twenty-First Century* (New York: Monthly Review Press, 2006), 19–20; David McNally, *Another World Is Possible: Globalization and Anti-Capitalism*, 2nd ed. (Winnipeg: Arbeiter Ring, 2006), 375.

124. ASOFAC–DG, *Avances, Riesgos y Retos del Juicio de Responsabilidades a Gonzalo Sánchez*

de Lozada y sus Colaboradores (La Paz: Asociación de Familiares Caídos por la Defensa del Gas [ASOFAC-DG], Defensor del Pueblo, Comunidad de Derechos Humanos, 2007), 3.

125. "Se Abren Tres Piquetes de Huelga de Hambre," *Opinión*, October 16, 2003.

126. Suárez, *Una Semana Fundamental*, 53.

127. "Se Abren Tres Piquetes."

128. Hylton and Thomson, *Revolutionary Horizons*, 116.

129. "Opositores, COB y COR El Alto Respaldan Sucesión Constitucional de Vicepresidente," *Opinión*, October 17, 2003.

130. "Mesa Apuesta a ser Neutral en Conflicto Social en Curso," *La Prensa*, October 17, 2003.

131. Larry Rohter, "Bolivian Leader Resigns and His Vice President Steps In," *New York Times*, October 18, 2003.

132. Suárez, *Una Semana Fundamental*, 59.

133. Sánchez de Lozada cited a poll published on the website of Radio Fides. It was revealed the next day by Radio Fides that its website had been hacked and that the results of the poll were precisely the inverse: 75 percent of Bolivians were in favor of the president stepping down. Suárez, *Una Semana Fundamental*, 59–61.

134. Gómez, *El Alto de Pie*, 134.

135. García Linera, "Crisis de Estado," 33–66.

136. "El ex Presidente está en Miami," *La Razón*, October 18, 2003. Also fleeing the country for fear of facing trial for their roles in the sixty-seven deaths and four hundred injured were minister of government, Yerko Kukoc (to Mexico); minister of the presidency, José Guillermo Justiniano; and vice-minister of government, José Luis Harb (both to Argentina).

137. "Mesa Gobernará Sin Políticos y Hará Referéndum y Constituyente," *La Razón*, October 18, 2003.

138. "Mesa Pasa de la Pantalla a la Silla Presidencial en una Carrera Fugaz," *La Razón*, October 18, 2003.

139. "Mesa Pasa de la Pantalla."

140. Vaca Díez and Cossío had been constitutionally entitled to assume the presidency in the event of Mesa's resignation, as they were head of the Senate and Chamber of Deputies, respectively. Instead, the president of the Supreme Court, Eduardo Rodríguez Veltzé, became the interim president, and general elections, originally scheduled originally for August 2007, were pushed forward to December 2005.

141. Many leaders and rank-and-file activists in this array of social movement and union organizations sought revolutionary change of the structures of society, economy, and polity. They frequently invoked the Constituent Assembly as a body that would *replace* the existing legislative, executive, military, and judicial apparatuses. On this view, the assembly would be a process through which Bolivia would be fundamentally *refounded* by, and in the interests of, the poor indigenous urban and rural majority.

Chapter 7: Argentina 2001: Our Year of Rebellion

1. Translator's note: the concept of "lo constituyente," or elected popular assemblies, was central in the debates within popular movements across the whole of Latin America in the first decade of the twenty-first century; see the chapter by Mike Gonzalez in this volume.

Chapter 8: The Pink Tide in Latin America: Where the Future Lay?

1. It is significant that the concept of the "historic compromise" was first articulated in November 1973 by Enrico Berlinguer, of the Italian Communist Party, in the course of a speech analyzing the Chilean experience.
2. David Hasselhof, of Baywatch fame, takes pride in his 360 pieces of the Berlin Wall. But that is not to suggest that he can be considered part of the Left!
3. A continuation of the corruption of language that gave us "humanitarian war," "collateral damage," and "friendly fire," among other terms to cover violence, destruction, and unjust war.
4. The Zapatista National Liberation Army (EZLN) was named in honor of the peasant revolutionary Emiliano Zapata, murdered in 1919. See Tom Hayden, ed., *The Zapatista Reader* (New York: Nation Books, 2002).
5. In 2018, Donald Trump delayed its renewal after the election of Andres Manuel López Obrador to the Mexican presidency.
6. See Jorge Orovitz Sanmartino's chapter on Argentina in this volume.
7. The issue of the armed struggle strategy belongs here, but it is too complex an issue to address within the confines of this essay. Whatever the limitations of the guerrilla strategy (which I have discussed elsewhere), the vicious and sustained repression unleashed for so long by authoritarian regimes is testimony to the fact that they had felt themselves seriously threatened by that generation of young revolutionaries whom they so relentlessly destroyed. See Mike Gonzalez and Houman Barekat, eds., *Arms and the People: Popular Movements and the Military from the Paris Commune to the Arab Spring* (London: Pluto Press, 2012).
8. See Subcomandante Marcos, "Letter from the Lacandon Jungle," in *Our Word Is Our Weapon* (London: Serpent's Tail, 2001).
9. See John Beverley, *Latinamericanism after 9/11* (Durham, NC: Duke University Press, 2013).
10. Exemplified of course by Oliver North and the Contra affair.
11. Though the Sandinistas made their own contribution to the defeat as well. See my *Nicaragua: What Went Wrong* (London: Bookmarks, 1990) and Dan Le Botz, *What Went Wrong? The Nicaraguan Revolution: A Marxist Analysis* (Leiden: E. J. Brill, 2018).
12. How profound that defeat was has emerged throughout 2018, as three hundred people have already died at the hands of the Ortega regime, killed by Sandinista police and troops.
13. They formed the Concertación coalition, which governed under the Christian Democratic president Patricio Aylwin. It was an irony that Aylwin had been a militant

advocate of the so-called soft coup (using economic means) to bring down Allende in 1973; but that seemed to have been forgotten.

14. Jorge Castañeda, "A Tale of Two Lefts," *Foreign Affairs*, May/June 2006.

15. See Phillip O'Brien, Jacqueline Roddick, and Ian Roxborough, *State and Revolution in Chile* (London: Palgrave Macmillan, 1995).

16. Emir Sader, *The New Mole: Paths of the Latin American Left* (London: Verso, 2011), 76.

17. John Holloway: *Change the World without Taking Power* (London: Pluto Press, 2002).

18. Michael Hardt and Toni Negri, *Empire* (Cambridge, MA: Harvard University Press, 2000); *Multitude* (Cambridge, MA: Harvard University Press, 2006).

19. George Ciccariello-Maher, *We Created Chávez: A People's History of the Venezuelan Revolution* (Durham, NC: Duke University Press, 2013).

20. Jeffery R. Webber, *Red October: Left-Indigenous Struggles in Modern Bolivia* (Leiden: E. J. Brill, 2012). Jeffery R. Webber, "Revolution against 'Progress': Neo-Extractivism, the Compensatory State, and the TIPNIS Conflict in Bolivia," in *Crisis and Contradiction: Marxist Perspectives on Latin America in the Global Political Economy*, ed. Susan J. Spronk and Jeffery R. Webber, 79 (Leiden, Netherlands: Brill, 2014), 302–33.

21. See Jeffery R. Webber's chapter on Bolivia in this volume.

22. Oscar Olivera and Tom Lewis, *Cochabamba! Water Wars in Bolivia, Mike Gonzalez and Marianella Yanes, eds.* (Chicago: South End Press, 2004).

23. Marcela Olivera, "Letter from Cochabamba," in *The Last Drop: The Politics of Water*, Mike Gonzalez and Marianella Yanes, eds. (London: Pluto Press, 2015).

24. See Jorge Orovitz Sanmartino's chapter on Argentina in this volume.

25. D. L. Raby, *Democracy and Revolution: Latin America and Socialism Today* (London: Pluto Press, 2006).

26. As a declaration from the indigenous organizations immediately after Morales's election made very clear.

27. In fact Cardoso had also launched some similar cash transfer schemes.

28. "Catastrophic equilibrium" is the term used by Bolivian vice president Álvaro García Linera to describe the situation there between 2002 and 2005.

29. Mike Gonzalez, "The Reckoning: The Future of the Venezuelan Revolution," *International Socialism*, second series, *143* (Summer 2014).

30. See Jeffery R. Webber, "Bolivia: Burdens of a State Manager," April 6, 2015, https://socialistproject.ca/2015/04/b1102/.

31. See Luis Macas interview in Jeffery R. Webber, *The Last Day of Oppression, and the First Day of the Same: The Politics and Economics of the New Latin American Left* (Chicago: Haymarket, 2017). See too John Vidal's interview with Alberto Acosta in *The Guardian* (December 2, 2010), and his interview with Jose Luis Exeni on ALICE CES, March 29, 2012, at youtube.com/watch?v=GJ9LTdOjWRU.

32. Edgardo Lander and Hugo Prieto, "Venezuela Must Face Its Civilizational Crisis," September 29, 2016, https://venezuelanalysis.com/ZPn.

33. "Venezuela Crisis: UN Says Security Forces Killed Hundreds," BBC News, June 22, 2018, https://www.bbc.com/news/world-latin-america-44575599.

34. "La ruina de Venezuela no se debe al 'socialismo' ni a la 'revolución,'" (The ruin of Ven-

ezuela has nothing to with "socialism" or "revolution"), in *Nueva Sociedad*, March/April 2018, www.nuso.org.

Chapter 9: The Tragedy of the Egyptian Revolution

1. See, respectively, Asef Bayat, *Revolution without Revolutionaries: Making Sense of the Arab Spring* (Stanford: Stanford University Press, 2017) and Robert Springborg, *Egypt* (Cambridge: Polity Press, 2018).

2. Leon D. Trotsky [1932–33], "Preface," in *The History of the Russian Revolution* (London: Pluto Press, 1977), 17.

3. Charles Tilly, *From Mobilization to Revolution* (New York: Random House, 1978), 190–93.

4. See Peter Curtin, *The World and the West: The European Challenge and the Overseas Response in the Age of Empire* (Cambridge: Cambridge University Press, 2000.)

5. See Roger Owen, *Cotton and the Egyptian Economy, 1820–1914: A Study in Trade and Development* (Oxford: Oxford University Press, 1969).

6. Gabriel Baer, *Studies in the Social History of Modern Egypt* (Chicago: Chicago University Press, 1969), 100.

7. Sven Beckert, *Empire of Cotton: A New History of Global Capitalism* (Harmondsworth: Penguin Books, 2016). This not only provides a fresh look at the centrality of cotton and cotton textiles to world capitalism since the Industrial Revolution, but also shows that the history of capitalist development in many of the countries of the global South, including Egypt, could only be understood in the context of how it related to the history of cotton trade and textile industries.

8. Rosa Luxemburg [1913], *The Accumulation of Capital* (London: Routledge and Kegan Paul, 1963). See especially chapter 30, "International Loans."

9. Roger Owen calculates the proportion of peasants who were landless in the 1870s at around one-third. Owen, *Cotton and the Egyptian Economy*, 148.

10. It must be remembered that this was taking place in a country with a literacy rate that continued to be less than 5 percent until the early twentieth century.

11. Owen, *Cotton and the Egyptian Economy*, 199.

12. Many of the leaders were themselves large landowners. See Abdel Azim Ramadan, *Development of the Nationalist Movement in Egypt: 1918–1936* (Cairo: Egyptian General Authority for Books, 1998; in Arabic).

13. For an informative account of political and class struggles during the first half of the twentieth century in Egypt, see Joel Beinin and Zackary Lockman, *Workers on the Nile: Nationalism, Communism, Islam and the Egyptian Working Class, 1882–1954* (Cairo: American University in Cairo Press, 1998).

14. The Wafd (The Delegation Party) was the main bourgeois nationalist party formed after the 1919 revolt.

15. Tariq Al-Bishry, *The Political Movement in Egypt: 1945–1953* (Cairo: Al-Shorouk Press, 2002; in Arabic)

16. For a detailed discussion of the nature of postcolonial regimes such as Nasser's in

Egypt in terms of Trotsky's theory of permanent revolution, Tony Cliff's theory of deflected permanent revolution, and other theories of revolution from above, see Neil Davidson, *How Revolutionary Were the Bourgeois Revolutions?* (Chicago: Haymarket Books, 2012), 284–308, 446–65; see also Joseph Choonara, "The Relevance of Permanent Revolution: A Reply to Neil Davidson," *International Socialism*, second series, 131 (Summer 2011).

17. See Vivek Chibber, *Locked in Place: State Building and Late Industrialization in India* (Princeton: Princeton University Press, 2003).

18. See Nigel Harris, *Of Bread and Guns: The World Economy in Crisis* (Harmondsworth: Penguin Books, 1983), and *The End of the Third World: Newly Industrializing Countries and the End of an Ideology* (Harmondsworth: Penguin Books, 1986).

19. It is sometimes forgotten that Egypt signed its first deals with the IMF for loans in 1962, the second year of its first "five-year plan," implementing an austerity program and devaluing the Egyptian pound. See J. Waterbury, *The Egypt of Nasser and Sadat: The Political Economy of Two Regimes* (Princeton, NJ: Princeton University Press, 1983).

20. Gilles Kepel, *The Prophet and the Pharaoh: Muslim Extremism in Egypt* (London: Zed Books, 1985).

21. Carrie Rosefsky Wickham, *Mobilizing Islam: Religion, Activism, and Political Change in Egypt* (New York: Columbia University Press, 2005).

22. The argument that the process of globalization would continue in a linear fashion to industrialize and develop the whole of the global South was always a myth. The number of failures far exceeded the success stories from Korea to China. The case of Egypt is one of several, where there are similar beginnings during the twentieth century, creating processes of industrialization, urbanization, and development but with the countries failing to become competitive centers of capital accumulation. For comparative and historical statistics putting the Egyptian case in global context, see United Nations Industrial Development Organization (UNIDO), *Industrial Development Reports*; also World Trade Organization, *World Trade Statistics*.

23. See Maha Mahfouz, *Egypt's Long Revolution* (London: Routledge, 2013).

24. Adam Hanieh, *Lineages of Revolt: Issues of Contemporary Capitalism in the Middle East* (Chicago: Haymarket Books, 2013), 52.

25. Hanieh, *Lineages of Revolt*, 149.

26. David Harvey, *A Brief History of Neoliberalism* (Oxford: Oxford University Press, 2005).

27. Jack Shenker, *The Egyptians: A Radical Story* (London: Allen Lane, 2015), 64.

28. Founded in the mid-1990s and emerging out of several Marxist study circles, the Revolutionary Socialists had become a significant voice on the left by the end of the twentieth century. They had adopted several critical stances that would distinguish them from the rest of the Left. Firstly, they did not view the collapse of the Soviet Union as the end of socialism. In fact, they viewed the Soviet Union as a form of state capitalism, so they were not as devastated as the rest of the Left when it collapsed. Secondly, radicalized by the first Palestinian Intifada of 1987, they considered the Palestinian question central to their politics. Thirdly, they believed that the project of rebuilding the Egyptian Left would only be successful if the Left challenged the Islamist alternative

from a politically independent position. The explicit or implicit alliance of the Left with the state was one of the main reasons for its demise. Fourthly, for the Revolutionary Socialists, the struggle for democracy needed to be linked to the struggles of workers and peasants against neoliberalism and the state.

29. *Kefaya* means "Enough" in Arabic.

30. It is true that some of the leaders of the Kefaya movement had no intention of sparking a mass movement and wished to keep the movements strictly within the limits of an elite pressure group. (For an elaboration of that argument, see Hugh Roberts, "The Revolution That Wasn't," *London Review of Books*, September 2, 2013). However, the widespread effects of this limited mobilization could hardly be controlled by the intentions of some of its leaders. The subsequent capitulation of most of those leaders to the army command and its later coup in 2013 should not retrospectively distort our reading of the events of 2004–6.

31. Carrie Rosefsky Wickham, *The Muslim Brotherhood: Evolution of an Islamist Movement* (Princeton, NJ: Princeton University Press, 2013), 111.

32. For an excellent analysis of the strike waves before and during the revolution, see Anne Alexander and Mustafa Bassiouny, *Bread, Freedom, Social Justice: Workers and the Egyptian Revolution* (London: Zed Books, 2014).

33. Alexander and Bassiouny, *Bread, Freedom, Social Justice*, 103.

34. Alexander and Bassiouny, *Bread, Freedom, Social Justice*, 104.

35. For a slightly exaggerated account of divisions within and between the different state apparatuses since Nasser, see Hisham Kandil, *Soldiers, Spies and Statesmen: Egypt's Road to Revolt* (London: Verso, 2012).

36. This slogan is sometimes wrongly translated as "The people want the downfall of the regime." This translation, besides being wrong linguistically, betrays an assumption of passivity that is also wrong in terms of understanding the mood and confidence of the masses at that time.

37. Wickham, *The Muslim Brotherhood*, 162.

38. Neil Ketchley, *Egypt in the Time of Revolution: Contentious Politics and the Arab Spring* (Cambridge: Cambridge University Press, 2017), 28.

39. One of the peculiarities of the mass demonstrations of those days was that despite police stations and vehicles being attacked, there was no significant attempt to occupy them or take the weapons. The same transpired with major government buildings: they would be attacked, surrounded, in many cases burnt, but not occupied. The joint weight of both the Muslim Brotherhood and reformist youth movements on the streets played a self-limiting role. The revolutionary Left was not large enough to break that dominance. This contrasts strongly with previous revolutionary upheavals where an integral part of the process was occupying government and police buildings and then using arms to defend them. Compare this with the struggle for Shanghai during the Chinese Revolution of 1925, in which postal and telegraph offices, government buildings, and police stations were occupied and defended. See Harold Isaacs [1938], *The Tragedy of the Chinese Revolution* (Chicago: Haymarket Books, 2010).

40. Soccer fan associations in Egypt had both a history of confrontation with the police

through years of clashes at stadiums across the country and a history of opposition to neoliberal economic policies that had led to the privatization of televised football matches. They were also highly organized, so it is not completely surprising that they ended up playing such a prominent role and eventually paying such a terrible price in lives lost.

41. The calling and mobilization for revolutionary days bears some resemblance to the *"journées"* of the French Revolution of 1789–94. It also continued long after the fall of Mubarak and only ended with the massacres of 2013.

42. The history of the Stalinist Left in Egypt, represented most recently by the Tagammu and the Egyptian Communist Party, has always been one of mistrust of mass movements and riding the coattails of the state and those in power. In the 1940s they allied with the bourgeois nationalist Wafd Party and in the 1960s dissolved their organizations to join Nasser's "Socialist Union." During Mubarak's reign, they supported the state in its struggle against Islamist terrorism and extremism. They later played a prominent role in the political alliance supporting the army and the coup of 2013, openly endorsing the massacre, torture, and arrest of Muslim Brotherhood supporters.

43. *Al-Masry al-Youm*, February 8, 2011.

44. Alexander and Bassiouny, *Bread, Freedom, Social Justice.*

45. Alexander and Bassiouny, *Bread, Freedom, Social Justice*, 203.

46. Anthony Shadid, "Suez Canal Workers Join Broad Strikes in Egypt," *New York Times*, February 15, 2011.

47. Shenker, *The Egyptians*, 236.

48. Although millions were involved in the mass mobilizations during the eighteen days, this was still a minority of the population. Rural provinces were generally not involved at this stage, and significant sections of the urban population, particularly the middle classes, watched the events unfold on television either in direct hostility to the revolution or in fear of the consequences of getting involved.

49. *Al-Masry al-Youm*, February 18, 2011.

50. Theories of conspiracy against Egypt, its unity, its state, and its security and stability dominated and continue to dominate the discourse of counter-revolution in Egypt.

51. Shenker, *The Egyptians*, 245.

52. Shenker, *The Egyptians*, 256.

53. Ikhwanonline.com/section/87689.

54. *Al-Masry al-Youm*, March 24, 2011.

55. "Cleansing" spread as a demand to remove corrupt managers and get more accountability.

56. The Copts, Egypt's Christian minority, represent around 10 percent of the population. Discrimination against this minority increased during the Sadat and Mubarak eras. The growing role of religious establishments in the provision of essential services as the state retreated, coupled with the rise of Islamist identity politics and retreat of many of the Copts into the perceived protection of the Church establishment, fueled sectarian tension, which accelerated in the last years of Mubarak's rule.

57. *Nile Television*, night of October 9, 2011.

58. Mohamed Mahmoud Street, which would become one of the main symbols of the

deadly battles between revolutionary youth and the police, had an interesting history. It was named after Mohamed Mahmud Pasha, who together with Saad Zaghlul led the anti-colonial movement that started with the 1919 revolution. He was also a major landowner with more than 8,000 feddans (8,300 acres); see Gabriel Baer, *Studies in the Social History of Modern Egypt* (Chicago: Chicago University Press, 1969). Although he played a leading role in a struggle against colonial rule, he was unable to mobilize masses that would threaten his property. This was a contradiction that plagued the Wafd leadership in the 1920s and '30s, and also would plague many Islamist and secular opposition forces during the 2011 revolution.

59. A major theme in the divisions within the revolutionary camp was over the choice between street fighting and occupations on the one hand and elections and ballot boxes on the other. Many of the young revolutionaries who were politicized during the revolution saw participation in elections as a betrayal of the revolution rather than an opportunity to strengthen the revolutionary camp and win over wider layers of people who were voting freely for the first time in their lives.

60. Wickham, *The Muslim Brotherhood*, 250–51.

61. Wickham, *The Muslim Brotherhood*, 252.

62. *Nour* means "light" in Arabic.

63. See Ashraf al-Sherif, *Egypt's Salafists at the Crossroads*, Carnegie Endowment for International Peace, 2015.

64. Alexander and Bassiouny, *Bread, Freedom, Social Justice*, 260.

65. Khaled Ali, a leftist labor lawyer and human rights activist, was also a presidential nominee but, relatively unknown and with limited resources, his campaign failed to attract much attention.

66. Wickham, *The Muslim Brotherhood*, 254.

67. Wickham, *The Muslim Brotherhood*, 263.

68. One of the major factors, both in the attempts at paralyzing and sabotaging the Mursi presidency and later legitimizing and facilitating the coup and military rule, was the Egyptian judiciary. Ideologically, the battle between Mursi and the judiciary was portrayed as a dictatorial president attempting to curtail the powers of an independent judiciary. In reality, it involved a highly politicized judiciary, one of the main pillars of the old regime, paving the way for the military. For a detailed account of the history of the Egyptian judiciary and in particular the Supreme Constitutional Court and their relation to other sections of the Egyptian state since Nasser, see Tamir Moustafa, *The Struggle for Constitutional Power: Law, Politics and Economic Development in Egypt* (Cambridge: Cambridge University Press, 2007).

69. Wickham, *The Muslim Brotherhood*, 265.

70. Wickham, *The Muslim Brotherhood*, 277.

71. Maha Abdelrahman, "In Praise of Organization: Egypt between Activism and Revolution," *Development and Change* 44, no. 3 (2013): 130.

72. Gilbert Achcar, *Morbid Symptoms: Relapse in the Arab Uprising* (Redwood City, CA: Stanford University Press, 2016), 180.

73. Hanieh, *Lineages of Revolt*, 170.

74. Alexander and Bassiouny, *Bread, Freedom, Social Justice*, 272.

75. Alexander and Bassiouny, *Bread, Freedom, Social Justice*, 305.

76. Ketchley, *Egypt in the Time of Revolution*, 108.

77. Ketchley, *Egypt in the Time of Revolution*, 111.

78. Adam Hanieh, in *Lineages of Revolt*, provides the most detailed account on the extent of Gulf capital involvement in the Egyptian economy during the Mubarak era and the logic of its support of the counter-revolution.

79. For an archive of statements, analysis, and positions of the Revolutionary Socialists between 2011 and 2013, see revsoc.me.

80. Some commentators would claim that the military coup of 2013 was not fundamentally different from the "coup" that removed Mubarak from power in 2011, since real power had always remained in the hands of the military; see, for example, Achcar, *Morbid Symptoms*. Others, utilizing Gramscian terminology, have seen the rise of Abdel Fattah al-Sisi and his coup as an example of some form of Bonapartism, seeing the SCAF coup of 2011 and the Sisi coup of 2013 as examples of "Caesarist passive revolution." Brecht de Smet, *Gramsci on Tahrir: Revolution and Counter-r evolution in Egypt* (London: Pluto Press, 2016).

81. There are many parallels between the evolving role of General Sisi between 2011 and 2013 and that of Chiang Kai-shek in the Chinese revolution and counter-revolution in the years 1925–27. As Harold Isaacs describes the Chinese leader in words befitting the Egyptian general: "Chiang Kai-shek is another of those historical personalities who emerge from a class to lead it because their personal ambitions, background, and history fit them to serve the given needs of their class at a given historical moment. What Engels called an 'endless array of contingencies,' which we term chance because their inter-connections are so often untraceable, brings them forward when these needs arise." Sisi, like Chiang Kai-shek, presented himself at first as a defender and supporter of the revolution, supporting the mobilization against Mursi and claiming that this was a new stage of the revolution, that there was a continuity between the January 2011 revolution and the June 2013 revolution. Like Chiang Kai-shek, he utilized nationalism and the confusion and ambiguity about the role of the army to appear as a different creature to different segments of the population. Another "three-headed Cerberus who stood at the gates of Hades." See Isaacs, *The Tragedy of the Chinese Revolution*, 88, 101.

82. Another similarity between Sisi's government and the one Chiang Kai-shek formed after his coup was that Chiang appointed several communist leaders as ministers, including the labor and agriculture ministers.

83. Egyptian Communist Party statement, August 16, 2013, www.cp-egypt.com.

84. Ketchley, *Egypt in the Time of Revolution*, 203.

85. See Corey Robin, *The Reactionary Mind: Conservatism from Edmund Burke to Sarah Palin* (Oxford: Oxford University Press, 2013).

86. In a speech in early 2016 at one of the military bases, Sisi openly discussed the old regime's fear of imposing harsh neoliberal measures. He said that when Sadat raised bread and other food prices in the 1970s and there were riots, the regime backed down and had been scared ever since. Sisi, however, was not scared and would carry out the

economic reform program by any means necessary. Also, just before the new IMF austerity deal in November 2016, he announced that the army was prepared to be deployed in all Egyptian cities within six hours.

87. See Steven A. Cook, *Ruling but Not Governing: The Military and Political Development in Algeria, Egypt and Turkey* (Baltimore: John Hopkins University Press, 2007).

Chapter 10: The Actuality of the Revolution

1. Anyone foolish enough to attempt a chapter on the scale of this one would be well advised to do what I have done and seek help and advice from comrades and colleagues before sending the finished article to the publisher. I am therefore grateful to Jamie Allinson, Tithi Bhattacharya, Satnam Virdee, and especially Gareth Dale for their enormously supportive but probing comments on various versions. Perhaps my biggest debt, however, is to Colin Barker, Gareth's and my fellow editor, who died during the final stages of the book's preparation. Even during what he knew was his final illness, Colin devoted part of his remaining time to making extensive notes on what I had written. Given how important Colin was in my own intellectual and political development, I will always be grateful for this kindness and proud to be associated with what was his final project.

2. For the best-known examples, see Karl Marx and Friedrich Engels [1848], "Manifesto of the Communist Party," in *The Revolutions of 1848*, vol. 1 of *Political Writings*, David Fernbach, ed. (Harmondsworth: Penguin Books/New Left Review, 1973), 79; and Karl Marx [1867], *Capital: A Critique of Political Economy*, vol. 1 (Harmondsworth: Penguin Books/New Left Review, 1976), 929.

3. Marx and Engels, "Manifesto of the Communist Party," 68.

4. Friedrich Engels [1877], *Anti-Dühring: Herr Eugen Dühring's Revolution in Science*, in *Collected Works*, vol. 25 (London: Lawrence and Wishart, 1987), 145. Marx had written: "Revolutions are the locomotives of history." See [1850], "The Class Struggles in France: 1848 to 1850," in *Surveys from Exile*, vol. 3 of *Political Writings*, David Fernbach, ed. (Harmondsworth: Penguin Books/New Left Review, 1973), 117. The metaphor of revolution as humanity pulling the "emergency brake" on a runaway train was reused by Walter Benjamin in the preparatory notes for his last great essay. See [1940], "Paralipomena to 'On the Concept of History,'" in *Selected Writings*, vol. 4, *1938–1940*, Howard Eiland and Michael J. Jennings, eds. (Cambridge, MA: Belknap Press of Harvard University Press, 2003), 402.

5. Friedrich Engels [1887], "Introduction [to Sigismund Borkheim's pamphlet, *In Memory of the German Blood and Thunder Patriot, 1806–1807*]," in *Collected Works*, vol. 26 (London: Lawrence and Wishart, 1990), 451. See also Frederick Engels [1891], "Socialism in Germany," in *Collected Works*, vol. 27 (London: Lawrence and Wishart, 1990), 245.

6. Rosa Luxemburg [1915], "The Junius Pamphlet: The Crisis in the German Social Democracy," in *Rosa Luxemburg Speaks*, Mary-Alice Walters, ed. (New York: Pathfinder Press, 1970), 269 (my emphasis).

7. Mike Davis, "Old Gods, New Enigmas: Notes on Revolutionary Agency," in *Old Gods,*

New Enigmas: Marx's Lost Theory (London: Verso, 2018), 154.

8. Michael Mann, *The Sources of Social Power*, vol. 4, *Globalisations, 1945–2011* (Cambridge: Cambridge University Press, 2013), 398.

9. Adrian Parr, *The Wrath of Capital: Neoliberalism and Climate Change Politics* (New York: Columbia University Press, 2013), 6.

10. Parr, *The Wrath of Capital*, 145–46.

11. David Wallace-Wells, "This Is Not a Drill," *The Guardian* (Weekend), February 2, 2019, 23.

12. Tamsin Green, "World Weatherwatch: From Drifts in Paris to Drought in Cape Town," *The Guardian*, February 14, 2018.

13. See, for example, George Lefebvre [1932], *The Great Fear of 1789: Rural Panic in Revolutionary France* (London: New Left Books, 1973).

14. James Davis, "At War with the Future: Catastrophism and the Right," in Sasha Lilley, David McNally, Eddie Yuen, and James Davis, *Catastrophism: The Apocalyptic Politics of Collapse and Rebirth* (Oakland, CA: PM Press, 2012), 106.

15. Jeet Heer, "Republic of Fear," *New Republic*, https://newrepublic.com/article/132114/republic-fear (posted March 21, 2015). Trump did not create fear out of nothing, but built on a public mood that has existed in the US for decades at least; see, for example, Barry Glassner, *The Culture of Fear: Why Americans Are Afraid of the Wrong Things* (New York: Basic Books, 1999).

16. Razmig Keucheyan, "Not Even Ecological Disaster Can Kill Capitalism," *The Guardian*, March 7, 2014.

17. György Lukács [1924], *Lenin: A Study in the Unity of His Thought* (London: New Left Books, 1970), chapter 1.

18. Engels, *Anti-Dühring*, 269–70.

19. William Morris [1890], *News from Nowhere: Or, an Epoch of Rest, Being Some Chapters from a Utopian Romance* (London: Longman, Green and Co., 1920), chapter 17, "How the Change Came."

20. Vladimir I. Lenin [1918], "Extraordinary Seventh Congress of the R.C.P.(B.): 9: Report on the Review of the Programme and on Changing the Name of the Party," in *Collected Works*, vol. 27, *February–July 1918* (Moscow: Progress Publishers, 1965), 131, 130.

21. Leon D. Trotsky [1908–1909/1922], *1905* (Harmondsworth: Penguin Books, 1972), 333.

22. Leon D. Trotsky [1906], *Results and Prospects*, in *The Permanent Revolution* and *Results and Prospects*, 3rd ed. (New York: Pathfinder, 1969), 100.

23. One of the most puzzling aspects of an essay by Jodi Dean—which, like this chapter, takes its title from Lukács' book—is that it discusses Lenin's view that the Russian Revolution would be proletarian rather than bourgeois, without considering Trotsky's earlier and more coherent version of this position. See Jodi Dean, "The Actuality of the Revolution," *Socialist Register 2017: Rethinking Revolution*, Leo Panitch and Greg Albo, eds. (London: Merlin Press, 2016), 62–64. For the differences between Trotsky and Lenin's respective arguments, see Neil Davidson, *How Revolutionary Were the Bourgeois*

Revolutions? (Chicago: Haymarket Books, 2012), 225–36.

24. Lenin's comments to this effect are legion but, for a selection, see Leon D. Trotsky [1930–32], *The History of the Russian Revolution* (London: Pluto Press, 1977), 1227–38.

25. Vladimir I. Lenin [1918], "Report on the Activities of the Council of People's Commissars, January 11 (24)," in *Collected Works*, vol. 26, *September 1917–February 1918* (Moscow: Foreign Languages Publishing House, 1964), 464–65, 470.

26. See also Davidson, *How Revolutionary Were the Bourgeois Revolutions?*, 280–84.

27. Davidson, *How Revolutionary Were the Bourgeois Revolutions?*, 236–42.

28. Lukács, *Lenin*, 10–12.

29. Massimo Salvadori [1976], *Karl Kautsky and the Socialist Revolution, 1880–1938* (London: Verso, 1990), 218–93.

30. Jeffery R. Webber, *From Rebellion to Reform in Bolivia: Class Struggle, Indigenous Liberation, and the Politics of Evo Morales* (Chicago: Haymarket Books, 2011), 168–69.

31. Yanis Varoufakis, "Confessions of an Erratic Marxist in the Midst of a Repugnant European Crisis," https://yanisvaroufakis.eu/2013/12/10/confessions-of-an-erratic-marxist-in-the-midst-of-a-repugnant-european-crisis/ (posted December 10, 2013).

32. Samir Amin, *Class and Nation Historically and in the Current Crisis* (New York: Monthly Review Press, 1980), 256.

33. Peter Wollen, "Our-Post Communism: The Legacy of Karl Kautsky," *New Left Review*, no. 202 (November/December 1993), 92, 93.

34. Meghnad Desai, *Marx's Revenge: The Resurgence of Capitalism and the Death of Statist Socialism* (London: Verso, 2002), 9, 10.

35. Desai, *Marx's Revenge*, 115–16, 119.

36. Benjamin Kunkel, "The Capitalocene," *London Review of Books* 39, no. 5 (March 2, 2017): 28. A postclimate catastrophe socialism involving "equality and scarcity" is discussed as one possible global development in Peter Frase, *Four Futures: Life after Capitalism* (London: Verso, 2016), 91–119.

37. Karl Marx et al. [1850], "Meeting of the Central Authority: September 15, 1850," in *Collected Works*, vol. 10 (London: Lawrence and Wishart, 1978), 626.

38. Che Guevara [1961], *Guerrilla Warfare* (Harmondsworth: Penguin Books, 1969), 13.

39. Fidel Castro [1962], "The Second Declaration of Havana," in *The First and Second Declarations of Havana: Manifestos of Revolutionary Struggle in the Americas Adopted by the Cuban People*, Mary-Alice Walters, ed. (New York: Pathfinder Press, 2007), 72–73.

40. Fidel Castro [1967], "On the Latin American Revolution," in *Fidel Castro Reader*, David Deutschmann and Deborah Shnookal, eds. (New York: Ocean Press, 2007), 296.

41. Samuel Farber, *The Politics of Che Guevara: Theory and Practice* (Chicago: Haymarket Books, 2016), 19–23.

42. Ernesto Che Guevara [1965], "Socialist Planning," in *Venceremos! The Speeches and Writings of Ernesto Che Guevara*, John Gerassi, ed. (London: Panther Books, 1969), 557.

43. Alasdair MacIntyre [1969], "Marxism of the Will," in *Alasdair MacIntyre's Engagement with Marxism: Selected Writings, 1953–1974*, Paul Blackledge and Neil Davidson, eds. (Leiden: E. J. Brill, 2008), 376.

44. NLR, "The Marxism of Régis Debray," *New Left Review*, no. 45 (September/October

1967): 8.

45. The Invisible Committee, *The Coming Insurrection* (Los Angeles: Semiotext(e), 2009), 95, 96.

46. John Holloway, "No," *Historical Materialism* 13, no. 4 (2005), 271.

47. "Many people, including some who call themselves Marxists, still think that to radically criticize a society you have to take a standpoint outside that society. They do not recognize that a critique can be both internal to what it criticizes, and radical in its demands for transformation." Does the position criticized here sound familiar at all? See Andrew Collier, *Marx* (Oxford: Oneworld Publications, 2004), 56.

48. Lukács, *Lenin*, 12–13.

49. Benjamin, "Paralipomena to 'On the Concept of History,'" 402.

50. Antonio Gramsci, "Problems of Marxism," in *Selections from the Prison Notebooks*, Quintin Hoare and Geoffrey Nowell Smith, eds. (London: Lawrence and Wishart, 1971), 438, Q11§15.

51. Antonio Gramsci and Palmiro Togliatti [1926], "The Italian Situation and the Tasks of the PCI ('Lyons Theses')," in *Selections from the Political Writings, 1921–1926*, Quintin Hoare, ed. (London: Lawrence and Wishart, 1978), 370.

52. Vladimir I. Lenin [1899], "On Strikes," in *Collected Works*, vol. 4, *1898–April 1901* (Moscow: Progress Publishers, 1960), 317.

53. Lukács, *Lenin*, 12.

54. Andrew Abbott [1997], "On the Concept of Turning Point," in *Time Matters: On Theory and Method* (Chicago: Chicago University Press, 2001), 257.

55. Lenin, "The Collapse of the Second International," 213–14.

56. Leon D. Trotsky, "In Defense of the Russian Revolution," in *Leon Trotsky Speaks* (New York: Pathfinder Books, 1972), 247; William Shakespeare, *Julius Caesar*, Act 4, Scene 3.

57. China Miéville, *October: The Story of the Russian Revolution* (London: Verso, 2017), 247.

58. György Lukács [1925], "Tailism and the Dialectic," in *A Defence of History and Class Consciousness* (London: Verso, 2000), 58.

59. Vladimir I. Lenin [1915], "The Collapse of the Second International," in *Collected Works*, vol. 21, *August 1914–December 1915* (Moscow: Progress Publishers, 1964), 214.

60. Leon D. Trotsky [1931], "What Is a Revolutionary Situation?," in *Writings of Leon Trotsky (1930–31)*, George Breitman and Sarah Lovell, eds. (New York: Pathfinder Press, 1973), 352.

61. Leon D. Trotsky [1921], "Flood Tide," in *The First Five Years of the Communist International*, vol. 2 (London: New Park Publications, 1974), 76.

62. Alexis de Tocqueville [1856], *The Ancien Regime and the French Revolution* (London: Fontana, 1966), 196.

63. Trotsky, "Flood Tide," 82, 83.

64. Antonio Gramsci, *Prison Notebooks*, vol. 2, Joseph A. Buttigieg, *ed.* (New York: Columbia University Press, 1996), 182, Q4§38.

65. Leon D. Trotsky [1932], "Revolution and War in China," in *Leon Trotsky on China*, Les Evans and Russell Block, eds. (New York: Monad Press, 1976), 584.

66. Leon D. Trotsky [1908–9/1919], *1905* (Harmondsworth: Penguin Books, 1972), 68.

67. Trotsky, *The History of the Russian Revolution*, 906; my italics.

68. Trotsky, *The History of the Russian Revolution*, 30; my italics.

69. Trotsky, *The History of the Russian Revolution*, 27.

70. Trotsky, "For the Internationalist Perspective," in *Leon Trotsky Speaks*, 199.

71. Eric J. Hobsbawm [1951], "Economic Fluctuations and Some Social Movements since 1800," in *Labouring Men: Studies in the History of Labour* (London: Weidenfeld and Nicolson, 1964), 126, 127, 147.

72. Kim Moody, *On New Terrain: How Capital Is Reshaping the Battleground of Class War* (Chicago: Haymarket Books, 2017), 75.

73. Vladimir I. Lenin [1916], "The Discussion on Self-Determination Summed Up," in *Collected Works*, vol. 22, *December 1915–July 1916* (Moscow: Progress Publishers, 1964), 355–56.

74. Vladimir I. Lenin [1917], "Letters from Afar: First Letter: The First Stage of the Revolution," in *Collected Works*, vol. 23, *August 1916–March 1917* (Moscow: Progress Publishers, 1964), 302.

75. Leon D. Trotsky [1924], "For the Internationalist Perspective," 182–83.

76. Louis Althusser [1962], "Contradiction and Overdetermination," in *For Marx* (London: Verso, 2005), 99.

77. Rex Wade, *The Russian Revolution, 1917* (Cambridge: Cambridge University Press, 2000), 283.

78. Hermann Gorter [1920], "Open Letter to Comrade Lenin: An Answer to Lenin's Pamphlet, '"Left-wing" Communism: An Infantile Disorder,'" in *International Communism in the Era of Lenin: A Documentary History*, Helmut Gruber, ed. (New York: Anchor Books, 1972), 217, 223.

79. Juliet Mitchell, *Woman's Estate* (Harmondsworth: Penguin Books, 1971), 14–15.

80. Tithi Bhattacharya, "Introduction: Mapping Social Reproduction Theory, in *Social Reproduction Theory: Remapping Class, Recentering Oppression*, Tithi Bhattacharya, ed. (London: Pluto Press, 2017), 3.

81. György Lukács [1923], "Reification and the Consciousness of the Proletariat," in *History and Class Consciousness: Studies in Marxist Dialectics* (London: Merlin Press, 1971), 168; my emphasis.

82. Bertell Ollman [1979], "Marxism and Political Science: Prolegomenon to a Debate on Marx's Method," in *Dance of the Dialectic: Steps in Marx's Method* (Urbana: University of Illinois Press, 2003), 139–40.

83. Angela Davis, *Women, Race and Class* (London: The Women's Press, 1982), 66.

84. Edward P. Thompson [1978], "The Poverty of Theory or an Orrery of Errors," in *The Poverty of Theory and Other Essays* (Fourth impression, London: Merlin Press, 1981), 64.

85. For different assessments of the extent to which *Capital* remained unfinished and reviews of the main contributions to this debate, see, Michael A. Lebowitz, *Beyond Capital: Marx's Political Economy of the Working Class* (Houndmills: Macmillan, 1992), 11–34, and Alex Callinicos, *Deciphering Capital: Marx's Capital and Its Destiny* (London: Bookmarks, 2014), 54–64.

86. See, for example, John Sanbonmatsu, *The Postmodern Prince: Critical Theory, Left Strate-

gy, and the Making of a New Political Subject (New York: Monthly Review Press, 2004), 196–202.

87. See, for example, Bob Pease, *Undoing Privilege: Unearned Advantage in a Divided World* (London: Zed Books, 2010), 17.

88. Marx to Weydemeyer, March 5, 1852, in *Collected Works*, vol. 39 (London: Lawrence and Wishart, 1983), 60.

89. Karl Marx [1875], "Critique of the Gotha Programme," in *The First International and After*, vol. 3 of *Political Writings*, David Fernbach, ed. (Harmondsworth: Penguin/New Left Review, 1974), 347.

90. Stuart Hall, "Race, Articulation and Societies Structured in Dominance," in *Sociological Theories: Race and Colonialism*, UNESCO, ed. (Paris: UNESCO, 1980), 341.

91. Karl Marx [1844], "Economic and Philosophical Manuscripts," in *Early Writings* (Harmondsworth: Penguin Books/New Left Review, 1975), 326.

92. Karl Marx [1867], *Capital: A Critique of Political Economy*, vol. 1 (Harmondsworth: Penguin Books/New Left Review, 1976), 481, 482. As Marx acknowledges (ibid., 483), the point had been made earlier by Adam Smith; see [1776], *An Inquiry into the Nature and Causes of the Wealth of Nations*, Edwin Cannan, ed. (Chicago: University of Chicago Press, 1976), Book V, chapter 1, 302–3.

93. I am grateful to Tithi Bhattacharya for bringing this point and some of the references in this paragraph to my attention; I look forward to her own important research on the subject appearing in print soon.

94. Marx, *Capital*, vol. 1, 695.

95. Friedrich Engels [1847], "The Reform Movement in France," in *Collected Works*, vol. 6 (London: Lawrence and Wishart, 1976), 377.

96. Lenin, "On Strikes," 315.

97. Vladimir I. Lenin [1905], "Socialism and Religion," in *Collected Works*, vol. 10, *November 1905–June 1906* (London: Lawrence and Wishart, 1962), 83.

98. As we have already seen in relation to the Russian Revolution, Marxists of the time were of course aware of the oppression of women and sought to end it, but they did not tend to use the term; in fact, the only specific oppression that was actually conceived as such was *national* oppression. Contemporary use of "oppression" in relation to "gender," "sexuality," "race," etc., seems to have been adopted from the concept of national oppression.

99. See John Smith's powerful description of the conditions under which three commodities—a T-shirt, iPhone, and cup of coffee—are produced: *Imperialism in the Twenty-First Century: Globalization, Super-Exploitation, and Capitalism's Final Crisis* (New York: Monthly Review Press, 2016), 9–34.

100. James Bloodworth, *Hired: Six Months Undercover in Low-Wage Britain* (London: Atlantic Books, 2018), 64–65, 67, and 11–76 more generally; for call centers, see Jamie Woodcock, *Working the Phones: Control and Resistance in Call Centres* (London: Pluto Press, 2017), 34–59.

101. Arlie Russell Hochschild [1983], *The Managed Heart: Commercialization of Human Feeling* (updated with a new preface; Berkeley: University of California Press, 2012), 5,

6–7, 8–9, and 3–9 more generally.

102. David Graeber, *Bullshit Jobs: A Theory* (London: Allen Lane, 2018), xviii.

103. Chuck Barone, "Political Economy of Classism: Towards a More Integrated Multilevel View," *Review of Radical Political Economy* 30, no. 2 (March 1998): 6.

104. Friedrich von Hayek, *The Road to Serfdom* (London: George Routledge and Sons, 1944), 104.

105. Terry Eagleton, *The Illusions of Postmodernism* (Oxford: Blackwell, 1996), 57–58. As someone of Irish Catholic heritage, Eagleton is of course aware that racism need not involve skin color or indeed any physical characteristic at all; but it always involves *some* essential quality or characteristic. Elsewhere he describes racism as involving "the superiority of one cultural identity over another." *The Idea of Culture* (Oxford: Blackwell, 2000), 58.

106. Ellen Meiksins Wood, "The Use and Abuses of 'Civil Society,'" in *Socialist Register 1990: The Retreat of the Intellectuals*, Ralph Miliband and Leo Panitch, eds. (London: Merlin Press, 1990), 76; see also *Democracy against Capitalism: Renewing Historical Materialism* (Cambridge: Cambridge University Press, 1995), 259.

107. Meiksins Wood, *Democracy against Capitalism*, 270.

108. Wendy Brown. "Feminism Unbound: Revolution, Mourning, Politics," in *Edgework: Critical Essays on Knowledge and Politics* (Princeton: Princeton University Press, 2005), 105–6, and see 104–12 more generally.

109. David McNally, "Intersections and Dialectics: Critical Reconstructions in Social Reproduction Theory," in *Social Reproduction Theory*, 107. For a recent discussion of precisely how racism was integrated with the origins and development of capitalism, see Satnam Virdee, "Racialized Capitalism: An Account of Its Contested Origins and Consolidation," *Sociological Review* 67, no. 1 (2019): 11–19.

110. Alexander Anievas and Kerem Nişancioğlu, *How the West Came to Rule: The Geopolitical Origins of Capitalism* (London: Pluto Press, 2015), 279.

111. I discuss this at greater length in "Capitalist Outcomes, Ideal Types, Historical Realities," *Historical Materialism* 27, no. 1 (2019): 210–76.

112. David Harvey, *Seventeen Contradictions and the End of Capitalism* (London: Profile Books, 2014), 68.

113. David Harvey, "Reply: Response to Alex Dubilet," *Syndicate* (April 1, 2015), https://syndicate.network/symposia/theology/seventeen-contradictions-and-the-end-of-capitalism/.

114. David Roediger, "Introduction: Thinking Through Race and Class in Hard Times," in *Class, Race, and Marxism* (London: Verso: 2017), 2.

115. The term was first used by Kimberlé Crenshaw, "Demarginalizing the Intersection of Race and Sex: A Black Feminist Critique of Antidiscrimination Doctrine, Feminist Theory and Antiracist Politics," *University of Chicago Legal Forum*, special issue: *Feminism in the Law: Theory, Practice and Criticism* (1989).

116. Edward Said, "Travelling Theory," in *The World, the Text, and the Critic* (Cambridge, MA: Harvard University Press, 1983); for an application of the analysis to intersectionality, see Sara Salem, "Intersectionality and Its Discontents: Intersectionality as

Travelling Theory," *European Journal of Women's Studies*, online first: http://journals. sagepub.com/doi/full/10.1177/1350506816643999 (posted April 22, 2016).

117. C. T. Mohanty, "Transnational Feminist Crossings: On Neoliberalism and Radical Critique," *Signs* 38, no. 4 (2013): 971–72.

118. Ashley Bohrer, "Intersectionality and Marxism: A Critical Historiography," *Historical Materialism* 26, no. 2 (2018): 69.

119. McNally, "Intersections and Dialectics," 97–99, 110–11 (quote).

120. Holly Lewis, *The Politics of Everybody: Feminism, Queer Theory, and Marxism at the Intersection* (London: Zed Books, 2016), 195.

121. Karl Marx, "Instructions for the Delegates of the Provisional General Council: The Different Questions," in *Collected Works*, vol. 20 (London: Lawrence and Wishart, 1985), 192.

122. Vladimir I. Lenin [1902], "What Is to Be Done? Burning Questions of Our Movement," in *Collected Works*, vol. 5, *May 1901–February 1902* (Moscow: Progress Publishers, 1961), 423.

123. Richard Stites [1978], *The Women's Liberation Movement in Russia: Feminism, Nihilism, and Bolshevism, 1860–1930*, new ed. (Princeton, NJ: Princeton University Press, 1991), 333.

124. S. A. Smith, *Russia in Revolution: An Empire in Crisis, 1890–1928* (Oxford: Oxford University Press, 2017), 338–45; Sharon Smith, *Women and Socialism: Class, Race, and Capital* (fully revised and updated edition; Chicago: Haymarket Books, 2015), 189–201; and Stites, *The Women's Liberation Movement in Russia*, 329–45, 358–76, 416–21.

125. Michael Haynes, *Russia: Class and Power, 1917–2000* (London: Bookmarks, 2002), 153–56; Stites, *The Women's Liberation Movement in Russia*, 376–406 ("the sexual Thermidor").

126. One possible reason why Lukács fails to identify such periods may be his conflation of Actuality 1 with Lenin's "era' of wars and revolutions," or at least the sense that the latter grew out of the former and would continue until the victory of the socialist revolution, or what he would later call the "illusions and extravagances" of the period; see "Postscript 1967," in *Lenin*, 90.

127. I discuss these revolutionary conjunctures, with special focus on "1968," in a book-length version of this chapter, due to appear as *The Actuality of the Revolution* (Chicago: Haymarket Books, forthcoming).

128. David Harvey, *The Condition of Postmodernity: An Inquiry into the Origins of Cultural Change* (Oxford: Basil Blackwell, 1989), 237.

129. Trotsky, "In Defense of the Russian Revolution," 249.

130. Perry Anderson, "Preface," in *The Antinomies of Antonio Gramsci* (London: Verso, 2017), 25.

131. Alain Badiou, *The Rebirth of History* (London: Verso, 2011), 38–39, 86.

132. I attempt to explain the non-occurrence of revolutionary conjunctures after 1975–76 in the forthcoming book-length version of this chapter.

133. Fredric Jameson, "Secondary Elaborations," in *Postmodernism, or, the Cultural Logic of Late Capitalism* (London: Verso, 1991), 309–10.

134. Perry Anderson, *The Origins of Postmodernity* (London: Verso, 1998), 121.

135. Fred Halliday, "Revolution in the Third World: 1945 and After," in *Revolution and Counter-Revolution*, E. E. Rice, ed. (Oxford: Basil Blackwell, 1991), 151.

136. Jeff Goodwin, *No Other Way Out: States and Revolutionary Movements, 1945–1991* (Cambridge: Cambridge University Press), 300.

137. Anderson [1976], *The Antinomies of Antonio Gramsci*, 106–7.

138. Goodwin, *No Other Way Out*, 44, 46–47.

139. Peter Thomas, *The Gramscian Moment: Philosophy, Hegemony and Marxism* (Leiden: E. J. Brill, 2009), 226. Although Thomas writes "a class" throughout this passage, what he describes here is only comprehensible as the *modus operandi* of a single class: the bourgeoisie.

140. Jeremy Lester, *Dialogue of Negation: Debates on Hegemony in Russia and the West* (London: Pluto Press, 2000), 72; see also Kate Crehan, *Gramsci's Common Sense: Inequality and Its Narratives* (Durham, NC: Duke University Press, 2016), 60.

141. Mark Fisher [2012], "Not Failing Better, but Fighting to Win," in *K-Punk: The Collected and Unpublished Writings of Mark Fisher (2004–2016)*, Darren Ambrose, ed. (London: Repeater, 2018), 521.

142. Philippe Le Goff, "Capitalism, Crisis and Critique: Reassessing Régis Debray's 'Modest Contribution' to Understanding May 1968 in Light of Luc Boltanski and Eve Chiapello's *Le nouvel esprit du capitalisme*," *Modern and Contemporary France* 22, no. 2 (2014): 241.

143. Daniel Chirot, "A Turning Point or Business as Usual?," in *Business as Usual: The Roots of the Global Financial Meltdown*, Craig Calhoun and Georgi Derluguian, eds. (New York: New York University Press, 2011), 136.

144. Arlie Russell Hochschild, *Strangers in Their Own Land: Anger and Mourning on the American Right* (New York: The New Press, 2016), 228.

145. William E. B. Du Bois [1935], *Black Reconstruction in America: An Essay Towards a History of the Part Which Black Folk Played in That Attempt to Reconstruct Democracy in America, 1860–1880* (New York: Atheneum, 1969), 700–701.

146. David R. Roediger, *The Wages of Whiteness: Race and the Making of the American Working Class* (London: Verso, 1991), 12–13 and 11–13 more generally; see also "Accounting for the Wages of Whiteness," in *Class, Race, and Marxism*, 61–72.

147. Friedrich Nietzsche [1887], *The Genealogy of Morals: A Polemic*, vol. 8, *The Complete Works of Friedrich Nietzsche* (Edinburgh: T. N. Foulis, 1913). 72.

148. China Miéville, "On Social Sadism," *Salvage* 2 (November 2015), 24.

149. Philip Mirowski, *Never Let a Serious Crisis Go to Waste: How Neoliberalism Survived the Financial Meltdown* (London: Verso, 2013), 130 and 129–38 more generally.

150. Fintan O'Toole, *Heroic Failure: Brexit and the Politics of Pain* (London: Head of Zeus, 2018), 132–133 and 123–51 more generally. One need not accept Snyder's liberal paranoia about the ubiquity of Russian influence in the West to acknowledge that in "sadopopulism" he has identified a real disposition; see Timothy Snyder, *The Road to Unfreedom: Russia, Europe, America* (London: Bodley Head, 2018), 273.

151. See, respectively, Danny Dorling and Sally Tomlinson, *Rule Britannia: Brexit and the*

End of Empire (London: Biteback, 2019), 28 and 21–37 more generally; and Charles Post, "We Got Trumped: Results and Prospects after the 2016 Election," *International Socialist Review* 104 (Spring 2007): 35–41.

152. Moody, *On New Terrain*, 84.

153. Daniel Bensaïd, "Leaps! Leaps! Leaps!," *International Socialism*, second series, 95 (Summer 2002): 77.

154. Moody, *On New Terrain*, 75–76.

155. See the discussion of "opportuneness" or "right-ness for the times" in Antonio Gramsci, *Prison Notebooks*, vol. 3, Joseph A. Buttigieg, ed. (New York: Columbia University Press, 2007), 209, Q7§78.

156. Walter Benjamin [1934–35], "Convolute N: On the Theory of Knowledge, Theory of Progress," in *The Arcades Project*, Rolf Tiedemann, ed. (Cambridge, MA: Belknap Press of Harvard University Press, 2002), 473.

157. Adam Tooze, *Crashed: How a Decade of Financial Crises Changed the World* (London: Allen Lane, 2018), 615–16.

158. Naomi Klein, *This Changes Everything: Capitalism versus the Climate* (London: Allen Lane, 2014), 40–41 and 38–44 more generally.

159. Ashley Dawson, "The Global Calculus of Climate Disaster," *Boston Review*, http://bostonreview.net/science-nature/ashley-dawson-global-calculus-climate-disaster (posted September 6, 2017).

160. Wallace-Wells, "This Is Not a Drill," 25.

161. Susan Ferguson and David McNally, "Precarious Migrants: Gender, Race and the Social Reproduction of a Global Working Class," *Socialist Register 2015: Transforming Classes*, Leo Panitch and Greg Albo, eds. (London: Merlin Press, 2014), 6.

162. Ferguson and McNally, "Precarious Migrants," 19.

163. Deng Yunxue, "Space and Strike Diffusion in a Decentralized Authoritarian Country: A Study of the Auto Parts Industry in South China," in *Worker's Movements and Strikes in the Twenty-First Century: A Global Perspective*, Jörg Nowak, Madhumita Dutta, and Peter Birke, eds. (London: Rowan and Littlefield, 2018), 48–52. For a more general discussion of migration in China, see Wen Tiejun, "How China's Migrant Labourers Are Becoming the New Proletariat," in *Labour and the Challenges of Globalization: What Prospects for Transnational Solidarity?*, Andreas Bieler, Ingemar Lindberg, and Devan Pillay, eds. (London: Pluto Press, 2008).

164. Aditya Chakrabortty, "College Cleaners Defeated Outsourcing. They've Shown It Can Be Done," *The Guardian*, September 12, 2017; "'Between Thorns and Roses': How Migrant Workers Beat Outsourcing at SOAS," Luke Stobart interview with SOAS Justice for Workers, *Historical Materialism* website, http://www.historicalmaterialism.org/interviews/between-thorns-and-roses-how-migrant-workers-beat-outsourcing-soas.

165. Satnam Virdee, *Racism, Class and the Racialized Outsider* (Houndmills: Palgrave Macmillan, 2014), 164.

166. Cinzia Arruzza, Tithi Bhattacharya, and Nancy Fraser, "Notes for a Feminist Manifesto," *New Left Review*, no. 114 (November/December 2018), 116.

167. Daniel Bensaïd [2004], *An Impatient Life: A Memoir* (London: Verso, 2013), 63.

168. Prisca Bachelet, interviewed in Mitchell Abidor, *May Made Me: An Oral History of the 1968 Uprising in France* (London: Pluto Press, 2018), 60.

169. Mark Elbaum, *Revolution in the Air: Sixties Radicals Turn to Lenin, Mao and Che* (London: Verso, 2002), 57.

170. Abidor, *May Made Me*, 8. Some revolutionaries, notably in Italy, did understand that '68 had the potential to be a moment of revolutionary rupture: "In their minds, they were not witnessing an Italian version of the Russian 1905, a dress rehearsal of some future event, rather these were the 'April Days,' the immediate prelude to the revolution." See Michael Hardt, "Into the Factory: Negri's Lenin and the Subjective Caesura (1968–73)," in *The Philosophy of Antonio Negri: Resistance in Practice*, Timothy S. Murphy and Abdul-Karim Mustapha, eds. (London: Pluto Press, 2005), 7.

171. *Revolutionary Rehearsals*, Colin Barker, ed. (London: Bookmarks, 1987).

172. John Berger [1968], "The Nature of Mass Demonstrations," in *Selected Essays and Articles: The Look of Things* (Harmondsworth: Penguin Books, 1972), 247, 249–50.

INDEX

NOTE: Page references noted with an *f* are figures; Page references with an *n* are notes.

419

ABOUT HAYMARKET BOOKS

Haymarket Books is a radical, independent, nonprofit book publisher based in Chicago. Our mission is to publish books that contribute to struggles for social and economic justice. We strive to make our books a vibrant and organic part of social movements and the education and development of a critical, engaged, international left.

We take inspiration and courage from our namesakes, the Haymarket martyrs, who gave their lives fighting for a better world. Their 1886 struggle for the eight-hour day—which gave us May Day, the international workers' holiday—reminds workers around the world that ordinary people can organize and struggle for their own liberation. These struggles continue today across the globe—struggles against oppression, exploitation, poverty, and war.

Since our founding in 2001, Haymarket Books has published more than five hundred titles. Radically independent, we seek to drive a wedge into the risk-averse world of corporate book publishing. Our authors include Noam Chomsky, Arundhati Roy, Rebecca Solnit, Angela Y. Davis, Howard Zinn, Amy Goodman, Wallace Shawn, Mike Davis, Winona LaDuke, Ilan Pappé, Richard Wolff, Dave Zirin, Keeanga-Yamahtta Taylor, Nick Turse, Dahr Jamail, David Barsamian, Elizabeth Laird, Amira Hass, Mark Steel, Avi Lewis, Naomi Klein, and Neil Davidson. We are also the trade publishers of the acclaimed Historical Materialism Book Series and of Dispatch Books.

ALSO AVAILABLE FROM HAYMARKET BOOKS

Revolutionary Rehearsals
Edited by Colin Barker

Marxism and Social Movements
Edited by Colin Barker, Laurence Cox, John Krinsky, and Alf Gunvald Nilsen

Holding Fast to an Image of the Past: Explorations in the Marxist Tradition
Neil Davidson

How Revolutionary Were the Bourgeois Revolutions?
Neil Davidson

Nation-States: Consciousness and Competition
Neil Davidson

We Cannot Escape History: States and Revolutions
Neil Davidson

Alasdair MacIntyre's Engagement with Marxism
Selected Writings 1953-1974
Alasdair MacIntyre, edited by Paul Blackledge and Neil Davidson

African Struggles Today: Social Movements Since Independence
Peter Dwyer and Leo Zeilig

The Last Day of Oppression, and the First Day of the Same:
The Politics and Economics of the New Latin American Left
Jeffery R. Webber

Voices of Liberation: Frantz Fanon
Leo Zeilig, introduction by Mireille Fanon-Mendes France

Urban Revolt: State Power and the Rise of People's Movements in the Global South
Edited by Immanuel Ness, Trevor Ngwane, and Luke Sinwell

ABOUT THE EDITORS

Colin Barker lectured in sociology for many years at Manchester Metropolitan University. He co-organized annual international conferences on Alternative Futures and Popular Protest. He published many books and articles on social movements and revolutions and was an active supporter of rs21.

Gareth Dale teaches politics at Brunel University. His publications include monographs and volumes on Karl Polanyi, the GDR and Eastern Europe, green growth, and migrant labour. He is currently preparing a volume of Colin Barker's selected writings.

Neil Davidson (1957-2020) lectured in Sociology at the School of Social and Political Science at the University of Glasgow. He authored *The Origins of Scottish Nationhood* (2000), *Discovering the Scottish Revolution* (2003), for which he was awarded the Deutscher Memorial Prize, *How Revolutionary Were the Bourgeois Revolutions?* (2012), *Holding Fast to an Image of the Past* (2014) and *We Cannot Escape History* (2015). Davidson was on the editorial boards of rs21 and the Scottish Left Project website, and was a member of the Radical Independence Campaign.

ABOUT THE CONTRIBUTORS

Claire Ceruti grew up in apartheid South Africa and was catapulted into the anti-apartheid struggle in 1985, when she started at Wits University. By 1987, she had met and joined a group aligned with the International Socialist tradition and is still trying to foment revolution with its descendent Keep Left. To pay the bills, she's currently an academic pieceworker.

Peter Dwyer is a member of the *Review of African Political Economy* editorial board and has published on social movements and Marxism. He teaches politics and development at the University of Warwick.

Mike Gonzalez is emeritus professor of Latin American studies at the University of Glasgow. He has written extensively on Latin American politics, literature and history, most recently *The Ebb of the Pink Tide: The Decline of the Left in Latin America* (2019), *In the Red Corner: The Marxism of José Carlos Mariátegui* (2019), and *The Literary Travellers Guide to Cuba* (2020). He contributed a chapter to *Revolutionary Rehearsals* (ed. Colin Barker, 1987).

Sameh Naguib teaches sociology at the American University in Cairo and has written extensively on politics in Egypt and the Middle East. He is a founding member of the Revolutionary Socialist Movement in Egypt.

Tom O'Lincoln has been active in left politics as a Marxist and revolutionary socialist since 1967. He was active in the 1990s supporting political activists in Indonesia. For six years he ran an Indonesian-language email magazine and website called *Suara Socialis*, a project to produce Marxist material in that language. Tom's publications include *Into the Mainstream: The Decline of Australian Communism*, *Years of Rage: Social Conflicts in the Fraser Era*, and *Australia's Pacific War: Challenging a National Myth*.

Jorge Sanmartino is a sociology professor at the University of Buenos Aires and other universities in Argentina. He has written numerous articles on political science, as well as on Latin American political reality. His latest book is *La Teoría del Estado Después de Poulantzas* (*State Theory after Poulantzas*).

Jeffery R. Webber is an associate professor in the department of politics at York University, Toronto. He is the author several books on Latin America. Most recently, he is coauthor with Franck Gaudichaud and Massimo Modonesi, of *Impasse of the Latin American Left*.

Leo Zeilig is a writer and researcher. He has written extensively on African politics and history, including books on working-class struggle and revolutionary movements, and biographies of some of Africa's most important political thinkers and activists. Leo is an editor of *Review of African Political Economy*—the radical African studies journal founded by activists and scholars in 1974— and an honorary research associate at the Society, Work and Development Institute (SWOP) at the University of the Witwatersrand in Johannesburg, South Africa.